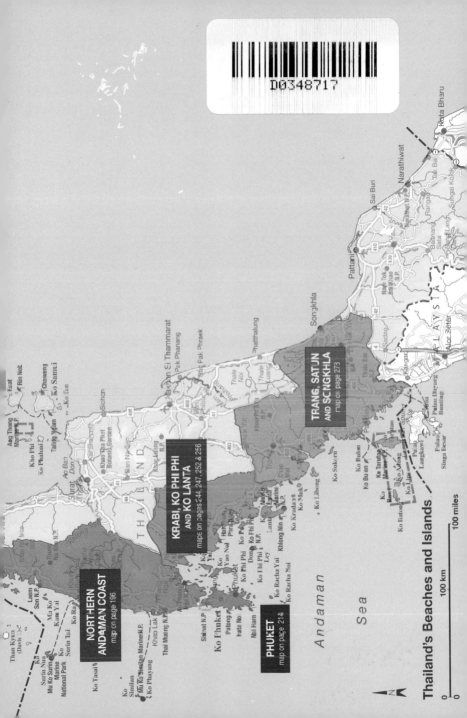

Thailand's Beaches and Islands

NORTHERN ANDAMAN COAST
map on page 196

KRABI, KO PHI PHI AND KO LANTA
maps on pages 244, 247, 252 & 256

PHUKET
map on page 214

TRANG, SATUN AND SONGKHLA
map on page 273

D0348717

Andaman Sea

MALAYSIA

0   100 km
0   100 miles

═══◎═══	Motorway with Junction
═ ═ ═ ═	Motorway (under construction)
═══ ═══	Dual Carriageway
━━━━━	Main Road
═══════	Secondary Road
━━━━━	Minor Road
──────	Track
─ ─ ─ ─	Footpath
━━ ▪ ▪ ━	International Boundary
─ ─ ─ ─	Province Boundary
─ • ─ • ─	National Park/Reserve
─ ─ ─ ─	Ferry Route
⊖	Border Crossing
✈ ✈	Airport
† ⸸	Church (ruins)
†	Monastery
▉ 🏰	Castle (ruins)
⸫	Archaeological Site
◑	Cave
★	Place of Interest
✳	Viewpoint
🌴	Beach
═══════	Motorway
═══════	Dual Carriageway
━━━━━ ┐	
━━━━━ ├ Main Roads	
━━━━━ ┘	
━━━━━ ┐	
━━━━━ ├ Minor Roads	
━━━━━ ┘	
─ ─ ─ ─	Footpath
━▬━▬━	Railway
▭	Pedestrian Area
▬	Important Building
▭	Park
❶	Numbered Sight
Ⓜ Ⓢ	Metro MRT/Skytrain BTS
🚌	Bus Station
❶	Tourist Information
✉	Post Office
✝	Cathedral/Church
☪	Mosque
✡	Synagogue
🗽	Statue/Monument
⌶	Tower
🗼	Lighthouse

INSIGHT GUIDES

THAILAND'S
BEACHES AND ISLANDS

☆ INSIGHT GUIDE

THAILAND'S
BEACHES AND ISLANDS

Editorial

Commissioning Editor
Sarah Clark
Series Manager
Carine Tracanelli
Publishing Manager
Rachel Fox
Art Editor
Tom Smyth

Distribution

UK & Ireland
**Dorling Kindersley Ltd, a Penguin
Group company**
80 Strand, London WC2R 0RL, UK
sales@uk.dk.com

United States
Ingram Publisher Services
One Ingram Blvd, PO Box 3006
La Vergne, TN 37086-1986
ips@ingramcontent.com

Australia and New Zealand
Woodslane
10 Apollo St, Warriewood
NSW 2102
Australia
info@woodslane.com.au

Worldwide
**Apa Publications GmbH & Co.
Verlag KG (Singapore branch)**
7030 Ang Mo Kio Avenue 5
08-65 Northstar @ AMK
Singapore 569880
apasin@singnet.com.sg

Printing

CTPS-China

© 2014 Apa Publications (UK) Ltd
All Rights Reserved

First Edition 2006
Third Edition 2014

ABOUT THIS BOOK

The first Insight Guide pioneered the use of creative full-colour photography in travel guides in 1970. Since then, we have expanded our range to cater for our readers' need not only for reliable information about their chosen destination but also for a real understanding of that destination. Now, when the internet can supply inexhaustible – but not always reliable – facts, our books marry text and pictures to provide that much more elusive quality: knowledge. To achieve this, they rely heavily on the authority of locally based writers and photographers.

How to use this book

The book is carefully structured to convey an understanding of the capital, Bangkok, as well as Thailand's main beaches and islands:

◆ The Best of Thailand's Beaches & Islands at the front helps you to prioritise what you want to see: top family attractions, the most idyllic beaches, the best dive sites, the most exclusive resorts and must-see temples, as well as the hottest restaurants and clubs.
◆ To understand this region better, you need to know about its past. The first section covers the region's history and culture in lively, authoritative essays written by specialist Thailand-based writers.
◆ The Places section provides a full rundown of all the attractions worth seeing. The main places of interest are coordinated by number with full-colour maps. In addition, a pull-out map at the back of the book gives details of Thailand's top beaches.

LEFT: Thailand's glorious coastline.

exploring the country as a magazine editor and freelance writer. His work includes time spent as the editor of Thailand's then biggest-selling English-language magazine, *Bangkok Metro*. An award-winning feature writer, he has also contributed pieces on food for the BBC's *Olive* magazine and on nightlife for *GQ*. When he is not writing, he relaxes at the drum kit in a blues, funk and jazz band.

The book was commissioned by Commissioning Editor **Catherine Dreghorn**, copyedited by **Paula Soper** and managed by Senior Commissioning Editor **Sarah Clark**.

This edition builds on earlier work by several writers, including **Steven Pettifor**, **Lauren Smith** and **Austin Bush**. The bulk of the features section (including History, People & Culture, and Religion) and the photo features were originally written by **Dr Andrew Forbes**, a long-time Thailand expert who runs a press agency, CPA, in Chiang Mai. The Nature & Environment chapter was written by fellow CPA associate writer/photographer **David Henley**. The Cuisine chapter was the handiwork of **Rob McKeown**, who lives and breathes varied Asian cuisines as roving reporter for several international food and travel publications.

Among the photographers whose images bring Thailand's beaches and islands to life are **John W. Ishii**, **Austin Bush**, **Jock Montgomery**, **David Henley**, **Jason Lang** and **Marcus Wilson-Smith**.

The book was indexed by **Isobel McLean**.

◆ Photo features illustrate various facets of Thailand, from temple architecture to festivals and marine life.

◆ Photographs throughout the book are chosen not only to illustrate geography and landscape but also to convey the different moods of the region and the pulse of its people.

◆ Each Places chapter is accompanied by a Travel Tips section covering transport, accommodation, restaurants and activities in that specific region. At the end of the book is a A–Z listing of practical tips, plus language and further reading sections.

The contributors

This third edition was thoroughly updated by Bangkok-based writer **Howard Richardson**, who lives beside Bangkok's Chao Phraya River, and has spent over 10 years

CONTACTING THE EDITORS

We would appreciate it if readers would alert us to errors or outdated information by writing to:

Insight Guides, P.O. Box 7910, London SE1 1WE, England. insight@apaguide.co.uk

NO part of this book may be reproduced, stored in a retrieval system or transmitted in any form or means electronic, mechanical, photocopying, recording or otherwise, without prior written permission of *Apa Publications*. Brief text quotations with use of photographs are exempted for book review purposes only. Information has been obtained from sources believed to be reliable, but its accuracy and completeness, and the opinions based thereon, are not guaranteed.

www.insightguides.com

LEFT: Aleenta resort,
Pranburi, at dusk.

6

THE BEST OF THAILAND'S BEACHES AND ISLANDS: TOP ATTRACTIONS

At a glance, here are the attractions you can't afford to miss, from idyllic beaches and diving hotspots to lush national parks and awe-inspiring temples.

◁ **Chinatown, Bangkok.** One of the most authentic Chinatowns outside of China. The narrow alleyways are full of temples and shrines, and stalls selling wonderful foods, spices and anything else you can imagine. *See page 88.*

▽ **Full Moon Parties, Ko Phangan.** Anything goes at these wild all-night raves on the beaches of Phangan. They draw thousands of visitors every month from all over the world. *See page 176.*

▷ **Vegetarian Festival, Phuket.** In this annual Chinese Taoist event, people abstain from meat and sex and perform acts of self-mutilation that are only for the robust of heart. *See page 35.*

▽ **Wat Phra Kaew, Bangkok.** No one visits the capital without seeing the Temple of the Emerald Buddha, located in the grounds of the Grand Palace. There are wonderful murals and several museums inside. *See page 74.*

▷ **Ao Phang Nga, Northern Andaman Coast.** A surreal seascape of limestone pinnacles rising out of the water invites exploration by sea canoe. Pass through underwater caves to hidden lagoons. See page 202.

△ **Ko Tarutao National Park, Satun.** This island chain, a former penal colony, mixes isolated and party destinations, and is one of only a few places in the world to see the manatee. *See page 275.*

▽ **Chatuchak, Bangkok.** Touted as the world's biggest flea market, with 8,000 stalls and an estimated 400,000 shoppers every weekend. You can buy whatever you want here, from local crafts to snakes and violins. *See page 97.*

△ **Khao Sok National Park** Good for trekking, caves, lakes and waterfalls, the amazing variety of flora and fauna here includes the world's second-largest flower. *See page 203.*

▽ **Railay Bay, Krabi.** These three beaches are among Thailand's most beautiful. The surrounding area has hundreds of sheer limestone cliffs that attract rock climbers from across the world. *See page 248.*

▽ **Surin Islands.** One of a clutch of dive havens off the Andaman coast, it includes the famous Richelieu Rock. Other class diving areas such as the Burma Banks are close by. *See page 199.*

THE BEST OF THAILAND'S BEACHES AND ISLANDS: EDITOR'S CHOICE

Setting priorities, making choices, unique attractions... here are our recommendations for travellers of all kinds, from families and culture vultures to night owls.

BEST FOR FAMILIES

• **Dino Park and Mini Golf: Phuket**. An 18-hole mini-golf course that trails over rocks and across rivers and waterfalls, past dinosaurs with smoking nostrils. *See page 224.*

• **Elephant trek: Pattaya**. See elephants bathing and feeding, then take a trek on one's back into the forest. *See page 125.*

• **National Discovery Museum: Bangkok**. Explore Thailand's history and cul-

ture at the country's best interactive museum. *See page 82.*

• **Phuket Fantasea: Phuket**. An exciting stage extravaganza combining dance, drama and acrobatics with pyrotechnics and performing elephants. *See page 222.*

• **Siam Ocean World: Bangkok**. See more than 30,000 marine animals in a giant Oceanarium, observe different marine species on a glass-bottomed boat ride and go diving with the sharks. *See page 92.*

• **Underwater World: Pattaya**. Explore the varied wonders of the briny depths without ever getting wet. *See page 125.*

• **Monkey Theatre: Ko Samui**. Watch monkeys scamper up trees at lightning speed to pluck coconuts from the palms. *See page 169.*

ABOVE: kitsch Dino Park. **LEFT:** elephant at the Phuket Fantasea. **ABOVE RIGHT:** red Thai curry.

FOOD AND DRINK

• **Cookery Schools: Bangkok, Hua Hin and Ko Samui.** There's nothing like learning how to cook Thai food while you're in Thailand and these are some of the best schools on offer. *See pages 117, 165, 192.*

• **Night Markets: Trang and Songkhla.** For some of the best southern-style streetfood, plus local colour and a great atmosphere. *See pages 282, 283.*

• **Nahm: Bangkok.** Voted one of the

world's best restaurants, it produces sensational traditional Thai flavours. *See page 110.*

• **Sirocco: Bangkok.** The stupendous city views are the main attraction at this famous alfresco rooftop restaurant and bar. *See page 110.*

• **Sra Bua: Bangkok.** Modern Thai cuisine by Copenhagen's Michelin-starred restaurant Kiin Kiin includes dishes like red curry ice cream. *See page 109.*

TEMPLES

- **Khao Luang Cave: Petchaburi**. More than 100 Buddha images fill this cave temple in several underground chambers. See page 149.
- **Wat Chalong: Phuket**. The island's largest and most important Buddhist temple contains a relic of the Buddha's bones. See page 226.
- **Wat Mahathat: Petchaburi**. A 14th century temple, Petchaburi's most important and known for its fine carvings and murals. See page 149.
- **Wat Matchimawat: Songkhla**. The town's most famous temple, with paintings that are over 200 years old. See page 277.
- **Wat Pho: Bangkok**. The capital's largest temple is best known for the gigantic statue of the reclining Buddha found here. See page 80.
- **Wat Tham Seua: Krabi**. "Tiger Cave Temple" is surrounded by forests and cliffs with truly fantastic views of the neighbouring area. See page 244.

ABOVE: Wat Chalong – the most important of Phuket's 29 Buddhist temples. **BELOW LEFT:** detail of the Sanctuary of Truth, Pattaya. **BELOW RIGHT:** Phuket night lights.

CULTURAL SIGHTS

- **Bangkok Art & Culture Centre**. Eleven storeys high and featuring some of Bangkok's best art and multimedia shows. See page 92.
- **Khao Wang: Petchaburi**. A vast hilltop complex of temples, pagodas and the winter palace buildings of King Rama IV. See page 148.
- **Sanctuary of Truth: Pattaya**. This awe-inspiring all-wood edifice pays homage to traditional Thai and Asian religious imagery. See page 125.
- **Thaksin Folklore Museum: Songkhla**. This regional museum highlights the culture, traditions and handicrafts of South Thailand. See page 278.

- **Vimanmek Mansion: Bangkok**. Billed as the world's largest golden teak structure, this former 19th century royal summer home has lots of period artefacts. See page 87.

HOTTEST NIGHTLIFE

- **Ku De Ta: Bangkok**. A huge entertainment complex with several restaurants, a club with top DJs and live music areas. See page 113.
- **Moov: Ko Tao**. Chilled-out club-bar with a tree house that caters to the island's diving crowd. See page 193.
- **'Lady-boy' cabarets: Bangkok, Pattaya, Ko Samui and Phuket**. Men in various stages of cross-dressing and sex change perform Vegas-style cabaret. See pages 114, 126, 191, 238.
- **Seduction Beach Club & Disco: Phuket**. A hot club on three floors with good house DJs and international imports. See page 238.
- **Reggae Bar: Ko Phi Phi**. The island's biggest and best party venue has its own Thai boxing ring. See page 269.

THAI.MASS
OIL
HEAD } ← M
FOOT }

LAZY DAYS AND ISLAND WAYS

With an ever-growing number of chic luxury resorts and spas, Thailand always has something for those seeking style and sophistication. And for those who simply want to get away from it all, there are still remote islands and virtually deserted beaches to choose from.

Thais have good reason for their famous welcoming smiles – their country is so enticing that it is ranked among the world's most popular tourist destinations. Holiday-makers now exceed 14 million a year, making tourism the country's top industry. With a unique culture and a piquantly delicious cuisine, year-round sunny weather, palm-studded and powdery white-sand beaches, forested mountains cloaked in dawn mists, time honoured ancient ruins and old temples, and the excitement of a bustling megalopolis such as Bangkok, it's easy to see why planeloads of visitors keep touching down on this exotic land.

For the majority of them, a Thai sojourn consists of a brief flirtation with the bright lights of Bangkok before escaping to the thousands of kilometres of sun-kissed coastline, or to an island getaway. The clear azure waters of the Eastern Seaboard, Andaman Coast to the west and the Gulf of Thailand along the east, are among the world's best for scuba diving and snorkelling, sailing and fishing.

Thailand's islands and beaches offer plenty of attractions for those who like swimming with vibrant marine life among kaleidoscopic coral reefs, but there is also plenty to please less energetic visitors. These regions of Thailand, which border Burma to the west, Cambodia to the east and Malaysia to the south, have a topography where Thai royal palaces and the statues and spires of Buddhist temples contrast with the blue waters and lush verdant forests. And family attractions are abundant in the shows and theme parks in places such as Pattaya and Phuket.

Once extensively the preserve of cash-strapped backpackers and tour groups, many of the country's beach areas now cater to a broader mix of travellers, with stylish boutique resorts, spas, clubs and fine restaurants. Holiday-makers cross paths with hedonistic Full Moon party animals, and starry-eyed honeymoon couples with spa lovers and New Age junkies seeking spiritual awakening or the ultimate massage.

Lest you think that tranquil hideaways no longer exist, Thailand still has near-desolate beaches and remote islands that the chain hotels have yet to discover. It is a safe, family-friendly country, despite the ongoing restlessness in the southernmost provinces. Who needs an excuse for a beach holiday anyway? ❑

PRECEDING PAGES: the bow of a longtail boat in Phi Phi Don; sign for massages on Hat Rin beach in Ko Phangan. **LEFT:** walking along the beach at Coral Island, Phuket.

PEOPLE AND CULTURE

Warm smiles, a pleasant disposition and a sense of calm: these are the qualities which are readily discerned by visitors to Thailand. And the traits seem to run equally through most of the country's diverse ethnic communities.

The overwhelming majority of Thailand's population is ethnic Tai, with the Central Tais predominating in the southeastern region between Bangkok and Cambodia, as well as down the peninsula about as far south as Prachuap Khiri Khan. Further to the south, their close cousins, the Southern Tais, gradually increase in numbers until, by Ranong and Surat Thani, they are the majority.

The Tais are relative newcomers to the region, having slowly migrated south from southern China between the 10th and 12th centuries. By about 1350, they had extended their control over all of present-day Thailand, as well as far into the Malay Peninsula, taking over territory previously controlled by the Khmers, Mon and Malays.

Living among the Tais today are a number of minorities who add considerably to the cultural, religious, linguistic and culinary diversity of the region. There are Vietnamese in the southeast, Malays in the far south, ethnic Chinese in all areas, and aboriginal groups such as the Mani and the "sea gypsies" *(see page 21)*, the former in isolated communities in the remoter parts of the mountainous interior and, the latter, along the Andaman Coast. Finally, there are smaller numbers of ethnic Khmer near the Cambodian border, as well as Mon, Burmans and Karen along the frontier with neighbouring Burma.

The present monarch, King Bhumibol Adulyadej *(see page 30)*, has made a point of embracing all the citizens of Thailand – including

non-Tais and non-Buddhists – as Thai. During his long reign, cultural and linguistic diversity has increasingly been celebrated rather than discouraged, although some groups, particularly hill tribes along the northern and western borders still don't enjoy full citizenship rights.

Karen and Mon

West of Bangkok, in the mountainous interior stretching from Ratchaburi to Chumphon and Ranong in the south, the Karen and Mon peoples, often seeking refuge from military persecution in Burma, or simply looking for work and a better life (often illegally), scratch a poor living from the soil. More prosperous descend-

LEFT: Thai boys playing on the beach in Chan Am.
RIGHT: a passenger at Hua Hin station.

ants of the Mon live in Greater Bangkok, on the island of Ko Kret and further south in Phra Pradaeng, where, in times past, they served as loyal bulwarks against possible Burmese aggression. The Mon, traditionally opposed to Thailand's old enemy Burma, have therefore been trusted by the Thais.

The Muslim community

As one moves further south on the Isthmus of Kra, minarets begin to appear among the palm trees, a clear indication of the presence of Thai-speaking Muslims. Even further south, on the Malaysian frontier, are four provinces with a Malay-speaking Muslim majority. Here, Thai-

The term "Tai" is used (loosely) to refer to an ethnolinguistic group of peoples spread across Southeast Asia. "Thai" refers to a citizen of Thailand, regardless of ethnicity or language spoken.

speaking Buddhists are in a small minority, but control the administration and schools.

The farmers and fishermen of this region are overwhelmingly Malay, yet even among this apparently homogenous group there are differences. To the west, the Andaman Coast province of Satun has the highest Muslim population in Thailand, with more than 80 percent of the total. Yet the people here seem content to be Thai citizens, and have never become involved in the region's separatist movement.

To the east, in the predominantly Malay provinces of Pattani, Narathiwat and Yala, disenchantment with rule from Bangkok is more widespread and Islamic practice more rigorous. This parallels the situation in the neighbouring Malaysian state of Kelantan, long the power base of PAS, the conservative Islamic Party of Malaysia.

The Sino-Thais

In the Bight of Bangkok, just off the coast of Chonburi Province, the tiny island of Ko Si Chang was once the main disembarkation point for migrants arriving in Thailand from southern China. It is not surprising, therefore, that Bangkok's substantial Chinese community (around 14 percent of the population) trace their ancestry mainly to the Guangdong, Fujian and Guangxi provinces. The neighbouring coastal provinces, from Chanthaburi in the east to Petchaburi in the west, have a very Chinese feel to them, too, as do the commercial sections of every provincial capital in the southern peninsular region and the small island towns of the Samui Archipelago.

The ethnic Chinese occupy a unique position in Thai society. Because they have excelled particularly at trading, the Chinese have come to dominate commerce throughout Southeast Asia, often causing resentment and hostility among the host populations. In Indonesia,

THE IMPACT OF TRADE

The narrow Isthmus of Kra long served as an overland route for merchants seeking to avoid the lengthy and dangerous voyage around the Malay Peninsula. The impact of this overland trade cannot be overestimated. In the early centuries AD, South Indian traders brought Hinduism with them. Buddhism followed, introduced from about 700 AD by Mon traders, then reinforced by missionaries from Sri Lanka. From the 10th century onwards, Islam appeared on the Andaman Coast, carried by Arab and Indian seafarers. Finally, the arrival of Europeans added to the cultural mix. In many ways, commerce made southern Thailand the melting pot it is today.

Malaysia, Burma and Vietnam, this has some-times led to anti-Chinese sentiments, ethnic tensions and occasional expulsions and massacres. There was discrimination against the ethnic Chinese in Thailand in the past, but it rarely led to the violence seen elsewhere in the region. In general, the Tais are well aware of the commercial skills of the overseas Chinese and have tended to intermarry with them rather than victimise or expel them. As a result, the two groups live side by side in almost complete harmony. In urban centres they have intermarried to the extent that most "overseas Chinese" now consider themselves to be as much Thai as Chinese. Making up an estimated 11 per-

especially in Bangkok and the provincial towns of the south – that it is often impossible to make an absolute distinction between the two. Indeed, Thailand's approach to its citizens of Chinese origin has been of inestimable value to the nation, and stands as an example to the rest of Southeast Asia.

Southern character

While the people of Thailand all share some common traits, there are interesting cultural distinctions between the southern Thais and those from other regions of the country.

The central and northern Thais often consider the southern Thais to be somewhat

cent or more of the total population, these are called *luk chin*, or "children of China".

Today, few can read Mandarin, though many older people still converse in southern Chinese dialects, predominantly Teochew, Hakka and Hainanese. They are very well integrated into Thai society, having adopted Theravada Buddhism and Thai names, cultural values and tastes. In return, the Thais have also absorbed much from the Chinese in matters linguistic, cultural and even culinary. Indeed, so well integrated have the two peoples become –

LEFT: a Muslim man outside a mosque in Khao Lak.
ABOVE: members of Bangkok's Chinese community.

THE TAMILS OF PHUKET

Most of Phuket's Tamils migrated from neighbouring Malaysia in the 19th century, though some came directly from India. A number were prosperous moneylenders from the rich Chettiar class, while others found employment on rubber plantations. By the early 20th century, the island had a sizeable Tamil community, though it has since diminished significantly due to remigration. Today, the Tamils live mainly in or near Phuket Town, where community life centres on Thandayudapani Temple on Suthat Road, one of the few functioning Hindu temples in Thailand. Here, the birthday of the god Ganesh is celebrated in August or September.

"hasty" – they can be quick-tempered and as fiery as their southern cuisine. They also speak faster, using a clipped dialect that, while comprehensible to other Thais, is distinctively southern. From a negative perspective, some southern Thai towns have acquired persistently shady reputations. Chonburi, southeast of Bangkok, has long been known for its *chao poh*, or "godfathers", gangsters who are often of ethnic-Chinese origin. These Thai mafiosi made huge amounts of money from a mixture of legitimate, semi-legal and openly criminal businesses, running everything from transport companies and petrol stations to underground lotteries, prostitution and cigarette smuggling.

action and partly because this kind of lawless behaviour has become unacceptable to many of today's urban Thais. Still, Chonburi and Nakhon Si Thammarat may have to wait for some years before their reputation for lawlessness disappears.

Of course, not all southern Thais are quick-tempered, and the great majority are law-abiding citizens. For their part, they sometimes see northern and northeastern Thais as too easy-going and unadventurous, lacking the southern ambition.

National ethos

Yet, despite these apparent differences, a shared reverence for the monarchy and a fervent belief

These *chao poh* had their heyday in the 1990s, but many have since met violent ends.

The infamous Sia Yai of Angthong, for instance, was blown apart by a mine outside the provincial courthouse in 1989. Sa Jiew of Chonburi was killed in 1991 when his Mercedes was blown off the road by a rocket-propelled grenade. To counter the constant threat of assassination, many *chao poh* used bulletproof cars and employed Uzi-toting gunmen – many of whom came from Nakhon Si Thammarat, a southern town famed across Thailand for the ruthlessness of its gunmen.

In recent years, the power of the *chao poh* has diminished considerably, partly through police

in religion serve as the unifying glue that binds Thai society. A pride in the country's long independence has also bred a quiet cultural confidence in Thais, whether southern or otherwise.

One of the nation's greatest treasures is intangible – the famous Thai appreciation of *sanuk*, or "fun" – that is, enjoying life. Perhaps less appreciated by outsiders, but no less essential, is the Thai trait of *supap*, or "politeness". If you are consistently smiling and polite, life in Thailand – even in Chonburi and Nakhon Si Thammarat – should be plain sailing. ❑

ABOVE LEFT: at a Ganesha shrine, Bangkok. **ABOVE RIGHT:** the Thais' friendly demeanour is well known.

Thailand's Sea Gypsies

Southern Thailand is home to a substantial community of people who, for centuries, have chosen to live and work on the waters of the Andaman Sea.

The "sea gypsies" of southern Thailand, known in Thai as *chao lay*, or "people of the sea", are divided into three groups, though they sometimes intermarry and generally consider themselves as one kindred people. Numbering between 4,000 and 5,000, they live only along the Andaman Sea, either in huts by the shore, or on itinerant craft that ply the coastal waters south from Ranong to Ko Tarutao.

The Urak Lawoi people, numbering around 3,000, form the largest sea-gypsy group. They live in simple shacks on beaches from Phuket to Ko Tarutao. Their two largest settlements are at Ko Sireh and Rawai in the southeast of Phuket.

Two smaller groups also exist – the 1,000 strong Moklen community living between Ko Phra Thong, near Takua Pa, and Phuket, and the 500 or so Moken, living north from Ko Phra Thong to the Burmese frontier. The Moken are the least adapted to modern life; they still use dugout canoes and avoid contact with settled people, especially local authorities. The Thais distinguish them from the more assimilated groups by calling them *chao ko tae* or "real island folk". The Moken rarely build on land, preferring a completely nomadic existence on the Andaman Sea.

Indigenous people

An indigenous people, it is likely the *chao lay* people were among the earliest inhabitants of the region, predating the arrival of the Tais from the north by many centuries. They are shorter, stockier and darker than the Tais, are related to the "Sea People" of Malaysia, and perhaps also to the Mani or Negrito peoples who inhabit the southern Thai interior. Little is known of the *chao lay*'s past as they have no written language or records. Their spoken languages are related to Malay, though the Moken have borrowed more vocabulary from Thai and Burmese.

Chao lay religion is neither Buddhist nor Muslim, but rests on spirits associated with the wind, waves and islands. The Moken venerate the sea, and every year, during the full moon of the fifth lunar month, they stop working for three days and nights to feast, dance, sing and drink alcohol. The Moken say that their earliest ancestor was washed ashore, but on land-

ing refused to become Muslim or Buddhist, choosing instead to return to the sea. Certainly, the sea gypsies remain a people apart, living on the fringes of southern Thai society. They are some of the poorest and least technologically sophisticated people in the country.

Yet the *chao lay* have some natural advantages. During the 2004 tsunami, although many sea-gypsy households sustained damage and some loss of life, they seemed to have instinctively understood the cataclysmic event better than their Thai neighbours, many saving themselves by moving early to higher ground. ❑

RIGHT: a sea gypsy on Ko Lanta mending nets.

DECISIVE DATES

BEGINNINGS

c.250 BC
Maritime trade established between India and Southeast Asia; Hindu influences begin to filter into region.

c.AD 200
Chen La culture established in lower Mekong region. Chinese culture makes an impact.

c.500
Srivijaya kingdom encompasses parts of Sumatra and peninsular Thailand; Hindu-Buddhism now dominant in region.

6th–9th centuries
Mon kingdom of Dvaravati flourishes in Chao Phraya River valley, giving boost to Buddhist religion.

790
Khmer kingdom of Kambuja established by King Jayavarman I.

889–915
King Yasovarman I founds new Khmer capital, later to become Angkor.

1113–50
Surayavarman II oversees building of Angkor Wat; height of Khmer Empire.

10th–12th centuries
Tai-speaking peoples start migration from southern China into mainland Southeast Asia.

SUKHOTHAI AND AYUTTHAYA

1238
First independent Thai state of Sukhothai founded by King Indraditya.

1279–98
Golden Era of Sukhothai under King Ramkhamhaeng. Thai culture flourishes and Thai script is developed.

1296
Thai kingdom of Lanna founded by King Mengrai at Chiang Mai.

c.1300
Thai political control extends to Andaman Sea, Nakhon Si Thammarat and Gulf of Thailand.

1350
King Ramathibodi establishes rival Thai kingdom at Ayutthaya; Sukhothai and Khmer kingdom of Angkor in decline.

1393
Ayutthaya conquers Angkor.

1438
Ayutthaya eclipses Sukhothai.

c.1540
Ayutthaya controls peninsular Thailand and parts of northern Malaysia.

1569–90
Ayutthaya is temporarily a tributary to Burma.

c.1600
First major economic and cultural ties with Europe.

1656–88
European (especially French) influence at court of Ayutthaya reaches zenith.

1767
Burmese forces sack Ayutthaya, killing or exiling Thai royal court. General Taksin organises resistance.

1768
Taksin proclaims himself king and establishes a new capital at Thonburi.

1779
Taksin's main generals, brothers Chakri and Sarasin, drive back the Burmese and conquer Chiang Mai.

1782
Taksin is murdered. Chao Phaya Chakri founds the current Chakri Dynasty (becoming King Rama I).

FOUNDING OF BANGKOK TO WORLD WAR II

1782–1809
King Rama I moves capital to Bangkok. The restored kingdom is consolidated and expanded.

1785
Burma's last major invasion defeated by King Rama I at Kanchanaburi. Thai authority established as far as Kedah and Terengganu in present-day Malaysia.

1809–24
Reign of King Rama II. Relations reopened with the West, most notably Britain.

1824–51
Reign of King Rama III. Rebellion against Thai rule in northern Malay states.

1851–68
Reign of King Mongkut (Rama IV), the Chakri Dynasty's first monarch.

1868–1910
Reign of King Chulalongkorn (Rama V), the father of modern Thailand.

1902
Pattani, Narathiwat and Yala brought under Bangkok control, sowing the seed of present-day insurgency.

1932
A military coup ends absolutism and ushers in a constitutional monarchy.

PRESENT-DAY
1946
Current King Bhumibol Adulyadej (Rama IX), ascends the throne.

PRECEDING PAGES: Chan-am fishermen carrying their catch. LEFT: The king of Siam on an elephant in 1690.
ABOVE: an elephant at Khao Lak is used in salvage efforts following the December 2004 tsunami.

1949
Siam's name officially changed to Thailand.

1973–91
Series of coups and right-wing military governments.

1975–85
Malay separatism brews in southern provinces.

1992
Coup attempt by General Suchinda ended by royal intervention. Increasing democratic progress.

1997
Thai economy suffers in Asian financial crisis.

2001
Billionaire Thaksin Shinawatra and Thai Rak Thai Party win elections.

2003
Islamic separatist struggles in far south.

2004
Tsunami devastates much of Andaman Coast.

2005–06
Thaksin re-elected despite accusations of corruption. He becomes focus of demonstrations by the PAD (Yellow Shirts) and is forced into exile in London.

2007
Thaksin banned from politics. His followers, the UDD (Red Shirts), protest. A Thaksin proxy, the PPP, wins December election.

2008
PAD occupies Government House and the airport. The courts disband the ruling party. Democrat Party leader Abhisit Vejjajiva becomes prime minister.

2009
UDD protests disrupt ASEAN summit in Pattaya. Riots in Bangkok; PAD leader is shot, but survives.

2010
Thaksin found guilty of abuse of power. UDD protesters occupy parts of Bangkok, 85 people killed.

2011
Thaksin proxy Pheu Thai Party, led by his sister, wins landslide victory. Yingluck becomes Thailand's first female prime minister.

2012–13
The Pheu Thai Party begins attempts to change the Constitution and create an amnesty largely seen as paving the way to return Thaksin's assets and allow him to return. Pro and anti-Thaksin demonstrations continue, although at a lower level.

HISTORY

Southern Thailand's sun-drenched beaches and islands were not always a playground for wintering tourists. In times past, the peninsula's central location in maritime Southeast Asia made it an important stopover for merchants along the region's lucrative trade routes.

In the early 10th–14th centuries, before the consolidation of the Siamese kingdom, the peninsula was a confluence of diverse cultural and religious influences fought over by local warlords and a vassal state to regional powerhouses.

In the beginning

The earliest known civilisation in Thailand dates from around 3600 BC, when the people of Ban Chiang in the northeast developed bronze tools, fired pottery and began to cultivate rice. The Tai people, after whom the kingdom is named, did not even inhabit the region of present-day Thailand during this time, but are thought to have been living in loosely organised groups in what is now southern China.

Little is known of the history of Thailand's coastal regions until around two millennia ago, by which time it seems certain that Malay peoples had settled in southern peninsular Thailand, along both the Andaman Sea and Gulf of Thailand coasts. Inland, in the wild hills and jungles of the central spine, small groups of Negrito hunter-gatherers eked out a precarious living. Further to the north, Mon people had settled the Tenasserim region and the southern Chao Phraya valley, while further east the Khmers had settled along the southeastern Gulf Coast and in the Mekong delta. Of the Tais, still living far to the north, there was as yet no sign.

The first civilisations to develop on Thailand's coasts and islands were not Tai, but Malay, Mon and Khmer, each shaped by the advanced

Indian and Chinese civilisations that came to exercise powerful and distinct influences across Southeast Asia.

The Golden Land and Srivijaya

As early as 300 BC, the Malay world, including peninsular Thailand, was already being Indianised by visiting traders in search of fragrant woods, pearls and especially gold, leading the Indians to name the region Suvarnabhumi or "Golden Land". By about AD 500, a loosely knit kingdom called Srivijaya had emerged, encompassing the coastal areas of Sumatra, peninsular Malaya and Thailand, as well as parts of Borneo. *Maharajas*, or kings, ruled its people, who prac-

LEFT: an artist's impression of Bangkok in 1846. **RIGHT:** Grand Palace mural depicting Thai history in Wat Pho.

tised both Hinduism and Buddhism and flourished through brisk trade with India and China.

A series of wars with the Javanese from the
10th century weakened Srivijaya, and the power
of the Hindu *maharajas* was undermined in the
region by the arrival of Muslim traders and
Islam. By the late 13th century, the new Siamese
kings of Sukhothai brought much of the Malay
Peninsula under their control.

The Mon kingdom of Dvaravati

At about the same time that Srivijaya dominated
the southern part of the Malay Peninsula, the
Mon people established themselves as the rulers
of the northern part of the peninsula and the

Chao Phraya valley. The kingdom of Dvaravati
flourished from the 6th to the 11th century,
with Nakhon Pathom, U-Thong and Lopburi its
major settlements. Much like Srivijaya, Dvaravati was strongly influenced by Indian culture
and religion, and the Mon played a central role
in the introduction of Buddhism to present-day
Thailand and, in particular, the Andaman Coast.
It is not clear whether Dvaravati was a single
unitary state under the control of a powerful
ruler, or a loose confederation of small princi-
palities. By the 12th–13th centuries, the Tais had
moved south, conquering Nakhon Pathom and
Lopburi and absorbing much of Mon culture,
including the Buddhist religion.

The Khmer empire

As the coastal regions of western Thailand
were dominated by Srivijaya and Dvaravati,
another major power was asserting its control
over what is now eastern Thailand. This was
the Khmer empire of Angkor, forerunner of
present-day Cambodia.

Strongly influenced by Indian culture,
Khmer civilisation reached its zenith under
the reign of Suryavarman II (1113–50), during
which time the temple of Angkor Wat in Cambodia was built. He united the kingdom, conquering Dvaravati and the area further west to
the border with the kingdom of Pagan (modern
Burma), expanding as far south into the Malay
Peninsula as Nakhon Si Thammarat, and domi-
nating the entire coast of the Gulf of Siam.

The next great Khmer ruler was Jayavarman
VII (ruled 1181–1219), who defeated the Chams
and initiated a series of astonishing building
projects. Yet this was to be the last flowering of
Khmer independence until modern times, as the
Khmer empire fell victim to the emerging power
that would later become known as Thailand.

Sukhothai, the first Thai kingdom

Sukhothai was part of the Khmer empire until
1238, when two Tai chieftains seceded and
established the first independent Tai kingdom.
This event is considered to mark the found-
ing of the modern Thai nation, although
other less well-known Tai states, such as Chiang Saen and Lanna in north Thailand were
established about the same time. Sukhothai
expanded by forming alliances with the other
Tai kingdoms. It adopted Theravada Buddhism

THE KINGDOM OF PATTANI

The Kingdom of Pattani was formerly a Malay sultanate
comprising the present-day provinces of Pattani, Yala and
Narathiwat. It became Muslim in the 11th century, but
Siamese influence increased until, in the mid-17th cen-
tury, Pattani became a tributary state of Ayutthaya. It later
rebelled against Thai control during the reign of King
Rama I, and its ruler, Sultan Muhammad, was killed in
battle. Then, a series of attempted rebellions prompted
Bangkok to divide Pattani into seven smaller states.
Despite a long association with Thailand, the Malays of
Pattani were never culturally absorbed into mainstream
Thai society, and the area remains fractious even today.

as the state religion with the help of Sri Lankan monks. Under King Ramkhamhaeng (ruled 1279–98), Sukhothai enjoyed a golden age of prosperity. During his reign, the Thai writing system evolved and the foundations of present-day Thailand were securely established. He expanded his control over the south, as far as the Andaman Sea and Nakhon Si Thammarat on the Gulf Coast, as well as over the Chao Phraya valley and even southeast into what is within the borders of present-day Cambodia.

With the creation of the Sukhothai kingdom, a new political structure came into being across mainland Southeast Asia. At the same time, the Thai newcomers, an ethnically Sinitic people,

In 1350, the ambitious ruler U-Thong moved his capital from Lopburi to a nearby island on the river – a more defensible location – and gave the new city the name Ayutthaya, proclaiming himself King Ramathibodi (ruled 1351–69). He declared Theravada Buddhism the state religion, invited monks from Sri Lanka to help spread the faith, and compiled a legal code, based on the Indian Dharmashastra, which remained in force until the 19th century.

Ayutthaya soon eclipsed Sukhothai as the leading Thai polity. By the end of the 14th century, Ayutthaya was the strongest power in Southeast Asia. In the last year of his reign, Ramathibodi seized Angkor in what was

intermarried with the inhabitants of the states they had supplanted and adopted their Indian-ised culture.

The kingdom of Ayutthaya

The glories of Sukhothai were short-lived, however. In the early 14th century, a rival Thai kingdom began to develop in the lower Chao Phraya valley, not far from present-day Bangkok.

the first of many successful Thai assaults on the Khmer capital. Forces were also sent to subdue Sukhothai, and the year after Rama-thibodi died, his kingdom was recognised by China's Hongwu Emperor, of the newly founded Ming dynasty, as Sukhothai's right-ful successor.

During the 15th century, much of Ayut-thaya's energies were directed southwards toward the Malay Peninsula, where its claims of sovereignty over the great trading port of Malacca were contested. The Malay states south of Nakhon Si Thammarat had become Muslim early in the century, and Islam served as a unify-ing symbol of Malay solidarity against the Thais

Left: Head Singha mythical lion Dvaravati style 8th–9th Century AD.
Above Left: a bas relief at Angkor depicting King Suryavarman II holding court.
Above Right: the Sukhothai King Ramkhamhaeng.

The Monarchy

Since the first independent Thai kingdom was established in 1238, the Thais have been ruled over by kings. To this day, the monarchy is loved by the people.

Although Thailand is officially a constitutional monarchy, an army-led bloodless coup in 1932 having removed the absolute powers of Thailand's King Prajadhipok, the monarchy remains one of

the most influential institutions in the land, and its presence is felt everywhere.

The official representation is seen in the blue bar of the Thai tricolour (red is nation, white is religion); photographs of the current King Bhumibol Adulyadej adorn government buildings and public spaces; and lese majeste laws carry a maximum penalty of seven years' imprisonment for anyone convicted of insulting the royal family.

Radio and TV stations play the national anthem regularly, as do schools, cinemas and railway and bus stations, when people will stand respectfully for the duration.

King Bhumibol's subjects have a famed love of him and will generally take offence at anyone speaking ill of the monarchy. His photograph is frequently found in shops and homes of Buddhists and non-Buddhist minorities alike. In many Muslim homes it is common to find a print of the king next to a picture of the Kaaba at Mecca, as a statement of both spiritual and secular loyalty. There may even be photos of his predecessors hanging alongside, particularly King Mongkut and King Chulalongkorn, the modernisers of Thailand in the late-19th and early 20th centuries.

Books and films about King Mongkut based on *The English Governess at the Siamese Court*, the memoirs of Anna Leonowens, are all banned in Thailand, including Hollywood favourite *The King & I*. Leonowens was a tutor of the royal children, but is regarded as having misrepresented her role and life in the palace.

King Bhumibol ascended the throne in 1946 after the mysterious death of his brother King Ananda Mahidol.

Man of the people

Respect for the king is enhanced by a sense of his morality and representation of traditional Thai values in the face of corrupt governments. He was seen as the ameliorating figure in the conflicts of 1973, 1976 and 1992, when the army and police killed many civilians. In recent years, though, he has been criticised by some supporters of Thaksin Shinawatra, who believe elements of the traditional elite were involved in the overthrow of the fugitive ex-prime minister. The *lese majeste* laws have been used more widely than usual during recent years to silence political rivals of all sides. King Bhumibol is also seen as a man of the people, particularly through his work in the King's Project, which helps small agricultural communities, and his subjects are genuinely proud of his achievements in the field of jazz; he has jammed with players Stan Getz and Benny Goodman. Huge crowds turn out for the king's birthday celebrations in Sanam Luang each December. ❑

LEFT: Prime Minister Yingluck Shinawatra.

thereafter. Although Ayutthaya failed to make Malacca a vassal state, it established control over much of the peninsula.

The rise of Burma

The 16th century witnessed the rise of Burma, which, under a powerful and aggressive dynasty, waged war on the Thais. In 1569, Burmese forces captured the city of Ayutthaya. King Naresuan the Great (ruled 1590–1605) succeeded in restoring Siamese independence, but in 1767, the Burmese armies once again invaded Ayutthaya, destroying Siam's capital.

Despite this, Siam made a rapid recovery. A noble of Chinese descent named Taksin led the

divine powers, and attacked the economically powerful Chinese merchant class. In 1782, a rebellion broke out, and Taksin was murdered.

The Chakri dynasty of Bangkok

In 1782, General Chakri assumed the throne and took the title Phra Phutthayotfa (King Rama I). One of his first decisions was to move the capital across the Chao Phraya River from Thonburi to the small settlement of Bang Makok, the "place of olive plums", which would become the city of Bangkok. His new palace was located on Rattanakosin Island, protected from attack by the river to the west and by a series of canals to the north, east and south. Rama I

resistance. From his base at Chanthaburi on the southeast coast, he defeated the Burmese and re-established the Siamese state. Taksin also set up the capital at Thonburi and was crowned king in 1768. He rapidly reunited the central Thai heartlands, and marched south to re-establish Siamese rule over all southern Thailand and the Malay states as far south as Penang and Trengganu.

Although a brilliant military tactician, Taksin was, by 1779, in political trouble. He alienated the Buddhist establishment by claiming to have

ABOVE: The city of Ayutthaya was ruined by the Burmese invasion.

restored much of the social and political system of Ayutthaya, promulgating new law codes, reinstating court ceremonies and imposing discipline on the Buddhist monkhood. Six great ministries headed by royal princes administered the government, one of which – the Kalahom – controlled the south.

In 1785, underestimating the resilience and strength of the new king, the Burmese once again invaded, driving far to the south to attack Phuket, Chaiya and Phattalung before being defeated by Rama I near Kanchanaburi. By the time of his death in 1809, Rama I controlled the Malay Peninsula as far south as Kedah and Trengganu, as well as the Gulf Coast as far east as the Cambodian frontier with Vietnam. Siam had become an empire considerably larger than Thailand today.

But despite these amazing successes, Thailand's present frontiers were not yet fixed. In 1825, the British sent a mission to Bangkok. They had annexed southern Burma and were extending their control over Malaya. The king was reluctant to give in to British demands, but his advisers warned him that Siam would meet the same fate as Burma unless the British were accommodated. In 1826, therefore, Siam concluded its first commercial treaty with a Western power. Under the treaty, Siam agreed to establish a uniform taxation system, to reduce

taxes on foreign trade and to abolish some of the royal monopolies. As a result, Siam's trade increased rapidly, many more foreigners settled in Bangkok and Western cultural influences began to spread. The kingdom became wealthier and its army better armed, but it now faced new challenges from Europe, rather than the old rivals Burma and Vietnam.

Under the threat of military pressure from France, a colonial power in Indochina since 1883, King Chulalongkorn (Rama V) was obliged to yield territory in the east, including western Cambodia, to the French. The British interceded to prevent further French aggression, but their price, in 1909, was British sovereignty over Thai-controlled Kedah, Kelantan, Perlis and Terengganu (part of present-day Malaysia) under the Anglo-Siamese Treaty of 1909. Only when this had been signed did Siam finally assume its present frontiers.

Military rule and modern times

In 1932, the Thai military staged a coup and ended the absolute power of the Chakri dynasty. Three years later, in 1935, King Rama VII abdicated, and Ananda Mahidol (Rama VIII, 1935–46), who was then at school in Switzerland, was chosen to be the next monarch. For the next 15 years, Siam was without a resident monarch for the first time in its history, and power lay with the military. In 1939, military strongman Luang Phibunsongkhram ordered that the name of the country be changed from Siam to Thailand and adopted the current national flag.

In 1940, moving to align Thailand with the Japanese, Phibun launched a small-scale war against the Vichy French in Indochina, retaking western Cambodia, including Angkor and much of the coast. Subsequently, on 8 December 1941, Japan invaded Thailand as a springboard for its attack on the British in Malaya and Singapore. The Thai armed forces resisted for a few hours, but Phibun, now confident of a Japanese victory over the Allies, decided to enter a formal alliance with the Japanese. As a reward, he was permitted to occupy certain

REEL LIFE BEACH

Numerous scenes from the movie *The Beach* (2000), starring Hollywood heart-throb Leonardo DiCaprio and based on the critically acclaimed novel by Alex Garland, were filmed on Phuket (at Surin, Ko Kaew and Kata beaches, Laem Promthep and Thalang), while the major part of the movie was shot at Maya Bay, Ko Phi Phi Ley. The film put the spotlight on the country in a positive way – indirectly promoting the attractions of Phuket to a worldwide audience – although at the time the filmmakers provoked criticism for allegedly altering the landscape. The main criticism today, ironically, is that the film caused excessive tourism on the island.

LEFT: Chakri monarchs in order of reign (left to right, from top), kings Mongkut (Rama IV), Chulalongkorn, Vajiravudh, Prajadhipok, Ananda and Bhumibol.
RIGHT: Thai leader Phibunsongkhram (bottom right) with US President Eisenhower in the 1950s.

territories lost to the British, including northern Malaya. But in 1945, following the defeat of Japan, the new Thai government of Khuang Aphaiwong withdrew unilaterally from Malaya. Two years later, Thailand withdrew from western Cambodia as well.

In June 1946, King Bhumibol Adulyadej (Rama IX) ascended the throne, and remains king today, the longest reigning head of state in the world *(see page 30)*.

The Post-war era
Since 1932, Thailand has endured 19 coups and had nearly 60 prime ministers, although some have served several terms. All governments were led by the military between 1946 and 1973, when a clique of generals dubbed "the Three Tyrants" employed martial law. Clashes on 14 October 1973 between troops and protesting students at Democracy Monument left many students dead, and the Three Tyrants fled to the US.

After a brief civilian government, in 1976 one of the generals, Thanom, returned, sparking protests. On 6 October, police, troops and paramilitary organisations stormed Thammasat University. Within hours, the army regained power.

For the next decade, relatively moderate military rule laid the foundations for new elections, which ushered in a civilian government, until another coup, this one bloodless, in 1991. The following year, more than 100 pro-democracy demonstrators were wounded or killed.

King Bhumibol brokered reconciliation, and a series of elected governments followed. In 1997, Thailand's economic crash triggered the Asian financial crisis.

Thaksin Shinawatra
Following the 2001 elections, the new prime minister Thaksin Shinawatra proved immediately controversial. He faced corruption charges and was condemned for suppressing the media and for his "War on Drugs", in which hundreds were killed. But he also introduced loans and cheap health care for the poor. As he became wildly popular in poorer rural areas, he was irritating traditional powers in Bangkok.

In 2005, anti-Thaksin demonstrators adopted the colour yellow to show allegiance to the monarchy, becoming known as the Yellow Shirts. In September 2006, Thaksin was ousted in a military coup.

PATTAYA AND SEX TOURISM

Tourism really began to develop along Thailand's southeast coast in the 1970s, gradually transforming and enriching a region that had traditionally been dependent on farming and fishing. Perhaps the most infamous and uncontrolled transformation occurred in Pattaya, where prostitution is rife.

Prostitution was made illegal in 1960, although the law is rarely enforced, and sex is openly for sale in go-go bars, brothels and massage parlours. In part this is because it is an accepted and common practice for Thai men to patronise prostitutes or have a *mia noi* ("little wife"), or mistress.

Sex tourism escalated with American troops taking R&R during the Vietnam War, and, by the 1980s, planeloads of men were flying in for the purpose. Many sex-workers, both male and female, come from northeast Thailand, where incomes are the lowest in the country. Many cross-cultural marriages have started in a brothel, and government figures often cite foreign husbands in northeastern villages as being significant contributors to GDP.

NGOs estimate between 200,000 and 300,000 sex workers in Thailand. Having found that few are motivated to leave the business, extricating workers is no longer their primary focus. Organisations such as Empower instead educate workers about the dangers of HIV, and teach them English so they are less likely to be exploited by clients.

As Thaksin lived in exile, his followers, calling themselves the United Front for Democracy Against Dictatorship (UDD), and wearing red shirts, also protested. A Thaksin proxy, the People Power Party (PPP) won the next general election in December 2007, and Thaksin returned the following year, only to later skip bail on corruption charges and flee once again to London.

Red Shirt, Yellow Shirt

Yellow Shirt demonstrations resumed and, during late 2008, they seized the airport, bringing the country to a standstill. In December 2008, the courts disbanded the ruling party and, in a deal widely seen as brokered by the army, the

In 2011, the Thaksin proxy Pheu Thai Party, led by his sister Yingluck, won a landslide election victory and Yingluck became Thailand's first female prime minister. Her early months, already difficult, were severely tested by the worst floods in decades, which saw large parts of the north, northeast and central regions inundated. The government endured heavy criticism for diverting flood waters towards poorer communities to save central Bangkok.

During 2012 the government pushed for a change to the Constitution and a general amnesty for post-coup events, seen as an attempt to return Thaksin's confiscated assets and allow him a comeback to the country.

Democrat Party took office, with Abhisit Vejjajiva as prime minister, bringing the Red Shirts back to the streets.

In April 2009, the Red Shirts disrupted the ASEAN summit in Pattaya, and heads of state were airlifted to safety; Songkran riots erupted in Bangkok; and PAD (Yellow Shirts) leader Sondhi Limthongkul was shot, but survived.

In February 2010, Thaksin was found guilty of abuse of power and had assets of B46 billion confiscated. In April and May, thousands of Red Shirts occupied parts of Bangkok, closing Pathumwan shopping malls for several weeks. Eighty-five people were killed and nearly 1,500 injured in clashes with the army.

The outcome is unclear. The king's age and health problems cause uncertainty about the succession, and the Red Shirts are a complex alliance of previously voiceless groups that include the rural poor, democracy supporters and grass roots movements. By February 2010 these consisted of 459 previously disparate causes.

As one Red Shirt leader said about the coup makers: "They have turned Thaksin the big capitalist into Thaksin the revolutionary." Another warned that, "Thaksin sees himself as the destination, but he is just an island along the way." ❑

ABOVE: Thaksin spearheaded a goodwill gesture in 2004 to airdrop paper cranes over the troubled south.

Phuket's Vegetarian Festival

Devotees striking their heads with axe blades, cutting their tongues with knives and rolling in broken glass are common sights at the Vegetarian Festival.

According to legend, early Chinese settlers who arrived in Phuket 200 years ago witnessed the origins of the island's most unusual event, the Phuket Vegetarian Festival. The festival is celebrated in the first nine days of the ninth month of the Chinese lunar calendar, usually in late September or early October.

During the event devout Taoist Chinese and many other Thais abstain from eating meat. In Phuket Town, the festival's activities centre on six Chinese temples, with Jui Tui Temple *(see page 217)*, on Thanon Ranong, the most important, followed by Bang Niew Temple and Sui Boon Tong Temple. The festival is also observed around the country, including Kathu Town in Phuket (where the Vegetarian Festival is believed to have originated), Bangkok and also at Trang Town in Trang Province.

Bizarre and extraordinary

Devotees at the Vegetarian Festival organise processions, make temple offerings, stage cultural shows and consult with mediums. They also perform a series of bizarre and extraordinary acts of self-mortification that, to the uninitiated, seem scarcely credible. Devotees enter into a trance designed to bring the gods to earth to participate in the festival, then walk with bare soles on red-hot coals, climb ladders made of razor-sharp sword blades, stab themselves with all manner of sharp objects, and pierce their cheeks with sharpened stakes, swords, daggers and even screwdrivers. It can be a bloody and disconcerting sight. Miraculously, little permanent damage seems to be done.

RIGHT: ritual self-mortification at the festival.

The opening event is the raising of the 10-metre (30ft) -tall lantern pole to notify the gods that the festival is about to begin. Meanwhile, altars are set up along major roads bearing offerings of fruit and flowers, incense, candles and nine tiny cups of tea. These are for the Nine Emperor Gods of the Taoist pantheon invited to participate in the festival and in whose honour the celebrations are held. Thousands of locals and visitors line the streets to observe the events, which are accompanied by loud music and frenzied dancing.

Phuket's Chinese community claims that a visiting theatrical troupe from Fujian

almost two centuries ago first began the festival. The story goes that the troupe was stricken with a strange illness because its members had failed to propitiate the Nine Emperor Gods. In order to recover, they had to perform a nine-day penance, after which they became well.

Everyone can enjoy specially prepared vegetarian food at street stalls and markets all over the island. Strangely, these vegetarian dishes, in Thai or Chinese style, are made to resemble meat. Though made from soy or other vegetable substitutes, the food looks and often tastes very much like chicken, pork or duck. ❑

A Calendar of Celebrations

Whether religious or secular, national or local, festivals in Thailand are truly fantastic displays of celebration.

There can be no doubt that the Thais place great importance on their festivals. Some date back centuries, like Loy Krathong, which began in the 13th century. Others, like Lamphun's Lamyai Fruit Festival, are more recent creations. In fact, new festivals are thought up every year, sometimes to promote tourism and often just for a bit of *sanuk* (fun). Some festivals are weighty events upon which the future of the nation depends. Some are more spiritual, allowing one to "make merit" and ensure a better karmic rebirth, while others are purely secular celebrations of the joy of living. Note: as Buddhist festivals fall within or depend upon the lunar calendar, their exact dates vary each year.

Above: the King's Birthday is celebrated on 5 December nationwide, but most spectacularly at Rattanakosin in Bangkok. The Grand Palace is illuminated, and there is a fireworks display.

Above: held in May at Sanam Luang in Bangkok, the Brahmin rituals of the Royal Ploughing Ceremony mark the start of the rice-growing season and divine whether the coming year's harvest will be plentiful.

Left: Visakha Puja, on the 15th day of the sixth lunar month, marks the birth, enlightenment and passing of the Buddha. It is Thailand's most important religious event, marked by candlelit processions at temples.

ABOVE: on 3 December is the Trooping of the Colour, held outside the old Thai Parliament in Bangkok. The King, Queen and other members of the royal family review the elite Royal Guard, who are clad in elaborate, brightly coloured dress uniforms and tall plumed helmets. The monarch arrives in style in his personal yellow Rolls-Royce.

BELOW: every 13 April, Thais mark the traditional lunar new year – which coincides with the height of the hot season – with an extraordinary bout of good-humoured water throwing throughout the country. Don't expect to stay dry for long when in public. Songkran festivities may last as long as four or five days, and involve music, dancing and, very often, liberal amounts of alcohol.

BELOW: Makha Puja is observed on the full moon of the third lunar month, to mark one of the Buddha's most important sermons. "Merit-making" ceremonies are held at temples across Thailand. In a quiet and dignified tradition that goes back centuries, people strive to atone for past misdeeds and perform good deeds. Food and robes are offered to monks, candlelit processions wind around stupas (shrines), flowers and incense are offered to Buddha images, and caged animals are released.

BELOW: perhaps Thailand's loveliest festival, Loy Krathong is celebrated on the full-moon night in November to pay respects to Mae Khongkha, goddess of the country's life-bringing rivers and lakes. The festival is supposed to have started at Sukhothai, the first Thai capital, during the time of King Ramkhamhaeng, when a court lady prepared a *krathong*, or float, for the king. Banana-stem floats, beautifully decorated with flowers, incense, candles and small coins, are released on waterways across the country.

RELIGION

All over Thailand, the visitor will see saffron-robed Buddhist monks and hear the soft chanting of Pali scriptures and the tinkling of temple bells. But look beyond the elaborate, brightly coloured temples and you will see the influence of spirit worship on everyday life.

Thailand is an overwhelmingly Buddhist nation. Around 95 percent of the population follow Buddhism, and its influence is apparent almost everywhere. Only in the very far south of the country, on the border with Malaysia, does Islam predominate.

The Way of the Elders

The main form of Buddhism practised is Theravada, or the "Way of the Elders", though in Chinese temples, the Mahayana, or "Greater Vehicle" tradition, may be found alongside Taoist and Confucian images. Both traditions teach that desire for worldly things leads to suffering, and that the only way to alleviate this suffering is to cast off desire. Theravada Buddhism emphasises personal salvation rather than the Mahayana way of the *bodhisattva*, which is the temporary renunciation of personal salvation in order to help humanity achieve enlightenment. The goal of the Theravadin is to become an *arhat*, or "worthy one".

In practice, most Thais hope that by "making merit" and honouring the *triratna*, or "Three Jewels" – the Buddha, the *sangha* (order of monks) and the *dharma* (sacred teachings) – they will attain a better rebirth and ultimately attain *nirvana*, or enlightenment. To do this, one should strive to build up positive *karma*. This may best be achieved by not taking life, abstaining from drinking alcohol and other intoxicants, avoiding gambling and sexual promiscuity, keeping calm and not becoming angry,

as well as honouring the elderly, monks and the Thai monarchy. Most Thai Buddhist men will join the *sangha* and become monks at least once in their lives. Women, too, may be ordained as nuns, though fewer are, and the act is usually delayed until old age, when the task of raising children has been completed.

Appeasing the spirits

Spirit worship plays a major, if informal, role in Thai religious life, alongside the practice of Buddhism. It is widely accepted that there are spirits everywhere – spirits of the water, wind and woods, and both locality spirits and tutelary spirits. These spirits are not so much good

LEFT: Khao Luang cave temple, Petchaburi.
RIGHT: a Buddhist monk carrying an alms bowl.

or bad, but are powerful and unpredictable. Moreover, they have many of the foibles of humans, being capable of vindictiveness, lust, jealousy, greed and malice. To appease them, offerings must be made, and since they display many aspects of human nature, these offerings are often what people would value themselves.

To counteract the spirits and potential dangers in life, protective spells are cast and kept in small amulets mostly worn around the neck. Curiously, the amulets are not bought, but rather rented on an indefinite lease from "landlords", often monks considered to possess magical powers. Some monasteries have been turned into highly profitable factories for the

production of amulets. There are amulets that offer protection against accidents while travelling or against bullet and knife wounds; some even boost sexual attraction. All this has no more to do with Buddhism than the protective blue-patterned tattoos sported by some rural Thais to ward off evil.

The city pillar

It is not known exactly when the Thai people first embraced a belief in spirits, but it was most probably long before their migration south into present-day Thailand, and certainly before their gradual conversion to Buddhism around 700–1200 AD. When the first Thai migrants established themselves in the plains around Sukhothai, their basic unit of organisation was the *muang*, a group of villages under the control and protection of a *wiang*, or fortified town. Of crucial importance to each *muang*, and located at the centre of each *wiang*, was the city pillar, or *lak muang*. To this day, it is a feature of towns in Thailand.

The *lak muang* – generally a rounded pole thought to represent a rice shoot – is the home of the guardian spirits of the city and surrounding district. It should be venerated on a regular basis, and an annual ceremony, with offerings of incense, flowers and candles, must also be held to ensure the continuing prosperity and safety of the *muang*. Long ago, during the region's animist past, the raising of city pillars was often associated with brutal rituals involving human sacrifice.

Fortunately, such rituals have long since disappeared from the scene, as gentler traditions

---

CONSECRATING A SPIRIT HOUSE

Setting up a spirit house, or *san phra phum*, is not a casual undertaking, but one that requires the services of an experienced professional. Usually, this is a Brahmin priest called a *phram* (dressed in white, in contrast to the Buddhist saffron robes), or at least someone schooled in Brahmin ritual.

The consecration ritual is commenced by scattering small coins around the site chosen for the new spirit house, and in the soil beneath the foundations. Then the spirit house is raised and offerings are made. These include flowers (usually elegant garlands of jasmine), money, candles and incense – the last often stuck into the crown of a pig's head.

The *phram*, together with the householder and his various relatives and friends, then prays to the spirits, beseeching the local *chao thii*, or Lord of the Locality, to take up residence in the new spirit house.

Spirit houses are often beautifully decorated, and to entice the *chao thii* into its new home, various inducements are generally added. These may include traditional offerings such as statues of dancers, ponies, servants and other necessities made of plaster or wood. In more recent times, items such as cars and other modern consumer desirables have been offered as well, each carefully chosen to catch the spirit's fancy.

associated with Theravada Buddhism have modified spirit beliefs. Today, some *lak muang* are topped by a gilded image of the Buddha.

Spirit houses

For many centuries, offerings have been made when land had to be cleared for agriculture or building. After all, the spirits of a place are its original owners, and their feelings have to be taken into consideration. At some point, it was decided that an effective way of placating a locality spirit was to build it a small house, or *san phra phum*, of its own. That way, it would be comfortable, content and, above all, would not want to move in with its human neighbours!

worship has been a two-way process. There is hardly a Buddhist temple in the country that does not incorporate an elaborate spirit house in its grounds – built at the same time as the consecration of the temple in order to accommodate the displaced locality spirits.

As if this weren't enough, the Thais also feel obliged to consider the world outside the *muang*. If the *lak muang* is the centre of civilisation and safety, the jungled hills and inaccessible mountains are the opposite. It is no surprise that the Thais erect spirit houses along the roads linking their settlements, paying particular attention to threatening or ominous landscapes. Even today, every pass or steep section of road

Thai Buddhists believe that every human house should have its own spirit house for the wellbeing of the locality spirit. These may be anywhere in the garden (even, in big cities, on the roof), with the important proviso that the shadow of human habitation should never fall on the spirit house. Shops and commercial establishments have their own spirit houses as well, often positioned to counteract the power of rival establishments' spirits.

The association of Buddhism with spirit

PHALLUS SHRINE

Certain spirit shrines, or their residents, are thought to have powers to redress specific problems. An example is the shrine of Chao Mae Thapthim, a female deity considered to reside in a venerable banyan tree, just behind Bangkok's Swissôtel Nai Lert Park. Mae Thapthim has the power to induce fertility, and many young women seeking to become pregnant visit the shrine. They leave the usual presents of flowers and incense, as well as a less common type of offering – wooden phalluses that come in all sizes, from a few centimetres long to giant representations extending over a metre and a half, standing on legs or even wheels.

LEFT: the city foundation pillar of Bangkok.
ABOVE LEFT: a typical spirit shrine in Thailand.
ABOVE RIGHT: Bangkok's Chao Mae Thapthim shrine.

is topped by a spirit house to accommodate the inconvenienced locality spirit. Passing drivers beep their horns in salutation, and many stop to make offerings. Spirit houses are also raised in fields to ensure the safety of the crop.

Islam in the south

It is only in the furthest south of peninsular Thailand, in Malay-speaking territory, that temples and spirit houses disappear, replaced by minarets and mosques. Islam first came to this region in the 8th century. Carried across the Indian Ocean by Arab and South Indian traders, it found fertile ground among the region's Malay-speaking people. The Muslim tradition

of Thailand's deep south is Sunni Islam of the Shafi'i school, as in neighbouring Malaysia.

When the first Muslims arrived, they settled and intermarried with the local Malay population, most of whom at the time practised a syncretic Hindu-Buddhist belief. By Islamic law, the children of such unions were raised as Muslims, and, over the centuries, a combination of intermarriage and proselytising led to the conversion of almost all the indigenous Malay peoples.

Comprising less than 5 percent of the population, Thai Muslims are a tiny minority, only dominant in the four southern provinces of Satun, Pattani, Yala and Narathiwat. In this

WITCH DOCTORS

There is an older spirit tradition practised by many Thai Muslims in the Malay-speaking south. Though widely believed in by most ordinary folk, it is officially condemned by orthodox Muslim teachers. This tradition is represented by the *bomoh*, or Malay "witch doctor", who can foretell future events, cure physical, mental and spiritual diseases, curse individuals or lift such curses. The witch doctors rely on a fascinating mix of folk Islam overlaying a deep vein of other traditions that predate Islam in the region. Because of this syncretism, which is completely forbidden in orthodox Islam, much of *bomoh* practice is concealed from outsiders.

region, the people are conservative, generally working as farmers or fisherfolk, studying the faith in religious schools, and saving to go on the haj, or pilgrimage, to Mecca. The Shafi'i school is traditional and not overly rigorous. However, home-grown radicalism and fundamentalist influences from abroad have injected new fervour into the small insurgent groups behind the increasingly violent separatist movement in Pattani, Yala and Narathiwat provinces. Satun Province, although largely Muslim, has steered clear of such strife and unrest, and is safe to visit. ❑

ABOVE: boys at a Muslim school in Kamala, Phuket.

From Buddhism to Modern Spa

Massage, with its Buddhist origins, is an inherent part of normal life in Thailand and this makes spa treatments a natural Thai experience.

Travelling monks arrived in Thailand in the 2nd or 3rd century AD, bearing not only Buddhism, but also *nuad paen boran* (ancient massage), which legend says was developed from Indian Vedic treatments by Shivakar Kumar Baccha, the Buddha's own medical adviser. Nearly 2,000 years after it entered the country, the world now calls it simply Thai massage. It is one of many treatments that are now available in the modern spas that are an enticing feature of the Thailand beach holiday.

The association with the country's religious philosophy means that the most dedicated masseurs still perform the service within the Buddhist concept of mindfulness. Before they start, true adherents will make a *wai* (a slight bow with hands clasped together) to pay respects to their teacher and focus on *metta* (loving kindness), thought to be the ideal state of mind in which to give massage.

Places of healing

For centuries, throughout Thailand, temples were places of healing, and they administered many of the treatments we now associate with modern spas, such as herbal compresses and herbal medicines.

As it is based on ancient Indian teachings, Thai massage includes the stretching elements of yoga alongside acupressure and reflexology. There should also be a meditative quality, although low-budget shops may have music or TV playing that scupper this. The massage principle revolves around 10 energy lines, called *sip sen*, believed to carry physical, emotional,

and spiritual energy between meridian points around the body. When the lines become blocked, illness or emotional stress occurs, so they must be reopened.

The experience is usually vigorous, employing push-and-pull stretching of tendons and joints and deep-tissue kneading with elbows, knees and feet and fingers, so it is not a suitable treatment for people with back, neck or joint problems. *Bow bow, kap/ka* is a useful phrase, meaning "softer, please". Sometimes an ointment is used on painful muscles – Tiger balm is the most famous brand – but generally there are no oils involved.

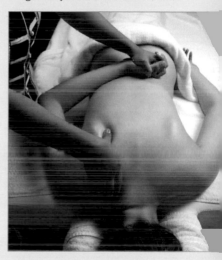

The most common operations are in small houses consisting of little more than several mattresses on the floor, curtained off from each other. These places can be found on many streets, particularly in tourist areas, and provide exquisite relaxation for as little as B200 an hour.

Urban spas, often in traditional teak houses, may include beauty elements such as body scrubs and facial treatments, while luxurious resort spas offer the gamut of "wellness" options, from massage to Traditional Chinese medicine, reiki, meditation, hypnotherapy and New Age treatments such as crystals and floral essences. ❑

RIGHT: massages in Thailand aim to reopen blocked lines of energy around the body.

SOUTHERN THAI CUISINE

Southern Thai food is the stuff of poetry: 'Mussaman curry is like a lover. As peppery and fragrant as the cumin seed / Its exciting allure arouses / I am urged to seek its source' – *Boat Songs*, King Rama II.

Dramatic limestone outcrops, white sands and pellucid waters are, for many visitors, among the many well-loved attractions of Thailand's islands and beaches. Very few, however, have any knowledge of *aahaan pak tai*, the south's distinctive cuisine, arguably the kingdom's most dynamic style of cooking.

Even though the influence of cookbooks, international restaurants and travel shows (not to mention the Thai government's highly active efforts to promote the cuisine) has helped to assure Thai food a place among the world's great cuisines, general awareness of Thailand's culinary traditions has yet to reach the level enjoyed by countries such as Italy and France. While many foodies are aware of the distinct regional variations of Italian and French cooking, Thai cuisine is still often judged as a monotypic tradition, represented simplistically by a menu of dishes characteristic of Bangkok's central cuisine.

Diverse influences

Of all the regional styles of cooking, southern Thailand's bears all the hallmarks of substantial cross-cultural influence. History, trade, religion and empire are stirred into the mix. The great Srivijaya rulers of Indonesia and their long-reaching influence, the 8th-century pilgrims of Islam who arrived before the Thai polity coalesced, the presence of Portuguese envoys, and the influence of Chinese festivals all played a part in the evolution of southern Thai cuisine.

The recurrent waves of trading that occurred from the 16th to 18th century contributed Persian spices such as cardamom and cumin. In much the same way, the Portuguese trading ships introduced ingredients from the New World, such as tomatoes, aubergines, cashews and chillies.

Aromatic curries can be almost Indian in their rich palette of spices and vibrant colours, and indeed, much of the cuisine's character was influenced by the Tamil and Keralan workers who have since migrated to neighbouring Malaysia. The Chinese, on the other hand, in places such as Phuket and Trang, brought their taste for coffee and dim sum with them.

LEFT: a spicy red curry and its many ingredients.
RIGHT: a Bangkok fruit stall.

Fierce and spicy flavours

So, what does southern Thai food taste like? Along with Isaan cooking of the northeast, it wields the most aggressive flavours of all Thai food. Indeed, visitors unaccustomed to it will immediately notice the fiery hot flavour that southerners are so fond of – *rot phet*, imparted by sharp hits of the numerous types of chilli used. But, like all Thai cuisine, this is balanced by sour, salty and sweet flavours. It is a richly woven meld of spices (which in some places can be so wide-ranging as to taste almost Persian) with a wondrous aroma hinting at its Indian influence, and pungent dashes of shrimp paste (a locally made speciality).

With technique at a premium, the artistry and complexity of preparation is almost jazz-like, with individual cooks improvising endlessly on old favourites, and occasionally yielding unlikely new combinations. The building blocks of flavour include *masala*-like curry blends, fermented vegetables and fish, various pickled bamboo shoots and greens, and an array of fruit that, like the versatile papaya, range from astringent when green and unripe to sugary sweet when ripened to maturity.

Bounteous ingredients

Natural bounty is a huge southern advantage. The Gulf of Thailand and the Andaman Sea

CHINESE FOOD IN TRANG TOWN

Though only a 10-minute ride from the limestone mountains of the coast, the sleepy trading town of Trang has something more than natural beauty: it is a little-known stronghold of Chinese food culture in the south.

With a large population of second- and third-generation ethnic Chinese immigrants, the flavours here are Thai in influence, but also traditional enough to be heartily welcomed in China. Dim sum can be found on street corners in the morning, when blue-collar workers load up on noodles and tiny dumplings of shrimp, pork or crab. Come nightfall, the town's vaunted barbecued pork – an unctuous and sweet creation permeated with just enough grill smoke to qualify it as a savoury – takes centre stage.

But the real draw here is black, heady and liquid. Trang, above all, is a coffee town. Shop owners of Hokkien Chinese descent roast their own beans and prepare coffee in a big, sock-like filter according to tradition. Every strip of houses has a coffee shop, so it is worth making the rounds. Some are rickety, the size of a pick-up truck, and made of clapboards. Others are near mini temples and always full of monks. Near the train station are several coffee shops where the cups of traditional thick, black brews are replaced by sugar-laced iced coffees and plates of sweet *roti*, loved by the youthful student clientele.

harbour troves of white snapper, horse mackerel, marbled goby (*soon hock*), squid, prawns and rock lobster. And because the Isthmus of Kra, which separates these bodies of water, is so narrow, there is rarely a catch that does not end up, often within a day, in both Ko Samui (in the Gulf) and Ko Lanta (in the Andaman).

Whether in the markets that spring up by the light of dawn, or at roadside stands under neon lights come nightfall, fruit is piled high. Phuket has a luscious sweet pineapple with a taste that hints at vanilla, apricots and rose; it is so tender that even the core can be eaten dipped in sugar. The spiky, stinky durian (especially the *kan yao* variety) is most prolific in the deep-south province of Yala, while the cooling, purple-skinned mangosteen is excellent south of Nakhon Si Thammarat. Water greens, jungle ferns, ginger buds, snake beans, lemongrass, galangal shoots – there is an abundance of vegetables and herbs, too.

Of course, rice is still the staple. In the past, it sustained workers through the day with just small portions of chilli, curry or sauce added for flavour. Even now, rural Thais eat large helpings of rice with just morsels of dried or salted fish. Thankfully, long-grain jasmine-scented Thai rice is one of the most delicious to be found in Asia.

Representative dishes

The seafood of the south is so fresh that it warrants little fuss in preparation. The best of the catch, such as Phuket's famed rock lobster or Trang's soft shell crab, is simply grilled or stir-fried with assertive seasonings such as lemongrass, black pepper and garlic. Squid is treated in the same way or, like many fish dishes, served with dipping sauces of chilli, lime and garlic. Deep-frying is a favourite, too, whether served in a sweet-sour Chinese style or in a very southern way with turmeric and garlic.

The curries are fiercely spicy and leave their milder cousins of the central region looking a bit boring. One signature dish is *kaeng leuang*, a southern-style curry stained yellow-orange by turmeric and bristling with chillies, pickled bamboo shoots, shrimp paste, cucumber and syrupy-sweet pineapple. Another, *kaeng tai pla*,

---

LEFT: fresh bounty from Thailand's coastal waters.
RIGHT: pineapples grown on Phuket.

> Pak kred, *a dish of flower buds, ginger roots, bean pods, cashew leaves, and many other mysterious items, is a tangle worthy of a botanist. It helps cool the menacing spice of southern curries.*

is a vicious stew of chillies, pickled bamboo shoots, fermented fish and black pepper that broadcasts its scent in all directions. A gentler speciality to try is *khao yam*, a seemingly innocuous salad of rice, vegetables, slivers of green mango, kaffir lime leaves, coconut flakes, dried

shrimp and a strong fish sauce called *budu*. The flavour is floral and feminine, yet unmistakably southern in its lingering strength – all the more so if prepared with *sataw*, a large lima-bean lookalike with a pungent flavour and aroma.

Muslim cooking

The Muslim cookery of the south eschews pork, of course, but goat, beef and chicken more than make up for it, as evidenced in the Indian *biryani* like rice dishes eaten here. The fragrant spices of cumin, cardamom, turmeric, as well as black and white pepper, are often at work, along with the different textures imparted by the use of yoghurt and ghee. Early morning and midday are the best times to find oxtail soup with torch ginger, shallots, chillies and coriander. *Roti*, the beloved Indian flatbread, is fun to watch being made, thanks to the often balletic slapping, pulling and whipping of the dough. It can be paired with a variety of curries and stuffed with egg or bananas according to preference. *Roti* stands live or die by the quality of their curries, and are a good place to try the distinctive spice-rich *mussaman* curry, sometimes thickened with pulverised nuts.

Localised variations

The south of Thailand is home to some of the most highly localised strains of regional cooking in the country. The flavours, the ingredients and the specialities vary with the town and which-ever communities are dominant there. Locating any given speciality is as easy as locating where the people renowned for cooking it live.

A stronghold of culture and a regional centre in earlier times, the mid-peninsula hub of Nakhon Si Thammarat is renowned for its balanced but vigorously hot *kaeng tai pla* and stir-fries such as *kaeng khua kling*, a dry curry with bird's-eye chillies, Thai aromatic ginger and garlic.

The booming border city of Hat Yai is known for its night markets. Those in the know head straight for the fried chicken, crispy and redo-lent of lemongrass, shallots and garlic. Pattani

HOW TO EAT THAI FOOD

Most Thai meals consist of several dishes placed in the centre of the table to be shared by all; the larger the group, the more dishes one can try. Except for dessert, there are no courses, as in a Western meal. Rather, the various dishes are enjoyed at the same time. Place a heap of rice on to your plate, together with small portions of various dishes at the side (it's polite to take only a little at a time). Eat with a fork and spoon, using the fork in the left hand to push food on to the spoon. Chopsticks are only for Chinese and noodle dishes. In the far south, the traditional way of eating with the fingers is still practised by ethnic Malays.

and Yala boast old, wooden Islamic architecture and a hot and salty cooking style of their own. Songkhla has a fine seafood tradition, and the border outpost of Satun, a sleepy ocean hamlet, is where the curries combine the characteris-tics of Thai and Indo-Malay food. Meanwhile, Ranong is an unsung star for its Chinese-style coffee houses, not unlike Trang *(see page 46)*.

Of course, another advantage of the culinary experience in southern Thailand is its stunning setting. A meal here is never too far from a picture-perfect beach. ❑

ABOVE: a food stall in Songkhla offering a wide selection of Thai curries.

Eating Out in Bangkok

Bangkok has always been one of the world's best places to eat. One could spend a month here slurping and spooning up the many varieties of food on offer.

Each of Thailand's four regions has a distinct cuisine, and the beauty of dining in Bangkok is that they're all available, from the sweet northern curry *khao soy* to the spicy Isaan classic *somtam* and pungent *gaeng tai pla* from the south. They're often discovered at street stalls and markets serving the city's migrant communities. Just head for the busiest spots and look for fresh produce and attention to food presentation – all indications of a good cook.

Whether tucked down the Old City alleys or nestled against the modern blocks of Sukhumvit, street food is everywhere – a legion of mango and durian sellers, roast-duck specialists and vendors wielding cleavers to hack off slices of crispy pork.

Of many seafood set-ups in Chinatown, a pair of the most famous battle it out on opposite corners of Soi Texas, both dealing in swimming-fresh squid, prawns and mussels, simply grilled or steamed, then slathered with sauces (*naam jim*) of garlic, herbs, lime juice, fish sauce and everything from fermented bean to tamarind juice.

Traditional flavours

Away from the street, Bangkok also sizzles. The long-time practice of Thai restaurants catering to tourist tastes is now challenged by a movement towards authentic traditional flavours epitomised by places like Bo.lan, Supanniga Eating Room and a branch of Nahm, in London, which was the world's first Michelin-starred Thai restaurant. Another Michelin winner, Copenhagen's Kiin Kiin, also has an outlet here, Sra Bua, serving modern inventions like red-curry ice cream.

Other well-represented Asian cuisines are Indian – including the excellent Gaggan, which uses molecular techniques – Japanese (check out Zuma) and Chinese, a huge influence on Thai dining, particularly in the ubiquitous lunchtime noodle dishes. Mei Jeang and China House in the Peninsula and Oriental hotels, respectively, are among the best upmarket Chinese.

There's also a recent clutch of places filling a gap in the market for decent food at mid-range prices. The French-owned chain Wine Connection does bistro fare and wallet-friendly wines, at least by Thailand standards, which are plagued by very high

taxes. Other mid-range picks are Quince, Smith, the Spanish El Osito and the Mexican La Monita. Bangkok's favourite Western food, though, is Italian, with an estimated 100-plus outlets.

There's a fun local café scene at Kuppa, Coffee Beans by Dao and Greyhound Café, where Thai-spiced pasta dishes, roti and curries reveal an East-West blend. In the warm weather many people head for the cool breezes and glorious views of alfresco rooftop restaurants such as Sirocco and Red Sky. Bangkok, long celebrated for its Thai streetfood, is fast maturing into a city of sophisticated international dining. ❑

RIGHT: Vertigo Restaurant at the Banyan Tree Hotel.

NATURE AND ENVIRONMENT

Apart from its white sandy beaches, Thailand's natural treasures include lush tropical rainforests teeming with wildlife, stunning karst formations and pristine coral reefs. Sadly, preservation efforts cannot quite halt their destruction by human activities and natural calamities.

Thailand's biological treasures and diverse landforms derive from its geographical position at the crossroads of Southeast Asia. Just as the nation has accommodated many peoples and cultures, so has it served as a conduit dispersing varied plant and animal life.

Covering some 513,115 sq km (198,115 sq miles), Thailand's overall shape resembles the head of an elephant, with the southern peninsula forming the trunk. The vast valley called the Central Plain stretches about 450km (280 miles) to the Gulf of Thailand. Over the years, rich silt that the overflowing tributaries habitually deposited have created an agricultural rice bowl, watered nowadays by intensive irrigation

drawn from a network of large dams.

Endowed with heavy rainfall and humidity, Thailand's south encompasses the Isthmus of Kra right down to the Malay Peninsula. The coastal forests of the south were cleared to make way for rubber and palm plantations in the late 19th and early 20th centuries. The provinces of Petchaburi and Prachuap Khiri Khan form the narrow neck of land connecting the Central Plain with the peninsular south, where some of Thailand's most stunning white-sand beaches are found. At its narrowest point, the slender strip of Thai territory from the Gulf of Thailand to Dan Singkhon, on the Burmese border, is a mere 12km (7 miles) wide.

Flora

Up to the mid-20th century, forests covered about 70 percent of Thailand's land area. By 1960, the figure had dropped to 50 percent. Today, probably only about 15 percent of undisturbed forest remains. Perhaps another 15 percent has been replanted, often with non-indigenous species, or else turned into plantations of trees for palm oil, and, especially in the south, rubber and pineapples. In all of Southeast Asia, the scale and rate of deforestation in Thailand was once second only to that of Singapore. Following several fatal landslides, logging was outlawed in Thailand in 1989, and the situation is now more stable.

forests can still be found in the Khao Luang, Ko Surin, Ko Tarutao and Thale Ban national parks, all of which are in the south. Of special note, too, is Khao Sok National Park *(see page 203)*, the largest nature preserve in peninsular Thailand and dominated by thick forest-covered limestone peaks, some rising as high as 1,000 metres (3,280ft).

Fauna

Of the world's approximate 4,000 species of mammal, 287 are found in Thailand, including 18 hoofed species, 13 species of primates, nine types of wild cat (including tigers and clouded leopards), two species of bear, two of wild dog

Tropical rainforests are most abundant in the uplands of both the south and southeast, where rainfall is plentiful even in the dry season. These harbour the densest concentration of species, with herbs, shrubs, ferns and fungi forming the lowest layer of vegetation. Above ground level is a relatively open layer of palms, bamboos and shrubs. Mid-level trees, festooned with vines, mosses and orchids, create a 25-metre (82ft)-high canopy, with the more well-spaced trees of the uppermost canopy soaring as high as 60 metres (200ft). Thriving rain-

---

LEFT: Cheow Lan Lake at Khao Sok National Park.
ABOVE LEFT: tropical bloom. **ABOVE RIGHT:** a gibbon.

KRABI'S MANGROVE FORESTS

Mangroves are considered to be the rainforests of the coast, and though many have been decimated by human activities, the mangrove forests of Krabi remain remarkably intact. They are home to many types of fish, shrimp and mollusc, provide shelter for dugongs, monkeys, lizards and sea turtles, and are also nesting grounds for hundreds of bird species, including the white-bellied sea eagle, ruddy kingfisher, mangrove pitta and the great knot. In mud and shallow waters, fiddler crabs and mud skippers abound. Fortunately, plans to develop Krabi's Deep Water Port were shelved to protect this unique environment.

and eight varieties of dolphin. Bats are abundant, with 107 species identified so far. But tigers and the larger deer could soon join the list of mammals that have vanished since 1900: this includes rhinoceros, several species of deer, two otter species and the kouprey, a wild ox discovered in Thailand in the 1930s.

The Asian elephant – Thailand's national symbol – which was declared the kingdom's first protected species in 1921, is perilously close to extinction. From more than 20,000 a century ago, fewer than 8,000 survive in Thailand today. Khao Yai National Park, north of Bangkok, offers the best chance of observing some of Thailand's remaining wild elephants.

Thailand also harbours four types of reptile and three types of amphibian. Among the 175 species of snake are deadly cobras, kraits and vipers. No doubt most of the insect species have yet to be identified, but there are 1,200 variegated butterflies. Beetle species may number in the tens of thousands, but have been so little studied that entomologists occasionally discover new ones.

Visitors to national parks may not see any large animals, but they will be rewarded with bird sightings. There are around 900 species permanently resident in the region, while about 240 non-breeding and wintering migratory species routinely pass through annually.

Coastal geography

With some 3,000km (2,000 miles) of coastline and more than 1,000 islands washed by two seas, littoral geography is a significant draw of southern Thailand's environment. Tourists are continually drawn to the region's powdery-sand beaches and clear waters rich in tropical marine life *(see pages 54–5 and 61)*. Geologically, the region is noted for its dramatic karst formations jutting out of the sea. Soft and easily eroded, the limestone once formed the seabed. Spectacular caves carved out by underground streams and lagoons hidden within the karsts make for fun-filled exploration on inflatable kayaks.

Ao Phang Nga National Park *(see page 202)* comprises an eye-popping series of crumbly cliffs, jutting islets and karst rocks. Though the sea has abundant marine and coastal creatures, most people visit to marvel at and sail around the many looming karst towers.

Environment at risk

Thailand's environment is in danger of irreversible damage. With the destruction of habitats, many species of wildlife could disappear, not just from Thailand, but from the world.

The Forestry Department is underfunded and understaffed. In the past few decades, at least 40 rangers have been murdered in the line of duty. Earning less than a factory worker, many rangers also collude with loggers and poachers. The country's poorest people also inadvertently contribute to the environmental degradation by farming on protected lands. The endangered populations of tiger, bear and deer are further threatened by the demand for medicinal products among the Chinese, and for gourmet "jungle" dining.

The coastal environment, too, has not been spared. Illegal construction, surreptitious land-grabs, oil spills and poor sewage disposal remain a problem at some of the Eastern Seaboard resorts, notably Pattaya and Si Racha. Even national parkland is not sacrosanct. Ko Samet, for instance, is part of a marine national park, but unbridled development along its coast has progressed despite the law.

Elsewhere, new legislation, or existing legislation more rigorously applied, is slowly making a difference. But it is less-developed islands such as Ko Lanta that stand to benefit most from the environmental lessons learnt.

About 17km (10 miles) west of Krabi is the unique and unusual Shell Fossil Beach. Here, fossilised shells dating back an estimated 75 million years have formed great stone slabs that project into the sea.

The situation is somewhat better on the western coast of the Gulf of Thailand and also along the Andaman Coast, although Phuket's Patong beach in particular suffers from overbuilding and has taken on some of the problems associated with Pattaya.

The coral reefs of southern Thailand's coastal waters are home to a diverse and spectacular range of marine life. Unfortunately, they are menaced by various human activities, including dynamite and poison fishing, both now strictly outlawed, anchor drag and overfishing.

Also damaging is global warming, which is especially severe in the Indian Ocean. It causes coral bleaching, which in 1998 killed an estimated 90 percent of the inner reefs in the Seychelles. In a bid to counter this threat, "reef balls" of hollow, reinforced concrete were sunk to rehabilitate reefs, notably in the Andaman Sea off Phuket and at Khao Lak, but also in the shallower Gulf of Thailand.

The disastrous tsunami of December 2004 had some positive environmental spin-offs, as illegal buildings and ramshackle resorts were literally swept away by the gigantic waves, most notably at Ko Phi Phi. But despite the Thai authorities' stated aim to prevent illegal rebuilding, forceful opposition and corruption allowed land-grabs and construction to begin again almost immediately, even on a national park such as Ko Phi Phi. Influential people and big business displaced many poorer familes.

Tourism undoubtedly plays a part in the mistreatment of coral, and the situation is now deemed severe enough for the Department of National Parks, Wildlife and Plant Conservation to close many dive sites for part of the year, including some of the most poular in Ko Surin, the Similan Islands and Ko Tarutao. Yet there are also encouraging signs that tourism may become a positive force in the preservation of what remains of Thailand's ecology. Some Thais – among them trekking guides, local Green groups and even a few progressive politicians – are becoming aware that environmental caretaking will sustain tourism longer than continued destruction. ❑

LEFT: Shell Fossil Beach.
ABOVE: Asian elephands at Khao Yai National Park.

UNDERWATER LANDSCAPE

Thailand's coral reefs are an outstanding wonderland of colour, home to myriad species of fish and other marine life.

Off the west coast, the flora and fauna of the Andaman Sea are characteristic of the Indian Ocean. Off the east coast, in the Gulf of Thailand, they are characteristic of Indo-Pacific seas. Coral reefs off both coastlines have been little surveyed, but they support at least 400 species of fish and 30 kinds of sea snake. Bottlenose dolphins, and sometimes whales, are found in Thai waters. The gentle dugong, or "sea cow", is increasingly hard to find among the sea grasses of Phang Nga, Phuket, Trang and Satun provinces. Thailand's coral species number almost 300, with the Andaman Sea boasting an even greater diversity. Intact reefs, however, survive only in areas far from human habitation, such as the vicinity of the Surin and Similan islands.

ABOVE: vast gardens of cabbage-patch coral share the reefs with outcrops of brain coral, organ-pipe coral, soft coral, staghorn, sponges, sea fans, gorgonians and black coral – a plethora of beautiful but fragile life forms.

LEFT: the octopus inhabits many regions of the Andaman and South China seas, and is especially at home in coral reefs. Its soft body can squeeze through narrow gaps in the reef, providing refuge from predators and a hiding place from which to pounce on its prey.

ABOVE: found in Thai waters are four species of turtle – green, leatherback, hawksbill and olive ridley. All are endangered.

ABOVE: the Andaman Sea is deeper, clearer and more saline than the Gulf. It has coral reefs that are more interesting and widely distributed, extending from Ko Tarutao Marine National Park on the frontiers with Malaysia to the reefs and shoals of Burma's Tenasserim region.

BELOW: the scorpionfish camouflages innocuously on the seabed, but can deliver an extremely poisonous sting if stepped on its venomous sharp spines. Thailand's waters are estimated to support almost 2,000 fish species, including 600–700 freshwater fish. But data is incomplete, and the total number of both freshwater and saltwater fish may in fact be 30–40 percent higher.

ABOVE LEFT: clownfish are found throughout the warm waters of the Indian and Pacific Oceans. These colourful fish live in a symbiotic relationship with sea anemones or stony corals. Once an anemone or a coral has been selected as home, the clown fish becomes very territorial and will defend it spiritedly.

BELOW: contrary to popular belief, only a few varieties of shark pose a threat to humans. Out of more than 350 species, only four have been confirmed to have killed appreciable numbers of humans in unprovoked attacks. These are the great white, oceanic whitetip, bull and tiger sharks. Fortunately, the first two species are not found in Thai waters, while the last two are rarely seen. Relatively common shark species found here include the non-aggressive nurse, leopard, silvertip, grey, blacktip, plus the gargantuan whale shark.

OUTDOOR ACTIVITIES

The south has rocky karsts, fecund tropical rainforests and extensive coastlines along the Gulf of Thailand and the Andaman Sea. Graced with some of the world's most idyllic beaches, bays and islands, the region's varied topography makes a stunning backdrop for a host of outdoor activities.

Thailand's diverse terrain has some breathtaking views and some equally breathtaking experiences to enjoy for sports and adventure enthusiasts of all ages and abilities. The jungles offer elephant treks, white water rafting, and off-road biking; elsewhere there's freefall parachuting, bungy jumping, and much else besides to make the adrenalin rush. And that's before we even get to the open seas and experiences like sailing, diving, paragliding, game fishing and deep water climbing of the jagged limestone karsts that jut from the seas off Thailand's southern shores.

Responsible tourism

Thailand has been very proactive in preserving areas on both land and water as national parks, although policing the resources within them has to a wide degree failed. Fish, coral, wildlife and forest areas are all under threat from illegal poaching, logging, development and poor environmental practices. Nonetheless, recent developments in ecotourism leave some scope for optimism in the tourism industry.

While some operators are only concerned with profit, more proactive companies realise that long-term profits depend on environmental sustainability. Good practice ranges from using reusable containers on nature tours to training and hiring local guides. If you are concerned about damaging the environment, ask the operator about the preservation measures it takes before signing up for an outdoor adventure.

LEFT: scaling on a cliff face at Railay Bay, Krabi.
RIGHT: parasailing at Ko Hae, off Phuket.

On water

Thailand's mild, clear, aquamarine waters are ideal for water-borne activities. The more populous beach resorts of Phuket, Pattaya, Ko Samui, Hua Hin and Ko Chang are typically enlivened (or plagued, depending on how you see it) by noisy jet-skis. The family-friendly inflatable banana-boat rides are always a hoot as well, but be sure to wear a life-jacket for those inevitable bouncing spills.

The relatively calm seas are well suited to water-skiing and the trendier wakeboarding, though novices may first prefer to refine their technique at a cable-ski lake in Phuket, Pattaya, or on the outskirts of Bangkok. More environmentally sound (minus the speedboat), and even more "in" than wakeboarding, is the relatively new sport of kite-surfing. Costing around B4,000 for a day, surfing behind a wind-propelled kite is a sport that is rapidly becom-

> *Considering that jet-skis are the cause of frequent accidents and occasional deaths, it is no surprise that some beaches ban them. If you hire a jet-ski, be careful where and how you ride it.*

ing increasingly popular at beaches in Hua Hin, Cha-am, Phuket and Ko Samui.

For a unique and lofty perspective of Thai beach life, a 15-minute parasailing ride, floating high above the sea strapped to a parachute, is exciting yet safe. Back at sea level, windsurfing equipment and instruction is widely available.

Deep-sea fishing trips can be as laid-back or as rod-pumping as the fish decide to make them. Most major resorts can arrange charters, where the evening meal depends on how well you do battle with a resistant giant tuna, a powerful barracuda or marlin.

For the unique opportunity to interact with the ocean's most developed species, Oasis Sea

World in Chanthaburi Province offers the family the chance to swim with dolphins (www.swimwithdolphinsthailand.com).

Sailing

Prices for sailing in Thailand are still reasonable compared with many established international centres, with a day's outing running from around B1,500 per person, including crew and hotel pick up. As more charter companies emerge, there's an increasing variety of boats available, from day sailing in dinghies to longer trips with facilities for fishing, diving and sea canoeing. It's even possible to get butler service. Weather conditions are generally favourable, and with relatively low boat traffic you can enjoy a large degree of solitude amid the south's dramatic scenery, possibly dropping anchor in the silvery bay of an uninhabited isle.

There are marinas in Pattaya, Ko Chang and Krabi and several in Phuket, with more in the pipeline. Increased interest has brought greater publicity for December's annual Phuket King's Cup Regatta, which has won several awards, including Yachting Event of the Year at the Christofle Asia Boating Awards. Other popular highlights include Pattaya's Top of the Gulf Regatta and the Ko Samui International Regatta, both usually held in May. All attract sailors from around the world, have opportunities for crewing and, of course, involve many parties.

Kayaking and white-water rafting

Blessed with thousands of kilometres of pristine waterways and shoreline, a kayaking tour is the most rewarding, eco-friendly and scenic way to explore the many limestone crags, secluded lagoons and tidal caves (known as *hong*) that are scattered in the waters around Ao Phang Nga and Trang in the Andaman Sea, or Ang Thong Marine National Park near Ko Samui in the Gulf of Thailand.

Embark on a day-long or several-day adventure at a gliding pace that even the least physically fit will find comfortable. It's a great way to view undisturbed wildlife and meet new friends. Paddle from the coast and listen to the cacophony of sounds made by small animals and birds that permeate the dense growth as

LEFT: jet-skiing and windsurfing off Pattaya.
RIGHT: rock climbing in Railay.

you negotiate the kayak through sinewy mangrove swamps. If an organised tour sounds too ambitious, then sea kayaks are also available for hourly rental on the beaches of Ko Chang, Ko Samui, Ko Phangan, Phuket, Krabi, and Ko Phi Phi. Those who regard kayaking as too tame can tumble over bumpy rapids on a dramatic knuckle-clenching white-water rafting expedition along the rivers that flow through wildlife sanctuaries and national parks in Phang Nga Province and elsewhere.

On land

Energetic, exercise-minded visitors are well catered for in Thailand's forests, with experiences such as hiking, rock climbing or mountain biking all very popular. A good guide will ensure you not only witness the native flora and fauna, but also learn about it and the surrounding habitat.

Thailand's rock-climbing sites are well known the world over, and the towering limestone karsts that have made the Krabi coast so famous are the perfect challenge for both novices and experts. There are several climbing schools operating along the Andaman coast, especially at Krabi, and Ko Tao also has some climbing and bouldering sites.

If teetering against the rock face attached to a rope sounds too nerve-wracking, a steady

NATIONAL PARKS OF SOUTH THAILAND

Thailand has more than 110 national parks, sanctuaries and marine parks to investigate. Most are low on accommodation, but organised birdwatching and hiking tours, as well as boat trips to deserted islands, are a way to explore these protected areas.

Apart from Khao Sok National Park *(see page 203)*, the following are worth highlighting. Located some 60km (40 miles) from Petchaburi, Thailand's largest park, Kaeng Krachan *(see page 150)* is a haven for numerous species of large mammal, including tigers, elephants, leopards, bears, deer, gibbons and monkeys.

Khao Sam Roi Yot National Park *(see page 155)* trans-

lates as "Three Hundred Mountain Peaks", in reference to the limestone pinnacles jutting up from the park's mangrove swamps to heights above 600 metres (2,000ft). Wildlife includes crab-eating macaques and the rare serow – a mountain goat-antelope. Birdwatchers shouldn't miss a trip to Thailand's largest wetland bird reserve, Thale Noi Waterfowl Park. At the tip of Songkhla Lake, it is home to nearly 200 species of waterfowl.

Mu Ko Lanta National Park *(see page 250)* and Ko Tarutao Marine National Park *(see page 275)* are island chains whose waters teem with marine life such as sharks, whales and the rare dugong.

hike though forest trails presents a relatively gentle up-close-and-personal experience of Thailand's wildlife. The best hikes are made in national-park land *(see pages 51 and 59)* and should only be undertaken in the company of an experienced guide. Park rangers, who offer their services for a fee, are one option, although most will not speak much English. Otherwise, several tour companies organise day and overnight treks into the bigger parks.

Elephants are the symbol of Thailand, and in the past played a very important role in the country, transporting heavy goods such as logs, and carrying mounted troops into battle. Riding an elephant on treks gives a small hint at

age-old modes of travel, when much movement through the jungle involved climbing on an elephant's back. A few minutes will give you an appreciation of travel when it often took days or weeks to reach your destination. Capitalising on this exotic image, elephant rides are also widely available at all major beach destinations, although the experience is somewhat less romantic, with elephant camps or villages conducting hour-long to half-day tours around well-worn trails.

In the shadow of the mighty pachyderm, horse riding has been slow to catch on in Thailand and is still largely a pursuit of the wealthy. However, the most accessible spot to saddle up is on Hua Hin beach, where a stable of old nags are led up and down the sands. Riding clubs in Pattaya and Phuket are open to non-members, with reasonable hourly and daily rates.

For those who prefer horsepower of a different kind, try out the All Terrain Vehicle (ATV) tours that are becoming more common at the major resort areas. Unfortunately, some ATV operators restrict their rides to unexciting fenced-off circuits. More thrilling tours venture through thick muddy forest. Alternatively, mountain biking is another great way of navigating the dense undergrowth behind Thailand's beaches.

Golf

Golf remains a popular pastime for Thailand's middle and upper classes, as well as being a lure for dedicated visitors to the wide choice of internationally designed championship courses. The history of the sport in Thailand dates back to the 1920s, when King Rama VI and members of the aristocracy played their first rounds at the country's first-ever golf club, the Royal Hua Hin Golf Course. Aside from being a relaxing way to improve your swing while on vacation, golf on Thailand's fairways provides incredible locations and lush backdrops and often reasonable course and caddy fees for visitors.

Most of the country's fairways are located in the central region around Bangkok and along the Eastern Seaboard region towards Pattaya. Hua Hin also has several golf courses, as does Phuket. Ko Samui currently has one 18-hole course. ❑

ECO-FRIENDLY TOURS

While Thailand is only just waking up to the impact of ecotourism and environmental conservation, more and more people visit the country expressly to participate in conservation activities.

In Phang Nga Province, one can volunteer to monitor sea-turtle breeding grounds, or help to restore local mangroves (www.losthorizonsasia.com). On Phuket, the Gibbon Rehabilitation Project prepares rescued and abused gibbons for reintroduction to the wild, and is in constant need of volunteers (www.gibbonproject.org). When volunteering in Thailand it's important to organise ahead as officially a work permit is required whether or not you are being paid.

LEFT: elephant riding in Phuket.

Diving and Snorkelling

With long coastlines skirting either side of the Isthmus of Kra, Thailand is a major international diving and snorkelling destination.

I t's not difficult to see why Thailand is popular with divers and snorkellers. The waters are clear and warm year-round, and a plethora of colourful coral reefs attract a huge variety of marine life, including turtles, sharks and rays. With dive shops and live-aboard tours accessing more remote dive sites as far as Malaysia to the south, Burma to the west and Cambodia to the east, Thailand is one of the most affordable places in the world to discover subaquatic vistas.

The Thai coast is split into three shores. Sharing the waters of the Gulf of Thailand, the Eastern Seaboard stretches from Bangkok to Ko Chang, while the Gulf Coast runs down from Bangkok to the deep south. To the west, the Andaman Sea is a part of the expansive Indian Ocean, licking the shores of Ranong, near Burma, all the way down to Satun on the Malaysian border.

The Andaman Sea is generally considered better in terms of reef and marine diversity, water clarity and its wealth of idyllic islands at which to anchor. Reached primarily via live-aboard trips from Phuket, the remote Similan and Surin Island chains are considered the country's premier sites, while the waters off Phuket, Krabi, Ko Phi Phi and Ko Lanta are also popular drop points. For an even greater sense of adventure, live-aboard trips sail into Burmese waters to dive the less-explored reefs of the Mergui Archipelago and the deep, shark-abundant Burma Banks.

Many overseas visitors learn how to dive while holidaying in Thailand. A number of these head to Thailand's dive capital Ko Tao, which has a large number of dive schools, as do more experienced divers,

as there are plenty of employment opportunities for wannabe dive instructors.

Dive sites

Most dive trips from the neighbouring islands of Ko Samui and Ko Phangan head to Ko Tao for the better sites, which unfortunately makes for frequent sightings of other dive groups as well as fish. Pattaya's waters offer little in terms of coral and water clarity, although this is compensated by a number of wreck dives. Ko Chang is now a mature dive destination, with several dive schools running excursions to the 50-island archipelago's many dive sites.

The majority of dive schools offer PADI Open Water certification courses from around B10,000. Fun dives for qualified divers cost from B1,600, discounted if you bring your own equipment. Before embarking on any dive trip, ask the operator if they operate their own boats, offer insurance, hotel pick-ups, and if there is an instructor or dive master who speaks your language.

Remember that the cheapest dive shops available are not always the safest. If you should get into trouble while submerged, there are emergency hyperbaric chambers situated in or around all of the major dive centres.   ❑

RIGHT: a diver jumping into the water at Ko Tao.

PLACES

A detailed guide to Bangkok and Thailand's beaches and islands, with the principal sites clearly cross-referenced by number to the maps.

Blessed with some 3,000km (2,000 miles) of stunning coastline and more than 1,000 paradisiacal islands washed by two seas – the Gulf of Thailand and the Andaman Sea – Thailand attracts a wide range of visitors, from gregarious party animals to reclusive honeymooners.

Barely 90 minutes from the capital, the brash and saucy coastal resort of Pattaya, with its golf courses and the energy of a cosmopolitan playground, has been dubbed the "Riviera of the Eastern Seaboard". Further east, the small, pretty island of Ko Samet is a favourite weekend escape for young Bangkokians, while Ko Chang, Thailand's second-largest island and part of an extensive marine national park, is rapidly developing.

Heading south, the Gulf of Thailand's winding coast has shores fringed with powdery white-sand beaches backed by mountains. The most accessible from Bangkok is family-friendly Hua Hin, which has an air of exclusivity due to its patronage by Thai royalty. Pranburi is fast making a name for itself, too, with its clutch of cutting-edge and design-conscious resorts. Out at sea, Ko Samui, the biggest of some 80 islands constituting the Samui Archipelago, is a significant draw, and can be combined with visits to neighbouring Ko Phangan, notorious for its anything-goes full-moon raves, and Ko Tao, a renowned diving Mecca.

Thailand's largest island, Phuket, the kingdom's premier island holiday spot. It has some of the world's most luxurious hotels, but it's still possible to explore rustic fishing villages and fragile mangrove forests.

Close by are Ao Phang Nga and Krabi, and islands such as Ko Phi Phi and Ko Lanta. With their ancient landscape and craggy limestone towers teetering skyward from clear azure waters, these are the preserve of intrepid rock climbers. At sea, kayakers are drawn to caves carved out by underground streams and lagoons hidden within limestone cliffs. Further out are renowned dive sites, near Similan and Surin islands, that beckon the world's scuba-diving fraternity.

Heading south, Trang, Satun and Songkhla, all breathtakingly beautiful, remain relatively untouched by tourism. It's important to check security updates for Songkhla. This book leaves out the insurgency-ravaged deep-south provinces of Pattani, Yala and Narathiwat. ❏

PRECEDING PAGES: aerial view of Ko Nang Yuan; a couple pose with a coconut drink on Coral Island, Phuket. **LEFT:** drinking in the scene at Ao Maya (Maya Bay), Ko Phi Phi Ley.

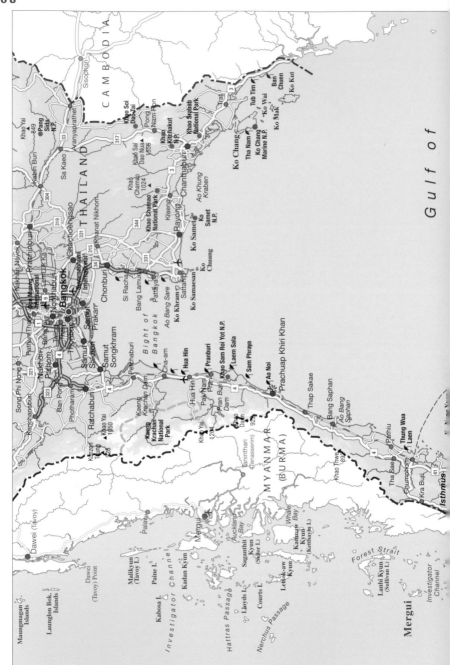

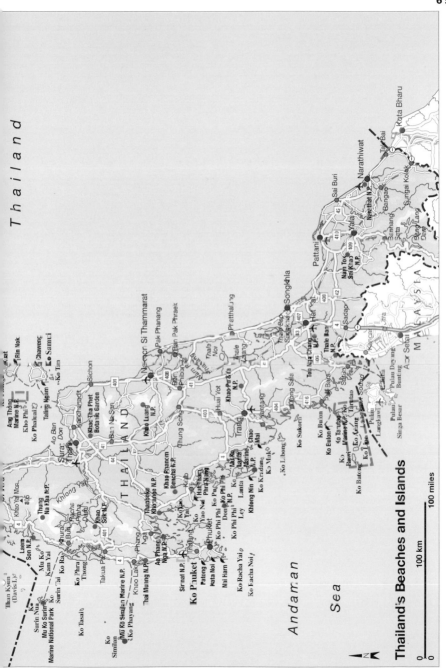

Thailand's Beaches and Islands

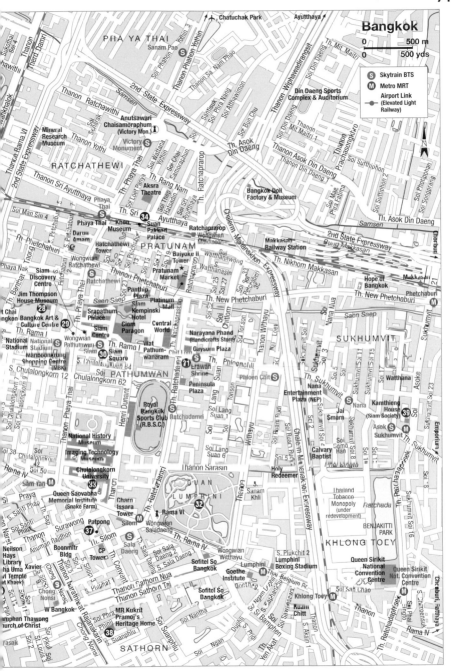

Bangkok

0 — 500 m
0 — 500 yds

- **S** Skytrain BTS
- **M** Metro MRT
- ● Airport Link (Elevated Light Railway)

PHA YA THAI

Chatuchak Park
Ayutthaya

Din Daeng Sports Complex & Auditorium

Anutsawari Chaisamoraphum (Victory Mon.)

Victory Monument

RATCHATHEWI

Mineral Research Museum

Bangkok Doll Factory & Museum

Aksra Theatre

Phaya Thai
Khan Museum

Suan Pakkad Palace

Ratchaprarop

Makkasan Railway Station

Darun Amarn

Ratchathewi Tower

PRATUNAM

Baiyoke II Tower

Hope of Bangkok

Siam Discovery Centre

Ratchathewi

Pratunam Market

Makkasan

Jim Thompson House Museum

Panthip Plaza

Platinum Mall

Kempinski Hotel

Siam Kempinski Hotel

Bangkok Art & Culture Centre (BACC)

Srapathum Palace

Siam Centre

Central World

Narayana Phand (Handicrafts Store)

Gaysorn Plaza

SUKHUMVIT

National Stadium

Mahboonkrong Shopping Centre (MBK)

Siam Square

Wat Pathumwanaram

Erawan Shrine

Phloen Chit

Nana Entertainment Plaza (NEP)

Kamthieng House (Siam Society)

National History Museum

Imaging Technology Museum

Chulalongkorn University

Royal Bangkok Sports Club (R.B.S.C)

Peninsula Plaza

Jai Smarn

Asok Sukhumvit

Calvary Baptist

Queen Saovabha Memorial Institute (Snake Farm)

Charn Issara Tower

Rama VI

SUAN LUMPHINI

Holy Redeemer

Thailand Tobacco Monopoly (under redevelopment)

BENJAKITTI PARK

Patpong

Silom

Wongwian Saladaeng

KHLONG TOEY

Neilson Hays Library

Boonmitr Bldg

CP Tower

Sala Daeng

Sofitel So Bangkok

Goethe Institute

Lumphini Boxing Stadium

Queen Sirikit National Convention Centre

Queen Sirikit Nat. Convention Centre

W Bangkok

MR Kukrit Pramoj's Heritage Home

Sofitel So Bangkok

Khlong Toey

Kuan Chitt

SATHORN

BANGKOK

Thailand's steamy capital offers a mind-blowing array of experiences and sights: royal architecture at Rattanakosin, spirituality at ancient Buddhist temples, and unparalleled shopping at raucous street markets and hip mega-malls. Come evening, there's a vast choice of eateries and nightspots.

A s Bangkok races into the 21st century, the skyline fills with hotels, shopping malls and apartments housing a middle class fast becoming "ample rich", as former Prime Minister Thaksin Shinawatra so memorably called his offshore company. The best ways to get around are the expanding Skytrain and Metro systems and the Chao Phraya River, which cradles many important sites on its eastern bank. On the western side, Thonburi's canals thread through colourful residential neighbourhoods.

In the late 18th century King Rama I dug a canal between two river bends, slicing off a parcel of land into an artificial island called Rattanakosin. This is where you'll find the Grand Palace and glittering Wat Phra Kaew, an essential part of any city tour. Just south are enclaves where foreigners originally settled: Chinatown, Little India (Pahurat) and Thanon Silom. Today, Silom, Thanon Sathorn and Thanon Sukhumvit further east, are important business and commercial centres.

In lovely pockets, wooden houses teeter on stilts beside canals, dragon costumes hang in Chinatown alleys, and golden spires shade saffron monks in old town temples. And, as the city hurtles on, one constant remains – the Thai ability to enjoy it. The overriding concept of fun, or *sanuk*, is never far away.

RATTANAKOSIN

The establishment of the old city of **Phra Nakorn**, royal district, centred on the island of **Rattanakosin**, marked Bangkok's rise as the new capital of Thailand in 1782. Rattanakosin's foundations were based on the former capital of Ayutthaya,

Main attractions
WAT PHRA KAEW AND
GRAND PALACE
NATIONAL MUSEUM
WAT PHO
WAT ARUN
THANON KHAO SAN
VIMANMEK MANSION
THE GOLDEN BUDDHA
JIM THOMPSON'S HOUSE
PATPONG
CHATUCHAK MARKET

LEFT: Khao San Road. **RIGHT:** Bangkok's motorcycle taxis wait for customers.

TIP

The dress code for Wat Phra Kaew and the Grand Palace is strict. Visitors must be dressed smartly – no shorts, short skirts or revealing tops, sandals or flip-flops. Suitable clothing may be borrowed from an office near the Gate of Victory.

which was abandoned after the Burmese ransacked it in 1767. With the Grand Palace at its centre, the defensive moats and walls formed a stronghold, while canals were dug to transport people across the marsh and swampland.

Rattanakosin brims with architectural grandeur; it contains many government offices and two of Thailand's most respected universities – Thammasat and Silpakorn – in addition to being the religious and ceremonial nucleus of the nation.

The area is best explored on foot. Its proximity to the river means that it can be conveniently accessed by water transport.

Wat Phra Kaew and the Grand Palace complex

The dignified splendour of two of Bangkok's principal attractions – Wat Phra Kaew and the Grand Palace – is breathtaking in spite of the heaving crowds. These structures are an arresting spectacle of form and colour: glistening golden *chedi*, glass mosaic-studded pillars, towering mythological gods, and fabulously

ornate temple and palace edifices.

The site originally spread over 160 hectares (65 acres) at this strategic location on the Chao Phraya River's banks. It was begun by King Rama I in 1782, who ordered a new residence built to house the Emerald Buddha, the country's most revered religious image, as well as a palace befitting the new capital of Bangkok. The entire compound was surrounded by high crenellated walls, securing a self-sufficient city-within-a-city, including the king's and king's wives' quarters, ceremonial buildings, military and civil wings, and a prison.

The only entrance (and exit) to the **Wat Phra Kaew and Grand Palace ❶** complex is along Thanon Na Phra Lan to the north (daily 8.30am–3.30pm; charge includes entry to Vimanmek Mansion and several other sights in Dusit; tel: 0-2222 8181; www.palaces.thai.net). Make sure you are dressed appropriately (*see margin tip*) and disregard touts who linger outside the complex telling you that it is closed.

The complex is loosely divided into two, with Wat Phra Kaew

BELOW LEFT: golden stupa at Wat Phra Kaew.
BELOW RIGHT: Phra Mondhop, the library in Wat Phra Kaeo.

encountered first to the left, and the Grand Palace and its peripheral buildings to the right. Most of the Grand Palace's interiors are inaccessible to the public, but the exteriors are still interesting to see.

Wat Phra Kaew

Wat Phra Kaew (Temple of the Emerald Buddha) serves as the Grand Palace's royal chapel. The magnificent temple compound is modelled after palace chapels in the former capitals of Sukhothai and Ayutthaya, and contains typical monastic structures, except living quarters for monks, a feature found in most other Thai temples.

At the main entrance to the temple compound you are greeted by a statue of Shivaka Kumar Baccha, reputed to be the Buddha's private physician. First to capture the eye on the upper terrace on the left are the gleaming gold mosaic tiles encrusting the Sri Lankan-style **Phra Si Rattana**

Chedi  – said to enshrine a piece of the Buddha's breastbone.

In the centre is **Phra Mondop ❸** (Library of Buddhist Scriptures), a delicate building, studded with blue and green glass mosaic, and topped by a multi-tiered roof fashioned like the crown of a Thai king. The library is surrounded by statues of sacred white elephants.

Adjacent to it is the **Prasat Phra Thep Bidom ❹** (Royal Pantheon). This contains life-sized statues of the Chakri kings and is open to the public only on Chakri Day, 6 April. Around the building stand marvellous gilded statues of mythological creatures, including the half-female, half-lion *aponsi*. The original pantheon was built in 1855, but was destroyed by fire and rebuilt in 1903. Flanking the entrance of the Prasat Phra Thep Bidom are two towering gilded *chedi*.

Behind Phra Mondop is a large sandstone model of the famous

Temple of the Emerald Buddha (Wat Phra Kaew).

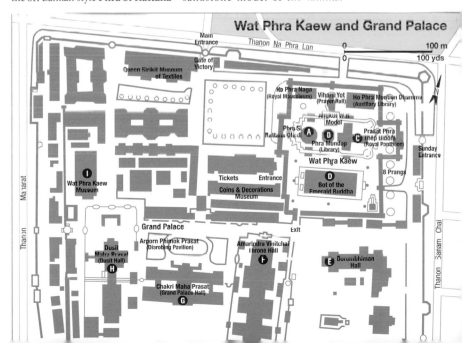

Wat Phra Kaew and Grand Palace

Thanon Na Phra Lan

Main Entrance

Gate of Victory

Queen Sirikit Museum of Textiles

Ho Phra Naga (Royal Mausoleum)

Viharn Yot (Prayer Hall)

Ho Phra Montien Dhamma (Auxiliary Library)

Angkor Wat Model

Phra Si Rattana Chedi ❹

Phra Mondop ❸ (Library)

Prasat Phra Thep Bidom ❹ (Royal Pantheon)

Wat Phra Kaew

Sunday Entrance

❶ Wat Phra Kaew Museum

Tickets Entrance

Coins & Decorations Museum

❹ Bot of the Emerald Buddha

8 Prangs

Thanon Maharat

Thanon

Grand Palace

Exit

❽ Dusit Maha Prasat (Dusit Hall)

Arporn Phimok Prasat (Disrobing Pavilion)

Amarindra Vinitchai Throne Hall ❻

❺ Borombhiman Hall

Chakri Maha Prasat (Grand Palace Hall) ❼

Thanon Sanam Chai

0   100 m
0   100 yds

Khmer temple of Angkor Wat in Cambodia. The model was built during King Rama IV's reign, when Cambodia was a vassal Thai state.

The walls of the cloister enclosing the temple courtyard are painted with a picture book of murals telling the *Ramakien* epic, the Thai version of the Indian *Ramayana*. Originally painted during the reign of King Rama III (1824–50), they have been meticulously restored.

Around the cloisters, six pairs of towering stone *yaksha* (demons), characters from the *Ramakien*, stand guard, armed with clubs, protecting the Emerald Buddha. At the complex's eastern edge are eight *prang* structures, which represent Buddhism's Eightfold Path.

The Emerald Buddha

Finally, you come to Wat Phra Kaew's most sacred structure, the **Bot of the Emerald Buddha** ⦁. Outside this main hall, at the open-air shrine, the air is always alive with the suppliants' murmured prayers and heavy with the scent of floral offerings and joss sticks.

At the top of the elaborate golden 11-metre (36ft) altar, in a glass case and protected by a nine-tiered umbrella, sits the country's most celebrated image, the diminutive 75cm (30ins)-tall Emerald Buddha, which, surprisingly, is not made of emerald but carved from a solid block of green jade. Despite the statue's size (it's hard to get a clear view of it from ground level), its power and importance should be instantly apparent from the demeanour of the pilgrims inside the hall.

Of unknown origin – legend claims that the Emerald Buddha image was carved in India, but stylistically, its design is 13th- or 14th-century Thai – the statue was found in Chiang Rai in 1464. Kept hidden in a *chedi* there for some reason, the image was revealed when the *chedi* was struck by lightning during a storm. The Lao army took the figure back to Vientiane, Laos, in the mid-16th century, where it stayed put until 1779 when it was seized by the Thais. After Bangkok was established as the new capital, King Rama I brought the statue back with him in 1784. The statue is claimed to bestow good fortune on the kingdom that possesses it.

The Grand Palace

Adjoining Wat Phra Kaew is the **Grand Palace**. Embodying Thailand's characteristic blend of temporal and spiritual elements, the Grand Palace has been added to or modified by every Thai king. The result is a mélange of architectural styles, from traditional Thai, Khmer and Chinese to British, French and Italian Renaissance. Following the mysterious death of his brother and predecessor King Rama VIII at the Grand Palace in 1946, the current King Rama IX moved permanently to Chitralada Palace in Dusit *(see page 86)*, with the Grand Palace now reserved for special ceremonies and state visits.

BELOW: gilded *garuda* encircle the main hall of Wat Phra Kaew.

Palace buildings

Exit from Wat Phra Kaew. On your left, tucked behind a closed gate guarded by sentry, is the French-inspired **Borombhiman Hall **. Built in 1903 as a residence for King Rama VI, it is now reserved as a state guesthouse for dignitaries.

To the right lies the **Amarin Vinitchai Throne Hall** , part of the three-building Phra Maha Montien complex. Originally a royal residence, it contained the bedchamber of King Rama I.

Next to it in a large courtyard, stands the triple-spired royal residence – and the grandest building in the complex – the **Chakri Maha Prasat** (Grand Palace Hall). This two-storey hall was constructed during King Chulalongkorn's reign (1868–1910) to commemorate the 100th anniversary of the Chakri dynasty in 1882. An impressive mixture of Thai and Western architecture, it was designed by British architects.

The Thai spires, however, were added at the last moment, following protests that it was improper for a hallowed Thai site to be dominated by a European-style building.

The top floor contains golden urns with ashes of the Chakri kings. The first floor still functions as an audience chamber for royal banquets and state visits. The ground floor is now a **Weapons Museum**. Outside, the courtyard is dotted with ornamental ebony trees pruned in the *bonsai* style.

The next building of interest is the **Dusit Maha Prasat** (Dusit Hall), built in 1789 by King Chakri (Rama I) to replace an earlier wooden structure. A splendid example of classical Thai architecture, its four tiered roof supports an elegant nine-level spire. To its left stands the exquisite **Arporn Phimok Prasat** (Disrobing Pavilion). It was built to the height of the king's palanquin so that he could alight from his elephant and don his ceremonial hat and gown before proceeding to the audience hall.

Opposite, don't miss the collection of small Buddha images made of silver, ivory, crystal and other materials at the **Wat Phra Kaew Museum** . On the way out, next

A Chinese-style statue outside the Dusit Maha Prasat.

Below: Chakri Maha Prasat, a mix of Thai and Western styles.

A Mythical Zoo

A stroll around any Thai temple is like exploring a bestial forest of the imagination. Fantastical creatures act as sacred guardians, each with its own special powers.

Many of these creatures from folklore were born in the Himaphan Forest, the mythical Himalayan forest surrounding the heavenly Mount Meru in Hindu and Buddhist scripture. Though Himaphan is invisible to human eyes, Thai artisans have spent centuries refining their imaginative depictions of its denizens. Here's a quick safari ride through some of the more common beasts you may encounter.

Garuda: Considered the most powerful creature of the Himaphan Forest, this half-eagle, half-man demigod is the mount of the Hindu god Vishnu. *Garuda* is sworn enemy of the magical water serpent *naga*. *Garuda* is often depicted with *naga* caught in his talons. Since Ayutthayan times, the *garuda* has been a symbol for the Royal Seal, and today, brightly coloured represen-

tations are emblazoned across official documents as well as on the facades of royally approved banks and corporations.

Naga: Brother and nemesis of *garuda*, the *naga* is a semi-divine creature with multiple human heads and serpent tails. A great *naga* is said to have provided shelter to the meditating Buddha. A resident of the watery underworld, the *naga* is associated with water's life-giving force, as well as acting as a bridge between the earthly and divine realms. *Naga* are typically represented along steps leading into temples.

Erawan: The magical elephant *erawan* was the steed for Indra, the Hindu king of the gods. The gigantic pachyderm has 33 heads, each with seven tusks so long that thousands of angels live inside them. Obviously, with such a gargantuan beast, a more modest three-headed version is usually represented. For proof of *erawan*'s importance to Thais, head to Erawan Shrine, where wooden elephants are presented as offerings.

Kinnaree and Aponsi: *Kinnaree* has the head and body of a woman with the tail and legs of a swan. Known for her talent in song and dance, beautifully crafted *kinnaree* sculptures can be seen at the Wat Phra Kaew. Perhaps a distant relative, *aponsi* is similarly portrayed as half-female, half-lion. The Golden Kinnaree is the Thai film-industry equivalent of the Oscar.

Hongsa: This bird-like creature has similarities to the swan and goose, and is a prevalent motif in traditional arts and crafts. In Hindu mythology, the *hongsa* is the mount of Brahma, the god of creation. Take a drive along Utthayan Avenue in Bangkok's western suburb of Puttha Monthon; some 1,000 golden *hongsa* birds decorate the tops of lamp-posts along this stretch of road.

Yaksha: Although these giant half-demon, half-god creatures appear forbidding as they guard the entrances to the temple structures at Wat Phra Kaew and Wat Arun, they are actually protectors of earthbound wealth. Led by Kuvera, they are worshipped as symbols of fertility and are also believed to protect newborn infants. ❑

LEFT: a fearsome *yaksha* statue at Wat Phra Kaew.

The Lak Muang is a good place to catch performances of Thai dance. People who have their prayers answered sometimes hire the resident dance troupe here to perform.

to the ticket office, is the **Coins and Decorations Museum**. It has a collection of coins dating from the 11th century and also royal regalia, decorations and medals made of gold and precious stones. Close to the gate by the road, the **Queen Sirikit Museum of Textiles** has items from around Southeast Asia.

Lak Muang

Every Thai city has a foundation stone *(see page 40)*, around which the city's guardian spirits gravitate, protecting and bringing good fortune to faithful worshippers. Bangkok was officially founded in 1782, when King Rama I erected the **Lak Muang ❷**, or City Pillar (daily 5am–7pm; free) across Thanon Sanam Chai from the eastern wall of the Grand Palace, to mark the official centre of the capital. The gilded wooden pillar resembles the Hindu Shiva *lingam*, which represents potency, and has the city's horoscope, rewritten by King Rama IV (1851–68), buried inside. Thonburi's taller Lak Muang was also moved here when Bangkok was founded.

Sanam Luang

North of Wat Phra Kaew and the Grand Palace, the large oval turf of **Sanam Luang ❸** (Royal Field) is where royal cremations and other important ceremonies are held. The field is particularly lively on the birthdays of the Thai king and queen, Songkran festival and the Ploughing Ceremony in May.

National Museum

West of Sanam Luang, at Thanon Na Phra That, is the **National Museum ❹** (Wed–Sun 9am–4pm; charge; guided tours at 9.30am Wed and Thur; tel: 0-2224 1333; www.national museums.finearts.go.th). Besides housing a vast collection of antiquities from all over Southeast Asia, the museum has an interesting history of its own. Its grounds and some of the principal rooms were part of the former Wang Na (Front Palace) of the king's second-in-line, called the Prince Successor, a feature of the Thai monarchy until 1870.

The oldest buildings in the compound date from 1782, including the splendid **Buddhaisawan**

BELOW: an example of ancient Thai painting.

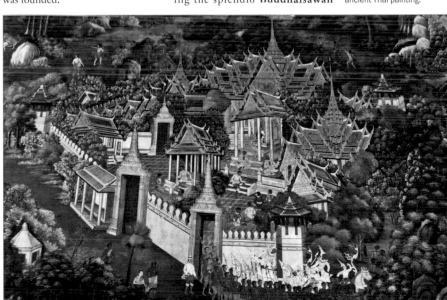

Located outside Wat Mahathat is one of Bangkok's more popular amulet markets. Thais use these amulets to ward off evil and attract good fortune. The amulets are mostly worn as pendants on heavy neck chains.

BELOW: Wat Pho's giant reclining Buddha.

Chapel. Built by the Prince Successor as his private place of worship within the palace, it contains some of Thailand's most beautiful and best-preserved murals dating from the 1790s, as well as the second-most-sacred Buddha image in Thailand, the famous 13th-century Phra Buddha Sihing.

To the left of the entrance is the **Sivamokhaphiman Hall**, which houses a prehistoric art collection. The front of the building is devoted to the **Thai History Gallery**, documenting the country's history from the Sukhothai period (13th century) to the present.

Also on site is the **Red House** (Tamnak Daeng), an ornate Ayutthaya-style golden-teak dwelling that once belonged to King Rama I's elder sister. Built in the Ayutthaya style, the house has an ornate wood finish.

The central audience hall of the Wang Na is divided into rooms (Nos 4–15) containing various ethnological exhibits such as elephant *howdah*, wood carvings, royal furnishings, weapons, *khon* dance masks and other royal treasures.

Wat Mahathat

Nestled between Silpakorn and Thammasat universities is **Wat Mahathat ❺** (daily 7am–8pm; free), which can be accessed from Sanam Luang or Thanon Maharat. Founded in the 1700s and home to the **Maha Chulalongkorn Rajavidyalaya University**, one of the two highest seats of Buddhist learning in the country, the temple exudes a more genuine work atmosphere compared to the more ceremonial temples in the area. King Rama IV spent almost 25 years studying as a monk here before taking the throne in 1851.

You can get in tune with your inner self at the temple's **International Buddhist Meditation Centre** (tel: 0-2623 5881), which conducts regular classes in English, and beyond the temple's western gate, **herbal medicine** and **amulet markets** (*see margin picture*) pitch along Thanon Maharat and in the alleys opposite.

Wat Pho

South of the Grand Palace and Wat Phra Kaew complex, on Thanon Thai Wang, is **Wat Pho ❻** (daily 8am–5pm; charge), Bangkok's largest and oldest surviving temple. Apart from its historic significance, visitors also come here to pay homage to the monumental Reclining Buddha, and to unwind at the city's best-known massage centre.

Also known to Thais as Wat Phra Chetuphon, the temple dates back to the 16th century. However, it did not achieve significance until Bangkok was established as the capital. Wat Pho was a particular favourite of the first four Bangkok kings, all of whom added to its treasures. The four coloured *chedi* to the west of the *bot* (ordination hall) are memorials to the past monarchs, and around the hall are 90-plus other *chedi*. The temple cloisters contain 394 bronze Buddha images, retrieved from ancient ruins in Sukhothai and Ayutthaya.

One of the most important additions was the Reclining Buddha by King Rama III in 1832. He also converted the temple into the country's earliest place of public learning. The monarch instructed that the walls be inscribed with lessons on astrology, history, morality and archaeology.

Wat Pho's giant Reclining Buddha, 46 metres (150ft) long and 15 metres (50ft) high, depicts the resting Buddha passing into nirvana. The flat soles of the Buddha's feet are inlaid with mother-of-pearl designs, illustrating the 108 auspicious signs for recognising Buddha. Also numbering 108 are the metallic bowls that span the wall; dropping a coin in each supposedly brings goodwill to the devotee.

Wat Pho massage school

Wat Pho is one of the best places to study traditional medicine, particularly massage and meditation. The temple's medicine pavilion displays stone tablets indicating beneficial body points for massage. Skirting the temple grounds are several small rock gardens that contain statues of her-mits striking poses; these were used as diagnostic aids. The **Wat Pho Thai Traditional Massage School** (daily 10am–6pm; tel: 0-2221 2974; www.watpomassage.com) offers cheap hour-long massages, and also offers courses for those wanting to learn the art of Thai massage while on holiday.

Wat Ratchabophit

Located on the opposite bank of Khlong Lord canal, on Thanon Fuang Nakhon, is **Wat Ratchabophit** **❼** (daily 5am–8pm, chapel 9–9.30am and 5.30–6pm; free). It's recognisable for its characteristic amalgamation of Thai temple architecture and period European style, an unusual design fusion that places the main circular *chedi* and its circular cloister in the centre. Started in 1869 by King Chulalongkorn (Rama V), the complex took well over two decades to complete.

The ordination hall is covered in *bencharong* ceramic tiles. The hall's windows and entrance doors are also exquisite works of art, with tiny pieces of mother-of-pearl inlaid in lacquer. The doors open on to one

TIP

When having a Thai massage, try to relax completely and believe that you're in safe hands. The massage will involve some contortionist-like poses and the natural inclination is to resist when you are sometimes bent into awkward positions. Don't fight it; just relax and go with the flow.

BELOW: Wat Ratchabophit marries Thai and European styles of architecture.

TIP

One of the best times to visit Wat Arun is late afternoon, when there are fewer visitors. When you are done, take the ferry across the river to Tha Tien pier, where you will enjoy great sunset views of Wat Arun from the popular but rundown bar-shack on the wooden pier.

of the most surprising temple interiors in Thailand – a Gothic-inspired chapel of solid columns that looks more like a medieval cathedral than a Thai temple.

National Discovery Museum

Just south of Wat Pho is the **National Discovery Museum** ❽ (Tue–Sun 10am–6pm; charge; tel: 0-2622 2777; www.ndmi.or.th). This excellent interactive, multimedia museum, housed in the old Commerce Ministry at the corner of Thanon Sanam Chai and Thanon Seethakarn, has a child-friendly environment and explores more than 3,000 years of Thai history, its envisioned future, and the kingdom's diverse peoples, cultures and beliefs.

THONBURI

Established by King Taksin after the fall of Ayutthaya in 1767, Thonburi served as Thailand's third capital for 15 years prior to Bangkok's establishment in 1782. Taksin spent most of his reign conquering factions of rebels who wished to lay claim to

his throne, leaving time only late in his reign to embellish his city. While Thonburi, which can be reached by numerous bridges, is short on major tourist attractions and only has a few high-end hotels, one of the most pleasing activities in the capital is a tour of the area's canals.

With rickety teak houses, vendors selling produce from boats, fishermen dangling rods out of windows and kids frolicking in the water, the sights along Thonburi's canals are reminiscent of a more peaceful bygone era. Those worth exploring include **Khlong Bangkok Noi**, which winds into **Khlong Bangkok Yai** downstream, as well as connecting to **Khlong Om** upstream. Once a source of fresh daily produce, the floating markets at **Wat Sai** and **Taling Chan** have become little more than tourist souvenir stops, but are still worth a look, and there's an artist community centred on Baan Silapin (daily 9am–6pm; tel: 081 -258 9260) with coffee shops and a traditional Thai puppet show.

Canal and river cruising

The major canals are serviced by public longtail boats. But as these can be erratic at certain times of the day, it is better to hire your own private longtail boat for a more leisurely exploration of the canals (*see page 103*).

Getting from pier to pier along the Chao Phraya River is best by **Chao Phraya Express** boats, which operate from the southern outskirts up to Nonthaburi in the north. For shuttling from one side of the river to the other, make use of the cheap cross-river ferries, including those close to the Chao Phraya Express boats (*see page 103*).

Wat Arun

When King Taksin first moored at the Thonburi bank of the Chao Phraya River at sunrise after sailing down from the sacked capital of

BELOW: longtail boats on the Chao Phraya River.

Ayutthaya in 1768, he found an old temple shrine and felt compelled to build a fitting holding place for the sacred Emerald Buddha. Eventually known as **Wat Arun** ❾, or the Temple of Dawn (daily 8.30am–5.30pm; charge), the temple was originally attached to Taksin's new palace (Wang Derm).

After Taksin's demise, the new King Chakri (Rama I) moved the capital (and the Emerald Buddha) to Bangkok, but the temple kept the interest of the first five kings. Over the years, the temple grew in size and ornamentation. In the early 19th century, King Rama II enlarged the structure and raised the central *prang* (Khmer-style tower) to 104 metres (345ft), making it the country's tallest religious structure.

Recycling piles of broken ceramic that was leftover ballast from Chinese merchant ships, Rama III introduced the colourful fragments of porcelain that cover most of the temple's exterior. The great *prang* represents the Hindu Buddhist Mount Meru, home of the gods with its 33 heavens. There are four smaller

prang standing at each corner of the temple, with niches containing statues of Nayu, the god of wind, on horseback. The entire complex is guarded by mythical giants called *yaksha*, similar to those that protect Wat Phra Kaew. There will be limited access to Wat Arun until 2015 due to renovations.

Museum of Royal Barges

On the north bank of the Khlong Bangkok Noi canal, which was a major waterway during King Taksin's reign, is the **National Museum of Royal Barges** ❿ (daily 9am–5pm; charge, photo fee extra; tel: 0-2424 0004). The dry-dock displays eight vessels from a fleet of over 50 that are rarely put to sail except on auspicious occasions. On such a day, a flotilla of 52 barges, manned by 2,082 oarsmen from the Thai navy, will carry the King along the Chao Phraya River to Wat Arun, where the monarch offers new robes to monks in a ceremony known as *kathin*.

The Royal Barges date back to 14th-century Ayutthaya, with the present fleet constructed in the early

An ornate garuda decorates the prow of a royal barge, seen at the National Museum of Royal Barges. This one is called the Narai Song Subhan.

BELOW LEFT: a young monk. **BELOW RIGHT:** Wat Arun, the Temple of the Dawn.

Located near Wat Suthat is the Giant Swing. In former days, young men would rock themselves back and forth to set the swing in motion, while trying to grab a bag of gold coins suspended on a nearby pole.

Below: seated Buddha images at Wat Suthat.

20th century. In the old days, the royal family, like everyone else, would travel by boat. The king would sit in the largest of the barges, the magnificent *Suphannahongse*, which was made from a single trunk of teak stretching over 46 metres (151ft). The model on display was built in 1911 and based on the design of its 18th-century predecessor.

OLD CITY AND DUSIT

Dominated by the wide boulevard of Thanon Ratchadamnoen, this section of the "Old City" contains all the peripheral buildings and temples that lie just outside Rattanakosin island. The area once marked the outskirts of the city, with the canals of Khlong Banglamphu and Khlong Ong Ang ferrying in supplies from the surrounding countryside. A strong sense of the past can still be found here, making this one of the city's most pleasant areas to explore.

Wat Suthat

Standing tall behind the Giant Swing, once the venue for a now-outlawed Brahmin ceremony, is **Wat Suthat ⓫** (daily 8.30am–9pm; charge), considered one of the country's six principal temples. Begun by Rama I in 1807, it took three reigns to complete. The temple is noted for its enormous *bot*, or ordination hall, said to be the tallest in Bangkok, and for its equally large *viharn* (sermon hall), both of which are surrounded by cloisters of many gilded Buddha images. The 8-metre (26ft)-tall Phra Sri Sakyamuni Buddha is one of the largest surviving bronze images from Sukhothai, and was transported by boat all the way from the northern kingdom. The temple courtyard is a virtual museum of statuary, with stone figures of Chinese generals and scholars. Originally ballast in rice ships returning from China, they were donated to temples.

Democracy Monument

Behind City Hall, north along Thanon Dinso, is a roundabout anchored by the **Democracy Monument ⓬**. Designed by Italian sculptor Corrado Feroci (also known as Silpa Bhirasri), the 1939 monument is a celebration of Thailand's transition from absolute to constitutional monarchy in 1932. Marked by four elongated wings, the central metal tray contains a copy of the constitution. The monument has been a rallying point for civil discontent, notably in 1973 and 1992, and again in 2010, when several people were killed and almost 1,000 injured in clashes between the army and Red Shirt demonstrators.

14 October Monument

A short walk west of Democracy Monument, along Thanon Ratchadamneon Klang towards the corner of Thanon Tanao, brings you to another chiselled edifice to the democratic struggle, the **14 October Monument**. This granite memorial

honours the people massacred by the army during the 1973 mass demonstrations against military rule in Thailand. Tragically, history repeated itself nearby with another violent crackdown on 6 October 1976.

Thanon Khao San

Along Thanon Tanao, on the left is **Thanon Khao San** ⓭, a self-contained ghetto for the backpacking globe-trotter since the early 1980s. Once a rather seedy gathering of cheap guest-houses, rice shops and pokey bars, as portrayed in Alex Garland's novel *The Beach*, Banglamphu's nerve centre has undergone a significant upgrade in recent years. The arrival of boutique hotels along with new bars and inter-national chains such as Starbucks have taken some of its edge away, but this neon-lit street is still full of character and party atmosphere, and is popular with younger Thais.

Wat Bowonniwet

At the end of Thanon Tanao, turn-ing right into Thanon Phra Sumen, is **Wat Bowonniwet** ⓮ (daily 8am–5pm; free), a modest-looking monas-tery with strong royal bonds. Built in 1826 during the reign of Rama III, King Mongkut (Rama IV) served as abbot of the temple for a small por-tion of his 27 years as a monk. More recently, the present King Bhumibol (Rama IX) donned saffron robes here after his coronation in 1946. Wat Bowonniwet is home to Thailand's second Buddhist university.

Thanon Ratchadamnoen

The wide **Thanon Ratchadamnoen** (Royal Passage), modelled at the turn of the 20th century on Paris's famous boulevards, splits into three sections and stretches all the way from the Grand Palace to the Dusit Park area. The tree-lined avenue has some of the city's widest and least cluttered pavements, and on royal birthdays becomes a sea of decorative lights, flags and royal portraits.

On the right of the road, east of Democracy Monument, **Rattana-kosin Exhibition Hall** (Tue–Fri 11am–8pm, Sat–Sun 10am–8pm; charge) displays the official history of the area, including architecture, tradi-tional arts and the Grand Palace.

During World War II, the Golden Mount served as a watchtower, with guards armed with signal flags to warn if the enemy invaders were drawing close.

BELOW LEFT: the Democracy Monument. **BELOW RIGHT:** metal spires of the Loha Prasat.

Ananta Samakhom Throne Hall, which dates back to 1907, is more European than Thai in character.

BELOW: backpacker haven, Thanon Khao San.

Loha Prasat and Wat Ratchanatda

Fifty metres/yds east, beside Pan Fah canal bridge, **Loha Prasat** (Metal Palace), on the right, is more evocative of Burmese temple structures. It shares the same grounds as **Wat Ratchanadda** (both daily 9am–5pm; charge). Originally meant to be the temple's *chedi*, and built by Rama III in 1846, Loha Prasat's unusual architecture is said to draw from an Indian design dating back some 2,500 years. The central tower has two tiers and 37 iron spires that symbolise the virtues needed to attain enlightenment. Just behind the temple is a thriving amulet market, similar to the one found at Wat Mahathat *(see page 80)*.

Golden Mount

On the corner by Pan Fah canal bridge are the ruined walls of Mahakan Fort. To the south, across the canal the **Golden Mount** (Phu Khao Thong) was for many years Bangkok's highest point (daily 7.30am–5.30pm; charge). Started by Rama III as a huge *chedi*, the city's soft earth made it impossible to build on

and the site became an artificial hill. King Mongkut added a more modest *chedi* to the top, and King Chulalongkorn completed work on the 78-metre (256ft)-high plot. A pathway to the summit curves around the side of the hill, shaded by trees and dotted with small shrines along the way. The gilded *chedi*, which is part of **Wat Saket** at the bottom of the Golden Mount, is said to contain a Buddha relic from India.

Dusit area

Crossing Khlong Banglamphu, Thanon Ratchadamnoen Klang turns into Ratchadamnoen Nok, with the pleasant, tree-lined boulevard leading down to a broad square in front of the old National Assembly building. Known as **Royal Plaza**, the square is watched over by a bronze **Statue of King Chulalongkorn** (Rama V) on horseback. Chulalongkorn was responsible for the construction of much of this part of Bangkok, which was once a rustic royal retreat from the city and the Grand Palace. With the present king residing in nearby **Chitralada Palace** and the day-to-day governance taking place in Parliament House, this area is the heartbeat of the nation, at least until 2017, when the new goverment site in Nonthaburi is planned for completion.

Ananta Samakhom

Beyond the statue, the **Ananta Samakhom Throne Hall** is a monumental Italian Renaissance-style hall of grey marble crowned by a huge dome (daily 8.30am–4.30pm; charge, or free with Grand Palace entrance ticket). It is the tallest building within the manicured gardens of **Dusit Park**, a royal oasis livened up by canals, bridges and fountains. Built in 1907 by King Chulalongkorn as a grandiose hall for receiving visiting dignitaries and other state ceremonies, the highlight of

the hall's rich interior is the dome-ceiling frescoes depicting all of the Chakri monarchs from Rama I to Rama VI.

Abhisek Dusit Throne Hall

Directly behind, still in Dusit Park, the **Royal Elephant National Museum** has displays of tusks and charms used by elephant handlers (*mahouts*), photos and articles about elephant capture and training, and a tableau of the ceremony performed during the white elephant presentation.

Across the lawn is **Abhisek Dusit Throne Hall** (daily 9.30am–4pm; charge, or free with Grand Palace entrance ticket), constructed in 1903 for King Chulalongkorn as an accompanying throne hall to Vimanmek (*see below*). It's a sumptuous meld of Victorian and Moorish styles, but retains its distinctly Thai sheen. The main hall is now used as a showroom-cum-museum for the SUPPORT foundation, a charitable organisation headed by Queen Sirikit that helps to preserve traditional Thai arts and crafts.

Vimanmek Mansion

Further into the park, **Vimanmek Mansion ⑱** is billed as the world's largest golden-teak building (daily 9.30am–4pm; charge, or free with Grand Palace entrance ticket; tel: 0-2628 6300; www.palaces.thai.net). Compulsory guided tours every 30 minutes; visitors dressed in shorts must wear sarongs that are provided at the door, and shoes and bags have to be stowed in lockers.

Originally built in 1868 as a summer house for King Chulalongkorn on the east-coast island of Ko Si Chang (*see page 120*), the king ordered that the three-storey mansion be dismantled and reassembled on the Dusit grounds in 1901. Made entirely from golden teak and without a single nail being used in its construction, the gingerbread fretwork and octagonal tower of this 72-room lodge looks more Victorian than period Thai. The king and his large family lived here for only five years, during which time no males were allowed entry.

The mansion eventually fell out of favour and lay abandoned until it

TIP

Be sure to keep your admission ticket to the Wat Phra Kaew and Grand Palace (*see page 74*). This allows you access to many of Dusit's sights for free, like the Ananta Samakhom Throne Hall, Vimanmek Mansion, Abhisek Dusit Throne Hall, and the Royal Elephant Museum.

BELOW LEFT: the Abhisek Dusit Throne Hall.
BELOW RIGHT: Vimanmek Mansion, the world's largest golden teak building.

An Ayutthaya-style Buddha image in the "abhaya mudra" (reassurance) posture at a gallery in Wat Benjamabophit.

BELOW: Wat Benjam-abophit.

was finally restored for the Bangkok bicentennial in 1982.

Vimanmek (meaning Palace in the Clouds) offers an interesting glimpse into how the royal family of the day lived. In the pavilion on the south side of the mansion are free performances of Thai dance and martial arts every day at 10.30am and 2pm.

Dusit Zoo

To the east of Dusit Park is **Dusit Zoo** (daily 8am–6pm; charge; tel: 0-2281 2000). The grounds were originally part of the Royal Dusit Garden Palace, where King Chulalongkorn had his private botanical garden. The 19-hectare (47-acre) site became a public zoo in 1938. The zoo has around 300 different species of mammal, almost 1,000 bird species and around 300 different kinds of reptile, but conditions at some of the animal enclosures are less than adequate.

Wat Benjamabophit

To the south of the Chulalongkorn statue, along Thanon Rama V, is **Wat Benjamabophit** , more popularly known as the Marble Temple (daily

8.30am–4.30pm; charge). It was the last major temple built in central Bangkok and the best example of modern Thai religious architecture.

Started by King Chulalongkorn at the turn of the last century, the *wat* was designed by the king's half-brother Prince Naris together with Italian architect Hercules Manfredi. It was completed in 1911, with dramatic fused elements of East and West, including a cruciform shape, walls of Carrara marble and unique European-crafted stained-glass windows depicting Thai mythological scenes. The *bot*'s principal Buddha is a replica of the famous Phra Buddha Chinarat of Phitsanulok. The base contains the ashes of King Chulalongkorn. Behind the *bot*, a gallery holds 53 significant Buddha images, originals and copies, from all over Asia.

In the early morning, merit-makers gather before the temple gates to donate food and offerings to a line of bowl-wielding monks, in contrast to common practice, when monks walk the streets for alms.

CHINATOWN

Chinatown was settled by Chinese merchants in the 1780s, after they were asked to relocate here so that the Grand Palace could be built. They lived mainly around the original dirt track of Sampeng (now officially Soi Wanit 1). Other adjacent plots of land were given to the Indian and Muslim communities. King Mongkut laid Thanon Charoen Krung (New Road) in 1863, the first paved street in Bangkok, and Chinatown soon began to spread outwards.

Packed with narrow roads and lanes teeming with commercial bustle, this is one of the capital's most traffic-clogged districts. Exploring on foot allows you to soak up the mercantile atmosphere. Away from downtown's plush mega-malls, Chinatown is a raw experience of Bangkok past: old shophouses, *godowns*

(warehouses), temples and shrines. The MRT expansion, due to operate in the area from 2015, should make it even busier.

Sampeng Lane

The **Sampeng** area, the old pulse of Chinatown, has a rowdy history as a raunchy entertainment district. By 1900, **Sampeng Lane** ㉑ had a reputation as "Sin Alley", with lanes leading to opium dens, gambling houses and brothels. Now devoid of sleaze it's a bustling area of small shops selling goods, frequently imported from China, particularly on the stretch running northwest up to Thanon Ratchawong. You'll find everything from cheap clothes and footwear to sticky confectionery, cosmetics and costume jewellery

Pahurat Market

Beyond Thanon Ratchawong, the lane continues on to Bangkok's Little India, centred on **Pahurat Market** ㉒ (daily 9am–6pm). This two-level bazaar has all manner of fabrics, Hindu deities and wedding regalia, together with traditional Thai dance costumes. On

Thanon Pahurat and parts of Thanon Chakraphet are cheap curry eateries and Indian tea and spice stalls. Indian migrants from the late 19th century converged here, and today, their presence is still strongly felt. Nearby at Thanon Chakraphet is the golden-domed **Sri Guru Singh Sabha** temple, the focal point of Bangkok's Sikh community.

Pak Khlong Talad

With floral garland offerings at temples and shrines all over the city, Bangkok needs a constant supply of fresh blooms. South of Pahurat Market, at the end of Thanon Tri Phet, near the riverfront, **Pak Khlong Talad** ㉓ (Flower Market) serves as the capital's flower and vegetable garden (daily 24 hours). The bunches of bargain-priced flowers are a riot of fragrance and colour.

Nakhon Kasem

East of Pahurat Market, between Thanon Yaowarat and Thanon Charoen Krung, at the corner with Thanon Chakrawat, is **Nakhon Kasem** ㉔, or Thieves' Market (daily

The flowers at Pak Khlong Talad may be unceremoniously wrapped in newspaper, but prices are very low

BELOW: bustling Thanon Yaowarat.

The solid-gold Buddha image at Wat Traimit was found purely by accident.

BELOW: swirl of shoppers at Mahboonkrong mall.

8am–8pm). A few decades ago, this was where you searched after being robbed, a likely place to recover stolen goods at very reasonable prices. It was later the haunt of antiques dealers, but now handles a variety of music shops and household items, although if you look hard enough, you may chance upon a few old treasures.

Wat Mangkon Kamalawat

Thanon Charoen Krung and **Thanon Yaowarat** are the two most important roads in the area. Yaowarat, which is the local name for Chinatown, is best known for its gold shops and, with its forest of neon signs, looks in parts very much like a Hong Kong street. On Thanon Charoen Krung, near Soi Itsaranuphap, is the towering gateway of ornate **Wat Mangkon Kamalawat** ㉕, or Leng Noi Yee (Dragon Flower Temple) as it's also known (daily 8.30am–3.30pm; free). Built in 1871, this is the most revered temple in Chinatown and Thailand's major centre for Mahayana Buddhism (most Thais practice Theravada Buddhism). Elements of Taoist and Confucianist worship can also be found at the temple

and it is the focal point for Bangkok's Vegetarian Festival each October.

Soi Itsaranuphap

Chinatown's most interesting lane is **Soi Itsaranuphap** (Soi 16), which runs south from Thanon Phlab Phla Chai and passes a 19th-century Thai temple called **Wat Kanikaphon** (daily 6am–4pm; free). Around the entrance to Soi Itsaranuphap are shops selling "hell money" (a form of joss paper) and miniature houses, Mercedes cars, and other items made of paper for the Chinese *kong tek* ceremony. The items are then taken to the temple and burnt as offerings to deceased relatives.

Talad Kao and Talad Mai

Soi Itsaranuphap has two of the city's best-known markets. **Talad Mai** (New Market), which has been selling its wares for over a century, trades until sundown. Further on, closer to Sampeng Lane, the two-century old **Talad Kao** ㉖ (Old Market) wraps up by late morning. Both have a reputation for high-quality fresh meat, fish and vegetables, and overflow during Chinese New Year.

Wat Traimit

Just east of the point where Thanon Yaowarat meets Thanon Charoen Krung, across from the Odeon Circle China Gate, is the unremarkable looking **Wat Traimit** ㉗ (daily 8am–5pm; charge), also known as The Temple of the Golden Buddha.

A 600 million-baht marble *mondop* (pavilion) was built in 2009 to house the 3-metre (10ft) -tall **Golden Buddha**, which was found by accident in the 1950s, when it fell to the ground during transportation. A crack in the stucco revealed a 5.5-ton solid-gold image. It is said to date from 13th-century Sukhothai, and was probably encased in stucco during the Ayutthayan period to conceal it from Burmese invaders. The *mondop*

is also home to historical displays in the **Yaowarat Chinatown Heritage Centre** (daily 8am–4.30pm; charge; tel: 0-2225 9775).

PATHUMWAN AND PRATUNAM

The commercial heart of downtown Bangkok, **Pathumwan** is a sprawl of shopping malls, all connected by the Skytrain. It's mainly a consumer's paradise, yet there are still plenty of sights more reminiscent of an older and more traditional Bangkok. Cleaved in the early 19th century, the man-made canal **Khlong Saen Saep** enabled the capital to spread north to **Pratunam** and beyond.

Jim Thompson's House

Just a short walk to the end of Soi Kasemsan 2 from the National Stadium Skytrain station is the protected oasis of **Jim Thompson's House** ㉘ (daily 9am–5pm; charge includes compulsory guided tours of the museum; tel: 0-2216 7368; www.jimthompsonhouse.com).

Jim Thompson was the American silk entrepreneur responsible for the revival of Thai silk. Thompson, an architect by training, first arrived in Thailand at the end of World War II, serving in the Office of Strategic Service (the forerunner of the CIA). Later, he returned to Bangkok to live, and soon became interested in the then almost-redundant craft of silk weaving and design.

Thompson mysteriously disappeared in the jungles of Malaysia's Cameron Highlands in 1967, but his well-preserved house still stands today by the banks of the Khlong Saen Saep canal. Thompson was an enthusiastic collector of Asian arts and antiquities, many of which adorn his traditional house-turned-museum.

The museum comprises six teak structures, which were transported from Ayutthaya to the silk-weaving enclave of Ban Khrua, just across Khlong Saen Saep, before being reassembled at the present site in 1959. From the windows of the house, it's easy to imagine how scenic the view would have been some 40 years ago, looking across the lush gardens, or "jungle" as Thompson called it.

SHOP

Resist the urge to shop at the rather pricey gift shop of Jim Thompson's House Museum. Better deals are available at the Jim Thompson Factory Outlet along 153 Th. Sukuhmvit Soi 93 (tel: 0-2332 6530).

BELOW LEFT AND RIGHT: interior and garden of Jim Thompson's House.

SHOP

The main shopping areas in downtown Bangkok are linked by the Skywalk – a covered elevated walkway beneath the Skytrain tracks – connecting National Stadium, Siam and Chit Lom Skytrain stations along Thanon Rama 1. This means you can walk from one mall to another under shade and without having to cross the streets.

Next to the old house is a restaurant, while opposite is the **Art Centre at Jim Thompson's House**, a contemporary gallery which holds regular exhibitions of local and international art and crafts.

Bangkok Art and Culture Centre

Leaving Soi Kasemsan 2 and turning left on Thanon Rama I brings you to the **Bangkok Art and Culture Centre** (Tue–Sun 10am–9pm; free; tel: 0-2214 6630; www.bacc.or.th). This 11-storey space stages some of Bangkok's best art and multimedia shows, featuring both local and international works. The retail outlets on its lower floors have imaginatively been issued to small independent galleries or organisations such as the Thai Film Foundation and Bangkok Opera. Art markets feature regularly on the concourse, and performances take place in a small auditorium on the ground floor.

Shopping along Th. Rama 1

Across the Skywalk *(see margin)* from the BACC is the bewildering mayhem of **Mahboonkrong**, better known as MBK. A monster mall, MBK is always busy with youngsters, and is known for its bootleg merchandise, art copiers and myriad mobile-phone shops.

Continuing on the Skywalk along Thanon Rama 1 brings you to the interconnecting malls of **Siam Discovery Centre** and **Siam Centre**. Both have been recently refurbished, the latter with a particularly funky modern design, and are home to a number of boutiques and expensive fashion brands. Siam Discovery has a branch of Madame Tussaud's.

The mammoth **Siam Paragon** next door is a shopper's paradise and hosts a slew of chichi brand-name shops and Southeast Asia's largest aquarium at **Siam Ocean World** (daily 9am–10pm, tel: 0-2687 2000; charge; www.siamoceanworld.com). The aquarium is divided into seven zones, including a massive oceanarium, and has more than 30,000 marine creatures. You can also ride in a glass-bottomed boat and dive with sharks. On the 5th floor is **Kidzania**, an edutainment complex for 4–14 year-olds.

Opposite, on Thanon Rama I,

BELOW LEFT: Erawan Shrine attracts worshippers all day long.
BELOW RIGHT: tranquil lake at Lumphini Park.

Siam Square ㉚, is located next to Chulalongkorn University, and is packed with students. For many years it was a hotbed of young fashion designers, and there are still pockets of boutique shops to drop into. But the sledgehammers have demolished most to make way for more malls.

Further along the Skywalk is **Central World**, Bangkok's largest mall, with scores of shops, restaurants, a multi-screen cinema and a Zen-lifestyle department store.

Erawan Shrine

Central World marks the end of Thanon Rama I, at a chaotic junction where the street intersects with Thanon Ratchadamri and changes its name to Thanon Ploenchit.

At the opposite corner is the popular **Erawan Shrine** ㉛ (daily 9am–5pm). The three-headed elephant Erawan, which features in Hindu mythology, makes many appearances in Thai life, but this shrine is dedicated to the four-headed Hindu god of creation, Brahma. Originally erected on the site of the former Erawan Hotel, rebuilt as the present Grand Hyatt Erawan, but deemed ineffective after a spate of accidents slowed the hotel's construction. This plaster-gilded 1956 replacement halted the unlucky run, and has been revered by locals for its strong talismanic powers ever since.

In early 2006, the shrine was smashed to pieces by a psychologically disturbed Thai man, who was subsequently beaten to death by an angry Thai mob. The site is so popular that four photographs of the shrine were displayed so that people could continue to worship until a new one was erected two months later when 1,000 people attended the unveiling.

Lumphini Park

At the western end of Thanon Ratchadamri, at the intersection of Thanon Rama IV, is **Lumphini Park** ㉜ (daily 4.30am–9pm; free), Bangkok's premier green spot. The park was given to the public in 1925 by King Vajiravudh (Rama VI), whose memorial statue stands in front of the main gates. Embellished with lakes (with pedal boats for hire) and a Chinese-style clock tower, sunrise or sunset sees elderly Chinese practising t'ai chi. In the cool season, from December to March, the park hosts open-air classical concerts every Sunday. If you are lucky you may come across a stall selling shots of snake's blood, believed to be a general cure-all and aphrodisiac.

Snake Farm

For an encounter with dangerous reptiles, slide along Thanon Rama IV to visit the **Queen Saovabha Memorial Institute** ㉝, popularly called the **Snake Farm** (Mon–Fri 8.30am–4.30pm, Sat–Sun 8.30am–noon; charge; tel: 0-2252 0161).

Founded in 1923 as the Pasteur Institute, the Institute's principal work lies in the research and treatment of snakebites and the extraction

A young volunteer at the Snake Farm gingerly handles a python as he poses for a photograph.

BELOW: the MBK shopping centre. It is situated at the National Stadium BTS skytrain station and S kywalk.

The Sala Rim Naam restaurant at the Oriental Hotel puts on a nightly show of traditional Thai dance-drama accompanied by a Thai set dinner.

BELOW: the Authors' Lounge at the Oriental.

of antivenins. Sessions of venom-milking (Mon–Fri 11am) and snake handling (Mon–Fri 2.30pm, Sat–Sun 11am) are the best times to visit, when snakes are pulled from the pit before a squealing audience.

Pratunam area

Northwards, over Khlong Saen Saep canal and Thanon Petchaburi, is **Pratunam Market**. This textiles market is a bustling warren of stalls, with piles of cheap clothing, fabrics and assorted fashion accessories. Across Thanon Petchaburi from Pratunam is **Platinum Fashion Mall**, home to hundreds of small clothes, textiles and accessories stalls. Just up the road is a mall entirely devoted to electronics and IT, **Panthip Plaza**.

Suan Pakkad Palace

Most tourists make a beeline for Jim Thompson's House, missing out on another equally delightful abode, the **Suan Pakkad Palace ㉞** (daily 9am–4pm; charge includes a guided tour; tel: 0-2245 4934; www.suanpakkad.com).

Located a short walk along Thanon Sri Ayutthaya from Phaya

Thai Skytrain station, Suan Pakkad or "Cabbage Patch", was the former residence of the late Prince and Princess Chumbhot, who were keen art collectors and gardeners. The compound's eight teak houses, amid a lush garden with lotus pond, now form a museum with a broad collection of antiques and artefacts from the prehistoric Bronze Age Ban Chiang period onwards. It also has the Khon Museum containing items about classical dance-theatre.

BANGRAK AND SILOM

Gravitating eastwards from the Chao Phraya River's premier real estate, Thanon Silom, together with Thanon Sathorn is the principal road of the business district, ending at Thanon Rama IV with Lumphini Park beyond. Parallel are Thanons Surawong and Si Phraya, all of which make up the district of **Bangrak**. But, come dusk, along Silom the office staff depart and a bevy of sex workers, male, female and *kathoey* (ladyboy), converge on the area.

Bangrak, however, is not all office blocks and unbridled sleaze. Between River City shopping centre and the Shangri-La hotel is the old *farang* (European) district, where the lanes still hold a few buildings from its days as a 19th-century settlement close to the beautiful old Customs House, which, still sadly dilapidated, is best seen from the river.

Mandarin Oriental Hotel

Next to the Custom's House is the **Mandarin Oriental Hotel ㉟**, founded in the 1870s and consistently rated as one of the world's best. Although the two newer blocks are nothing special to look at, you can get a good feel for the old-world atmosphere with afternoon tea in the elegant **Authors' Lounge**, among historical Thai photos and others of literary greats that have

passed through the doors, such as Somerset Maugham, Noël Coward and Graham Greene.

Assumption Cathedral

Turn right outside the Oriental Hotel, along Oriental Avenue, towards the river where a side road on the left leads to a small square dominated by **Assumption Cathedral** (daily 6am–9pm; free). Built in 1910, the red-brick cathedral is surrounded by a Catholic mission. Its ornate interior is topped with a beautiful domed ceiling hovering over a large sacristy with gilded pillars. Take a breather here and mull over Bangkok's secluded feats of architectural delight.

Asiatique

A ten-minute boat shuttle south along the river from Saphan Taksin pier, **Asiatique** (daily 5pm–midnight) is one of the city's few pedestrian friendly waterfront spaces. Its many restaurants and stalls sell a wide range of items such as handicrafts and home decor. Also here are *katoey* shows at **Calypso Cabaret** and traditional Thai puppetry at the **Joe Louis Theatre**.

Maha Uma Devi Temple

Looming behind Assumption Cathedral, at the corner of Silom and Charoen Krung, is the faux-classical **State Tower**, with fantastic views from its alfresco rooftop drink-and-dine venue Sirocco.

Continuing further along Thanon Silom on the right, on the corner of Soi Pan, is the vibrant Hindu **Maha Uma Devi Temple** ㊱ (daily 6am–8pm; free). Named after Shiva's consort, Uma Devi, the temple was established in the 1860s by the city's Tamil community, whose presence is still prevalent in the area. The temple is known to Thais as Wat Khaek, meaning "guests' temple" (*khaek* is also a less-welcoming term used by locals for anyone from the Asian subcontinent).

Patpong

Come nightfall, stall vendors set up a **night market** along Thanon Silom from Soi 2–Soi 8, commandeering the narrow pavements in either direction, including the fleshpot of **Patpong** ㊲ (Soi 1 and Soi 2). The market sells the usual wares, including counterfeit watches, fake name-brand bags and

The stepped facade of the Maha Uma Devi Temple.

BELOW: seamy streets and sights of Patpong.

SHOP

The market vendors around Patpong are among the toughest in the city, quoting ridiculously inflated prices that are some 50–75 percent higher than what they are actually prepared to accept. Bargain hard!

clothes, and bootleg CDs and DVDs. With its slew of trashy go-go bars and anything-goes strip clubs, Patpong's sleazy reputation is still deserved, although its heyday has long gone and many bars are being overtaken by boutique shops. Touts still proffer a freakish assortment of sex shows, including the notorious ping pong acrobatics, but today's tamer experience is more a blitz of neon lights, relentless techno beats and gyrating bikini-clad dancers on bar tops.

A few lanes east from Patpong, **Silom Soi 4** is a compact street of dance clubs, restaurants and bars that is a largely, but not exclusively, gay area. Nearby **Silom Soi 2** is dedicated to full-on gay party-goers. And further on still, the hostess bars along **Soi Thaniya** cater for mainly Japanese clientele.

Kukrit Pramoj's Home

Over on Thanon Sathorn, tucked away on Soi Phra Phinij, is **MR Kukrit Pramoj's Heritage Home ㊳** (Sat–Sun 10am–5pm; charge; tel: 0-2286 8185). Born of royal descent (signified by the title Mom Ratcha-

wong – MR), the late Kukrit Pramoj had a brief stint as prime minister during the politically disruptive times of the 1970s, but he is better remembered as a prolific author and cultural preservationist.

His splendid wooden home, surrounded by an ornate Khmer-style garden, is now a museum. Its five stilt buildings reflect the traditional architecture of the Central Plains; the *bonsai* garden adds a sense of serenity; and the interior displays beautiful *objets d'art*, antique pottery and even an ornate bed that belonged to Rama II.

SUKHUMVIT

Thanon **Sukhumvit**, a bustling, traffic-clogged artery, pushes the urban sprawl eastwards (it actually runs all the way to the Cambodian border). The efficient Skytrain provides the fastest means of public transport here between its many upmarket shops, restaurants and entertainment venues.

Although thin on key tourist attractions, Thanon Sukhumvit is the place that most of the city's growing expatriate community calls home.

BELOW: Kukrit Pramoj's home and garden

Sukhumvit's early blocks burst with a profusion of tailors, pool halls, beer bars, inns and hotels. A **night market** crowds the pavements from Soi 3–19, replaced later at night by makeshift food and drink stalls. The area has a lascivious veneer, anchored by the three-storey mall of go-go bars, **Nana Entertainment Plaza** (NEP), on Soi 4. Working girls soliciting for customers can be found along street corners from Soi 5 to Soi 19. Further along across the Asoke intersection (Soi 21) is Sukhumvit's other notorious neon strip devoted to pole dancing, **Soi Cowboy**.

However, Sukhumvit's overall character is far from sleazy, with many of the city's best nightspots dotted along its side streets. Head to **Soi 11** for the home of the **Q Bar** and the late night dance club, **Bash**

Kamthieng House

Turn left at Sukhumvit Soi 21 (Soi Asoke), after Terminal 21 shopping mall, and you come to one of Sukhumvit's oldest buildings, the headquarters of the **Siam Society** (Tue–Sat 9am–5pm; tel: 0-2661 6470-77; www.siam-society.org). It was founded in 1904 to promote the study of Thai culture, and has an excellent library full of rare books and Thai maps. On the same grounds is the **Kamthieng House** , a 150-year-old wooden home transplanted from Chiang Mai and turned into an ethnological museum.

Kamthieng House was moved from its former location in Chiang Mai to Bangkok.

Emporium area

On the corner of Soi 24, near Phrom Phong Skytrain station, is Sukhumvit's premier shopping mall, **Emporium**. The mall is big on both interiors and fashion, but it also hosts several cinemas and the excellent **Thailand Creative & Design Center**, with a design reference library and regular exhibitions (daily 10.30am–9pm; tel: 0-2664 8448; www.tcdc.or.th). The nearby side lanes are full of pubs, bars and restaurants. Further east, just off Thong Lo Skytrain station, is **Soi 55** (Soi Thonglor), a hot hangout for young Thais and home to some of the city's liveliest bars, restaurants and clubs. Notable destinations include Iron Fairies, The Water Library and Demo. ❏

BELOW: a fabric stall at Chatuchak Market.

Chatuchak Market

The final stop (Mo Chit) on the Skytrain's northern line drops you at the **Chatuchak Weekend Market** (Sat–Sun 7am–6pm). Reputed to be the world's biggest flea market, Chatuchak is a must-see for any visitor; even the least-enthusiastic shopper will be overawed by the sheer scale and variety of goods for sale. With an estimated 400,000 visitors weaving through the market's maze-like interior every weekend, Chatuchak is a heady assault on the senses; an early start (by 9am) is essential to beat the heat and the crowds. The fun is in stumbling across hidden pockets of culture or kitsch as you meander through the alleyways.

TEMPLE ART AND ARCHITECTURE

The temple *(wat)* plays a vital role in every community, large or small; for many visitors, Thailand's temples are the country's most memorable sights.

A typical Thai *wat* (temple) has two enclosing walls that divide it from the secular world. The monks' quarters are situated between the outer and inner walls. In larger temples, the inner walls may be lined with Buddha images and serve as cloisters for meditation. This part of the temple is called *buddhavasa* or *phutthawat*. Within the inner walls is the *bot* or *ubosot* (ordination hall), surrounded by eight stone tablets and set on consecrated ground. This is the most sacred part of the temple and only monks can enter it. The *bot* contains a Buddha image, but it is the *viharn* (sermon hall) that contains the principal Buddha images. Also in the inner courtyard are the bell-shaped *chedi* (relic chambers) or towering Khmer-style spires called *prang*, which are a variation of *chedi* and similarly contain the relics of either the Buddha or pious or distinguished people. *Salas* (pavilions) can be found all around the temple; the largest of these is the *sala kan prian* (study hall), used for saying afternoon prayers. Apart from Buddha images, various mythological creatures *(see page 78)* are found within the temple compound.

ABOVE: the cloisters at Wat Suthat are lined with Buddha statues, here in the "Subduing Mara" position, denoting a renunciation of worldly desire.

BELOW: gilded *chofa* (bird-like decorations), intricately carved gables, and green and ochre tiles are common features of Thai temple roofs.

ABOVE: temple exteriors are often very ornate, such as that of the *bot* of the Emerald Buddha at Wat Phra Kaew. Gold tiles, glass mosaic, lacquer and mother-of-pearl are some of the materials used.

BELOW: Thai temple murals are created on a background that has been prepared and dried before the artist paints on it using pigments mixed with glue. Often featured on the interior walls, such murals depict the classic subjects of Thai painting, including tales from the *Jataka* (Buddha's birth and previous lives) and other Buddhist themes, and also vignettes of local life. During the reign of Rama III (1824–51), mural painting reached its peak, with artists not only following the principles of traditional Thai art but also introducing new elements, such as Western perspective. The mural below, from Wat Suthat in Bangkok, is an example of the late-18th-century style (better known as the Rattanakosin Period).

BELOW: the gleaming Phra Si Rattana *chedi* at Wat Phra Kaew is bell-shaped with a ringed spire and a three-tiered base – a feature of Sri Lankan reliquary towers. Close inspection will reveal a surface made up of thousands of tiny gold mosaic pieces.

BELOW: these towering *chedi* at Wat Pho sit on square bases and have graceful and elegant proportions, reminiscent of the Lanna-style architecture of north Thailand. Decorated with coloured tiles, the *chedi* are memorials to the first four Chakri kings.

BELOW: Wat Arun features five rounded *prang* – reflecting Cambodian-Khmer influence – encrusted with thousands of broken porcelain pieces. These shards were leftover ballast from Chinese ships that visited Bangkok in its early days.

B ANGKOK

TRANSPORT

Getting There

By Air
Suvarnabhumi Airport
Bangkok's **Suvarnabhumi Airport** (pronounced "su-wa-na-poom"; www.suvarnabhumiairport.com) is about 30km (19 miles) east of Bangkok. It takes about 45 minutes to get to the airport from the city by taxi, depending on traffic conditions. The airport handles all international flights to Bangkok as well as many domestic connections.

Suvarnabhumi has one main passenger terminal with seven concourses, capable of handling 76 flights per hour with ease, according to the Airport Authority of Thailand (AOT). The airport has its fair share of complaints, usually sparse toilet facilities, a congested arrival hall and long walks between gates. But the experience is pretty hassle-free, the main bugbear being rogue taxis.

The airport has a good range of facilities on offer, including foreign-exchange outlets, ATMs, a Tourism Authority of Thailand (TAT) office, medical centre, internet connection, fitness centre and a wide array of shops and restaurants.

In line with the practice of major airports the world over, the airport tax for international flights out of Suvarnabhumi is now incorporated into the price of your air ticket.

For further information, check the airport website or phone any of the following numbers for assistance:
Airport Call Centre: 0-2132 1888
Departures: 0-2132 9324–7
Arrivals: 0-2132 9328–9

Don Muang Airport
Some low budget carriers use Bangkok's old **Don Muang Airport** (tel: 0-2535 1111; www.donmuangairportonline.com) for domestic and international flights. It takes about 45 minutes to get to the airport by taxi.

Note: If making a flight connection between Suvarnabhumi and Don Muang airports, be sure to allow sufficient time as taxi travel between the two airports could take up to 1½ hours.

By Rail
The **State Railway of Thailand** (hotline 1690; www.railway.co.th) operates trains that are clean, cheap and reliable, if a little slow. There are three entry points by rail into Thailand. Two are from Malaysia, the more popular of which is the daily train that leaves Butterworth, near Penang in northwest Malaysia, at 1.15pm for Hat Yai (south Thailand) and arrives at Bangkok's Hualam-phong Station at 10.50am the next day. Trains leave Hualam-phong Station daily at 2.45pm for the return journey to Malaysia. There is also a short line from Nong Khai, in northeast Thailand, to 3km (2 miles) across the Laos border. This will eventually extend to Vientiane.

By Road
Malaysia provides the main road access into Thailand, with crossings near Betong and Sungai Kolok. From **Laos**, there are four Friendship Bridges, at Mukdahan, Nakhon Phanom and Nong Khai, all in northeast Thailand, and at Chiang Khong, in Chiang Rai Province. There is also a land crossing at Huay Kon (in Nan Province). From **Cambodia**, the most commonly used border crossing is from Poipet, which connects to the Thai town of Aranyaprathet, east of Bangkok.

Getting Around
From the Airport
The journey from Suvarnabhumi International Airport to the city centre takes 45 minutes in good traffic. Times can more than double during rush hours or rain. If you already have a reservation at a hotel, a representative will have your name or hotel name written on a sign. If you haven't

made prior arrangements, take a taxi, limousine or the Airport Rail Link.

By Taxi

Operating 24 hours daily, all taxis officially serving the airport are air-conditioned and metered. When you exit from the Arrival Hall, there is an official taxi booth outside on the 4th floor concourse. Join the queue and tell the person at the desk where you want to go to. A receipt will be issued, with the licence-plate number of the taxi and your destination in Thai written on it. Make sure the driver turns on the meter. At the end of your trip, pay what is on the meter plus the B50 airport surcharge and the highway toll fees (about B90 in total to downtown). Depending on traffic, an average fare from the airport to the city centre is around B450 (including toll fees and airport surcharge).

By Limousine

There are two limousine operators stationed at the Arrival Hall. **Airports of Thailand Limousines** (AOT) (tel: 0-2134 2323–6) operates a variety of vehicles that can take you to the city centre for about B1,000. Luxury cars such as a top-end 7-series BMW will cost B2,200. Rates to Pattaya start at around B2,600, depending on the vehicle used. **THAI Airways Limousines** (mobile tel: 081-652 4444) also operates a premium car service. Prices are similar to those charged by AOT.

By Rail

The 28km (18-mile) **Suvarnabhumi Airport Rail Link** (SARL) connects the airport to the city with two services. The **City Line** to Phaya Thai calls at eight stations en route – Lat Krabang, Ban Thap Chang, Hua Mak, Ramkhamhaeng, Asoke, Makkasan, Ratchaprarop and Phaya Thai – and takes 30 minutes for the full journey. It links to the Skytrain system at Phaya Thai. The **Express Line** runs direct to Bangkok City Air Terminal, at Makkasan, where passengers can check in and drop their luggage. Makkasan will eventually link by walkway to Phetchaburi Metro station, but at the time of going to press it was not built. Tickets B15–45 (City Line), B90–B150 (Express Line). Journey time 15 mins to Makkasan, 30 mins to Phaya Thai. Both lines run 6am–midnight.

Public Transport

Skytrain (BTS)

BTS **Tourist Information Centre:** tel: 0-2617 7341; hotline: 0-2617 6000; www.bts.co.th.

The Bangkok Transit System's elevated train service, or Skytrain, is the perfect way of beating the city's traffic-congested streets. The network's ambitious plans are eventually to extend into provinces surrounding Bangkok.

It consists of two lines. The **Sukhumvit Line** runs from Mo Chit station in the north to Bearing in the southeast. The **Silom Line** runs from National Stadium, near Siam Square, south to Talad Phlu station, across the river in Thonburi. The lines intersect at Siam station.

The Skytrain is fast, frequent and clean, but suffers from overcrowding during peak hours.

BELOW: the Skytrain.

Accessibility, too, is a problem for the disabled and aged as there aren't enough escalators or lifts.

Trains operate from 6am to midnight (3 minutes peak; 5 minutes off-peak). Single-trip fares range from B15–42, depending on distance. There are self-service ticket machines on all station concourses. Tourists may find it more useful to buy the unlimited-ride 1-Day Pass (B130) and there's a Rabbit Card to which you can add discounted multi-trip packages running from B405 for 15 trips to B1,100 for 50 trips. The Rabbit Card is valid on the BRT *(see below)* and may eventually extend to the MRT *(see below)*. All are available at station counters.

MRT

Customer Relations Centre: tel: 0-2624 5200; www.bangkokmetro.co.th.

Bangkok's Mass Rapid Transport (MRT) has 18 stations, stretching 20km (12 miles) between Bang Sue in the northern suburbs of Bangkok to the city's main railway station, Hualamphong, near Chinatown.

Three of its stations – Silom, Sukhumvit and Chatuchak Park – are interchanges, and passengers can transfer to the Skytrain network at these points. More lines and extensions to both rail networks are planned.

Operating from 6am to midnight, the air-conditioned trains run frequently (2–4 minutes peak, 4–6 minutes off-peak). Fares range from B16-41 for single-trip tokens.

Unlike the Skytrain, coin-sized plastic tokens are used instead of cards. These are dispensed by self-service ticket machines at all stations. Also available at station counters are the unlimited-ride 1-Day Pass (B120); 3-Day Pass (B230); 30-Day (B1,400) and the stored-value Adult Card (B200; includes B50 deposit).

Taxis

Taxis are abundant in Bangkok. They are metered, air-conditioned, inexpensive, and comfortably seat 3 to 4 people.

Taxis are best hailed along the streets, as those parked outside hotels hustle for a non-metered fair. Metered taxis are recognisable by the sign on their roofs, with an illuminated red light above the dashboard indicating whether they are free or not.

The flag-fall charge is B35; after the first 1km (0.5 mile), the meter goes up by B5–8.5 every kilometre, depending on distance travelled. If stuck in traffic, a small per-minute surcharge kicks in. If your journey crosses town, ask the driver to take the expressway. Using the network of elevated two-lane roads can reduce travel time by half. The toll fare of B20–50 is given to the driver at the payment booth, not at the end of the trip.

Before starting any journey, check whether the meter has been reset and turned on. Generally, drivers are far better than their reputations in this regard, but will try it on occasionally. This happens particularly if there is heavy rain, when it is sometimes wise to negotiate anyway, as traffic moves more slowly and the meter keeps ticking. Fares, however, can be negotiated for longer distances outside Bangkok: for instance, Pattaya (B1,200); Ko Samet (B1,500) or Hua Hin (B1,500-B2,500).

Drivers don't speak much English. They should know the locations of major hotels. Otherwise, it's a good idea to have a destination written in Thai on a piece of paper. Thai drivers can usually understand street addresses written in capital Roman letters.

If you arrange for a pick-up, there is a B20 surcharge.
Siam Taxi: hotline: tel: 1661

Tuk-tuk

Tuk-tuk are the brightly coloured three-wheeled taxis whose name comes from the incessant noise their two-stroke engines make. Few tuk-tuk drivers speak English,

so make sure your destination is written down in Thai. Unless you bargain hard, tuk-tuk fares are rarely lower than those of metered taxis.

Expect to pay B30–50 for short journeys of a few blocks or around 15 minutes or less, and B50–100 for longer journeys. A B100 ride should get you a half-hour ride across most parts of downtown. Be sure to negotiate the fare beforehand.

Motorcycle Taxis

Motorcycle-taxi stands (with young men in fluorescent orange vests) are clustered at the entrance of most *soi* (small side-streets) and beside any busy intersection or building entrance. The drivers are experts at weaving through Bangkok's heavy traffic and may cut travel time in half, but they they can be reckless.

Hire only a driver who provides a passenger helmet. Fares must be negotiated beforehand, and they are rarely lower than taxi fares for the same distance travelled. Hold on tight and keep your knees tucked in because drivers tend to weave precariously in and out of traffic. If the driver is going too fast, ask him to slow down: *cha-cha khap/kha.*

Thai women usually ride side-saddle and it's common see entire families on one motorbike.

A short distance, such as the length of a street, will cost B10–20, with longer rides at B50–100. During rush hours (8–10am and 4–6pm), prices are higher.

Buses

Bus transport in Bangkok is very cheap but can be arduous, time-consuming and confusing. Municipal and private operators all come under the charge of the **Bangkok Mass Transit Authority** (tel: 0-2246 0973; www.bmta.co.th). With little English signage on show and few conductors or drivers speaking English, boarding the right bus is an exercise in frustration. Most bus maps are out of

date, so stick to Bangkok's alternative transport options. The **Bus Rapid Transit (BRT)** system uses dedicated lanes, but is limited to one route from Chong Nonsi BTS station to Wong Wian Yai on the Thonburi side of the river.

Boats

The most common waterborne transport is the **Chao Phraya Express Boat** (tel: 0-2623 6143; www.chaophrayaboat.co.th), which travels from Tha Nonthaburi pier in the north and ends at Ratburana in the south. Boats run every 15 minutes on the main services from 6am–7pm, and they stop at different piers according to the coloured flag on top of the boat: blue, green-yellow, yellow, orange and no flag. The first two offer restricted commuter services. Otherwise, yellow-flag boats are fastest and do not stop at many piers, while the orange-flag and no-flag boats stop at most of the marked river piers. If unsure, check before boarding. Fares cost from B10–40 and are paid to the conductor on board or at some pier counters.

The **Chao Phraya Tourist Boat** (tel: 0-2623 6143; www.chaophraya-boat.co.th) operates daily from 9.30am to 4pm and costs B150 per day for unlimited trips. After 3.30pm, you can also use the ticket on the regular express boats. A useful commentary is provided on board, along with a small guidebook and a bottle of water. The route begins at Tha Sathorn (Central Pier) and travels upriver to Tha Phra Arthit, stopping at 10 major piers along the way. Boats leave every 30 minutes.

Cross-river ferries are used for getting from one side of the river to the other. They can be boarded close to the jetties that also service the Chao Phraya River Express. Costing B3.50 per journey, the cross-river ferries operate daily between 5am and 10pm or later.

The **longtail canal boat taxis** ply the narrow inner canals of

Bangkok and are used for carrying passengers from the centre of town to the outlying districts. Many of the piers are located near traffic bridges and tickets cost B5–15, depending on the distance, with services operating roughly every 10 minutes until 6 to 7pm.

Rental Cars

Driving in Bangkok has some frustrations, but with adjustments and *jai yen* (a cool heart), the experience is generally comfortable. The potential problems include: drivers cutting in front of you with little warning, narrow and busy side streets, rare use of signalling and motorbikes everywhere, so use of wing mirrors needs to be constant. It might sound scary, but drivers generally stick to their lane, at least, and if you're used to city driving, there should be little to worry about.

An international driver's licence is necessary to drive a car. A small car can be hired for around B800 a day, check that insurance is included.
Avis, 2/12 Th. Withayu; tel: 0-2255 5300/4; and Suvarnabhami Airport (arrival hall); tel: 0-84 700 8157-9; Reservation Centre, tel: 0-2251 1131–2; www. avisthailand.com.
Hertz, Sukhumvit Soi 71; tel: 0-2266 4666; www.hertz.com.

Trips Out of Bangkok

By Road

Thailand has a good road system, with over 50,000km (31,000 miles) of motorways and more being built every year. Road signs are usually in both Thai and English and you should have no difficulty following a map. An international driver's licence is required.

Unfortunately, driving on a narrow but busy road can be a terrifying experience, with right-of-way determined by size. It is not unusual for a bus to overtake a truck despite the fact that the oncoming lane is filled with vehicles.

RENTING LONGTAIL BOATS

If you wish to explore the canals of Thonburi, private longtail-boat rentals can be negotiated from most of the river's main piers. A 90-minute to 2-hour tour will take you into the quieter canal communities. Find out which route the boat will take and ask to pull up and get out if anything interests you. Negotiate rates beforehand; an hour-long trip will cost B700–800, rising to B1,000 and more for 2 hours. The price is for the entire boat, which seats up to 16 people, not per person.

Another option is to hire a car or a van with driver for trips outside of Bangkok. Try **Thai Car Hire** (www. thaicarhire.com) or **Krungthai Car Rent** (tel: 0 2291 8888; www. krungthai.co.th). Rates start around B1,500 per day.

You can get to several places outside the city, such as Pattaya and Hua Hin, by simply flagging a taxi along a Bangkok street or booking one beforehand (see page 102). Be sure to negotiate a flat rate before boarding; don't use the meter.

By Air

Thai Airways International

(THAI) services a domestic network, with as many as 14 daily services to popular destinations such as Chiang Mai, Ko Samui and Phuket.
Bangkok Airways has several daily flights from Bangkok to Ko Samui, and to places including Krabi, Phuket and Trat. From Ko Samui, destinations include Krabi, Pattaya and Phuket. Among low-cost airlines, **AirAsia** has the widest portfolio, connecting with overseas and domestic destinations, including Hat Yai, Narathiwat and Surat Thani.

You can book and pay online with these airlines.
AirAsia: tel: 0-2215 9999; www.airasia.com.

Bangkok Airways: tel: 1771; www.bangkokair.com.
Nok Air: tel: 1318; www.nokair.com.
Orient Thai: tel: 0-2229 4100; Call Centre: 1126; www.flyorientthai. com.
Thai Airways International: tel: 0-2288-7000; www.thaiair.com.
Thai Smile: tel: 0-2356 1111; www.thaismileair.com.

By Bus

Air-conditioned buses service many destinations in Thailand. VIP coaches with extra legroom are the best for overnight journeys. The **Transport Company Ltd** (www.transport.co.th), known locally as **Bor Kor Sor (BKS)**, operates government-run buses. You can purchase bus tickets directly at BKS stations around the country or at a travel agency. Private buses, which are usually more expensive, depart either from BKS terminals or their own stations. In Bangkok, many leave from Thanon Khao San.

Bangkok BKS terminals are found at the following locations:
Eastern (Ekamai) Bus Terminal. Th. Sukhumvit opposite Soi 63; tel: 0-2391 2504.
Southern Bus Terminal: Th. Boromrat Chonnani, Thonburi; tel: 0-2435 1200.
Central, Northeast and Northern (Mo Chit) Bus Terminal: Th. Khampaengphet 2; Central, tel: 0-2936 1897; Northeast, tel: 0-2936 0667; Northern, tel: 0-2936 3660.

By Train

State Railway of Thailand (tel: 1690; www.railway.co.th) operates three principal routes – north, northeast and south – from **Hualamphong Railway Station** at Th. Rama 4; tel: 0-2225 0300. Express and rapid services on the main lines offer first-class air-conditioned or second class fan-cooled carriages with sleeping cabins or berths. In addition to the above, some trains depart from **Bangkok Noi Station**, tel: 0-2411 3102, in Thonburi.

BANGKOK

Choosing a Hotel

Hotels in Bangkok, with their first-rate service and range of facilities, are among the best in the world. Many moderately priced hotels in Bangkok would be considered first class in Europe, and even budget hotels will invariably have a swimming pool and at least one decent food outlet.

Those on a tight budget will find numerous guesthouses offering decent accommodation. Once of primary interest only to backpackers because of their sparse facilities, many have now been upgraded to include air conditioning and en suite bathrooms.

Prices and Bookings

Many mid- and top-end hotels charge a standard 7 percent VAT and 10 percent service to the bill, so check to see if the rate includes this or not. Depending on the season, discounts can exceed 50 percent or more off the published rack rate. Internet bookings are cheaper than the walk-in or call-up rate. Either check the hotel website directly or online hotel sites, such as www.agoda.com. As rates can be so elastic, relative price categories denoting the lowest priced rooms available are used in this section.

Be sure to book a room in advance during Christmas, New Year and Chinese New Year holidays, and if travelling outside Bangkok, during Songkran in mid-April.

RATTANAKOSIN

Arun Residence & Sala Arun
36 Soi Pratoo Nok Yoong, Th. Maharat
Tel: 0-2221 9158
www.arunresidence.com
This old, riverside Sino-Portuguese mansion with views of Wat Arun is a short walk from Wat Pho. Its Euro-Thai restaurant The Deck is an atmospheric spot, and they have a beautiful sister, Sala Arun (www.salaarun.com), just downriver. (6 rooms) **$$**

Chakrabongse Villa
396 Th. Maharaj
Tel: 0-2225 1290
www.chakrabongsevillas.com
This early-20th-century riverside compound was the home of a Thai prince. Its four elegant Thai-style villas overlook Wat Arun. Beautiful gardens and a secluded swimming pool add to its appeal, as does the 15-minute walk to the Grand Palace. (4 rooms) **$$$**

THONBURI

Anantara Bangkok Riverside Resort & Spa
257 Th. Charoen Nakorn

Tel: 0-2476 0022
www.marriotthotels.com
With verdant grounds and a wonderfully landscaped pool that fronts the river, this resort truly feels like an escape from the frenetic city. Located on the Thonburi side, it is quite far down the river, almost to the edge of town, but the free 15-minute boat shuttle to Tha Sathorn pier is part of the enjoyment of staying here. Self-contained, with six restaurants, three bars and a spa, the hotel is also part of a shopping complex. Its Riverside Terrace hosts nightly Thai dance performances along with dinner. (413 rooms) **$$$**

Millennium Hilton Bangkok
123 Th. Charoen Nakorn
Tel: 0-2442 2000
www.bangkok.hilton.com
The swish Hilton has a stylish modern-Asian interior designed by Tony Chi. All rooms have expansive windows with river views and the pool has a resort feel. There's a spa, four restaurants and two bars, including panoramic views from the 32nd floor Three-Sixty Lounge. A complimentary shuttle boat runs to the Bangkok side. (543 rooms) **$$$**

Peninsula
333 Th. Charoen Nakorn
Tel: 0-2861 2888
www.peninsula.com
The contemporary international decor has neat

Asian undertones, and all rooms overlook the Chao Phraya, although a new condominium, The River, now partially restricts views to the south. There's a lovely spa, a pool overlooking the river, and the superb Chinese restaurant Mei Jeang is one of the best in the city. A free shuttle boat is available to Saphan Taksin BTS station from 6am–midnight. (370 rooms) **$$$$**

OLD CITY AND DUSIT

Buddy Lodge
265 Th. Khao San
Tel: 0-2629 4477
www.buddylodge.com
Khao San's pioneering boutique hotel at the beginning of the century, Buddy Lodge has a rooftop swimming pool, fitness room and a well-run spa. The rooms are more pleasant than plush, but are en suite with louvred windows, small balconies and satellite TV. Located in a mini mall with bars, shops and a McDonald's downstairs. **$$**

D&D Inn
68-70 Th. Khao San
Tel: 0-2629 0526/8
www.khaosanby.com
Right in the middle of Khao San, this is more of a hotel than a guesthouse, with a rooftop swimming pool, bar and open pavilion for tradi-

tional massage. Rooms are well equipped with bathrooms, air con, TV, fridge and IDD phone. (200 rooms) **$**

Riva Surya Bangkok
23 Thanon Phra Arthit
Tel: 0-2633 5000
www.rivasuryabangkok.com
On the river in Bangkok's most culturally rich area, the Riva is close to the National Museum and Grand Palace, but also on the edge of the Khao San party zone. There's a bar, a pool, a fitness centre, and the Dabble & Rum café has riverview garden seating. (68 rooms) **$$**

The Siam
3/2 Thanon Khao
Tel: 0-2206 6999
www.thesiamhotel.com
Another riverside opening, these stylish Art Deco suites and villas are individually designed with nods to historic Siam. Along with artworks and antiques, each room has a personal butler and free Wi-fi. At the top end is Connie's Cottage, a 100 year-old wooden house brought from Ayutthaya by Jim Thompson and his close friend Connie Mangskau. (39 rooms) **$$$$**

ABOVE: the Siam.

Free Wi-fi in the rooms, a Chinese teahouse, jazz bar, spa and complimentary shuttle service. (76 rooms) **$$**

PATHUMWAN AND PRATUNAM

Amari Watergate
847 Th. Petchaburi
Tel: 0-2653 9000/19.
www.amari.com/watergate
This large tower isn't very attractive on the outside but has been refurbished within. Facilities, including a great gym and the basement Americana pub Henry J. Beans. Located just across from Pratunam Market and the main shopping district around Central World Plaza. The closest Skytrain station is Chit Lom, but unfortunately it's not within walking distance. (563 rooms) **$$$**

A-One Inn
25/13–15 Soi Kasemsan 1, Th. Rama I
Tel: 0-2215 3029.
www.aoneinn.com
The basic rooms have satellite TV and air con, and this is a good price

CHINATOWN

Shanghai Mansion
479–481 Th. Yaowaraj
Tel: 0-2221 2121
www.shanghaimansion.com
A classy boutique hotel in a part of town often written off as lacking in any decent lodgings. The rooms have lovely over-the-top chinoiserie furnishings, four-poster beds and bright colours.

so close to Siam Square shops and the SkyTrain. It also has an internet café with Wi-fi and a laundry service. If you can't find space here, this street has similar options. (20 rooms) **$**

Conrad Bangkok
All Seasons Place, 87 Th. Withayu
Tel: 0-2690 9999
www.conradhotels.com
Located near embassies and next door to the All Seasons Place shopping centre, the spacious and contemporary rooms are furnished with Thai silk and woods, with data ports for high-speed internet access and large bathrooms with rain-showers. There's a wide choice of eateries, as well as the jazzy Diplomat Bar. The serviced apartments here are a better deal for longer stays. Ploenchit Skytrain station is a 6-minute walk away. (392 rooms) **$$$**

Four Seasons
155 Th. Ratchadamri
Tel: 0-2251 6127.
www.fourseasons.com/bangkok
Five-star luxury, with a magnificent lobby decorated with hand-painted

silk ceilings and Thai murals by renowned local artists. Also has some of the city's best dining outlets, including the Italian Biscotti. (256 rooms) **$$$$**

Grand Hyatt Erawan
494 Th. Ratchadamri
Tel: 0-2254 1234.
www.bangkok.grand.hyatt.com
Smack in the middle of the downtown shopping district and beside the Erawan Shrine, its imposing formal lobby has huge classical columns. The range of restaurants includes the excellent traditional French-inspired Tables, and there's a basement restaurant-nightclub Spasso. (387 rooms) **$$$**

InterContinental Bangkok
973 Thanon Ploenchit
Tel: 0-2656 0444

PRICE CATEGORIES

Price categories show the starting price for a double room without breakfast and taxes:
$ = under US$70
$$ = US$70–130
$$$ = US$130–250
$$$$ = over US$250

www.ichotelsgroup.com
Linked to Chit Lom Sky-train station and Gaysorn Plaza, this hotel has spacious rooms with internet access and CD players. A rooftop swimming pool has fine city views, and there's a cute Italian bistro called Grossi, in the basement. **$$$**

Luxx
82/8 Soi Langsuan
Tel: 0-2684 1111
www.staywithluxx.com
The studios and suites run from stylish yet functional to luxurious, and come with open bathrooms, LCD TV screens, hi-tech MP3-USB compatible entertainment systems, picture windows and balconies. Free Wi-fi throughout the hotel. (51 rooms) **$$**

Novotel Bangkok
Siam Square Soi 6
Tel: 0-2255 6888
www.accorhotels-asia.com
Tucked into the buzzy Siam Square, a short walk to shopping malls and the Siam Skytrain station, location is a big draw here. It has several restaurants and its large basement entertainment complex, Concept CM2, is a frequently packed local nightspot. (429 rooms) **$$**

Siam Kempinski
991/9 Th. Rama I
Tel: 0-2162 9000
www.kempinski.com
Standing just behind Siam Paragon mall, the rooms in this hotel have garden views, flat-screen TVs, iPod connectivity and broadband internet. Other facilities include Sra Bua "molecular" Thai restaurant, a branch of Copenhagen's Michelin-starred Kiin Kiin. (303 rooms) **$$$**

BANGRAK AND SILOM

Baan Saladaeng
69/2 Saladaeng Soi 3
Tel: 0-2636 3038
www.baansaladaeng.com
A very tasteful budget operation with just nine themed-decor rooms with names such as Neo Siam, Moroccan Suite and Pop Art Mania. Each has air con, TV and Wi-fi. There's a small coffee bar, and it's a great location for transport, restaurants and nightlife. (9 rooms). **$**

Le Bua at State Tower
State Tower, 1055/111 Th. Silom
Tel: 0-2624 9999
www.lebua.com
Located on the corner of Thanon Silom and Thanon Charoen Krung, these contemporary Asian-style rooms and suites each have river – or city – view balconies. Just a 10-minute walk to Saphan Taksin Skytrain station, the 64-storey State Tower has established itself as a Bangkok landmark, with its opulent rooftop eating and drinking outlets that are collectively known as The Dome. (367 rooms) **$$$**

Dusit Thani
946 Thanon Rama IV
Tel: 0-2200 9999
www.dusit.com
Ideally located across from Lumphini Park, near Patpong's nightlife, and beside MRT and Skytrain stations, this was Bangkok's first luxury hotel when it opened in the 1970s. Recent refurbishments have added new millennium chic to the Asian-tinged

ABOVE: the Landmark Hotel.

interior. Enjoy a massage at the Devarana Spa, then float on to one of its 13 bars and restaurants. (517 rooms) **$$$**

The Heritage Baan Silom
Baan Silom, Th. Silom
Tel: 0-2236 8388.
www.theheritagehotels.com
The old world meets the new in these pleasant rooms with a mix of ancient Thai motifs, colonial-style chairs and iron baths, and a clean boutique elegance. Located in the low-rise Baan Silom courtyard complex, it is close to the gems district and a short taxi ride to the river. **$**

The Mandarin Oriental
48 Oriental Avenue
Tel: 0-2659 9000
www.mandarinoriental.com
Part of the history of East meeting West, the Oriental, established in 1876, is the most famous hotel in Bangkok, and is well known for its attention to detail and grand setting along

the Chao Phraya River. The Authors' Wing, the only surviving original structure in the hotel, has period suites and delightful tearooms. Le Normandie French restaurant is the only place in town that requires a tie for dinner. (395 rooms) **$$$$**

Pullman Bangkok Hotel G
188 Th. Silom
Tel: 0-2238 1991
www.pullmanhotels.com
This 38-storey hotel located in the quieter part of busy Thanon Silom is only a short walk to Chong Nonsi Skytrain station. Furnished in a chic modern style, it caters to both business and leisure travellers. Scarlett Wine Bar & Restaurant has stunning city views from its 37th-floor perch. (454 rooms) **$$**

La Résidence
173/8-9 Th. Surawong
Tel: 0-2266 5400.
www.laresidencebangkok.com
Small, friendly hotel with funky, individually deco-

rated rooms, including two modest suites, one with garden balcony and views. All accommodation has Wi-fi access. Patpong nightmarket is only a short cab-ride away. (26 rooms) **$$**

Sofitel So Bangkok
2 Thanon Sathorn Nua
Tel: 0-2624 0000
www.sofitel.com
The Sofitel's urban chic brand has lots of youthful elegance, from the chocolate "lab" by the entrance to the semi-alfresco Park Society bar-restaurant with great city views across Lumphini Park. The rooms have a five elements theme of Water, Earth, Wood, Metal and Fire, all from a different designer. Christian Lacroix designed the uniforms. (238 rooms) **$$$**

W Bangkok
106 Thanon Sathorn Nua
Tel: 0-2344 4000
www.whotels.com
The luxury W chain has its Bangkok flagship right beside Chong Nonsi Skytrain station, in the middle of the rapidly developing business district. The colour scheme includes lots of purple, silver and black, and rooms have iPad docking to link with TV screens. The casual all-day restaurant serves international food. The pool has underwater lighting and speakers. (407 rooms) **$$$**

SUKHUMVIT

Ambassador
171 Sukhumvit Soi 11
Tel: 0-2254 0444
www.amtel.co.th
A huge, rather dated

hotel, but with decent rooms in this price range, and only a 5-minute walk to Nana Skytrain station. It has a spa and outdoor pool, and lots of good restaurants and clubs are located nearby. (760 rooms) **$**

Atlanta
78 Thanon Sukhumvit Soi 2
Tel: 0-2252 1650
www.theatlantahotelbangkok.com
A quirky but charming 1950s throwback, rich in character, with a period interior, and a strong moral ethos that holds no truck with sex tourists and allows no room visitors. There is a pool in landscaped gardens and a good Thai restaurant. (59 rooms) **$**

Dream Hotel
10 Sukhumvit Soi 15
Tel: 0-2254 8500
www.dreambkk.com
Cutting-edge design is at the forefront of this unique glass-encased hotel with stylish restaurants, a cigar bar, club and Dalí-inspired lounge. Guest rooms come complete with 42-inch plasma TVs, iPod Nanos and a bar stocked with Veuve-Clicquot champagne. (195 rooms) **$**

Emporium Suites
622 Sukhumvit Soi 24
Tel: 0-2664 9999
www.emporiumsuites.com
Located above the Emporium mall, and connected to the Phrom Phong Skytrain station, this dapper serviced apartment complex offers options from studio and 1-bedroom suites to 3 bedroom apartments with a full range of facilities. Some rooms have views of

Benjasiri Park. (378 rooms) **$$$**

The Eugenia
267 Sukhumvit Soi 31
Tel: 0-2259 9011
www.theeugenia.com
This 12-suite accommodation in a 19th-century manor has old-world colonial charm. All rooms have antique furnishings and many have four-poster beds. The hotel's limousines are a fleet of vintage Jaguars and Mercedes-Benzs. (12 rooms) **$$$**

JW Marriott
4 Th. Sukhumvit Soi 2
Tel: 0-2656 7700.
www.marriotthotels.com
This classy five-star hotel is just around the corner from Bangkok's risqué Nana Entertainment Plaza, but don't let that deter you. All the usual amenities, plus Bangkok's largest fitness centre, efficient business facilities and spacious well-appointed rooms make this one of the best hotels in the city. Convenient location between the Nana and Ploenchit Skytrain stations. (441 rooms) **$$$**

Landmark
138 Th. Sukhumvit
Tel: 0-2254 0404
www.landmarkbangkok.com
Good location on Thanon Sukhumvit, with easy access to Nana Skytrain station and the "girly bar" enclave of Nana Entertainment Plaza. Geared toward the business traveller with a busy business centre. (415 rooms) **$$**

Seven
3/15 Sukhumvit Soi 31
Tel: 0-2662 0951
www.sleepatseven.com
Ultra-cool "concept" hotel with bar, gallery and

café. Features six rooms, each with their own colour and cosmological meaning. The 7th Heaven Bar, sun deck and free Wi-fi are all part of this small but stylishly functional hotel. One of the better newcomers to the city's hotel scene. (6 rooms) **$$**

Sheraton Grande Sukhumvit
250 Th. Sukhumvit
Tel: 0-2653 0333
www.sheratongrandesukhumvit.com
This hotel has a great location on Thanon Sukhumvit, and is well connected by Skywalk to Asok Skytrain and Sukhumvit metro stations. First-rate facilities include extra-large rooms, a landscaped pool and an excellent spa. It also has particularly good Italian and Thai restaurants, a nightclub and very talented musicians in the Living Room jazz bar. (445 rooms) **$$$**

Suk 11 Hostel
1/33 Th. Sukhumvit Soi 11
Tel: 0-2253 5927
www.suk11.com
No-smoking, bare rooms with no TV or fridge, but lots of wood and rustic decor at this family-run guesthouse. There is internet access in the lobby, plus a common room with TV and DVDs. A short walk from the Skytrain. (67 rooms) **$**

PRICE CATEGORIES

Price categories show the starting price for a double room without breakfast and taxes:
$ = under US$70
$$ = US$70–130
$$$ = US$130–250
$$$$ = over US$250

BANGKOK

RATTANAKOSIN

Thai

The Deck
Arun Residence, 36-38 Soi
Pratoo Nok Yoong
Tel: 0-2221 9158
Open: Mon–Thu 11am–
10pm; Fri–Sun 11am–
11pm.
Just two minutes' walk
from Wat Pho, this
pleasant restaurant has
outdoor seating and
river views of Wat Arun.
Its Thai and European
fusion menu offers
items such as carpaccio
of tea-smoked duck.
$$–$$$

THONBURI

Thai

Krua Rakang Thong
306 Soi Wat Rakang, Th. Arun
Amarin
Tel: 0-2848 9597
Open: daily 11am–
11pm.

This old-style riverfront
restaurant with views of
Wat Arun and the spires
of the Grand Palace is a
good sunset spot to dine
on king prawns in sweet-
and-sour tamarind
sauce, spicy northeast-
ern salads, and
"exploded" catfish,
diced and fried until
crumbly, then added to
coconut soup. **$**

OLD CITY AND DUSIT

International

Primavera
56 Th. Phra Sumen
Tel: 0-2281 4718
www.primavera-cafe.com
Open: daily 9am–11pm.
European coffee-shop
interior of mainly dark
woods. Top billing on a
short menu goes to
pizza, along with liver
pâté and fried calamari
as starters. There's a
reasonable choice of ice
creams and coffees.
$–$$

Thai

Chote Chitr
Th. Praengphutorn
Tel: 0-2221 4082
Open: Mon–Sat 10am–
9pm.
Five-table shophouse
opened 90 years ago by
a doctor of traditional
medicine. They've
served excellent food
(and medicines) ever
since. Try the dark, pun-
gent wing-bean salad, or
sour and peppery "old-
fashioned soup". **$**

May Kaidee
59 Th. Tanao
Tel: 0-2281 7137
www.maykaidee.com
Open: daily 8am–11pm.
Owner May has a repu-
tation for her vegetarian
cuisine. Second outlet at
nearby 33 Th. Samsen.
Isaan-style (from north-
east Thailand) vegetar-
ian dishes with
mushrooms, tofu and
soya beans, and deli-
cious massaman curry
with tofu, potatoes and
peanuts are good
options. May also gives
cooking lessons. It is

located behind Burger
King, east off Thanon
Tanao. **$**

Thai–Indian

Roti-Mataba
136 Th. Phra Arthit
Tel: 0-2282 2119
Open: Tue–Sun 7am–
10pm.
A whole army of women
make the Muslim-style
breads – such as flat,
unleavened roti and
meat-stuffed mataba –
by the hundreds in this
incredibly busy shop-
house. Dip the crisp roti
into their delicious mas-
saman and korma cur-
ries of fish, vegetable or
meat. There are only a
few tables inside
upstairs and on the
pavement, so be pre-
pared to wait. **$**

CHINATOWN

Chinese

**Hua Seng Hong
Yaowaraj**
438 Th. Charoen Krung Soi 14
Tel: 0-2627 5030
Open: daily 9am–9pm.
A former shophouse-
turned-restaurant with
marble-top tables and
air conditioning. A rau-
cous Chinese lunch
venue selling all-day dim
sum from an outside
counter and all manner
of congee, hot-and-sour
soup, barbecued pork,
fish maw and braised-
goose dishes inside.
$–$$

BELOW: dine at a dizzying height on the rooftop Sirocco restaurant.

Indian

Punjab Sweets and Restaurant
436/5 Th. Chakraphet
Tel: 0-2623 7606
Open: daily 8am–9pm.
Bangkok's Little India
(Pahurat) sits at the
western edge of China-
town. Its alleyways are
crowded with tailors and
tiny Indian cafés, of
which this is one of the
best. Its meat- and
dairy-free food includes
a good choice of curries
and dosa (rice-flour pan-
cakes) from South India,
and Punjabi sweets
wrapped in edible silver
foil leaf. $

Thai–Chinese

Soi Texas
Soi Padung Dao
Tel: 0-2224 5933
Open: daily 9am–2am.
Famed for its food, this
small Chinatown lane is
named after the Texas
Suki restaurant 50m/
yds on the right. It also
has two packed stalls at
the mouth of the soi, Rut
and Lek and T & K (open
from 6pm). They serve
great curried crab and
seafood that is superb
charcoal-grilled or fried
with garlic and chilli.
$–$$

PATHUMWAN AND PRATUNAM

French

Crepes & Co
59/4 Langsuan Soi 1
Tel: 0-2652 0208
www.crepesnco.com
Open: daily 9am–11pm.
A relaxed and reliable
crêperie that specialises
in unusual international

fillings along with the
crêpe suzettes. It also
serves tagines, briouats
and other Moroccan
dishes, plus Greek
favourites like melizana
salata. The spacious
open plan room has
thick, blond wood pillars
and beams, and sofas
and armchairs in the
centre to lend a living
room ambiance. There is
a popular Sunday brunch
on offer, too. $$

Le Beaulieu
Athénée Office Tower, 63 Wire-
less Rd
Tel: 08-1362 1362
www.le-beaulieu.com
Open daily 11.30am–
3pm and 6.30–11pm.
Chef Hervé Frerard has
forged one of the best
reputations in Bangkok
for French cuisine, and
this cosy, minimalist
interior provides a good
spot to try it. Typical
dishes include a superb
roasted Anjou pigeon
with truffle sauce. It's
part of a serviced resi-
dence, but doesn't feel
like it, and on one side
has a long outdoor bar
with chill-out sounds.
One of the best in town.
$$$$

Indian

Gaggan
68/1 Soi Langsuan
Tel: 0-2652-1700
Open: daily 6–11pm.
In a summer-house inte-
rior of white wood and
rattan, this "progressive
Indian" boasts El Bulli-in-
spired "molecular" cook-
ing techniques in dishes
such as roasted foie gras
with raspberry chutney.
It's interesting, but the
excellent traditional fare
such as bhunna mutton
curry is far more suc-
cessful. $$$

Japanese

Zuma
St Regis Hotel, 159 Th. Ratchadamri
Tel: 0-2252 4707
www.zumarestaurant.com
Open: daily noon–3pm,
6pm–11pm.
This branch of London's
modern Japanese Zuma
has all natural woods
and granite with an
electro-music back-
ground to bring stylish
energy. The great quality
product includes hot,
cold and sparkling
sakes and dishes like
miso marinated black
cod. The bar extends
through full wall win-
dows to a split level garden with sofas and
ornamental trees.
$$$$

Mexican

La Monita Taqueria
888/26 Mahatun Plaza, Th.
Ploenchit
Tel: 0-2650 9581
Open: daily 11.30am–
10pm.
Five-table Mexican diner
with cheap decor, good
food and a friendly
atmosphere. It serves all
the usual burritos,
nachos, wings and Moxi
or Cali tacos to wash
down with mojitos and
beer. There is good
smoky guacamole on
offer and free corkage.
$–$$

Spanish

El Osito
888/23-24 Mahatun Plaza, Th.
Ploenchit
Tel: 0-2650 9581
www.elositobkk.com
Open: Mon–Sat 11am–
11.30pm.
Spanish diner meets
New York deli amid pol-

ished concrete walls,
exposed wires and bare
bulbs hung from the ceil-
ing. The daytime menu
of sandwiches, such as
Reuben and home-
made pastrami, at night
morphs into Spanish
drinking snacks and full
meals like grilled rib-eye
and prawns with fried
parsley, olive oil, garlic,
and crispy French bread.
Good bottled beers and
cider are alternatives to
wine. $$

Thai

Somtam Siam Square Soi 5
392/2 Siam Sq Soi 5
Tel: 0-2251 4880
Open: daily 11.15am–
9pm.
Modern Isaan (north-
eastern Thailand) res-
taurant that is so
popular there are cush-
ions outside for people
waiting. The action
whirls around an open
kitchen where staff
make a great fiery
somtam nua, northeast-
ern sausage, and other
excellent Isaan dishes.
$

Sra Bua
Siam Kempinski Hotel, 991/9
Th. Rama I
Tel: 0-2162-9000
www.kempinskibangkok.com
Open Mon–Fri noon–
2.30pm, daily 6–11pm.
This outlet of Copenha-
gen's Michelin-starred
Kiin Kiin has a thrilling
modern slant on Thai

PRICE CATEGORIES
Price per person for a
three-course meal
without drinks:
$ = under US$10
$$ = US$10–25
$$$ = US$25–50
$$$$ = over US$50

food, with dishes such as green-curry mousse, *tom klong* soup served as jellies, and red-curry ice-cream. **$$$$**

BANGRAK AND SILOM

Chinese

China House
Mandarin Oriental Hotel,
48 Oriental Ave
Tel: 0-2659 9000
www.mandarinoriental.com
Open: daily 11.30am–2pm and 7–10pm. Beautiful 1930s Shanghainese Art-Deco interior of red lanterns, ebony pillars and Chinese calligraphy. A brass samovar steams in the central tearoom. It's a wonderful setting for good-quality dishes such as hot-and-sour soup filled with fresh herbs and sweet lobster meat. **$$$**

French

D'Sens
Dusit Thani Hotel,
946 Th. Rama IV
Tel: 0-2236 9999
Open: Mon–Fri 11.30am–2.30pm, Mon–Sat and public holidays 6–10.30pm. This excellent franchise of the three-Michelin-starred Le Jardin des Sens, in Montpellier, France, is full of intricate surprises such as steamed turbot with almond crust, fennel compote, orange-and-carrot syrup and oyster cannelloni. The muted pastel interior was refurbished in 2011. There are good views and it's located just metres from the Sky-

train and MRT. **$$$$**
Le Bouchon
37/17 Patpong Soi 2
Tel: 0-2234 9109
Open: Mon–Sat L and D, Sun D.
This lovely seven-table bistro gains a certain frisson from its location in Patpong – very French and slightly naughty, like a Marseille dockyard diner. Very popular with local French expats for its simple home cooking and friendly banter at the small bar where diners wait for seats while sipping aperitifs. **$$–$$$**

International

Eat Me
Fl 1, 1/6 Piphat Soi 2,
off Th. Convent
Tel: 0-2238 0931
www.eatmerestaurant.com
Open: daily D.
Chic, arty eatery serving modern Australian cuisine, featuring dishes such as charred scallops with mango, herb salad, pickled onion and citrus dressing. Low lighting and a fragmented layout lend intimacy. On cool nights, ask for a table on the terrace. **$$$**
Sirocco
Fl 63 State Tower Bangkok,
1055 Th. Silom
Tel: 0-2624 9555
www.thedomebkk.com
Open: daily D.
Spectacular 200-metre (656ft)-high rooftop restaurant with magnificent views over the river. Greco-Roman-style architecture and a jazz band add to the sense of occasion here. The Italian and Mediterranean food is inconsistent, but who cares? This is a must-visit, if only for the

views. In the same complex, there's good seafood in the classy Distil Bar, pan-Asian fare in Breeze, and an expensive Italian eatery called Mezzaluna. **$$$**

Italian

Zanotti
Gnd fl, Saladaeng Colonnade,
21/2 Soi Saladaeng
Tel: 0-2636 0002
www.zanotti-ristorante.com
Open: daily L and D.
Chef-owner Gianmaria Zanotti has created a restaurant that people visit for the buzz as much as for the food. The homely Italian fare from the Piedmont and Tuscany regions includes over 20 pasta dishes and seafood and steaks charcoal-grilled over orange-wood from Chiang Mai. A good selection of wines is available by the glass. **$$$**

Thai

Harmonique
22 Charoen Krung Soi 34
Tel: 0-2237 8175
Open: Mon–Sat 10am–10pm.
Charming restaurant occupying several antique-filled Chinese shophouses with leafy courtyards. Popular with Western diners, the spices are fairly quiet by Thai standards. But the food is generally good; it's a relaxing place to hang out; and it's handy for riverside hotels. **$–$$**
Nahm
Metropolitan Hotel,
27 Th. Sathorn Tai
Tel: 0-2625 3333
Open: daily noon–2pm, 6.30–10.30pm.

This standout restaurant is a branch of what was Europe's first Michelin-starred Thai restaurant, run by Australian chef David Thompson. The ultra-traditional menu includes intriguing flavours such as northern pork, prawn and tamarind relish served with braised mackerel, sweet pork, crispy acacia and soft-boiled eggs. **$$$$**
Somboon Seafood
169/7-11 Th. Surawong
Tel: 0-2233 3104
Open: daily 4–11pm. No-frills café of tubular metal furniture and good Chinese-style seafood. The fat curried crabs and prawns with spicy *nam jim* dipping sauce are excellent, along with whole fish cooked every-which-way. The canteen-like service may not win any awards, but the food just might. **$$$**

SUKHUMVIT

American

New York Steakhouse
JW Marriott Hotel,
4 Sukhumvit Soi 2
Tel: 0-2656 7700
www.marriott.com
Open: daily 6pm–11pm. This is a very fine restaurant with a relaxed atmosphere despite the formal club-like dark wood and high-backed leather chairs. Great quality beef and seafood backed by US-loved standards such as clam chowder are on offer, along with a very long list of martinis. **$$$$**

Indian

Hazara
29 Sukhumvit Soi 38
Tel: 0-2713 6048-9
www.facebars.com
Open: daily 6–10.30pm.
Tasty north-Indian fare,
such as peppery *khadai
kheenga* (shrimps stir-
fried with bell peppers),
in a glorious setting
embellished with Asian
antiques and artefacts.
This restaurant is
housed in a traditional
Thai cluster complex
and includes the trendy
Face Bar. **$$$**

International

Opposite Mess Hall
27/1 Sukhumvit Soi 51
Tel: 0- 2662 6330
www.oppositebangkok.com
Open: Tue–Sun 7pm–
1am.
Helmed by the popular
chef Jess Barnes, this is
the dining operation of
the art bar WTF, oppo-
site. It's small, with a
working men's vibe and
simple Aussie-Euro food
that's big on lesser used
ingredients in dishes
like smoked bone mar-
row dumplings with beef
broth, pumpkin and fer-
mented daikon. It's
tasty, and great with a
beer. **$$**

Quince
Sukhumvit Soi 45
Tel: 0- 2662 4478
Open: daily 11.30am–
1am.
Trendy European restau-
rant with earthy farm-
house presentation and
a stated commitment to
local produce where
possible. They're good
on fresh salads such as
blueberry beetroot with
feta cheese and rocket,
and homey international
fare, including chicken

tagine-style with lemon
and chickpeas. There's
a buzzy, pub-like atmos-
phere, occasional DJs,
arty cocktails and a good
wine list. **$$$**

Water Library @ Grass
Grass Thonglor, 264/1
Sukhumvit Soi 55 (Thonglor
12)
Tel: 0-2714 9292
www.mywaterlibrary.com/thonglor
Open: daily 6pm–1am.
Chefs serve very inven-
tive food to just ten din-
ers a night at a sushi
style counter. The
12-course menu
changes regularly, with
modern techniques and
funky presentation
dominant in dishes such
as Belon oysters with
beurre blanc ice-cream
and rib eye with porcini
marmade and violet
potatoes. There's also a
wine pairing menu
option. There's only a
single set dinner each
night at 7pm, so book-
ing is essential. **$$$$**

Italian

Enoteca
39 Sukhumvit Soi 27
Tel: 0-2258-4386
www.enotecabangkok.com
Open: daily 6–10.30pm.
A very good menu in a
small place with
exposed brickwork,
blackboard menu and
arty posters. Saffron
risotto flecked with liq-
uorice, suckling pig with
coffee laced chestnut
purée, and chocolate
foam on rum-seasoned
crushed ice are just
some of the typically
clever touches. **$$$**

Middle Eastern

Nasir Al-Masri
4/6 Sukhumvit Soi 3/1
Tel: 0-2253-5582

www.restaurant-shishah-nasir.com
Open: daily 24 hrs.
This area is often called
Soi Arab because of its
Middle Eastern opera-
tions selling kebabs and
Lebanese-style dips.
Along with standard
skewers 'Nasir the Egyp-
tian' also has speciali-
ties from home, such as
fuul (mashed beans in
oil) and *molokhaya* (a
spinach-like vegetable
mixed with garlic). **$**

Thai

Bo.lan
42 Soi Pichai Ronnarong,
Sukhumvit Soi 26
Tel: 0 2260 2962
www.bo.lan.com
Open: Tue–Sun 6.30–
10.30pm.
A cute town-house oper-
ation run by alumni of
London's Michelin-
starred Thai restaurant
Naam. Very traditional
recipes run through
mysterious regional fla-
vours in dishes such as
sweet cured pork in
coconut cream, and
deep-fried fish with an
eye-watering spicy sour
dipping sauce. **$$$**

Long Table
Floor 25, The Column
Residence, Sukhumvit Soi 16
Tel: 0-2302 2557-9
www.longtablebangkok.com
Open: daily 11am–2am.
Fantastic city views and
a long communal table
are focal points as you
dine to a funky sound-
track. Lobster and avo-
cado with a smoky *nam
prik* and green-mango
salad; and foie gras with
dried shrimp and tama-
rind are both standouts.
$$$

Thai Food Stalls
Sukhumvit Soi 38
Open: daily 4pm–2am.
There's a good mix of

rough-and-tumble food
stalls at the entrance of
this *soi* next to Thonglor
Skytrain station. Try rice
gruel, spring rolls, spicy
crab salad, crispy pork,
nam kaeng sai (desserts
with ice) and countless
others. Wash down with
fruit juice or beer. **$**

Vientiane Kitchen
8 Sukhumvit Soi 36
Tel: 0-2258 6171
Open: daily noon–
midnight.
Lao-Isaan food in a *sala*
complex where musi-
cians play traditional
music under trees laden
with fairy lights while
you eat. This is fun din-
ing, with rice whisky,
spicy salads, grilled
marinated chicken and
countryside faves such
as *kai mot daeng* (red
ant eggs). **$$**

Vegetarian

Govinda
6/6 Sukhumvit Soi 22
Tel: 0-2663 4970
Open: Wed–Mon
11.30am–3pm, 6pm–
11pm.
Good-standard, all-veg-
etarian Italian food that
includes a variety of pas-
tas, thin-crust pizzas,
cheesy risottos and
bakes. Even desserts
such as tiramisu and
cheesecake are egg-
free. Also serves bread
and ice cream made on
the premises and a
selection of imported
beers. **$$**

PRICE CATEGORIES

Price per person for a
three-course meal
without drinks:
$ = under US$10
$$ = US$10–25
$$$ = US$25–50
$$$$ = over US$50

ACTIVITIES

The Arts

While Thailand's traditional arts-and-crafts heritage is well acknowledged, there are surprisingly few venues in the capital in which to appreciate it fully. The contemporary-art scene, on the other hand, is simmering away, with numerous art galleries. There is no distinct cultural enclave in Bangkok; events and sites are found throughout the city.

Performing Arts Venues

Aksra Theatre: 8/1 Soi Rangnam; tel: 0-2677 8888; www.aksra theatre.com. This 600-seat theatre mixes Thai and other Asian puppetry with cultural performances (daily 12.30pm and 6.30pm) and mainstream popular theatre. Located in the King Power duty-free complex, so you can shop for gifts after the show.
National Theatre: Th. Ratchini; tel: 0-2224 1342. Grand old theatre that hosts a variety of traditional music and dance performances every month.
Sala Chalerm Krung: 66 Thanon Charoen Krung; tel: 0-2222 1854. A convenient space to hear some Thai classical music, as it hosts Khon masked drama performances every Friday and Saturday evening from 7pm. It's unusual to see this in a theatre setting; most other shows are in hotel restaurants and lobbies or themed tourist spots (see below).
Thailand Cultural Centre: Th. Ratchada Phisek; tel: 0-2247 0028; www.thaiculturalcenter.com. Stages everything from loud pop concerts to sophisticated high-brow works by the Bangkok Opera (www.bangkokopera.com). This is also where the Bangkok Symphony Orchestra performs.

Dinner Dance and Drama

There is traditional *khon* dance-drama, without dinner, at Chal-erm Krung Theatre (see above), and free performances at the **Erawan Shrine** (see page 93) in the Pathumwan area or **Lak Muang** (see page 79) near the Grand Palace, both of which have resident dance troupes who are paid by devotees to dance in thanksgiving for having prayers answered. Otherwise, traditional dance-drama is performed in condensed forms at a few restaurants around the capital, usually by dance-drama students. These shows are either performanced after a Thai dinner or as vignettes interspersed between the various courses.
Ruen Thep Room: Silom Village, 286 Th. Silom; tel: 0-2234 4581. A large hall of dark wood and Thai paintings and sculptures creates the right ambience for the nightly hour-long dance and drama performance at 8.30pm.
Sala Rim Nam: opposite Mandarin Oriental Hotel, 48 Oriental Avenue; tel: 0-2437 6211. Set on the opposite riverbank, the Oriental's riverside restaurant offers a set dinner menu accompanied by an entertaining dance and drama performance at 8.30pm nightly.
Siam Niramit: 19 Th. Tiamruammit, Huaykwang; tel: 0-2649 9222; www.siamniramit.com. A beautifully costumed extravaganza that traverses the country's history and diverse cultures in three acts. A nightly performance takes place at 8pm. Pre-show buffet dinner available at its restaurant.

Art Galleries

Most contemporary art on view in Bangkok is created by home-grown artists. There is also an increasing number of regional Asian artists who display their works here. Check the monthly free *BAM: Bangkok Art Map*, the *Bangkok Post*, *The Nation* and local magazines for details.
Bangkok Art and Culture Centre: 939 Thanon Rama 1; tel: 0-2214 6630-8; www.bacc.or.th. This 11-storey space has some of Bangkok's best art and multimedia shows (see page 92).
H Gallery: 201 Soi 12 Th. Sathorn; tel: 0-1310 4428; www.hgallerybkk.com. Run by an American, this gallery is located in an old converted wooden school building. Promotes a stable of young and eclectic commercially viable artists.
100 Tonson Gallery: 100 Soi Tonson, Th. Ploenchit; tel: 0-2684 1527; www.100tonsongallery.com. Attracts some of the country's best artists and holds high-profile exhibitions that create a lot of media buzz.
Museum of Contemporary Art (MOCA): Th. 499 Moo 3 Vibhavadi Rangsit; tel: 0-2953 1005; www.mocabangkok.com. A little trek to north Bangkok rewards with a private collection that is perhaps the best permanent exhibition of modern Thai art in the capital.
Queen's Gallery: 101 Th. Ratchadamnoen Klang; tel: 0-2281 5360; www.queengallery.org. Five-floor gallery with a steady exhibition schedule of modern and contemporary art, predominantly locally produced works.
Silpakorn University Gallery: 31 Th. Na Phra Lan, opposite the Grand Palace; tel: 0-623 6120 ext 1418. Thailand's oldest and most prestigious arts university; three galleries here display works by students, teachers and visiting artists.

Cinema

Bangkok's cinemas are comfortable and tickets are cheap; they mainly screen mainstream Hollywood pulp. Thai movies have improved dramatically in the last few years. There are numerous large and modern multiplexes but only one independent arthouse cinema called the House.
EGV Multiplexes: 6th Floor, Siam Discovery Centre, Th. Rama I; tel:

0-2812 9999 (all branches); www.egv.com.

House Boutique Cinema: RCA Plaza, Royal City Avenue; tel: 0-2641 5177/8; www.houserama.com.

Major Cineplex: Central World Plaza, 7th Floor, Th. Ratchadamri; Sukhumvit Ekkamai, Soi 61 Sukhumvit; and Ratchayothin, 1839 Th. Pahonyothin; tel: 0-2515 5555 (all branches); www.majorcineplex.com.

SF Cinema City: 7th Floor, Mahboonkrong Centre, 444 Th. Phayathai; tel: 0-2611 6444; and 6th Floor, Emporium, Sukhumvit Soi 24; tel: 0-2260 9333; www.sfcinemacity.com.

Nightlife

Bangkok's reputation as a centre for sex of every persuasion frequently overshadows its other night-time offerings, which include jazz clubs, cool bars and chic clubs aplenty. To enter clubs, the law requires ID proving you are over-20 and most clubs comply, so take a copy of your passport along.

For fleshy nightlife, head to Patpong (see pages 95–96), Soi Nana or Soi Cowboy (see pages 96–97).

Dance Bars and Clubs

Several clubs impose a door charge, usually including a couple of drinks.

Old City and Dusit

The Club: Khao San; tel: 0-2629 2255. A fairytale castle interior pulses to crowds of young Thais and foreign backpackers dancing to techno, house and electro with occasional live musicians and pro dancers.

Sukhumvit

Bash: 37 Sukhumvit Soi 11; tel: 0-2651 1037; www.bashbangkok.com. Billed as an upscale late nightclub, Bash is quietly affiliated with the nearby Q Bar. All purple and leather interior like a 70s New York pimp's paradise, it kicks off

at midnight with three floors of mixed sounds, including trance, hip hop and house and occassional imports like Danny Rampling. Drinks start around B220.

Demo: Thonglor Soi 10; tel: 0-2711 6970. Graffiti-covered walls help to generate the urban warehouse ambiance that characterises for this new Thonglor hotspot. It serves an exclusive menu of house music in all its forms and a long list of stiff drinks. Great sound system, mock-classical French furniture and a very cool crowd.

Q Bar: 34 Sukhumvit Soi 11; tel: 0-2252 3274; www.qbarbangkok.com. This lounge and dance bar has a very comfortable outdoor balcony area upstairs and inside hosts some of the city's coolest dance music. The nightly DJ line-up includes visitors such as Goldie, and the bar has an impressive drinks list, with 50 brands of vodka alone.

Silom and Bangrak

Ku De Ta: Sathorn Square Building, Th. Narathiwat; tel: 0-2108 2000; www.kudeta.com. The Singapore nightlife brand opened here with spectacular views at multiple venues, including modern Asian cuisine at one of three restaurants, several bars and a club with

BELOW: live jazz at the Saxophone.

top DJs and a cutting edge sound system.

Maggie Choo's: 320 Th. Silom; tel: 0-2635 6055; www.facebook.com/maggiechoos. A fantasy 1930s' Shanghai bordello, Maggie's has an evocative period noodle shop, and beyond that a large room modelled on a colonial era bank vault. Leather couches; busts of Queen Victoria; dry ice and girls in slit-to-the-thigh Chinese dresses complete the picture to funky electro sounds and live bands.

Tapas Café & Tapas Room: Soi 4 Th. Silom; tel: 0-2234 4737. A true survivor in the city's party scene, this compact two floored dance bar is packed with beautiful twentysomething locals and expats downing jugs of icy margarita. Choice of music genres, from lounge, to house and dance classics.

Bars and Pubs

Silom and Bangrak

Sky Bar/Distil: State Tower, Th. Silom; tel: 0-2624 9555; www.thedomebkk.com. Sixty-four floors up, Sky Bar is on the roof, the open-air extension of Sirocco restaurant. Distil has spectacular river views from a small balcony, and a chilled ambience. High flyers enjoy champagne and oysters at translucent onyx tables.

Sukhumvit

Cheap Charlie's: 1 Sukhumvit Soi 11; tel: 0-2253 4648. This legendary boozing hole takes the minimalist concept to new heights, by having only a bar – no roof, no walls – and a few stools in the street. You occasionally have to move aside for passing traffic, but who cares? It's cheap, and typical of the local penchant for setting up business wherever the mood takes you.

Iron Fairies: opp Soi 13, Soi Thonglor (Sukhumvit Soi 55), tel: 08-4425 8080; www.theironfairies. com. Combination of blacksmith's workshop, bar and restaurant. This tiny place manufactures metallic fairy characters from the owner's famous children's book series by day (it's full of old sewing machines, potion jars and iron machinery). At night it's a bar with absinthe, burgers and live jazz.

Oskar Bistro: 24 Sukhumvit Soi 11; tel: 02-255 3377; www.oskar-bistro.com. The smart but casual Oskar has loungey electro sounds that get dancier as the night matures, making it a good venue to linger or as an ideal warm-up for clubs in the same soi. They also have very tasty international food.

Live Music Venues

Ad Here: 13 Th. Samsen; tel: 08-9769 4613. Musicians turn up to play blues and jazz in a bar the size of a guitar case. You sometimes get pleasant surprises, such as Charlie Musselwhite playing when they're in town. Close to Khao San Road, there's a laid back vibe and a good mix of Thai and *farang* punters.

Bamboo Bar: Oriental Hotel, 48 Oriental Avenue; tel: 0-2236 0400. The perfect place to soak up jazz, this cosy, intimate bar, with its wicker furnishings.

The Living Room: Sheraton Grande Sukhumvit, 205 Th. Sukhumvit; tel: 0-2653 0333; www.starwood.com/bangkok. There is a very good house band at this open-plan circular venue, in addition to the occasional resident

NIGHTLIFE LISTINGS

The *Bangkok Post* and *The Nation* feature decent listings and entertainment information, alongside magazines such as *BK* and *Bangkok 101*.

singers and overseas visitors such as Ernie Watts and The Preservation Hall Jazz Band.

Saxophone Pub & Restaurant: 3/8 Th. Phayathai, Victory Monument; tel: 0-2246 5472. As much a monument as its neighbouring war memorial, this lively venue has been packing them in for close to two decades. You can hear good blues, rock and jazz music here.

Tawandang German Brewery: 462/61 Thanon Rama III; tel: 0-2678 1114-5; www.tawandang. com. A vast two-tier pub-cum-theatre with a wide-ranging programme of Thai music, costumed dancers, magic acts and even ballet. The house band Fong Nam, led by American avant-gardeist Bruce Gaston, plays a mix of traditional and modern styles. They also have occasional big-name Thai acts such as Ad Carabao, and good Thai food.

Kathoey Cabaret

For a night of camp fun, see a Vegas-style lip-synching show performed by transsexuals known as "lady-boys" or *kathoey*.

Calypso Asiatique: Th. Charoenkrung (btw Sois 72-76); tel: 0-2688 1415; www.calypsocabaret.com. One of the city's best *kathoey* (transsexual) cabarets performed by sequinned artistes, cross-dressing or at various stages of sex-change. Shows (8.15pm and 9.45pm), include anything from Marilyn Monroe impersonators to Thai classical dance.

Gay Venues

Balcony: 86-88 Soi 4 Th. Silom; tel: 0-2235 5891. Lively long-standing bar with a mixed crowd and tables on the street.

DJ Station: 8/6-8 Silom Soi 2;

tel: 0-2266 4029; www.dj-station. com. Bangkok's most popular gay club, this venue is packed throughout the night. The atmosphere is electric and patrons often dress outrageously.

Dick's Café: 894/7-8 Soi Pratuchai, Duangthawee Plaza; tel: 0-2637 0078; www.dickscafe. com. Taped jazz music and paintings by local artists create a mellow mood. This is a good place to unwind in.

Telephone Pub: 114/11–13 Silom Soi 4; tel: 0-2234 3279; www.telephonepub.com. Popular with expats and locals, this is Bangkok's original gay pub, named because tables have telephones, so you can contact people across the room.

Shopping
General

Shoppers love meandering through the new mega-malls and department stores, even if just for the air-conditioned respite. Most open daily from 10am–10pm. Every June–July and Dec–Jan, major department stores and malls take part in the Thailand Grand Sales, though many also offer a 5 percent tourist discount year round – simply show your passport at the point of purchase. You can also claim a 7 percent VAT refund at the airport *(see page 294)*.

Shopping Malls

Central World: Th. Ratchadamri; tel: 0-2640 7000; www.centralworld. co.th. Bangkok's largest mall includes Isetan department store, hundreds of brand names, a cineplex, beauty services, yoga studios and restaurants. You could spend all day here.

Emporium: 622 Th. Sukhumvit; tel: 0-2664 8000/9; www.empori umthailand.com. Mainly brand-name stores, as well as more practical electronics shops. The Thai section on the 4th floor has handicrafts and jewellery.

Erawan Bangkok: 494 Th. Ploenchit; tel: 0-2250 7777; www.erawan

bangkok.com. Connected to the Grand Hyatt Erawan, this boutique mall contains contains fashion and spa shops and eateries.

Gaysorn: 999 Th. Ploenchit; tel: 0-2656 1149; www.gaysorn.com. Another glitzy mall for high-fashion labels; go to the third floor if you are looking for home-decoration shops.

Mahboonkrong (MBK): 444 Th. Phayathai; tel: 0-2620 9000; www.mbk-center.co.th. Heaving crowds browse for a vast array, including cosmetics, cameras, phones, clothes and jewellery. You can bargain at many stalls here.

Siam Centre: 989 Th. Rama I; tel: 0-2658 1000; www.siamcenter.co.th Has a funky new interior, a range of international and local fashion stores, and the usual range of cafés and restaurants.

Siam Discovery Centre: 989 Th. Rama I; tel: 0-2658 1000; www.siamdiscovery.co.th. Packed with imported brands, there's also an Ice rink, the Grand EGV cinema and Madame Tussaud's waxworks museum.

Siam Paragon: Th. Rama I; tel: 0-2610 9000; www.siamparagon.co.th. There is something for everyone at this enormous mall, with top local and international clothing labels available, an Apple store, an excellent gourmet market and Siam Ocean World aquarium.

Markets

Colourful markets and street vendors (both day and night) are popular for cheap goods and basic necessities. The following places covered in the Bangkok chapter are worth seeking out:

Pratunam Market *(page 94)*; **Khao San** *(page 86)*; Chinatown's **Sampeng Lane** and **Pahurat Market** *(pages 88–89)*; **Patpong** *(page 95)*; **Sukhumvit** *(page 97)* and **Chatuchak Weekend Market** *(page 97)*.

What to Buy

Antiques

O P Place, Th. Charoen Krung Soi 38; tel: 0-2266 0186. Close to

the Mandarin Oriental hotel, this mall stocks quality antiques and reproductions.

River City: 23 Trok Rongnamkaeng; tel: 0-2237 0077/8. Bangkok's art and antiques centre, with the second to fourth floors selling such items. Antique auctions are held monthly in the Auction House, but beware of forgeries and artefacts pilfered from historical sites.

Electronics

Panthip Plaza: 604/3 Th. Petchaburi; tel: 0-2251 9724/8. A five-floor marketplace for computer gear and PC software (although much of it pirated).

Fashion and Clothes

Thais follow fashion trends closely and are quick to copy the latest collections from foreign design houses – and flog them at a fraction of the cost. The only downside for most Westerners is the clothes fit as the Thai physique is small and slim. Thai fashion houses include **Fly Now**, **Greyhound** and **Kloset**.

Fly Now: 1st Floor, Siam Paragon, Th. Rama I; tel: 0-2610 9410; www.flynowbangkok.com. Somchai Songwatana, lauded at British Designer 2000, still looms large

in Thai fashion. Get accessories here such as bags, wallets, belts and shoes, or have a classic modern dress made to order.

Jaspal: 2nd Floor, Siam Centre, Th. Rama I; tel: 0-2251 5918; www.jaspal.com. Local fashion chain with branches in most shopping malls in town. Influenced by British and European style trends. Unlike most Thai labels, sizes go up to XL.

Senada Theory: 2nd Fl Gaysorn Plaza, Th. Ploenchit; tel: 0-2656 1350. The flagship store of designer Chanita Preechawitayakul, who has an international profile for smart "vintage romantic" designs in Thai silks and Chinese cottons.

Tailors

There are nearly as many tailors as noodle shops in the capital, and while the craftsmanship isn't a stitch near to Savile Row, prices are a bargain. There is a proliferation around Sukhumvit's early sois, Siam Square, Silom and Thanon Khao San. Avoid the "suits made in 24 hours".

Textiles

Almeta Silk: 20/3 Th. Sukhumvit Soi 23; tel: 0-2258 4227; www.almeta.com. Made-to-order hand-

BELOW: on Khao San Road.

woven silk in stunning colour combinations that can be turned into home furnishings.

Doi Tung: 4th Floor, Siam Discovery Centre, Th. Rama I; tel: 02-658 0424/5; www.doitung.org. This royally initiated craft foundation sells traditional weaves infused with a funky sense of the contemporary.

Jim Thompson Thai Silk: 9 Th. Surawong; tel: 0-2632 8100/4; and **Jim Thompson Factory Outlet:** 153 Sukhumvit Soi 93; tel: 0-2632 5530; www.jimthompson.com. With several branches around the city, this famous silk company has had a contemporary makeover in recent years. Clothing, accessories and home furnishings are available.

ABOVE: Thai boxing.

Gems and Jewellery

Bangkok is well known for its gemstone scams. Buy only from reputable shops endorsed by the Tourism Authority of Thailand and the Thai Gem and Jewellery Traders Association. These shops carry the Jewel Fest (www.jewelfest.com) logo and issue a certificate of authenticity that comes with a money-back guarantee.

Handicrafts/Home Decor

In addition to Asiatique and Chatuchak Weekend Market, the shops below are worth a browse. Expect prices to be higher, though.

Narai Phand: Gnd Fl President Tower, 973 Th. Ploenchit, tel: 0-2656 0398; www.naraiphand.com. One-stop shop for all Thai crafts, from traditional musical instruments to ornamental headpieces.

Propaganda: 4th Floor, Siam Discovery Centre Th. Rama 1; tel: 0-2658 0430; www.propagandaonline.com. Quirkily designed home-decor items (think of a Thai version of Alessi) such as funky tableware and molar-shaped toothbrush holders. Other outlets at Central World and Emporium.

ThaiCraft: 242 Soi Akharn Songkroh; tel: 0-2676 0636-8; www.thaicraft.org. There's no retail out-

let here, rather, it's an organisation that holds regular shopping fairs in Bangkok selling crafts from around Thailand. They adhere to fair-trade practices. Check the website for latest events.

Outdoor Activities

Participant Sports

Bowling

SF Strike Bowl: 7th Floor MBK Centre; tel: 0-2611 7171; www.sfcinemacity.com. One of several SF locations in Bangkok, this 28-lane alley is part of a Game Zone with pool, table football and air hockey.

Flowboarding

Flow House Bangkok: A Square, Sukhumvit Soi 26; tel: 0-2108-5210; www.flowhousebangkok.com. A machine at this "urban beach club" jets a sheet of water on which to enjoy a combination of snowboarding, skateboarding and surfing. Instructors will get you started, and there are retail outlets, plus food and drinks at the Flow Bar & Grill.

Golf

Thais are golfing buffs, going so far as to employ some of the golfing world's stellar architects to

design international-class courses. Green fees run from around B900–B5,000 but may increase with items like compulsory golf carts. Look for happy hour promotions.

Bangkok Golf Club: 99 Moo 2 Thanon Tivanond; tel: 0-2501 2828; www.golf.th.com. About 40 minutes from the centre of Bangkok there is an 18-hole course and a nine-hole made up of only par threes, all modelled on famous golfing courses from all around the world.

Panya Indra Golf Course: 99 Moo 6, Km 9 Kannayao, Th. Ramindra; tel: 0-2943 0000; www.panyagolf.com. About 30 minutes from downtown, this well-kept course has a challenging 27-hole course.

Thai Country Club: 88 Moo 1, Bangna-Trad Km. 35.5; tel: 038-570 234; www.thaicountryclub.com. This 375yd, 18-hole course regularly hosts top tournaments such as the Volvo Masters Asia. Tiger Woods played here on his only vist to the country in 1997.

Go-karting

EasyKart.Net: 2nd Floor, RCA Plaza, Royal City Ave, Th. Rama IX; tel: 0-2203 1205; www.easykart.net. This facility, with a 600-metre (1,968ft)-long race circuit, is a well-managed outfit. The karts are extremely fast and light, reaching a top speed of around 60kmh (37mph). The stadium has a hi-tech computerised time clock, highlighting individual fastest laps.

Spectator Sports

Thai Boxing

Bangkok has two principal places to view Thai boxing, or *muay thai*.
Lumpini Boxing Stadium: Th. Rama IV; tel: 0-2251 4303. Matches are on Tue, 6.15–11pm, Fri–Sat 5–8pm and 8.30pm–midnight. Tickets at B500, B800 and B1,500.
Ratchadamnoen Boxing Stadium: 1 Th. Ratchadamnoen Nok; tel: 0-2281 4205. Matches at 6pm on Mon, Wed and Thu, and 5pm on Sun. Tickets: B500, B800 and B1,500.

Sightseeing Tours

Unfortunately, Bangkok has very little in the way of organised sightseeing tours. The few existing tours are often targeted at the domestic market, with guides speaking only Thai. However, all the major hotels have tour desks that can arrange visits (with private guide and car with driver) to the major tourist sites.

The **Chao Phraya Tourist Boat** (*see page 102*) is more of a shuttle service than a tour proper, but you do get a running commentary on board of the sights along the Chao Phraya River. For those wishing to explore the canals of Thonburi or Nonthaburi, **private longtail boats** (*see page 103*) can be rented from most of the river's main piers.

Dinner cruises (or evening cocktails) on board an authentic teak barge is a nice way of spending the evening and soaking up the sights along the river.
Amazing Bangkok Cyclist: 10/5-7, Soi Aree, Sukhumvit Soi 26; tel: 0-2665 6364; www.realasia. net. Cycling tours last from a morning to a full weekend (including a ride on a longtail boat) into the

capital's more scenic and traffic-free area (from B1,000 per person). Walking and canal boat tours are also available, plus an interesting train tour into the countryside at Samut Sakhon.
Anantara Cruises: tel: 0-2477 0770; www.bangkok-cruises.anantara. com. Two restored and converted rice barges go on three day-two night cruises to either Ayutthaya or Ang Thong. The trips include shore visits and the boats have luxury cabins with en suite bathrooms, a sundeck and a full bar and kitchen.
Loy Nava Dinner Cruise: tel: 0-2437 4932; www.loynava.com. A teak barge was refurbished and converted into the *Tahsaneeya Nava*. Its 2-hour dinner cruise (daily 6pm and 8.10pm) starts with a traditional welcome by hostesses. Dinner is a Thai set menu accompanied by live traditional music. Prices are B1,400 per person if you book online.
Oriental Escape: 98/7 Supalai Park Twanon Tower, Nonthaburi; tel: 0-2195 8875; www.oriental escape.com Offers a wide range of tours (including Thai-boxing and Thai dance-and-dinner shows) of Bangkok and its surroundings (Damnoen Saduak floating market, Ayutthaya, Kanchanaburi, etc), as well as other parts of Thailand.

Spas

Chi Spa: The Shangri-La hotel, 89 Soi Wat Suan Plu; tel: 0-2236 7777; www.shangri-la.com. Spacious, luxurious treatment rooms amid a hushed calm in which to enjoy signature therapies that aim to restore the balance of your chi (energy flow).
Devarana Spa: The Dusit Thani, 946 Th. Rama IV; tel: 0-2636 3596; www.devaranaspa.com. One of Bangkok's most stylish and evocative havens of wellbeing. Flowing with an abundance of natural light, this spa has a very calming Zen mood.
Divana Spa: 7 Sukhumvit Soi 25; tel: 0-2661 6784; www.divanaspa.

com. A hidden garden oasis in the heart of the city, this independent spa formulates many of the products used from its very own organic garden.
Oriental Spa: The Mandarin Oriental, 48 Oriental Ave; tel: 0-2659 9000; www.mandarinoriental.com. This spa is one of the capital's first and also one of the best temples dedicated to health and wellbeing. Situated in a century-old teak house on the banks of the Chao Phraya River.
Rasayana Retreat: 57 Soi Phrom Mitr, Sukhumvit Soi 39; tel: 0-2662 4803; www.rasayanaretreat. com. An independent spa complete with all the usual facilities and treatments, plus a raw-food restaurant.
S Medical Spa: 193/12, Lake Rajada Complex, Th. Ratchadapisek; tel: 0-2264 0999, www. smedspa.com. A chic spa with physicians and dermatologists on site, the treatments available here include Eastern and Western steam rooms, hydrotherapy pools and beauty-enhancement procedures such as laser face lifts and Botox.

Cookery Schools

Blue Elephant Cookery School: Blue Elephant Restaurant, 233 Th. Sathorn; tel: 0-2673 9353; www.blueelephant.com. Located in an old mansion, this cookery school offers half-day classes that begin with a trip to a Thai-produce market.
Mandarin Oriental Cookery School: Mandarin Oriental Hotel, 48 Oriental Avenue; tel: 0-2659 9000; www.mandarinoriental.com. The legendary hotel runs pricey cooking demonstrations rather than hands-on courses.
Thai House: Nonthaburi; tel: 0-2903 9611, 2997 5161; www. thaihouse.co.th. This venue combines Thai cookery lessons with a stay in a rustic Thai-style house located in the suburbs of Nonthaburi; 1-, 2- and 3-day courses are available with meals and lodging included.

EASTERN SEABOARD

Miles of sandy beaches, dozens of tiny islands waiting to be explored, wildlife centres and treks through jungled forest to hidden waterfalls... you can find these and more on Thailand's most developed and easily accessible shore.

Bangkok

The Eastern Seaboard is Thailand's most commercially and industrially developed shore, with the length from Bangkok to Rayong featuring numerous factories and oil refineries. Thankfully, the development has done little to deter tourism, and with miles of sandy beaches and dozens of islands lying just offshore, plus relatively calm seas all year round (see margin tip, page 121), it's easy to find your own secluded oasis.

This section of the Thai coast has just about something for everyone: the beaches around Pattaya and Rayong, along with the islands of Ko Samet and Ko Chang, abound with activities. Speckled with orchards and national parks, the region is also a golfer's paradise, with more than 25 international-standard fairways in close proximity to Pattaya.

Highway 3 is the principal road that trails through the provinces of Chonburi, Rayong, Chantaburi and Trat, all the way to Cambodia. There is a rail line as far as Pattaya, but services are limited and slow. Two small airports serve the vicinity, the closest being U-Tapao Airport near Pattaya. Further down the coast is Trat Airport, which cuts down on

travel times from Bangkok for travellers wishing to reach Ko Chang.

The easterly location of Bangkok's **Suvarnabhumi International Airport** significantly reduces travel times to destinations such as Pattaya, and many visitors are now opting to head straight to the coast, rather than spend a night in Bangkok. International hotel brands and luxury property companies are developing the area and it is likely that the region will see yet further growth in the coming years.

Main attractions

SRI RACHA TIGER ZOO
KO SI CHANG
SANCTUARY OF TRUTH
TIFFANY'S
KU SAMET
KO CHANG

LEFT: a laid-back beach bar on Ko Chang.
RIGHT: young Thais in Ko Samet.

Statue of a gilded fat Buddha at Wat Ko Loi, on the island of Ko Loi.

BANG SAEN

The elevated highway that leads out of Bangkok runs past **Chonburi**, which is considered the gateway to the Eastern Seaboard. Just south of Chonburi municipality, the 2km (1-mile)-long beach at **Bang Saen ❶** springs to life each weekend as hordes of middle-class Bangkokians arrive in cars and buses. The nearest stretch of beach from the capital, you will find it covered with a profusion of beach umbrellas and inflatable inner-tubes, the surf filled with bobbing bodies fully dressed to avoid a tan (many Thais associate tanned skin with working folk who toil in the sun).

SI RACHA

The run-of-the-mill coastal town of **Si Racha ❷**, about 100km (62 miles) from Bangkok, nestles between two hill ranges, with a busy harbour extending beyond its piers. Visitors and locals alike enjoy the waterfront restaurants here, dipping fresh shrimp

and crab into *nam prik si racha*, a spicy, thick red sauce that is famous throughout the land. Offshore, connected by a bridge, is the islet of **Ko Loi**, where the tree-shrouded **Wat Ko Loi** fuses Thai and Chinese elements on top of a rocky outcrop.

The **Sriracha Tiger Zoo** (daily 8am–6pm; charge; tel: 0-3829 6556/8; www.tigerzoo.com) claims to be the largest tiger zoo in the world, with around 100 Bengal tigers. The tigers star in the daily circus shows, which also feature crocodiles. There is also an elephant show, a bear show, pig racing, ostrich riding, and plenty of other entertaining animals and birds.

KO SI CHANG

A 45-minute boat ride from Si Racha is the island of **Ko Si Chang ❸**, known primarily as the coastal retreat of King Chulalongkorn (Rama V). The king built his summer palace here in the 1890s, only to abandon it after the French briefly

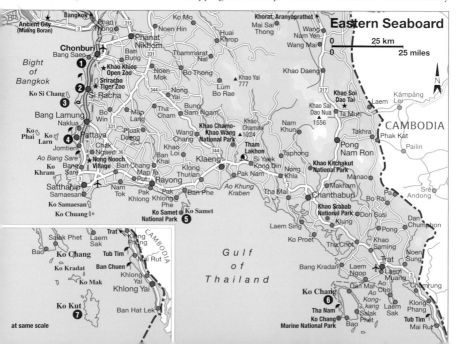

occupied the island a few years later. Once a customs point for cargo ships unloading on to smaller vessels to sail up the Chao Phraya River, the sea is always crowded with large freighters and rows of flat barges waiting to be supplied. Busy at weekends with Thai day-trippers, the island has a few passable beaches, though certainly not Thailand's best or cleanest.

Ko Si Chang provides an interesting slice of island living without the typical tourist presence. It can be visited as a day or overnight trip from the capital or as a stop-off en route east to Pattaya and beyond. Day trippers are approached as soon as they step off the ferry by drivers of motorcycle trishaws, who offer 3–4-hour-long tours around the island for B250.

Sights and activities

Once off the pier, and after exploring **Tha Bon**, the island's main fishing town, most visitors head straight for the grounds of **Judhadhut Palace** (daily 8am–6pm; free). Recently restored, the grounds double up as an ocean-front public park, with a small pebbly beach beside the rebuilt **Atsadang Bridge**. Once a colonnaded wooden pier used as Chulalongkorn's landing stage, this is now a popular spot for kids to leap from and swim around moored fishing boats.

While the main teak palace itself was dismantled and rebuilt in Bangkok as the Vimanmek Mansion *(see page 87)*, several of the palace's other structures have been remodelled, including the green wooden house **Ruen Mai Rim Talay**, which was used as a convalescent home for infirm Western visitors. The pretty gardens that extend up the hill are worth exploring; at the top is the white spire of **Wat Atsadang Nimit**. As with palace buildings of the day, the temple's design was a fusion of Thai and European architecture, with the circular *chedi* featuring unique stained-glass panels.

Strange as it may sound, ask any trishaw driver to take you to **Dracula's Castle** and they will pull up in the middle of nowhere beside a bizarre-looking house that towers eerily above the tree-line. The abode is a labour of love for a professor of

TIP

The best months of the year along the Eastern Seaboard are from Nov to Feb. Expect scorching temperatures from Mar to May, and rain from June to Oct. But even then, the wet season is not as intense as the Andaman coast, making for relatively calm seas even during the rainy months.

BELOW LEFT: Wat Atsadang Nimit
BELOW RIGHT: Atsadang Bridge.

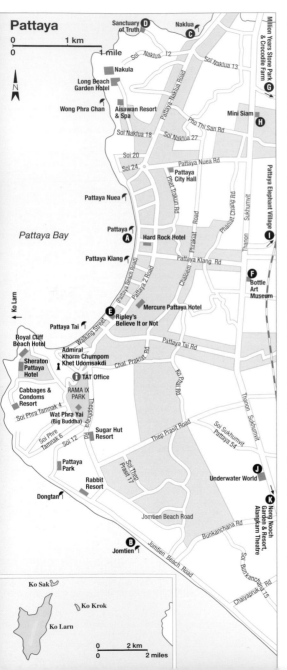

Pattaya

0   1 km

0   1 mile

Pattaya Bay

Ko Larn

Sanctuary of Truth **D**

Naklua **C**

Million Years Stone Park & Crocodile Farm

Sol Naklua 12

Sol Naklua 13

Nakula

Long Beach Garden Hotel

Wong Phra Chan

Aisawan Resort & Spa

Pho Thi San Rd

Mini Siam **H**

Sol Naklua 18

Sol Naklua 27

Pattaya Elephant Village

Sol 20

Sol 24

Pattaya Nuea Rd

Pattaya City Hall

Pattaya Nuea

Pattaya **A**

Hard Rock Hotel

Pattaya Klang

Pattaya Klang Rd

Bottle Art Museum **F**

Mercure Pattaya Hotel

Pattaya Tai

Ripley's Believe It or Not **E**

Pattaya Tai Rd

Royal Cliff Beach Hotel

Admiral Khorm Chumpom Khet Udomsakdi

Chai Prakiat

Sheraton Pattaya Hotel

TAT Office

Cabbages & Condoms Resort

RAMA IX PARK

Wat Phra Yai (Big Buddha)

Sugar Hut Resort

Thep Prasit Road

Sol Sukhumvit Pattaya 34

Underwater World **J**

Pattaya Park

Rabbit Resort

Nong Nooch Garden & Resort, Alangkam Theatre **K**

Dongtan

Jomtien Beach Road

Bunkanchana Rd

Jomtien **B**

Jomtien Beach Road

Sol Bunkanchana 15

Chaiyapruk Rd

Ko Sak

Ko Krok

Ko Larn

0   2 km

0   2 miles

architecture and isn't open to the public, but it provides a creepy photo opportunity before continuing on to the island's principal beach of **Hat Tham Pang** (Fallen Cave), on the west coast. Depending on the tide, the 1km (½-mile)-long beach can shrink in size, and is usually crowded with lines of beach umbrellas and food shacks located behind.

Religious retreats on the island include the meditation centre at **Wat Tham Yai Prik** (daily 8am–6pm; free), where monks and nuns meditate in caves that reach deep into the rocky hill that the temple rests against. Foreigners often come to stay here to find their spiritual "centre". There is no charge to stay at the temple, but donations are welcomed.

On steep Kayasira hill is **Sanjao Pho Khao Yai** (daily 8am–6pm; free), the Shrine of the Father Spirit of the Great Hill. This gaudy Chinese temple perched high on the rock has great views overlooking the town and port below. Said to date back to China's Ming Dynasty, the colourful temple is a popular stop for Chinese visitors, who pay homage at the damp cave shrines before hiking up further to a *sala* containing the Buddha's footprint.

There aren't many restaurants of note, but **Pan & David**, a simple streetside eatery, is recommended *(see page 138)*. Run by an American and his Thai wife, the restaurant is a good source of tourist tips. The couple can also help arrange fishing, scuba diving and boat trips to nearby islands such as **Ko Khang Khao**, which has the nicest beach in the area.

PATTAYA

Good and bad, the reputation of **Pattaya ❹** precedes it, with most people having formed their own opinion of this resort area even before they set foot here. This notoriety dates back to the Vietnam War, when boatloads of American GIs flocked to the then quiet beaches and bars for R&R. With the Thai Navy operating from the nearby port at Satthahip, battalions of visiting US marines still occasionally descend on Pattaya – much to the delight of the resort's entertainment spots.

Located 147km (91 miles) from Bangkok, or just under two hours by road, the seaside town has long been popular with Thai youth and families. In recent years, Europeans have been outnumbered by visitors from Asia and the Middle East, along with significant numbers from Russia.

The once-polluted beaches have been cleaned up, but they are nowhere near as pristine as those of the southern islands. However, whatever Pattaya lacks, it more than compensates for in other areas. There is a plethora of good-value accommodation and restaurants, a wide range of outdoor and indoor activities, as well as several cultural attractions. Beyond that, Pattaya's buzzing, if salacious, nightlife scene is something to be experienced, or avoided, depending on your sensibility.

Although Pattaya tries hard to cre

ate the ambience of a cosmopolitan playground, with glitzy malls and hotels, a pedestrianised shopping street and tree-lined paths, it still retains a provincial character.

Pattaya is also a popular spot for foreigners owning beach condos and houses, used as weekend getaways for Bangkok expats and as winter homes for retirees from Europe. Property is being built at an astonishing rate. There are some swanky residences on the market, and improvements to infrastructure, especially international schools, are drawing in more respectable residents. But its seedy reputation also attracts a strong criminal element. Thankfully, the underworld is rarely visible to the average tourist and Pattaya feels as safe as anywhere else in Thailand.

Pattaya's beaches

On the beach front is the 3km (2-mile)-long crescent-shaped **Hat Pattaya A**, the least attractive of the three beaches, with only a narrow and umbrella-crammed wisp of yellow sand. It is backed by a palm-lined promenade that has unfortunately

BELOW: Fishing boats off Jomtien beach.

Keep an eye out for jet-skiers when swimming at Pattaya or Jomtien beaches. Accidents have happened in the past.

become a pitching point for "working girls". The Phra Tamnak hill area separates the main resort splay from a huddle of mid- and high-end hotels (such as the Sheraton and Royal Cliff) that front several small but pleasant beaches.

Just a short ride south is the 6km (4-mile)-long **Hat Jomtien** Ⓑ, with a stretch of beach that is only marginally cleaner and better than Hat Pattaya. The nicest-looking (ie fewer umbrellas) and least-populated bays are found in north Pattaya, rounding the **Hat Naklua** Ⓒ headland towards the fishing village. Accessed from Naklua Soi 16 is **Hat Wongamart**, a pleasant stretch of sand backed by several condo towers and small hotels.

Beach activities

Pattaya and Jomtien are good locations for water sports, with windsurfing and sailing equipment available for rent, along with jet-skis, waterscooters and waterskiing equipment. Beware the scams associated with hiring these craft (*see Crime and Safety, page 287*). The brave can try parasailing, strapped into a parachute and towed aloft by a speedboat.

Ko Larn – identified in brochures as **Coral Island** but whose name actually translates as Bald Island – is one of Pattaya's most popular day-trip locations. Its once-pristine coral reefs have been destroyed by fishermen using dynamite to stun fish. Yet glass-bottomed boats still ferry visitors around its waters, the passengers peering in vain at the dead grey coral. However, Ko Larn has the wide, soft-sand beaches that Pattaya lacks and is a great place to spend a leisurely day. The shore is lined with seafood restaurants, and there are water-sports facilities for those who manage to get off their beach chairs.

Several scuba schools run dive trips to Pattaya's outlying islands; the surrounding waters harbour one of Thailand's best wreck dive sites, with no less than four sunken vessels scattered between Pattaya and Satthahip port. Ko Larn and the surrounding islands, such as **Ko Sak** and **Ko Krok**, see more tourist activity – visibility isn't crystal-clear but the waters are

BELOW: Ko Larn, also known as Coral Island.

fairly protected from currents, which make them suitable for diving beginners. The further islands of **Ko Rin** and **Ko Man Wichai** present better dive spots, with clearer visibility and an abundant range of marine life, and the opportunity to spot sharks and turtles. The **Hardeep Wreck**, **Bremen Wreck**, and the recently scuttled **HMS Kram Wreck** are frequently explored by more experienced divers.

Land attractions

On land, a must-see is the intricate wood-carved **Sanctuary of Truth D**, in Naklua Soi 12 (daily 8am–6pm; charge; tel: 0-3836 7229; www.sanctuaryoftruth.com). This awe-inspiring structure made of teak is intended to revive traditional artisan techniques as well as act as a spiritual beacon. Dramatically perched on the seafront, the fantastical tower blends ancient religious iconography from Thailand and Southeast Asia. Work began in 1901 and is expected to take at least another 10 years to complete. Aside from the cathedral-like structure filled with chiselled figures, there are regular dolphin shows and Thai cultural shows, plus horse and elephant riding.

Rather more kitsch is the branch of **Ripley's Believe It or Not E** (daily 11am–11pm; charge; tel: 0-3871 0294; www.ripleysthailand.com) at the Royal Garden Plaza. Its collection of oddities from around the world may appeal to some.

While many of Pattaya's visitors prefer to quaff bottles of cold beer, others can opt to view a unique collection of delicate miniatures displayed inside some 300 bottles at the **Bottle Art Museum F** on Thanon Sukhumvit (daily 8am–5pm; charge; tel: 0-3842 2957). All the items have been patiently assembled over a period of 15 years by a Dutchman, Pieter Bij De Leij and a Thai woman, Prapaisi Thaipanich.

Another of Pattaya's tourist stops is the **Million Years Stone Park & Crocodile Farm G** (daily 8am–6.30pm; charge; tel: 0-3824 9347; www.thaistonepark.org). This is a collection of weirdly shaped boulders set among a landscape of rare and exotic flora. Situated off Thanon Chaiyaphruek, there are also beasts aplenty at the park, such as crocodiles, bears, tigers, camels and even giant freshwater catfish.

Feel like a giant at **Mini Siam H** as you step around tiny scale models of many of the world's architectural landmarks (daily 7am–10pm; charge; tel: 0-3872 7333; www.minisiam.com). This Lilliputian world is on Thanon Sukhumvit in North Pattaya.

Families with young children will enjoy **Pattaya Elephant Village I** on Thanon Sukhumvit (daily 8.30am–7pm; charge; tel: 0-3824 9818; www.elephant-village-pattaya.com). It offers a daily elephant show as well as fun rides into the surrounding countryside.

If you want to keep your feet dry, a land-based view of marine wonders can be had at **Underwater World J** (daily 9am–6pm; charge; tel: 0-3875

TIP

Pattaya has a bad reputation for con artists – collecting donations for spurious causes, selling precious stones at "bargain" prices, or offering "free" trips to tourist sights, so keep your wits about you.

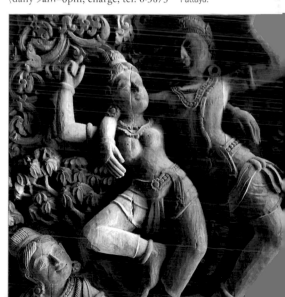

BELOW: detail of the Sanctuary of Truth in Pattaya.

Up close and personal with an elephant at Pattaya's Nong Nooch Village.

BELOW: bold signs beside the road make it clear what Pattaya's main entertainment is.

6879; www.underwaterworldpattaya.com), just after the Thanon Thep Prasit junction with Thanon Sukhumvit. The large aquarium has a 100-metre (328ft)-long fibreglass viewing tunnel, along with a "touch pool" for hands-on interaction with smaller marine animals, and a shark and ray tank. For an extra fee, you can also scuba dive among the sharks.

South of Pattaya, 163km (101 miles) along Thanon Sukhumvit is **Nong Nooch Garden & Resort** , a 243-hectare (600-acre) landscaped parkland enclosing two manmade lakes (daily 8am–6pm; charge; tel: 0-3870 9360; www.nongnoochtropicalgarden.com). Apart from one of the biggest collections of orchids and palms in the world, the park features a butterfly garden, mini-zoo and a daily cultural show with traditional dancing, boxing and an elephant circus.

Due to open opposite Nong Nooch on Thanon Sukhumvit, late 2014, **Cartoon Network Amazone** (charge; www.cartoonnetworkamazone. com) is a themed waterpark and has a beach and 150 features based on characters such as Ben 10, with a wave pool, an "adventure river" and a speed slide falling from a six-storey tower.

Pattaya's nightlife

Pattaya's main nightlife zones cluster around **Beach Road** and **Walking Street** in South Pattaya. There's a staggering range of bars, Irish pubs, German brew houses, live-music venues, nightclubs, plus many go-go bars, open-air "beer bars" and massage parlours. The strip called **Boyz Town** (Pattayaland Soi 3) follows the same theme for gay men. Of the lip-synching Vegas-style cabarets featuring *kathoey* or "lady-boys" (transsexuals), the best is **Tiffany's**, on Pattaya 2 Road (daily shows at 6pm, 7.30pm and 9pm; charge; www.tiffanyshow.co.th). More family-oriented, **Alangkarn Theatre** (Thu–Tue shows at 6pm; charge; www.alangkarnthailand.com) at Km 155 along Thanon Sukhumvit combines traditional dance and theatre in a spectacle of historic Thailand, complete with elephant battles, lasers and pyrotechnics. Pattaya has its own mini Chatuchak at **Thepprasit Market** (Fri–Sun 5pm–11pm), close to the junction

of Thepprasit and Sukhumvit roads, selling the usual knock-off watches, bags, T-shirts and interior decor.

KO SAMET

Located 200km (124 miles), or three hours by road, from Bangkok and a short boat trip across from the fishing harbour of **Ban Phe**, the postcard-perfect island of **Ko Samet** ❺ is a popular weekend getaway for Bangkokians. The island is well known among Thais as the place where Sunthorn Phu (1786–1855), a flamboyantly romantic court poet, retired to compose some of his works. Born in nearby Klaeng on the mainland, Sunthorn called the island Ko Kaew Phisadan, or "island with sand like crushed crystal", and it was here that his best-known poem, *Phra Aphaimani*, a tale about a prince and a mermaid, was set.

From a quiet poetic retreat, the island has gained popularity as a laid-back resort, helped by the fine, white sand beaches and clear turquoise waters. The island was declared part of a national marine park in 1981 (entry fee on arrival), so technically, most of the resort and bungalow operations are illegal. Ko Samet is very popular with Thai students and young professionals, making it extremely busy on public holidays, when room rates can increase by more than 50 percent. Its popularity has also led to the construction of new and upscale resorts on the island. Note: the island has a reputation for dengue fever, so take all of the necessary precautions.

Ko Samet's beaches

Almost all of the island's sandy beaches run down the east coast, starting near the larger northern tip with Hat Sai Kaew, and gradually getting more isolated as the island narrows to the southern bay of Ao Karang. Most of the island's infrastructure – school, clinic, temple, market and a few shops – is located near **Na Dan** ❹ pier and along the paved road to Hat Sai Kaew.

The island is relatively small, at only 6km (4 miles) long and 3km (2 miles) wide, and a hike from top to bottom, passing by all the east-coast beaches, can be done in a few hours, though the coastal track cuts across several rocky headlands. There is a single road running down the centre of the island, which turns to bumpy dirt track at its outer reaches.

The west coast's only beach, but the island's most exclusive, **Ao Phrao** ❻, has just a few upmarket hotels nestled into its small scenic bay. On the east, **Hat Sai Kaew** ❼ (Diamond Sand), a short walk from Na Dan pier, is the most developed beach, with a larger selection of air-conditioned hotels, bars and seafood restaurants, plus luxuriant powdery white sands. Consequently, it is also one of the most congested.

Further down the coast is the bay of **Ao Hin Khok** ❽, separated from Hat Sai Kaew by a rocky promontory, marked by a weathered mermaid statue inspired by Sunthorn

TIP

While the regular fishing boat ferries are much cheaper, taking a speedboat across to Ko Samet (around B800) from the mainland port is much faster, drops you on the bay of your choice, and usually means you escape the National Park entry fee of B200 per foreign person, which is pretty steep compared with the B20 that Thais are charged.

BELOW: Hat Sai Kaew on Ko Samet.

Banana-boat rides on Ao Wong Deuan. This beach has ample facilities but can get noisy as a result.

Phu's famous poem. Here, and at the next bay – **Ao Phai** ⓔ, which has an equally nice white sandy beach – is where foreigners tend to nest. Hotels such as **Naga Bungalows** (Ao Hin Khok) and **Silver Sand** (Ao Phai) frequently host late-night parties.

The next white-sand bay is small and intimate **Ao Tub Tim** ⓕ. There are only two places to stay here but the noisier attractions of Ao Phai are only a short walk away. There are two more quiet bays, **Ao Nuan** and **Ao Chao**, until you hit the picturesque, crescent-shaped **Ao Wong Deuan** ⓖ, which is becoming increasingly spoilt by boats, noisy jet-skis and the cram of bars and resorts (mostly middle- to upper-end price range). The facilities are good, with minimarts, motorcycle rental and internet cafés, but the scene is more akin to Pattaya, with older Western men being pampered by their hired female "guides".

After Ao Wong Deuan, the bays become very peaceful, such as scenic

BELOW: lounging at Ao Thian, Ko Samet.

Ao Thian ⓗ (Candlelight Beach), which is actually a series of small beaches separated by rocky outcrops, and the southern **Ao Kiu** ⓘ, which has the island's most exclusive accomodation, the **Paradee Resort**.

Sights and activities

Most activity at Ko Samet is relaxed and beach-bound – sunbathing, beach strolls, swimming and snorkelling are all options – though jet-skis and inflatable banana boats do occasionally interrupt the peace. Vendors hawk fruit, beer, ice cream, snacks and sarongs, and there's an army of women offering massage and hair-braiding on the busier beaches. There isn't much in the way of reef around the shoreline, and what few spots there are have been badly damaged, but you will still encounter colourful varieties of tropical fish. Several resorts offer snorkelling trips by speedboat around Ko Samet and to nearby islets.

A few places offer scuba diving off

BELOW: lounging at Ao Thian, Ko Samet.

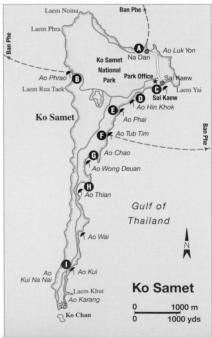

Ko Samet

the beach at Ao Phrao, while boat trips head out to nearby islands such as **Ko Talu**, where visibility is clearer but abandoned commercial fishing debris is an eyesore. Further east is **Hin Ploeng**, and off the island's southern tip is **Shark Point**, which can have strong currents and is best suited to experienced divers.

Ko Samet is to be avoided on public holidays, when visitors outnumber beds, and tents are pitched on any spare patch of land to be found. Evenings are relatively low-key; restaurants set up fresh-seafood beach barbecues, while some eateries entertain the purse-tight backpacker crowd with the latest pirated Hollywood movies. With local tourists making up the bulk of arrivals, Samet's service staff can be rather curt to foreign visitors and their needs.

KO CHANG

Thailand's second-largest island, at 492 sq km (190 sq miles), after Phuket, **Ko Chang** ❻ (Elephant Island) is part of a national marine park that includes some 52 islands. It has a rich ecology, with more than 60 species of tropical bird. Around a five-hour drive from Bangkok (or 45 minutes by plane to Trat on the mainland, then transfer by boat), the verdant island is part of Trat province, close to the Cambodian border. Located 20km (12 miles) southwest of Trat town, the mainland pier of **Laem Ngop** is the main setting-off point to the island.

For years, Koh Chang managed, to escape the rapid development of islands such as Phuket and Ko Samui, and remained a firm favourite almost exclusively with backpackers and low-budget travellers. However, building began in earnest after former Prime Minister Thaksin Shinawatra actively promoted Ko Chang as a playground for the rich in 2003. The official plan has since been abandoned, but the legacy is a boom in construction that now lines a large part of the single road that runs around (and will eventually loop) the island.

While the upsurge may detract from the island's untouched appeal, it does mean that there is a wider range of accommodation, including

Seashells from the beach at Ko Chang.

BELOW: sunset viewed from Ko Chang.

Hat Sai Khao has the best infrastructure on Ko Chang, including bars, cafés, restaurants and even ATM machines.

BELOW: Than Mayom Waterfall, Ko Chang.

stylish hotels with spas. There is a corresponding increase in foreign tourists and wealthier Thai vacationers, although, despite the lack of the old rock-bottom prices, several beaches do still attract the budget crowd. Car ferries from the mainland are also more numerous, and the loop road is now fairly busy in high season. This, and several hazardous hill passes with sharp bends, means more care needs to be taken if exploring the area on a rented motorcycle.

Ko Chang's beaches

Still, don't be put off by the changes taking place; the island still has a relatively untouched hilly interior, a mangrove forest and some lovely beaches. The main beaches line up along the west coast, with **Hat Sai Khao Ⓐ** (White Sand Beach) the most developed (and longest) stretch, with its swathe of powdery sands framed by a backdrop of casuarina trees.

South is **Hat Khlong Phrao Ⓑ**, one of the nicest yet quietest beaches on the island. It is effectively divided into the northern, central and southern sections by canals. Beyond that lies **Hat Kai Bae Ⓒ**, which has seen much recent development. Unfortunately, parts of its beach disappear when the tide is high. Next up is the last vestige of Ko Chang's hippie traveller scene, the lovely stretch of **Hat Tha Nam Ⓓ**, or Lonely Beach; it's no longer such a haven of solitude, with plush resorts starting to edge in. Just over 1km (½-mile)-long, this fine-sand beach gets a little coarser towards the south. It's the island's best beach for swimming, although there is a steep shelf at the northern tip. Next is **Ao Bai Lan Ⓔ**, a bay with rocks and reef but no beach.

At the bottom of the west coast is the stilted fishing village of **Ban Bang Bao Ⓕ**, which has become little more than a narrow concrete pier devoted to tourism, with seafood restaurants, dive shops, souvenir shops

and a guesthouse. This is also the departure point for dive and snorkel trips to surrounding islands.

The coastal road continues east but eventually arrives at a gate that claims private access to Ko Chang Grand Lagoona resort. Until the island loop is completed, this is where the journey ends.

Accessed from the east coast, in the next bay along the south coast nestles **Salak Phet** ⊙ fishing village, which has a more authentic and less developed feel than Ban Bang Bao.

Compared with the west coast, the eastern shoreline has little in the way of beaches and is largely ignored by most visitors. This makes a leisurely drive along the plantation- and hill-backed road a real pleasure, with few vehicles and the reward of a seafood lunch at Salak Phet. An alternative route runs along the east of Salak Phet where a newly built winding road continues all the way to **Hat Yao** ⊕, or Long Beach, on the southern tip.

Sights and activities

Most island-hoppers understandably confine themselves to the west-coast beaches, but just as appealing is the lush verdant mountainous backbone. The island's ecosystem features many avian species (including hornbills), macaques, pythons and cobras, monitor lizards, deer and boar, as well as striking wild flora. Day-long as well as overnight treks are conducted by the reputable **Trekkers of Ko Chang** (tel: 0-3952 5029), and many hotels organise trips with **Mr Anong** (mobile tel: 08-6152 5271).

With the island named after the noble pachyderm, it is no surprise that there are at least three elephant camps conducting treks into the interior. The best one, located deep in the forest, is the elephant camp of **Ban Kwan Chang** (tel: 08-9247 3161), which conducts well-organised half-

day treks and feeding sessions.

Other popular activities include kayaking and treks to the island's numerous waterfalls. The two most well-trodden are **Khlong Phlu Waterfall** and **Than Mayom Waterfall**, both of which have park offices that charge foreigners an inflated B200 for each fall, while Thais pay B20.

Snorkelling and scuba-diving trips usually head to the smaller outlying islands *(see page 132)* off the southern end of Ko Chang, going as far as **Ko Kut**, the second-largest island in the archipelago. There is fine diving at reasonably shallow depths, which is best done from November to March when the sea is calmer and visibility clearer.

Some of the best dive and snorkel sites include the pinnacles off **Ko Rang**, the reefs around **Ko Wai**, where sharks frequently hover, shallow dives off **Ko Khlum** and **Hin Luk Bat**, a rock pinnacle 30 minutes south by boat from Ban Bang Bao, and the **Thonburi Wreck** off Ko Chang's southeastern tip, where the warship *Thonburi* was sunk by French troops on 17 January 1941.

(see page 132)

TIP

Hat Tha Nam (also known as Lonely Beach) is one of Ko Chang's nicest beaches but beware of the strong undertow and currents at its northern end. A good number of drownings have occured in these treacherous waters.

Below: a sign for the waterfall at Khlong Phlu.

*Glowing sunset over the
Ko Chang coast.*

BELOW: excursion boat in
front of Ko Wai island.

Nightlife

Ko Chang's nightlife is subdued compared to Ko Samui or Phuket, with each beach having its own preferred watering holes. **Hat Sai Khao** is where the main energy is, where the large **Sabay Bar** sees the most action. Lying on cushioned beach mats is the typical set-up, and live music is a feature at many of the bars. As a sign of things to come, there is a block of raucous "beer bars" (nicknamed Mini Pattaya by residents) on the road at the southern end of Hat Sai Khao, with scantily clad bar girls to lure in customers.

Further down the west coast, **Hat Kai Bae** has a burgeoning nightlife scene, with a growing number of bars, restaurants and resorts. **Hat Tha Nam** has its own pocket of entertainment, with the Treehouse being its most popular hangout.

Ko Chang Archipelago

If Ko Chang feels a little too well-trodden, an alternative course of action is to head for the string of isolated islands off the southern tip. Many of Ko Chang's best snorkel and dive sites are found in the waters surrounding these islands. Around 10km (6 miles) off Ko Chang, the tiny island of **Ko Wai** has limited and basic accommodation, but the vibe here is very relaxed, the views of surrounding islands are spectacular, and there's a lovely coral reef just a short swim from the main beach.

An hour by speedboat from the mainland pier of Laem Ngop, the flat island of **Ko Mak** is dense with coconut trees and has two lovely beaches with few tourists but, unfortunately, plenty of sand flies; be sure to bring insect repellent. While the beaches are relatively unspoilt, the lack of development means that stretches of sand on **Ao Kao**, on Ko Mak's southwest coast, are littered with unsightly flotsam from fishing craft – a possible danger to barefooted walkers. **Ao Suan Yai**, on the opposite side of Ko Mak, is the island's prettiest bay. Both places have some basic accommodation and restaurants.

The southernmost island in the archipelago, and the closest to Cambodia, is **Ko Kut ❼**, Thailand's fourth-largest island and 2½ hours away by speedboat. Some 25km (16-miles) long and 12km (7-miles) wide, some of the island's populace is of Khmer origin, with most inhabitants earning a living from fishing or agriculture. Aside from several beaches and clear seas, attractions include **Khlong Chao Waterfall** and the fishing village at **Ao Sa Lad**. Due to its remote location, the island's development has been fairly low-key, attracting mainly organised tour groups.

Seasonal boats to Ko Wai, Ko Mak and Ko Kut leave from Laem Ngop pier on mainland Trat. From Ko Chang's Bang Bao pier, there are boats that organise tours to the more popular islands; resorts can also arrange for you to hitch a ride on a sightseeing tour boat. Speedboats can be arranged, but are expensive so are best hired for a group. ❑

E ASTERN SEABOARD

TRANSPORT

KO SI CHANG

Getting There
By Taxi
In Bangkok, a taxi can be booked to make the 100km (62-mile) journey to Si Racha, the jump-off point for the island of Ko Si Chang. The ride should take about 1–1½ hours. Make sure to negotiate a flat rate before boarding; it should cost around B1,000. Songthaew (pick-up trucks) on the pier can be negotiated for the return journey to Bangkok or for the onward journey to Pattaya (costing roughly B300–400).

By Bus
Air-conditioned buses leave every 40 minutes, from 5am to 9pm daily, from Bangkok's **Ekamai Bus Terminal** for Si Racha bus station (B98). The journey takes around 1½ hours. You can take a *tuk-tuk* (B40) from the bus station to Jarin pier.

By Boat
Ferries to Ko Si Chang leave from Jarin pier every hour from 7am to 8pm daily. The journey takes around 40 minutes and costs B50 one way. Ferries return to the mainland every hour from 8am to 6pm. Alternatively, private speed-

boats can also be hired at the pier for around B1,000 one way.

Getting Around
The easiest way to explore the island is on the local three-wheel motorcycle called *samlor*. Drivers can be hired for a 3- to 4-hour tour of the island for about B250. Agree on the number of places you want to stop at first. A single journey to anywhere on the island costs around B30.

Motorcycles can also be rented (B250–300 per day) if you wish to explore on your own.

PATTAYA

Getting There
By Air
U-Tapao Airport in Sattahip, about 1 hour east of Pattaya, caters largely to chartered flights from Europe as well as domestic flights. **Bangkok Airways** has once-a-day connections to both Phuket and Ko Samui.

By Taxi
Most hotels in Pattaya can arrange private transfers from Bangkok. Or you can book a taxi in Bangkok for the 147km (91-mile) trip to Pattaya. The ride takes 1½–2 hours

and costs around B1,200 (including toll fees). Be sure to agree on the rate before boarding the taxi. There is also a limousine service direct from Suvarnabhumi International Airport direct to Pattaya (from B2,600).

By Bus
Air conditioned buses leave every 40 minutes daily (5am–11pm) from Bangkok's **Ekamai Bus Terminal** to Pattaya (B120). The journey takes around 2 hours.

By Minivan
Shared minivans leave Suvarnabhumi Airport thrice daily: 9am, noon and 7pm (B300 per person).

Getting Around
The easiest way to get around Pattaya is by *songthaew* trucks that run along Thanon Pattaya 2 and Thanon Hat Pattaya (Beach Road). The fare starts at B10, but for longer rides towards Naklua and Jomtien, the fare goes up to B50. Motorcycle taxis are common, but be sure to agree on the rate first. Motorcycles (B200–700 per day) or cars (B800–2,500 per day) can be rented from private operators or **Avis** at the Dusit hotel (tel: 0-3836 1627). There is also the **Pattaya Beach Bus**, which runs between Pattaya and Jomtien. Tickets cost B20.

KO SAMET

Getting There

By Taxi

Taxis in Bangkok can be booked for the 200km (124-mile) journey to Ban Phe pier in Rayong province. The ride will take approximately 3 hours and will cost B1,500–1,800. Be sure to bargain the rate before boarding. Near the 7-11 store opposite Ban Phe pier, taxis await passengers for rides back to Bangkok, Pattaya (B500–1,000) or on to Trat (B1,500), the jump-off point for Ko Chang.

By Bus

Air-conditioned buses leave every hour (5am–9pm) from **Ekamai Bus Terminal** in Bangkok for Ban Phe pier in Rayong. The journey takes around 3–3½ hours and the fare is B175 one way.

By Minivan

Private tour companies in Bangkok operate tourist minivans departing from Thanon Khao San, Victory Monument and designated tour agents and hotels in Bangkok to Ban Phe pier for about B250 per person. Return trips can be arranged with resorts and tour counters on Ko Samet or at travel agents near Ban Phe pier. Typically, operators will try to cram the van full before leaving (11 pax), which may well add a considerable delay to your journey.

By Boat

Fishing boats leave Ban Phe pier, across from the bus station, every hour or when there are enough passengers. Decide which beach you will be staying at before picking your boat. The journey to the main Na Dan pier on Ko Samet takes around 30 minutes and costs B50 one way. Some boats continue on to Ao Wong Deuan, but there are also direct boats from Ban Phe to Ao Wong Deuan, the 40-minute ride costing B60. If

there are a few of you, consider hiring a speedboat as it is much faster. Expect to pay about B1,000 to Hat Sai Kaew or Ao Phai, and about B1,200 to Ao Wong Deuan.

Getting Around

With Ko Samet only 6km (4 miles) from north to south, walking to most places is relatively easy. The island has little in the way of paved roads and *songthaew* trucks are the only transportation option. These trucks shuttle visitors from Na Dan pier to the beaches for B10–50, depending on distance. Motorcycles are available for hire (B100–300 per day) but this is quite pointless with little more than one dirt track running down the centre of the island.

KO CHANG

Getting There

By Air

Bangkok Airways operates three daily flights from Bangkok to Trat airport. The journey takes less than an hour. From the airport take a 20-minute taxi or *songthaew* ride to Laem Ngop pier. Larger hotels will arrange transportation (by minivan from the airport and boat to Ko Chang) for around B200–250 per person for shared transfers and considerably more for private transfers (B750 and up).

By Taxi

Travelling by road from Bangkok is not the best way of getting to Ko Chang because of the 300km (190-mile) distance. You can arrange for a taxi in Bangkok to make the 5-hour ride to Laem Ngop pier in Trat Province for a flat rate of B3,000. Make sure you agree on the rate beforehand to avoid confusion at the end of the journey. For the return journey to Bangkok, private taxis are

ABOVE: Ko Chang ferry.

available near Laem Ngop pier for around the same price.

By Bus

Air-conditioned buses leave daily from Bangkok's **Ekamai Bus Terminal** for Trat every 90 minutes between 6am and 11.30pm. Tickets cost B230–290 one way, depending on the route. In addition there are five daily bus departures from **Northeastern (Mo Chit) Bus Terminal** between 6am and 11pm. The ride takes around 6 hours. From Trat bus station take a *songthaew* truck to Laem Ngop pier, about 17km (11 miles) away.

By Minivan

Private tour companies in Bangkok operate tourist minivans departing from Thanon Khao San, Victory Monument and designated tour agents and hotels in Bangkok to Laem Ngop pier in Trat for about B500–600 per person. Return trips can be arranged with resorts and tour counters on Ko Chang or at travel agents near Laem Ngop pier. Typically, operators will try to cram the van full before leaving (11 pax), adding considerable delay to your journey.

By Boat

Passenger and car ferries leave from three different piers in Laem Ngop. The journey on the passenger ferry to Tha Dan Kao pier on Ko Chang (which most people use) takes 50 minutes and costs B80 one way, B120 return. During the peak season from Nov to Apr, boats depart hourly from 6am to 5pm; at other times of the year, departures are once every two hours. Larger car ferries depart from other points on Laem Ngop, and they accept non-vehicular passengers as well.

Getting Around

With one paved road that runs almost all round the island, *song-thaews* are the only way of getting around. From Tha Dan Kao pier in Ko Chang, expect to pay B30 to Hat Sai Khao, B50 to Ao Khlong Phrao and Hat Kai Bae, B70 to Hat Tha Nam. Motorcycles (B250–300 per day) and cars (B1,000–2,000 per day) can be rented, but be careful as there are steep hills on both sides of the island.

ACCOMMODATION LISTINGS

KO SI CHANG

Sichang Palace
81 Moo 1, Th. Asdang
Tel: 0-3821 6276/9
www.sichangpalace.com
Slightly over-the-top appearance, this is as upmarket as it gets on the island. Near the pier in town. All rooms have air conditioning, TV and hot water, and there's also a pool, coffee shop, nightclub and billiards room. (60 rooms) **$**

Tiewpai Park Resort
8 Moo 2
Tel: 0-3821 6084
Popular with backpackers, this friendly place in the heart of the island has a variety of room types, from dormitory beds to Thai-style air-conditioned rooms with en suite bathrooms. Island tours by boat and motorcycles for hire (17 bungalows) **$**

PATTAYA

Amari Orchid Resort & Tower
Th. Hat Pattaya (Beach Rd) North Pattaya
Tel: 0-3841 8418
www.amari.com
Offering two options, the low-rise 4-star Garden Wing and the 5-star Ocean Tower Wing, which features oversized 50-sq-metre (538-sq-foot) ocean-view rooms. Whichever option guests choose, they will have access to a slew of facilities, including free-form and lap swimming pools, fitness centre, spa and seven food and beverage outlets, including the hip Mantra Restaurant & Bar. (529 rooms) **$$**

Birds & Bees Resort
366/11 Th. Phra Tamnak Soi 4
Tel: 0-3825 0556-8.
www.cabbagesandcondoms.co.th
Owned by former Senator Mechai, whose campaigning on Aids awareness has earned him the title "Mr Condom". The ocean and treetop suites all have teak decks and private jacuzzis, and there's a large sea-view pool surrounded by a pretty garden. Staying here means you also contribute money to help Thailand's less fortunate. (54 rooms) **$$**

Dusit Thani Pattaya
240/2 Th. Hat Pattaya
Tel: 0-3842 5611
www.dusit.com
This beach-front resort, with lush gardens, resplendent lobby and atrium, simply exudes class. The hotel directly fronts two beaches and maximises sea views from its well-appointed rooms. Facilities are very good, with a gym, lagoon pool and award-winning Devarana Spa. (462 rooms) **$$$**

Hard Rock Hotel Pattaya
Th. Hat Pattaya (Beach Rd)
Tel: 0-3042 8755
www.pattaya.hardrockhotels.net
Beachside fun in a contemporary setting. The rooms are fairly standard, with the flashy pop colours and music memorabilia typical of all Hard Rock outlets. The vast hotel pool comes complete with thatched pavilions for you to lie beneath, while Hard Rock's health club is the perfect foil to Pattaya's entertainment scene. (323 rooms) **$$**

Marsi Pattaya
378/39 Soi Kasetsin 2, Th. Phra Tamnak
Tel: 0-3825 0722
www.dynastyinn.com
This resort on a quiet street in the pleasant Phra Tamnak hill area has no sea view but is good value, with a secluded stretch of beach just a short walk away. Rooms are spacious, and were recently renovated. There's a large pool and friendly

PRICE CATEGORIES

Price categories show the starting price for a double room without breakfast and taxes:
$ = under US$70
$$ = US$70–130
$$$ = US$130–250
$$$$ = over US$250

staff. (49 rooms) **$**

Mercure Pattaya
484 Soi 15, Moo 10,
Th. Pattaya 2
Tel: 0-3842 5050.
www.mercurepattaya.com
Part of a reputable chain
known for its reliable
quality, this large hotel in
the heart of downtown
Pattaya is elegant con-
sidering its low rates.
The rooms are equipped
with modern conven-
iences. (245 rooms) **$$**

**Pullman Pattaya
Hotel G**
445/3 Moo 5, Wongamart, Th.
Naklua
Tel: 0-3841 1940
www.accorhotels.com
Set right on Wongamart
beach at Naklua Bay, this
large, modern-looking
hotel is popular with well-
heeled Asian travellers. A
stylish blend of tradi-
tional and contemporary
Asian design, the well-
equipped hotel features

two swimming pools and
three restaurants plus
conference facilities.
(374 rooms) **$$**

Rabbit Resort
318/84 Moo 12, Soi Dongtan
Police Station, Jomtien
Tel: 0-3825 1730
www.rabbitresort.com
Set slightly back from
Dongtan beach in Jomt-
ien, Rabbit is a Thai-style
resort set among pretty
gardens. The rooms are
decorated with tradi-
tional local furniture and
fabrics, giving the place
a homely feel. There are
two swimming pools, a
restaurant and a beach
grill. (49 rooms) **$$**

Sheraton Pattaya
437 Th. Phra Tamnak
Tel: 0-3825 9888
www.sheraton.com/pattaya
This hotel is in a
secluded spot on the
Phra Tamnak headland
looking directly out to Ko
Larn. More like a private

country club than a typi-
cal hotel, the beautifully-
landscaped resort has
calming water elements
and even its own beach.
Many of the rooms have
their own ocean-facing
sala (pavilion), and the
Amburaya Spa is there
for body-tuning. (156
rooms) **$$$**

The Siam Guest House
528/26 Moo 10, Soi 12, Th.
Pattaya 2
Tel: 0-3842-4245. **$**
www.siamgh.com
Close to the bars and
shops off Beach Road,
but far enough away for
peace when you need to
sleep. The simple, clean
rooms, with Wi-fi access
and satellite TV, are a
bargain at this price. (46
rooms) **$**

The Zign Hotel
555/65 Moo 5, 12 Th. Naklua
Tel: 0-3890 9800
www.thezignhotel.com
Contemporary Thai

ABOVE: morning drinks.

architecture and interior
design fuse modern
materials with natural
elements in this stun-
ning villa and tower
resort. Built around the
themes of stone, wicker
and terracotta, with
warm orange walls and
earthy colours. Its lead-
ing-edge design contin-
ues in its eight bars and
restaurants, as well as
its Zphora Spa. (959
rooms) **$$**

KO SAMET

Ao Prao Resort
60 Moo 4, Ao Phrao
Tel: 0-3864 4101/5
www.kohsametaoprao.com
This upscale resort is on
the only beach on the
sunset side of Ko
Samet. It therefore sees
fewer visitors, adding to
its exclusivity. The ele-
gant bungalows come
with modern conven-
iences, including cable
TV. (48 rooms) **$$**

Lima Coco
40/1 Moo 4, Ao Prao
Tel: 0-2129 1140
www.limasamed.com
This pioneer of upscale
Ko Samet accommoda-
tion may be in need of a
new lick of paint, but it is
still popular with Bang-
kokians and sees many

return visitors. Five
types of simple but ele-
gant villa offer plenty of
choice. (32 rooms) **$$**

Paradee Resort
Ao Kiew
Tel: 0-3864 4285/7
www.paradeeresort.com
Stunning contemporary
Thai-designed luxury
villa resort aimed at cou-
ples wanting to get away
from it all. All villas are
more than 100 sq
metres (1076 sq feet)
and feature sundecks
with garden or sea
views. Excellent spa on
site. (40 rooms) **$$$$**

Sai Kaew Beach
Resort
8/1 Moo 4, Hat Sai Kaew
Mobile tel: 0-3864 4195
www.samedresorts.com /saikaew

Decked out in summery
blues and whites, this
small-scale contempo-
rary resort is part of the
growing Samed Resorts
Group. Situated at the
northern tip of Hat Sai
Kaew, the resort has
rooms, cottages and vil-
las set either beachside
or around the swimming
pool. Ask about their
long-stay promotions.
(158 rooms) **$$$**

Tubtim Resort
13/15 Moo 4, Ao Tub Tim
Tel: 0-3864 4025.
www.tubtimresort.com
This rustic resort is a
longtime favourite with
Bangkok's youngsters.
Family-run, it offers
both cheap wooden
huts and concrete air-

conditioned bungalows.
The beach is one of the
prettiest, and the
evening barbecue
beside the bar fills up
fast. (75 rooms) **$**

Le Vimarn Cottages &
Spa
Moo 4, Ao Phrao
Tel: 0-3864 4104/7
www.levimarncottage.com
This teak-built resort
with sea-facing infinity
pool is located on a hillside overlooking the bay
on the more secluded
sunset side of the
island. There are three
types of cottage and villa
to choose from, deco-
rated in an elegant
blend of traditional and
contemporary. (31
rooms) **$$$**

KO CHANG

Amari Emerald Cove Resort
88/8 Moo 4, Ao Khlong Phrao
Tel: 0-3955 2000.
www.amari.com
A part of the successful Amari chain, this is one of the island's biggest and best sleeping options. The rooms are tastefully done up in a stylish contemporary Asian-design. The beachfront pool is large and rectangular, so suited to swimming laps. Also on site is the excellent Breeze Spa, a PADI dive centre, three restaurants and activities including Thai boxing, dance and cooking classes. (165 rooms) $$

Amber Sands
51/3 Moo 2 Dan Kao
Tel: 0-3958 6177
www.ambersandsbeachresort.com.
Amid the ongoing upmarket developments on Ko Chang, it is sometimes a good option to stay on the quiet side of the island. This smart resort with just seven rooms surrounding an infinity pool is right on the beach. All rooms are en suite, with air conditioning. They offer ferry collections and returns, and car and bike hire if you need to get away from the tranquillity. The beach-side restaurant serves Thai and western food. (7 rooms) $

Bang Bao Sea Hut
53 Bang Bao Village
Tel: 0-3955 8098
www.kohchang-seahut.com
A quirky setting with rooms on stilts on a private pier, with satellite TV, fridge and Wi-fi. Not much in the way of facilities, it's really the views and sea breezes you come for, but there is a fun waterslide at the end of the jetty. Organises a host of activities for guests, from snorkelling to mountain-biking, and they have free kayaks for trips to the beach. (14 rooms) $$

Barali Beach Resort
77 Moo 4, Ao Khlong Phrao
Tel: 0-3955 7091
www.baraliresort.com
These contemporary Asian-style villas come with TV, stereo, hairdryer and safe; some have beautiful sunken bath-tubs. The infinity pool almost touches the ocean. There is also a spa, pool bar, restaurant and small library. (40 rooms) $$$

Bhumiyama Beach Resort
Hat Tha Nam
Tel: 08-1860 4623
www.bhumiyama.com
The only upmarket resort to be set up on the backpacker retreat of Lonely Beach, this pleasant resort is built around a lovely tropical beach-front garden with ponds and a central swimming pool. Away from the main building, the better rooms are in two-storey houses with Thai accents. (46 rooms) $$

Centara Koh Chang Tropicana Beach Resort & Spa
26/3 Moo 4, Hat Khlong Phrao
Tel: 0-3955 7122.
www.kohchangtropicana.net
Lush gardens abound in this stylish eco-resort with wooden elevated walkways stretching over the sea. Thai-Balinese-style villas have cosy interiors, except for the bathrooms, which are a bit over the top. Features a beach-front restaurant with excellent barbecues every night and a good spa with daily yoga classes. (157 rooms) $$$

The Dewa Koh Chang
24/1/1 Moo 4, Hat Khlong Phrao
Tel: 0-3955 7339.
www.thedewakohchang.com
This high-end resort combines Ko Chang's tropical-paradise vibe with chic design and stellar facilities. Spectacular sea vistas, live acoustic music on the beach, regular shuttles to Khlong Phlu waterfall and Hat Sai Khao, and yummy Thai food all add to its allure. (59 rooms) $$$

Panviman Resort Koh Chang
8/15 Ao Khlong Phrao
Tel: 0-3955 1290
www.panviman.com
A rather grand resort, with sister properties in Chiang Mai and Ko Phangan. Its contemporary take on traditional

BELOW: poolside, Amari Emerald Cove Resort.

PRICE CATEGORIES

Price categories show the starting price for a double room without breakfast and taxes:
$ = under US$70
$$ = US$70–130
$$$ = US$130–250
$$$$ = over US$250

Thai architectural form extends from the capacious lobby to the large rooms. Bliss yourself out at the Viman Spa or, for a more adventurous alternative, hire a sea kayak for some marine exploring. (50 rooms) **$$**

The Spa Resort Koh Chang
15/4 Moo 4, Baan Salak Kok
Tel: 0-3955 3091
www.thespakohchang.com
Recharge your batteries at this holistic eco-resort. Detox and fasting programmes are available and bolster the yoga, meditation and massage sessions. Swim in the chemical-free pool and dine at the fine organic, vegetarian restaurant called Radiance, which was apparently

ranked by UK's *Restaurant* magazine as one of the world's 50 best restaurants. The resort even has its own dental clinic. (26 rooms) **$**

KO MAK

Koh Mak Resort
Moo 2, Ao Kao
Tel: 0-3950 1013
www.kohmakresort.com
Set amid pristine clipped lawns and coconut groves, accommodation at this resort ranges from basic rooms to seaside villas with outdoor jacuzzis and huge windows over the Gulf of Thailand. Dine alfresco at the jetty, or at the resort restaurant, which

serves up tasty Thai and Western dishes. (31 rooms) **$**

Monkey Island Resort
Mobile tel: 08-9501 6030
www.monkeyislandkohmak.com
This funky resort on a pretty beach has dive and snorkelling facilities and throws seafood barbecues. The accommodation consists of large 2-bedroom air-conditioned Gorilla Huts, smaller fan-cooled Chimpanzee Huts with outdoor showers, and the B600 shared bathroom Baboon Huts. Head to the Orangutan Bar for sundowners. Good for people who like a party atmosphere and jamming along to informal live music. (29 rooms) **$**

Plubpla Koh Mak Retreat
50/5 Moo 2, Ao Pai Beach
Tel: 087-802 7575
www.kohmakretreat.com
Wooden walkways link a series of smart villas beside the beach, some with jacuzzis. There's a good Thai restaurant, an infinity pool and free bicycles if you're feeling energetic. There's also free (but slow) internet access. (18 rooms) **$**

> ### PRICE CATEGORIES
>
> Price categories show the starting price for a double room without breakfast and taxes:
> **$** = under US$70
> **$$** = US$70–130
> **$$$** = US$130–250
> **$$$$** = over US$250

R E S T A U R A N T   L I S T I N G S

KO SI CHANG

Thai and Western

Pan & David
167 Moo 3,
Th. Makhaamthaew
Tel: 0-3821 6075
www.ko-sichang.com

Open: Wed–Mon L and D
Situated beside the quiet road that leads to the summer palace, this ever-popular restaurant is run by American expat David and his Thai wife Pan. The simple open-sided eatery has garden seating and is backed by the seaview Rim Talay resort. The wide menu here

includes breakfast options as well as fresh seafood, Italian, French and Thai as well as vegetarian dishes. A small wine selection is also available. **$**

PATTAYA

International

Bruno's
306/63 Chateau Dale Plaza,
Th. Thappraya
Tel: 0-3836 4600
www.brunos-pattaya.com
Open: daily L and D.
One of Pattaya's most popular expat-friendly

bistros, Bruno's offers a warm, welcoming vibe. Expect well-presented French-European dishes like pan-seared scallops and rack of lamb Provençal, and an extensive wine list. **$$$**

Cafe Des Amis
391/6, Thappraya Soi 11

Tel: 08-4026 4989
www.cafedesamispattaya.com
Open: Mon–Sat D.
This smart, friendly place has a good classic European menu. Diners might start with lobster bisque or beef carpaccio and move through to coq au vin and then

chocolate mousse. It's slightly out of the way, but they have a pick up service for B200 a trip anywhere in Jomtien or Pattaya. **$$$**

Café New Orleans
Pattayaland Soi 2
Tel: 038 710 805-6
Open: daily 5pm–mid-

night.
Located at the centre of the red light district, there's a frisson to the ambiance along with the standard Cajun dishes like clam chowder, blackened chicken and baby back ribs. Finish with Mississippi mud cake. **$$$**

Casa Pascal
Moo 10, Th. Pattaya 2
Tel: 0-3872 3660
www.restaurant-in-pattaya.com
Open: daily B, L and D, Sun brunch.
Centrally located opposite the Royal Garden Plaza. This Swiss-run place has a mixed European menu, with a nudge towards Germanic in dishes like Wiener schnitzel and pork knuckle with sauerkraut, plus steaks and even the occasional curry. **$$$**

Manhattans Restaurant and Bar
Nirvana Place, Th. Thappraya
Tel: 0-3825 9790
www.manhattans-pattaya.com
Open: Mon–Sat 5–10.30pm.
This resort has a plush interior, with a cocktail bar, as the name suggests, and a pianist, along with a modern French restaurant and tapas-style bistro-bar. Three courses might start with fresh oysters or tuna and *wakame*, followed by imported steak or lobster bisque and a dessert of chocolate soufflé. **$$$–$$$$**

Mantra Restaurant and Bar
240 Moo 5, Th. Hat Pattaya
Tel: 0-3842 9591
www.mantra-pattaya.com
Open: daily 5pm–1am.
A modern dining experience with a backdrop of funky lighting, polished concrete, glass, black lacquer and red velvet. Open interactive kitchens offer seven cuisines: Chinese, Japanese, Western, Indian, Mediterranean, seafood and charcoal-grill, and they serve a popular Sunday brunch. The signature starter of Mantra Quintetto carpaccio is hard to beat. Later in the evening, the bar is a great chill-out spot. **$$$–$$$$**

Sportsman Pub & Restaurant
482 Moo 10, Soi 13, Th. Pattaya 2
Tel: 0-3871 0609
www.sportsmanspub.com
Open: daily B, L and D.
This busy British-style alehouse is just as well known for its hearty menu of *farang*-friendly favourites as it is for its range of imported beers. Fill up here on breakfasts, pies, burgers, steaks and the all-you-can-eat Sunday roast-beef lunch. **$$–$$$**

Thai

Cabbages & Condoms
366/11, Th. Phra Tamnak Soi 4
Tel: 0-3825 0556/8
www.cabbagesandcondoms.co.th
Open: daily B, L and D.
Named after its owner, former Senator Mechai, whose work on birth control has earned him the nickname "Mr Condom", this restaurant is part of the Birds & Bees Resort. It serves OK-to-good Thai standards and has hillside views out to sea. **$–$$**

King Seafood
94 Walking Street
Tel: 0-3842 9459
Open: daily 2pm–1am.
Thai restaurant built on

ABOVE: fried snapper with chilli sauce.

stilts over the waves, with lobster, crab, shrimp and fish either live in tanks or displayed on ice, so you can choose your own. A lively place with lots of communal dining. **$$**

Mumarol
83/4 Naklua Banglamung
Tel: 0-3823-4352
Open: daily B, L and D.
Fantastic deep-fried sea bass, curried crab and spicy seafood salad with a view of fishing boats, old sea barges and the bamboo stakes of mussel farms out in the bay. **$–$$**

Nang Nual
Walking Street
Tel: 0-3842 8177
Open: L and D.
This well-known seafood establishment has a prime location, on beautiful Pattaya Bay. It certainly isn't glamorous, but for freshly caught fish and shellfish cooked Thai style, it's unbeatable. The sea food is laid out on ice or live in tanks for you to choose and order in a variety of cooking styles. **$$–$$$**

PIC Kitchen
Fl 2, 255 Th. Pattaya 2, Soi 5.
Tel: 0-3842 8374
www.pic-kitchen.com
This long-time favourite in Pattaya offers a Thai experience with floor seating in one of three garden-facing *salas* (pavilions), or regular table dining in air-conditioned comfort. Decent Thai such as duck red curry and deep fried chicken in pandanus leaf. **$$–$$$**

Other Asian

Ali Baba Tandoori & Curry Restaurant
1/13-14 Th. Pattaya Klang
Tel: 0-3842 9262
Open: daily L and D.
One of Pattaya's oldest Indian restaurants, this is something of an institution. Emphasis is on the subtle balance of spices, rather than blasting everything with chilli. The extensive

PRICE CATEGORIES

Price per person for a three-course meal without drinks:
$ = under US$10
$$ = US$10–25
$$$ = US$25–50
$$$$ = over US$50

menu has more than 70 dishes, including 16 different types of bread. The kebabs are sublime. **$$–$$$**
Le Saigon Bayview
Fl 23, Pattaya Hill Resort, 329/245 Moo 12, Th. Phra Tamnak Soi 2
Tel: 0-3825 0329
www.lesaigonbayview.com

Open: daily D. There are great views of Jomtien and Pattaya Bay from tables inside and out at this rooftop restaurant. The menu bolsters its Vietnamese dishes with a choice of Western and Thai, and it's open from late afternoon for drinks. **$$–$$$**

ABOVE: Thai fruits

KO SAMET

Ko Samet doesn't have much in the way of quality stand-alone restaurants. Almost all eateries and bars are contained within the small resorts.

Thai and Western

Breeze Restaurant
Ao Prao Resort, Ao Phrao
Tel: 0-3864 4101/5
www.kohsametaoprao.com
Open: daily B, L and D.
If you are looking for a

more elegant dining experience away from the slew of beach-barbecue food on offer, then this place is about as good as it gets. The selection of Thai food, steaks and international dishes is well presented but by no means a gastronomic epiphany. **$$$**
Naga Bungalows
Ao Hin Khok
Tel: 0-3864 4034
Open: daily B, L and D.

A longtime favourite with backpackers, this restaurant-bar is run by an Englishwoman and is known for its bakery and late-night revelry. The restaurant is located up the hill and serves decent Western breakfasts as well as sandwiches, pizzas, burgers and Thai dishes. Overlooking the beach, the bar gets busy during the evening happy hour. **$–$$**

Samed Villa
8/4, Ao Phai
Tel: 0-3864 4094
www.samedvilla.com
Open: daily B, L and D.
Under Swiss ownership, this resort is very popular with Bangkok expats. The beachside restaurant has a large selection of Thai and Western dishes, including barbecues of seafood and steaks. The service here is prompt and friendly. **$$**

KO CHANG

Thai and Western

Blue Lagoon
Ao Khlong Phrao
Mobile tel: 0-1940 0649
Open: daily B, L and D.
The lagoon certainly isn't very blue, but the Thai food here is considered among the island's finest. Also serves some decent international fare. Runs a cookery school and has some bungalows, too. **$**
Hungry Elephant
Opp Sky Bar, between Hat Sai Khao and Hat Khai Muk
Tel: 08-9985-8433
Open: daily L and D.
Few tourists venture to

this unassuming streetside restaurant, but it is well known among Bangkok expats. Run by a friendly Thai couple, the menu has Thai staples, and some good French dishes are on offer, too. Delicious steaks. **$$**
Invito Al Cibo
Hat Sai Khao
Tel: 0-3132 3583
Open: daily L and D.
Set in a beautiful cliffside location overlooking the sea, this friendly restaurant has good standard Italian and Thai classics. So if the mood takes, you could eat bruschetta, crab

curry, fried rice, homemade pasta and pizzas (cooked in an open wood-fired oven) all at the same table. And it's lovely at sunset. **$$$**
Iyara Seafood
24 Moo 4, Hat Khlong Phrao
Tel: 0-3955 1353
Open: daily B, L and D.
The sea views here are superb, but it may take you a while to notice because you'll be too busy tucking into its delicious seafood. The fish could only be fresher if it jumped on to your plate. Try the deep-fried kingfish with spicy mango salad, squid fried with garlic and black pepper,

or popular classics such as barbecued prawns. **$$–$$$**
Kai Bae Marina
Hat Kai Bae
Mobile tel: 0-7044 0385
Open: daily B, L and D.
Under Austrian ownership, this restaurant has a no-frills decor, but it fills up with eager customers every evening.

PRICE CATEGORIES

Price per person for a three-course meal without drinks:
$ = under US$10
$$ = US$10–25
$$$ = US$25–50
$$$$ = over US$50

The appeal is the broad menu that includes a Thai seafood section, as well as pizzas, steaks and dishes with a definite northern-European bias. Whatever your choice, it's all decent, honest food. **$$**

Saffron on the Sea
13/10 Moo 4, Hat Khai Muk
Tel: 0-3955 1253
Open: daily L and D.
Located not far from White Sands Beach, this cosy restaurant is attached to a small resort and has good sea views. They serve very good Thai standard dishes such as *somtam* and *massaman* currys and other several fish and seafood dishes cooked in a variety of ways. **$$**

Salak Phet Seafood
43 Moo 2, Salak Phet

Tel: 08-1429 9983
Open: daily B, L and D.
Considered by many to be the best seafood eatery on the island, this restaurant and resort is perched on stilts in the southeast of the island and is part of the fishing village of the same name. A great option for crab, squid, shrimp, and fish that you can choose yourself from the sunken nets below the pier. Steamed clams and prawn tempura on the menu. **$-$$**

Tonsai Restaurant
Hat Sai Khao
Mobile tel: 0-9895 7229
Open: daily L and D.
Located on the opposite side of the road from the beach, the novel setting of this restaurant – a banyan tree-house – is what initially attracts

customers, but it's the delicious selection of Thai and fusion cuisine at bargain prices that keeps diners coming back again for more. This is a very chilled-out establishment; lie back on cushions and sample cocktails from the extensive list before munching on tasty salads and curries. A great way to spend a lazy afternoon. **$-$$**

Vegetarian

Radiance Restaurant
Spa Koh Chang Resort, 15/4 Moo 4, Baan Salak Kok
Tel: 0-3955 3091
www.thespakohchang.com
Open: daily L and D.
Feast on what is possibly the healthiest eating option available on Ko Chang at this resort-op-

erated dining venue. Choose from a range of flavour-packed, MSG-free organic vegetarian food cooked in either Thai or Western style. **$$-$$$**

BELOW: red Thai curry.

ACTIVITIES

Nightlife
Dance Bars and Clubs

Club Insomnia Pattaya: Th. Hat Pattaya (Walking St), tel: 08-1177-7085. A large venue with a good sound system playing general electro and house music. They have occasional visiting DJs.

Lucifer Disko: Th. Hat Pattaya (Walking St); tel: 0 3871 0216. Lucifer opens on to Walking Street with a Latin bar in front drawing a slightly older clientele, while in the back is the pumped-up, hell-themed nightclub playing mainstream R&B and hip-hop. They also have live bands.

Marine: Th. Hat Pattaya (Walking St); tel:0-3842 8583; www.facebook.com/marinedisco. Trashy and loud, in a cavernous room, this is one of Pattaya's oldest clubs. The music is mainly Euro-dance and techno with live bands mixed in.

Mixx Discotheque: 311 Bali-Hai Plaza; tel: 0-3825 2790. A smallish venue heaving with action and a varied DJ schedule of house, trance and hip-hop, played in separate rooms. It's very popular and also stylish, which is why it's also among the more expensive spots in town.

Bars and Pubs

Hopf Brew House: 219 Th. Hat Pattaya (Beach Rd); tel: 0-3871 0653. Popular microbrewery that sees a steady flow of Pattaya's

more respectable types who come for the wood-fired oven pizzas and Italian and European dishes. In-house band livens things up.

Pattaya Beer Garden: Th. Hat Pattaya (Beach Rd); tel: 0-3871 0754; www.pattayabeergarden.com. A family-friendly bar with outdoor tables on the seafront, located just before Walking Street. They have lots of seafood choices within the usual Thai and pub menu, served from breakfast to dinner, and a standard bar list.

Rosie O'Grady's: J Soi 7, Pattaya Beach Rd; tel: 0-3836 1686; www.rosieogradyspattaya.com. A more middle-aged crowd at this standard Irish-themed pub with the usual mix of British ales, sport on TV and quiz nights. Lots of pub grub available, too.

Live Music Venues

The Blues Factory: 131/3 Moo 10, Soi Lucky Star (off Walking St); www.thebluesfactorypattaya.com. One of Pattaya's best music venues and suitable for all, including families. Features live blues and rock nightly by resident musicians, including Lam Morrison, the Blues Machine and the Rock Machine.

The Jazz Pit: Fl 2, 255 Th. Pattaya 2 Soi 5; tel: 0-3842 8374; www.pic-kitchen.com. With a logo claiming "it's not for everybody", this music bar with a cool, laid-back vibe adjoins the popular PIC Kitchen restaurant. Live bands and jam sessions feature resident ensembles and overseas acts.

Hard Rock Café: Th. Hat Pattaya (Beach Rd); tel: 0-3842 8755; www.hardrockhotelpattaya.com. This global brand differs little from place to place, except on Saturdays, when the foam party puts a soapy sheen on the merriment. House bands play from 10pm.

Kathoey Cabaret

For a night full of sequinned fun, Pattaya is well known for its Vegas-style lip-synching shows at Tiffany's, Alcazar and Simon Cabaret. The *kathoey* performers are cross-dressers and transgenders who have undergone various stages of sex change surgery.

Alcazar: 78/14 Th. Pattaya 2; tel: 08-1781 1703; www.alcazarthailand. com. Pattaya's second-most recognised *kathoey* cabaret offers a spectacular show in a 1,200-seat venue. Four nightly shows at 5pm, 6.30pm, 8pm and 9.30pm.

Tiffany's: 464 Moo 9, Th. Pattaya 2; tel: 0-3842 1700/5; www.tiffany-show.co.th. Probably Thailand's most famous *kathoey* or "lady-boy" (transsexual) cabaret routine, with three nightly shows (6pm, 7.30pm, 9pm; B500–600) in the 1,000-seat auditorium. Presents dance extravaganzas inspired by Broadway, historic Thailand and China.

Gay Venues

It's hard to miss Pattaya's main concentration of gay activity, with a big neon sign across the width of Pattayaland Soi 3 flashing "Boyz Town". For more information, visit www.utopia-asia.com.

Le Café Royale's Piano Bar: 325/102–9 Pattayaland Soi 3; tel: 0-3842 3515; www.caferoyale-pattaya.com. A hotel bar-restaurant in the heart of Pattaya's gay nightlife zone, they have live music, with an open mic if you want to perform, and a 24-hour coffee shop.

Copa Show Bar: 325/106 Pattayaland Soi 3; tel: 0-3848 8694; www.copapattaya.com. The show bar in this hotel has nightly cabaret and dancers trying to perform in a large water tank, which is more hilarious than titillating.

Shopping

Pattaya is the Eastern Seaboard's best shopping option, with several malls and a couple of outdoor tourist markets. Beyond the usual high-street brands, choices are basically limited to market-stall counterfeits and tacky tourist bric-a-brac, though there are replica-antiques and collectibles shops, and several recently opened galleries.

Shopping Malls

Central Festival Pattaya Beach: Th. Hat Pattaya (Beach Rd); tel: 0-3300 3999; www.centralfestival. co.th. Billed as "the largest beachfront lifestyle shopping complex in Asia", the mall has over 200 shops, including international fashion brands. There is also a wide selection of restaurants, plus cinemas (one of them open-air) and a bowling complex.

Mike Shopping Mall: Th. Hat Pattaya (Beach Rd); tel: 0-3841 2000. This long-standing mall was refurbished in 2012, and has lost a little of its market feel. It carries a wide range of goods, often of a more bargain-basement quality, but it is still good for essentials.

Royal Garden Plaza: Th. Hat Pattaya (Beach Rd); tel: 0-3871 0297; www.royalgardenplaza.co.th. Pattaya's original downtown mall has fewer exclusive brand names than Central Festival, but there is a good range of shops selling both imported and local goods. Also has eateries and a cinema.

Factory Outlet Malls

Fly Now: Th. Sukhumvit; tel: 0-3822 1744; www.fnoutlet.com. Located next to Cholchan Resort, Fly Now, one of Thailand's principal fashion houses, offers discounted export-quality clothing, household items, bedding and baskets.

Outlet Mall & Premium Outlet Pattaya: 666 and 888 Moo 12, Th. Thepprasit; tel: 0-3842 7764. Twinned American-style shopping complexes with discounts on legitimate name brands. Nothing too fancy but good basics from the likes of Lacoste, Levi's, Adidas, Diesel and such like.

Markets

Made in Thailand Market: Soi Buakhaow. Cheap clothing, handicrafts and the like. A good place to stock up on mementoes before heading home.

Thepprasit Night Market: Th. Thepprasit. Located close to the junction with Thanon Sukhumvit, this market runs from Friday to Sunday and sells the usual eclectic mass of knock-off watches, bags, T-shirts, interior decor.

World Gems Collection: 98 Moo 6, Th. North Pattaya; tel: 0-3841 2333; www.worldgemscollection.co.th. Claiming to be Asia's largest jewellery outlet, this monster showroom has a museum and a factory where you can see pieces being made. Thousands of stones and jewellery pieces to choose from.

Outdoor Activities
Diving

Mermaid's Scuba Diving Centre: 75/124 Moo 12, Th. Hat Jomtien (Jomtien Beach Rd); tel: 0-3823 2219; www.mermaiddive.com. A large, well-managed dive centre with three boats offering regular courses and fun dives, as well as speciality courses such as the PADI National Geographic Diver

Course and courses for disabled divers.

Pattaya Dive Centre: 219/3 Tipp Plaza, Th. Hat Pattaya (Beach Rd) Soi 6; tel: 0-3842 2133; www.dive-pattaya.com. A British-owned operation with over a decade's experience in Pattaya, and a retail shop, classroom and workshop all on site. Its PADI courses, from beginner to dive master, run at several locations including wrecks and islands.

Bungee Jumping

Pattaya Jungle Bungy Jump: 25/5 Moo 12 Thambon Nong Prue; tel: 08-9834 5712; www.thailand-bungy-jumping.com. They offer a 50-metre (165ft) launch over water, priced at B2,000 (inclusive of insurance and a "courage" certificate), and for B2,900 (including T-shirt, DVD and photos) you get a second jump free. There is also free transport for jumpers to and from the site.

Golf

The area around Pattaya has around 20 golf courses. At around B800–3,000, green fees are considerably lower than abroad, and most clubs are happy to allow non-members access. Check www.thaigolfer.com for more details.

Laem Chabang International Country Club: 106/8 Moo 4, Si Racha; tel: 0-3837 2273; www.laemchabanggolf.com. Rated one of the region's best, this 27-hole course (par 72) was designed by Jack Nicklaus.

Phoenix Golf Club: Th. Sukhumvit km 158, Pattaya; tel: 0-3823 9391. With sea views, this 27-hole course (par 72) was designed by Dennis Griffith and is ideal for long hitters.

St Andrews 2000: 5-9/36 Moo 7, Banchang; tel: 0-3803 0660; www.standrews2000golf.com. Designed by the late Scottish-born golf icon Desmond Muirhead, the course features elevated tees and greens, tight landing zones and split-elevation fairways. The 4th hole is an absolute beast.

Go-Karting

EasyKart: Bali Hai Pier; mobile tel: 08-6028 0880; www.easykart.net. Burn some rubber at either of two tracks here. Engine sizes are available from 100-270cc to suit both novice and experienced drivers, there's computerised timing and a bar-restaurant.

Horse Riding

Horseshoe Point: 100 Moo 9, Tambon Pong; tel: 0-3873 5050; www.horseshoepoint.com. Has two indoor riding rings, an outdoor sand field, jumping field, polo field and natural trails. Short 15-minute rides start at B350, 2-hour trail rides cost B1,650, and lessons run from B1,000. They also have accommodation.

Muay Thai

Fairtex Sports & Racquet Club: 179/185 Moo 5, Th. Pattaya-Nua; tel: 0-3825 3889; www.fairtexpattaya.com. Learn Muay (Thai boxing) Thai and a number of other sports, including tennis and rock climbing, at a centre that includes a spa, restaurants and accommodation.

Sailing

Ocean Marina Yacht Club: 274/1-9 Moo 4, Th. Sukhumvit km 157, Sattahip; tel: 0-3823

7311; www.oceanmarinayachtclub.com. Several yachts and catamarans are available to charter with crew for half-day, sunset or overnight cruises. Those inexperienced can arrange lessons, too.

Skydiving and Parachuting

Sky Dive Pattaya: Nong Kho Resevoir, Nong Kham, Sri Racha; tel: 08-5900 3412; www.thaiskyadventures.com. Located around 20km (12 miles) north of Pattaya, they offer tandem skydives and courses to qualify as a skydiver, daily except Tuesday. A single jump costs around B10,000, with group discounts available. Be aware the weather, particularly in the rainy season, may cause cancellations, although they estimate 300-plus jump days a year. Advance booking is required.

Thrill Rides

2Sky Pattaya Rocket Ball: Bali Hai Pier; www.2skypattaya.com. This exhilarating ride has two people strapped into a ball-shaped steel cage attached to an elasticated rope stretched tightly between two cranes. Then they catapult you 50 metres into the air at 100mph in one second, spinning as you go.

BELOW: therapist at Devarana spa.

Water Theme Park

Pattaya Park: 345 Hat Jomtien; tel: 0-3825 1201/8; www.pattaya park.com. Centred around Pattaya Tower, this water theme park, and amusement-ride area called "Funny Land", has plenty that will thrill both kids and adults. Ascend the tower for panoramic views, then descend by either the Sky Shuttle cable car, Speed Shuttle, or the adrenalin-pumping Tower Jump. The water park also has slides and a whirlpool.

Wind- and Kitesurfing

Blue Lagoon Water Sports Club: 24/20 Moo 2, Na Jomtiem Soi 14, Sattahip; tel: 08-5134 9588; www.bluelagoonpattaya.com. 3-day courses are offered in kitesurfing, which is probably what you'll need to get airborne. Alternatively, one day orientation courses help you decide whether the sport is for you. You can rent or buy equipment.

Zip Lining

Flight of the Gibbon: Khao Kheow Open Zoo, Sri Ratcha; tel: 08-9970 5511; www.treetopasia.com. They say that anyone of any age can fly, from five to 90 years, on 3km of zip lines that stretch through the rainforest canopy interspersed with 26 platforms. Sightings of giant squirrels, monkeys and barking deer are all part of the thrill. Extra challenges for various skills and ages include suspended bridges, spider nets and flying swings. It can take around three hours to complete, depending on numbers.

Spas

Cliff Spa: Royal Cliff Beach Resort, 353 Th. Phra Tamnak; tel: 0-3825 0421; www.royalcliff.com. Sits on a hill with wonderful views of the bay. It has 18 luxurious treatment suites plus a complete range of facilities. Spa Café serves healthy cuisine and herbal teas.
Devarana: Dusit Thani Pattaya, 240/2 Th. Hat Pattaya; tel:

0-3842 5611; www.devaranaspa.com. Devarana, meaning "garden in heaven", is one of Pattaya's most expensive spas, with plush suites for couples.
Oasis Spa Pattaya: 322 Th. Thappaya; tel: 0-3836 4070; www. pattayaoasis.com. A garden spa with seven private treatment rooms, saunas and steam rooms. Experience bliss with the signature Oasis Four Hands massage done by two therapists.

KO SAMET

Nightlife

Baywatch Bar: Ao Wong Deuan, mobile tel: 08-1826 7834. A beach-side bar with a choice of loungers on the sand or pub-like interior complete with a pool table. Imported beers, pizzas and a range of cocktails keep punters happy, as does Skype for those late-night and long-distance phone calls.
Lima Bar: Hat Sai Kaew, tel: 0-2129 1140. Enjoy lovely sunsets as DJs pump out mellow tunes. Part of Lima Bella resort.
Naga Bungalows: Hat Hin Kok;

tel: 0-3864 4034. Perched on a hillside looking down on to the beach, Naga has one of Ko Samet's busiest beach bars. Daily happy hour and decent upbeat music to chill to.
Silver Sand: Ao Phai, mobile tel: 0-1996 5720. With little else on offer late at night, the beach bar here is usually crammed to the hilt. Sprawling with beach mats, it occupies a large area, with the decibels cranked high, much to the ire of those trying to rest at the nearby hotels. Nightly fire-juggling entertainment draws the crowds, who don't seem put off by the somewhat moody bar staff.

Outdoor Activities
Diving

Ploy Scuba Diving: Hat Sai Kaew, mobile tel: 0-3864 4212; www. ploytalaygroup.com. Part of a reputable chain of dive shops. Professionally managed, with courses in several languages.
Samed Resorts PADI Dive Centre: Ao Prao Resort, Ao Phrao; tel: 0-3864 4100; www.samedresorts. com. This expensive resort-linked dive centre is well run and offers basic, open-water and advanced dive courses.

BELOW: Ko Chang windsurfing.

ABOVE: having fun snorkelling.

KO CHANG

Nightlife
Bars

Koh Chang Wine Gallery: Kai Bae Plaza, Hat Kai Bae; tel: 08-1668 7035. Wine wholesaler-cum-bar, with a huge range of good vino and bountiful beers that won't bust your wallet.

Lek Bar: Kai Bae Beach Resort, Hat Kai Bae; tel: 0-7065 4231. Also known as Nick's and Lek's bar, this popular hangout on Hat Kai Bae is run by a Brit and his Thai partner. Has a rustic-island look, with a garden and live music.

Oodies: 7/20 Hat Sai Khao, mobile tel: 08-1835 1271. Situated opposite the beach on Hat Sai Khao, this open-fronted music bar gets busy with a more mature set who gather here in the evenings to enjoy the live blues, folk, rock and Thai music.

Sabay Bar: 7/10 Moo 4, Hat Sai Khao; tel: 0-3955 1098. Whether you come here for sundowners, or later in the night to catch the live band while lying out on beach mats, Sabay is easily the busiest bar on Hat Sai Khao, possibly on the entire island. Nightly fire-juggling shows on the beach keep guests entertained.

Outdoor Activities
Adventure Parks

Tree Top Adventure Park: 115 Moo 1; tel: 08-4310 7600; www. treetopadventurepark.com. Zip through trees like Tarzan at this adventure park festooned with rope walkways, slides, high-level platforms and pulleys galore. Seriously good fun, but those with vertigo will go wobbly-kneed at the sight of these challenges.

Diving

Dolphin Divers: 38/7 Moo 4, Ao Khlong Phrao, mobile tel: 08-7028 1627; www.scubadivingkohchang.com. A small and friendly company with multilingual courses. Diving is done around the main island as well as nearby islands such as Ko Wai, Ko Rang, Ko Mak and Ko Kut.

Scandanavian Chang Dive Centre: 21/17 Moo 4, Ao Khlong Phrao, mobile tel: 0-3969 6530; www.changdiving.com. Professional and well-equipped outfit with courses from beginner to open water and beyond. Available from aged eight years and up.

Catamaran Sailing

Sea Adventures: Hat Sai Khao, mobile tel: 0-4728 6387. For a unique experience, book a seat on this 13 metre (40ft) British-owned catamaran. There are day-long tours (with snorkelling and barbecue lunch) off Ko Chang and several of the outer islands. Cost: B1,300 per person.

Trekking

Coco Dee Bo Tours: 16 /17 Moo 4, Chai Chet; tel: 08-7711 3390, www.cocodeebokohchang.com. This outfit runs a variety of activities including jungle treks, birdwatching and fishing trips.

Trekkers of Ko Chang: tel: 0-3952 5029, mobile tel: 08-1578 7513. Selling itself as an eco-friendly company, it has several full-day treks into Ko Chang's jungled interior, all led by experienced guides.

Elephant Treks

Jungleway: mobile tel: 0-9223 4795, www.jungleway.com. Offers a half-day tour where you get to see the elephants bathing and feeding at Ban Kwan Chang camp, followed by a 90-minute trek on elephant-back into the forest (B900 per person). Also organises treks to the island's interior.

Spas

Breeze Spa: Amari Emerald Cove Resort, Ao Khlong Phrao; tel: 0-3955 2000; www.amari.com. This could be the island's most expensive spa, but entering its soothing confines will transport you to seventh heaven. Excellent service.

Centara Koh Chang Tropicana Resort & Spa: 26/3 Moo 4, Ao Khlong Phrao; tel: 0-3955 7122; www.centarahotelsresorts.com. The spa at this tastefully designed resort offers several traditional Thai therapies as well as facials, scrubs and aromatherapy massages.

The Dewa Spa: The Dewa Koh Chang, Hat Klong Prao; tel: 0-3955 7339; www.thedewakohchang. com. Exquisite spa that offers hydrotherapy, salt scrubs, oil rubs and marvellous massages in 11 treatment rooms.

Cooking Classes

i-site Koh Chang: 23/9 Moo 4, Klong Prao; tel: 08-1773-4221; www.i-sitekohchang.com. This all-purpose company organises tours and activities on Ko Chang and the islands, including cooking classes, all-terrain vehicles, fishing and diving.

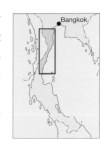
NORTHERN GULF COAST

This narrow strip of land, blessed with sandy beaches, good weather, rich forests and ancient towns, also contains two of Thailand's famous national parks. Popular destinations in this area include historically rich Petchaburi, beach getaways Cha-am and Hua Hin, and the celebrity-friendly Pranburi.

Wedged between the Gulf of Thailand and the Andaman Sea, southern Thailand geographically resembles an elephant's trunk snaking down narrowly from below the Central Plains to the tip of the Malay Peninsula. The Isthmus of Kra is the name for this land bridge connecting mainland Asia with the Malay Peninsula, which, at its narrowest point in Chumphon, is only 44km (27 miles) wide from coast to coast.

The 600km (373 miles) or so from Bangkok to Surat Thani province is blessed with seemingly endless sandy beaches and equable weather (*see margin tip, page 152*), plus lushly, forested interiors and historic towns that harbour plenty of attractions that are well worth exploring. The southern railway line and Highway 4, which is also known as Petch-kasem Highway, are the two principal links to the south, although there are also airports in Surat Thani and Hua Hin.

The upper section of the Gulf coast is home to two of the country's best-known national parks: Kaeng Krachan, also the country's largest, and Khao Sam Roi Yot. The town of Petchaburi, with its ancient temples,

is a worthy stop before travellers continue to the beach-side enclaves of Cha-am and Hua Hin, popular with Bangkokians as weekend getaways from the bustle of the city. Further south, Pranburi is growing in reputation as a high-end boutique-resort hideaway. Prachuap Khiri Khan and Chumphon see few foreign tourists, except those departing from Chumphon's port for the boat ride to Ko Tao (*see page 179*), although the island is in fact more easily accessed from Ko Samui.

Main attractions
PHRA NAKHON HISTORICAL PARK
KAENG KRACHAN NATIONAL PARK
HUA HIN
KHAO SAM ROI YOT NATIONAL PARK

LEFT: Petchaburi's Wat Kamphaeng Laeng.
RIGHT: making the trek up to Khao Wang.

Northern Gulf Coast

PETCHABURI

PETCHABURI

Historically rich **Petchaburi ❶** is one of Thailand's oldest towns and has been an important trade and cultural centre since the 11th century. Lying on the Petchaburi River some 120km (75 miles) south of Bangkok, the town has come under the influence of the Mon, Khmers and Thais at various times, and has over 30 temples that reflect the differing cultures and architectural styles of its various past invaders.

A pleasant place to while away a day or two, Petchaburi is easily navigable on foot. It has a laid-back provincial atmosphere with little in the way of modern conveniences.

Khao Wang

Just west of town, and providing a useful geographical reference, is the 92-metre (302ft) hill called **Khao Wang** (Mount Palace). Commissioned in 1860 as the summer residence of King Mongkut (Rama IV), the entire complex is now known as **Phra Nakhon Historical Park** (daily 8.30am–4.30pm; charge; tel: 0-3240 1006). It is a curious melange of Thai, Chinese and Western architectural styles taking the form of shrines, temples, pagodas and other structures. Many of these offer fabulous panoramas of the vicinity, especially around sunset.

The hilltop buildings include three throne halls (two of which have been turned into a museum housing an assortment of furniture and collectibles belonging to King Mongkut); a neoclassical observatory (the king was an avid astronomer); a large white *chedi*; and **Wat Maha Samanaram**. The steep cobblestone trail to the peak winds through forest and well-kept gardens populated by inquisitive monkeys. The easier option is to take the rickety cable car (daily 8am–5pm) on the Petchkasem side of the hill; its entrance is marked by a line of souvenir shops.

Other key temples

Some of Petchaburi's more important religious sites include the five laterite Khmer *prang* of the originally Hindu **Wat Kamphaeng Laeng** (daily 8am–4pm; free), which possibly marks the southernmost point of the Khmer kingdom. Located on Thanon Phra Song, the temple dates from the 12th century. Although the towers have undergone some restoration work, they are still dishevelled enough to look authentic.

Just around the corner from here, on Thanon Phongsuriya, is the 17th-century **Wat Yai Suwannaram** (daily 8am–4pm; free). The temple is best known for its fading murals of Hindu gods that date back to the 18th century. Its large grounds hold a lovely teak pavilion, as well as a catfish-filled pond. Jutting out into the pond is a small stilted *ho trai*, or scripture library.

Back across the river and along Thanon Damneon Kasem are the five white stucco-covered *prang* of the town's most dominant temple, **Wat Mahathat** (daily 8am–4pm; free). As with any Mahathat (Great

Relic) temple, the 14th-century site contains enshrined relics of the Buddha, but is probably better known for the intricate depictions of angels and other mythical creatures in the low-relief stucco on the gables of the main temple buildings.

Khao Luang cave

An interesting excursion only 5km (3 miles) from town is **Khao Luang cave** (daily 8am–5pm; charge). Shafts of sunlight filter down from naturally hewn holes in the cave roof, creating a breathtaking sight. Rays illuminate some of the hundred or more Buddha images that rest in the three main chambers of the cave, contributing to the spiritual aura.

Beside the entrance to the cave is **Wat Bunthawi**, a temple with wonderfully carved wooden door panels. The hilly approach to the cave is occupied by a large group of monkeys seeking handouts from visitors (avoid feeding them, however). Unofficial guides wait near the approach to the cave, offering to turn on the cave lights for a fee.

Avoid feeding the monkeys at Khao Wang, even if they seem tame.

Below: Khao Luang cave.

Suspension bridge spanning the river at Kaeng Krachan National Park.

BELOW: Pala-U Waterfall, Kaeng Krachen.

Ban Puen Palace

As the railway line south brought greater access to this part of Thailand, a number of palaces were erected for the royal family in times past. Situated beside the Petchaburi River, along Thanon Ratchadamneon, is the **Ban Puen Palace** (daily 8am–4pm; charge; tel: 0-3242 5555). The structure would look more at home in Germany's Black Forest than here in the coastal flats of Petchaburi. Built in 1910 for King Rama V (the year he died), this stately Germanic home was modelled on the summer palace of Keiser Wilhelm, and designed by a German architect. The grandiose two-storey palace was intended as a rainy-season hideaway for the king. Although little in the way of furniture remains to convey its original splendour, the porcelain-tiled dining room and inner courtyard, with its pond and fountain, are interesting enough to explore, as are the expansive gardens beside the river.

KAENG KRACHAN N P

Located some 60km (37 miles) southwest of Petchaburi town is the vast 3,000-sq-km (1,158-sq-mile) **Kaeng Krachan National Park ❷** (daily 6am–6pm; charge). The park – the largest in Thailand – is the source of the Petchaburi and Pranburi rivers and covers almost half of Petchaburi Province. It is a haven for numerous species of large mammal, including tigers, elephants, leopards, bears, deer, gibbons and monkeys. With around 300 species of resident and migratory birds, the park is also a prime birdwatching spot. The topography varies between rainforest and savannah grasslands, and features both a freshwater lake and rugged mountain ranges. It is possible to ascend the park's tallest peak, the 1,207-metre (3,960ft) **Phanoen Tung**, for superb views of the lush countryside, or trek to the 18-tier **Tho Thip Waterfall**. Swimming in and boating on the vast reservoir created by the **Kaeng Krachan Dam** are other activities popular with visitors.

Considering Kaeng Krachan's close proximity to Bangkok, surprisingly few tourists venture here. Trekking is the park's main activity; guides can be hired at the park's headquarters at the

end of the road beyond the dam. On the southern edge of Kaeng Krachan, towards the mountain range that divides Thailand from Burma, is the area's spectacular **Pala-U Waterfall.** Best seen during the rainy season, the fall has 11-tiers and is surrounded by dense forest. Accommodation consists of basic park lodgings, but the easiest way to visit the park is on a tour organised by hotels in Hua Hin.

Tours to Kaeng Krachan National Park often include a stop at the **Wildlife Rescue Centre** in Kao Look Chang, where you can visit animals that have been abused in captivity and hear about the centre's uphill battle to save local wildlife (by appointment only; tel: 0-3245 8135; www.wfft.org). Around 24km (15 miles) from Petchaburi, the centre cares and rehabilitates more than 30 rescued gibbons, as well as bears, macaques and langurs.

CHA-AM

Popular as a weekend getaway with Bangkokians is the long stretch of sand at **Cha-am ③**. Around 40km (25 miles) south of Petchaburi (or some 178km/111 miles from Bangkok), the beach has a different vibe from Hua Hin further down the coast, and is fairly quiet on weekdays, with plenty of seafood stalls and cheap restaurants along the beach-front Thanon Ruamchit to choose from. At weekends, however, the mood becomes more raucous as families and college students arrive in droves, picnicking (and boozing) under the casuarina trees and beach brollies, floating on rubber inner-tubes and riding on inflatable banana boats. The sand underfoot is a bit rough and the waters are less than pristine, but Cha-am does offer good value for money when it comes to hotels and food. In recent years chic minimalist hotels like the Veranda and Alila Cha-am have varied the accommodation options.

Maruekhathayawan Palace

Some 10km (6 miles) south of Cha-am, heading towards Hua Hin, is the seaside **Maruekhathayawan Palace** (daily 8am–4pm; charge; tel: 0-3250 8039). Built in 1923 from golden teak, the airy stilted structures were designed by an Italian architect and are European in style – supposedly based on sketches made by King Vajiravudh (Rama VI). Beautifully renovated in summery pastel shades, the three palace wings are interconnected by long raised and covered walkways.

The palace served as a retreat for King Vajiravudh during the two years before his death in 1925. After the king's death, the palace lay abandoned for decades before being restored and opened to the public. The magnificent audience chamber is the centrepiece of the palace structure, with many of the smaller fretwork topped rooms decked out in period furnishings. Despite its proximity to Hua Hin, the lovely palace grounds see few foreign visitors and only get busy at weekends with local visitors.

Maruekhathayawan Palace was used as a retreat by King Vajiravudh between 1923–5.

BELOW: fun on the sand at Cha-am beach.

TIP

The Gulf of Thailand coast covered in this chapter has weather similar to that of the rest of Thailand *(see page 287)* but although the rains here continue well into Nov, the effects of the monsoon are milder. The best months of the year are from Dec to Mar, while Apr and May are the hottest months. The rainy months stretch from July to Nov.

BELOW LEFT AND RIGHT:
aspects of the Hua Hin
Railway Station.

HUA HIN

Prachuap Khiri Khan is Thailand's narrowest province and its coast is fringed with mountains and lovely quiet beaches, the most popular of which is the 5km (3-mile)-long sandy beach at **Hua Hin** ❹. Located 203km (126 miles) from Bangkok, it's as little as two hours away by road and four hours by rail. Hua Hin has long had an air of exclusivity, thanks to the private residences maintained by Thai royalty and Bangkok's wealthy elite, and partly because of this, it retains more of a Thai family ambience than other beach destinations. Although it also has excesses if you look for them.

The royal connection can be seen at the seafront teak summer residency called **Klai Kangwon Palace**, which means "Far from Worries". Built in 1926 for King Rama VII, the Spanish-style villa is still regularly used by the royal family and is not open to the public.

One of the country's first rail lines linked Bangkok to Hua Hin at the start of the 20th century, transporting the capital's wealthy to the southern shores. Hua Hin thus had the aura of a European spa town, with the royals coming here for the clean air. Today, the coastal town is beginning to reclaim that mantle as several exclusive spa retreats – like the award-winning Chiva Som – cater to the needs of moneyed travellers. A string of large brand-name resorts, such as Hilton, Hyatt and Marriott, have also opened in recent years, along with local (and equally expensive) concerns such as the Dusit and Anantara.

Hua Hin sights

Today, some visitors still choose to take the train to Hua Hin, arriving at the charming **Hua Hin Railway Station**. Built in the early 1920s, the station evokes the romance of a bygone era, with the cream-and-red decorated royal waiting room, once used by King Rama VI and his entourage, still intact.

Thanon Damneon Kasem leads from the railway station directly to the beach and another historic landmark, the colonial-style **former Railway Hotel**. Constructed in 1922,

the Victorian-inspired building was the country's first resort hotel and has now been restored to its original wood-panelled glory as the **Centara Grand Beach Resort & Villas**. Even if you don't stay here, take afternoon tea or dine at one of its restaurants and then stroll through its large manicured gardens filled with topiary creatures, including a huge elephant that you can walk through.

Beside the hotel, Thanon Damnern Kasem ends at an alley that is the main access point to Hua Hin beach. The walkway is lined with stalls proffering tourist tat, and on the beach are boys with ponies for hire for trots along the beach.

Today, the wide and sweeping run of Hua Hin beach is backed by the summer homes of Bangkok's elite, along with a slew of faceless condo developments. Some of the beach front homes, which fuse elements of Thai and Western architecture, date back almost a century and are owned by influential families.

A few of these historic abodes have been restored and converted into unique boutique resorts, like Baan Bayan and **Baan Talay Dao**, while **Baan Itsara** is one of Hua Hin's better restaurants. Hua Hin is also fast gaining a reputation as a place to retire, and more and more condos and beach houses are being built to accommodate the upsurge.

The beach, punctuated by occasional boulders that give it a scenic beauty, lacks the character of Thailand's palm-fringed island bays, but is great for long undisturbed strolls. The beaches further south of town, **Suan Son** and **Khao Tao**, are nicer and more secluded, but again, not extraordinary. While the sea is generally calm during the low season period of May to September, the winds can whip up the water towards the end and start of the year. This is when windsurfers and kite-surfers take to the water (as the sea has jellyfish, it's advisable to wear long shorts).

Pony rides along the beach at Hua Hin are a popular activity.

Outside Hua Hin

For a bird's-eye view of Hua Hin, head up steep **Khao Hin Lek Fai** hill for some of the best panoramas of the beach. Around 3km (2 miles) west of town, turn down Soi 70 and

BELOW: Hilton Hua Hin is one of several luxury hotels on the beach.

A view of Wat Khao Takiab.

BELOW: at the World Elephant Polo Championships.

follow the signposts for the viewpoints (six different spots are marked around a recreational park) from which the scenery can be enjoyed. Dawn and sunset are the best times to stop here.

Visible a few kilometres south of town is **Khao Takiab** (Chopstick Hill), a rocky outcrop that marks the end of Hua Hin beach. It is a steep climb to the top but the views of the surrounding coast are worth the sweat. The hill is split into two windswept peaks, the nearest festooned with several small shrines and with a steep staircase that leads down to a towering 20-metre (66ft)-tall Buddha image. Dramatically standing just above the crashing surf, the image looks back toward Hua Hin beach with hands outstretched.

On the other brow is **Wat Khao Lad**, with its lofty pagoda atop a tall flight of stairs. A little further round the headland is a garish Chinese shrine with a large statue of the Goddess of Mercy, Kwan Im. A road splitting the two peaks leads to one of Hua Hin's most popular seafood restaurants **La Mer**, *(see page 161).*

Activities

These days, as tourism, with all its associated trappings, increases its grip, the image of the resort as a low-key family getaway is becoming a thing of the past. The town's nightlife has picked up in the last few years as more "beer bars" (but no go-go bars as yet) open, with more girls recruited to draw in customers. Despite this, Hua Hin retains its small seaside-town charm and is far removed in atmosphere from the raunchy red lights of Pattaya.

Along with this upsurge in nightlife, a number of new restaurants have appeared in the area, too. While Hua Hin was always known as a place for wonderfully fresh seafood, the diversity of culinary options has expanded beyond just Thai. These days, Japanese, Korean, Scandinavian, German, French and Italian eateries reflect the nationalities of the major tourist arrivals. The restaurants and bars are mainly clustered into a small area around Thanon Naresdamri and behind, on the parallel Thanon Phunsuk. Soi Bintabaht has the highest concentration of girly bars, and the pier area along Naresdamri serves some of the best grilled seafood in the town.

Hua Hin hosts a lot of activities and events, usually organised at weekends to cater to the Bangkok crowds. These include the annual **Hua Hin Jazz Festival**, generally held in June. It mainly consists of Thai bands, many of which would struggle to justify the jazz moniker, but has included the likes of Bill Bruford's Earthworks in the past. The **Hua Hin Regatta** falls in July or August and attracts sailors from around the region to compete in several classes. There may be crewing opportunities if you want to sail but have no boat. A more unusual event is the **King's Cup Elephant Polo** tournament, which attracts international teams in August or September.

In tune with the town's historical legacy, the **Hua Hin Vintage Car Parade** each December marked its tenth anniversary in 2012. It sees over 50 classic cars drive from Bangkok to Hua Hin's Centara Grand Beach Resort before taking a photo opportunity lap down the town's streets. For the latest information and listings, pick up a copy of *Hua Hin Today* newspaper.

Hua Hin may not boast as many golf courses as Pattaya, but what Hua Hin lacks in numbers, it makes up for in heritage. In the 1920s, the king and members of the country's aristocracy played their first game at the **Royal Hua Hin Golf Course**, the country's first ever golf course. Today, there are several courses within striking distance of the town, with more on the way.

PRANBURI

The beaches south of Hua Hin towards **Pranburi** ❺ continue to see development. Around 20 minutes' drive from Hua Hin, Pak Nam Pran, the mouth of the Pranburi River, marks the beginning of a clean but fairly unremarkable beach that runs down towards Sam Roi Yot National Park. Here are found some of Thailand's most exclusive beachfront hideaways, including the magnificent **Evason**, the north African themed **Villa Maroc** and the plush, celebrity-friendly **Aleenta**.

Most people who stay at these places may have no reason to leave the luxurious confines of their hotel, although some resorts organise tours to the mangrove-lined Pranburi River estuary and to Sam Roi Yot.

Located 63km (39 miles) south of Hua Hin is **Khao Sam Roi Yot National Park** ❻, which translates as "Three Hundred Mountain Peaks" and refers to the dramatic landscape of limestone pinnacles jutting up from the park's mangrove swamps to heights above 600 metres (1,968ft).

Carved from the rugged coastline, the 98-sq-km (38-sq-ft) park (daily 6am–6pm; charge) features beaches, marshes and brackish lagoons, forests, caves and offshore islands. Wildlife includes a multitude of migratory birds that congregate on the freshwater marsh and mudflats, unusual crab-eating macaques and the rare serow – a mountain goat-antelope. At certain times of the year, pods of dolphins also swim along the park's shores.

The park's most famous attraction, the huge cave of **Tham Phraya Nakhon** is reached by boat or by foot along a steep half-hour trail from Hat Laem Sala. Its large sinkhole allows shafts of light to enter and illuminate the grand Thai-style pavilion or *sala* called **Phra Thinang Khuha Kharu-hat**. It was built in the 1890s for a visit by King Chulalongkorn (Rama V). Other noteworthy caves are **Tham Sai** and **Tham Kaeo** (Jewel Cave), the latter with glistening stalactite and rock formations. The park's best viewpoint is at the 300-metre (984ft) **Khao Daeng** outcrop at the southern end of the park.

Limestone pinnacles at Khao Sam Roi Yot National Park.

Below: the plush Aleenta resort in Pranburi.

In 1868, King Mongkut, an astute astronomer, visited Khao Sam Roi Yot National Park to view a total eclipse of the sun, which he had foretold. The king's prediction, to the astonishment of local astrologers, was only four minutes off the mark. Sadly, Mongkut contracted malaria from this trip and died a week after his return to Bangkok.

Most Hua Hin and Pranburi hotels organise day trips to the park, but independent travellers can catch a train or bus to Pranburi, and from there take a *songthaew* to the fishing village of Bang Pu, inside the park. From here, catch a short boat ride or walk across the headland from the village to the park checkpoint on **Hat Laem Sala** beach.

There is accommodation run by the Forestry Department here, but a better alternative is to stay at a hotel, such as the family-friendly **Dolphin Bay Resort** *(see page 160)*, located at **Hat Phu Noi** beach, a few kilometres north of the park.

SOUTH OF PRANBURI

The coastline south of Khao Sam Roi Yot is still miles and miles of sandy beaches, yet most foreign tourists make the jump directly to Chumphon for ferry connections to Ko Tao *(see page 179)*, or to Surat Thani and then by boat to either Ko Samui *(see page 166)* or Ko Phangan *(see page 172)*.

While this stretch of the Gulf of Thailand coast may not be geared towards pampering foreign visitors, you will be rewarded with the less commercial face of Thai tourism.

Prachuap Khiri Khan ❼, about 85km (53 miles) from Hua Hin, is an interesting town to explore, as are the beaches of **Ao Manao**, 4km (3 miles) south of Prachuap town, and **Ban Krut**, 70km (43 miles) south. Both beaches have limited facilities in the way of accommodation and restaurants. Offshore from the town of **Bang Saphan Yai**, further south, is **Ko Thalu**, one of the first islands south of Bangkok that is good enough for snorkelling and diving.

Located 184km (114 miles) from Prachuap Khiri Khan, and considered the start of southern Thailand, is **Chumphon ❽**. It has several good beaches, including **Thung Wua Laem**, 12km (7 miles) north of Chumphon town, and **Ao Thung Makam Noi**, about 25km (16 miles) south. Some 20km (12 miles) offshore are the reef-fringed islands of **Ko Ngam Yai** and **Ko Ngam Noi**, popular with divers, while 80km (50 miles) away is **Ko Tao** *(see page 179)*, another diving hotspot. ❑

BELOW: the famous *sala*, or pavilion, at Tham Phraya Nakhon.

NORTHERN GULF COAST

TRANSPORT

PETCHABURI

Getting There
By Taxi
A taxi in Bangkok can be booked for the 120km (75-mile) ride to Petchaburi. The ride will take 2 hours and cost B1,000–1,500. Be sure to agree on the rate before boarding.

By Bus
Express buses leave Bangkok's **Southern Bus Terminal** every two hours between 11am and 5pm, stopping at Petchaburi and Cha-am before heading to Hua Hin. The journey to Petchaburi takes around 1½ hours (B112).

By Train
There are 12 departures on the Southern Line from Bangkok's **Hualamphong Station** between 8.05am and 10.50pm daily. Trains take around 4 hours (depending on the service) to get to Petchaburi. Ticket prices vary, depending on the choice of train and class of travel.

Getting Around
Samlor (three-wheel motorcycles) and songthaew trucks are Petchaburi's principal mode of public transport. Rates for trips around town average between B10 and B20. Motorcycle taxis are common, with fares ranging from B20–30 for a short journey. If you prefer to get around on your own, motorcycles (B250 per day) and bicycles (B120) can be rented at the Rabieng Rim Nam Guest house (tel: 0 3242 5707).

CHA-AM

Getting There
By Taxi
A taxi in Bangkok can be booked for the ride to Cha-am, 178km (111 miles) away. The cost is about B1,500–2,000, and it will take about 3 hours to get there. Resorts in Cha-am can also arrange for car or minivan transfers. Limousines can be arranged at Bangkok International Airport to Cha-am. Depending on the car used, it will cost between B2,800 and B5,000.

By Bus
Buses leave from Bangkok's **Southern Bus Terminal** every 30 minutes daily between 6.30am and 5.30pm, stopping at Petchaburi and then at Cha-am. Travel time is approximately 3 hours to Cha-am; the one-way ticket price is B142. The airport shuttles to Hua Hin (see below) will stop at Cha-am if you tell the driver beforehand.

By Train
There are 2 departures on the Southern Line from Bangkok's **Hualamphong Station** at 9.20am and 3.35pm daily. Trains take around 4 hours to get to Cha-am. Ticket prices vary, depending on the choice of train and class of travel.

Getting Around
Cha-am is best suited for those with their own transport. Motorcycles, bicycles and cars can be rented from numerous resorts. Along the beach road you can take a two-seater samlor for around B20, while vendors also rent three-person bikes for B60 an hour. Motorcycle taxis are common, with fares ranging from B20–30 for a short ride.

HUA HIN AND PRANBURI

Getting There
By Air
In 2013, **Nok Air** (tel: 1318; www.nokair.com) launched evening flights on Thursdays, Fridays and

Sundays from Don Mueang Airport to Hua Hin (B1,299). Most hotels will pick up from the airport. Many companies have tried this route and later withdrawn, so don't count on it lasting.

By Taxi

A taxi from Bangkok to Hua Hin, 203km (126 miles) away, will take approximately 3 hours. Expect to pay between B1,500 and B2,500 and make sure you agree on the rate beforehand. Limousines can be arranged at Bangkok International Airport to Hua Hin for B2,800 to B5,000, depending on the type of car and location of the drop-off. Pranburi, for instance, is 23km (14 miles) south of Hua Hin and transfers will cost more. Resorts in Hua Hin and Pranburi can also arrange for transfers by car or minivan. Make enquiries at the time of booking.

By Bus

Buses leave from Bangkok's **Southern Bus Terminal** every 30 minutes between 6.30am and 5.30pm, making stops at Petchaburi and Cha-am first before arriving at Hua Hin. Journey time is roughly 3 hours to Hua Hin. One-way tickets cost B160. There

ABOVE: a trishaw driver at the Hua Hin Railway station.

are also six shuttle buses between 7.30am and 7.30pm from Suvarnabhumi airport to Hua Hin, priced B350.

By Train

There are 12 daily departures on the Southern Line from Bangkok's main **Hualamphong Station** between 8.05am and 10.50pm. Trains take from 3½ hours (depending on the service) to get to Hua Hin, which has a quaint colonial-style station. Ticket prices vary, depending on the choice of train and class of travel.

Getting Around

Samlor (three-wheel motorcycles) and *songthaew* trucks are Hua Hin's principal mode of public transportation. Rates for short rides around town average between B10 and B20, while a ride to resorts located in Pranburi cost between B40 and B50. Motorcycle taxis are common, with fares ranging from B20–30 for a short journey.

For independent travel, motorcycles and cars can be hired by visiting the various stands and shops all over town.

A C C O M M O D A T I O N   L I S T I N G S

PETCHABURI

Fisherman's Resort
170 Moo 1, Hat Chao Samran
Tel: 0-3244 1370
www.thefishermansresort.com
This boutique resort is 15km (10 miles) from town on the beach at Hat Chao Samran and promotes the merits of its undeveloped location as an alternative to Hua Hin. Built in classic Asian style, it has a

swimming pool, a spa and a beachfront restaurant with Thai and western food. (32 villas) **$$**

Rabieng Rim Nam Guesthouse
1 Th. Chisa-In
Tel: 0-3242 5707
This popular backpacker haunt is centrally located beside a busy bridge over the

river. It is a cheap option but don't expect too much. There are just small box-like rooms and shared bathrooms. It is a good place to glean local info, however, and also has one of the best restaurants in town. (9 rooms) **$**

Sun Hotel
43/33 Moo 5 Baan-Mor

Tel: 0-3240 0000
Well situated for Phra Nakon Historical Park, a short walk away, the Sun has basic, large rooms with air conditioning. There's also free Wi-fi and a reasonable Thai café/restaurant. You'll need a *samlor* from here to the temples, but it's not too far. **$**

CHA-AM

Dusit Thani Hua Hin
1349 Th. Petchkasem
Tel: 0-3252 0009
www.dusit.com
Located midway between Cha-am's main beach front and Hua Hin, this is a large hotel with expansive gardens, sea views and plenty of water features on show. The decor is a blend of colonial-style and traditional Thai features. (296 rooms) $$

Hotel De La Paix
115 Moo 7, Tambol Bangkao
Tel: 0-3270 9555
www.hoteldelapaixhh.com
This deluxe boutique resort on the beach uses natural materials in its clean, minimalist, contemporary design. The luxurious, comfortable rooms and villas are capacious, with free Wi-fi, flat screen TVs, oversized bathrooms and rain showers. Two restaurants, a stunning lap pool, spa and fitness centre complete the scene. (77 rooms) $$

Rungaran de Challet
263/26 Soi. Cha-am Tai 4, Th. Ruamjit
Tel: 0-3247 1226
www.rungaran-chaam.com
This clean little hotel, designed in traditional Thai style, is excellent value. The generous rooms have flat screen TVs, there's free Wi-fi and a garden with ornamental pond, but no pool. It's close to the beach in Cha-am village, so restaurants and shops are nearby. (32 rooms) $

Veranda Resort & Spa Hua Hin Cha Am
737/12 Th. Mung Talay
Tel: 0-3270 9000
www.verandaresortandspa.com
Veranda is making waves for its contemporary elegance and style. The large pool and pond are the central features of this boutique-style resort and it has a trendy beachfront brasserie. The regular rooms are slightly cramped, but the sea-view villas are very spacious. (118 rooms) $$$

HUA HIN AND PRANBURI

HUA HIN

Anantara
43/1 Th. Phetchkasem
Tel: 0-3252 0250
www.huahin.anantara.com
Luxurious hideaway tucked among verdant gardens and fronting the beach. Rooms are spacious and have strong Thai accents, with the more expensive ones facing the beach and lagoon. Highly rated spa, plus restaurants including Italian and Thai. (187 rooms) $$$

Baan Bayan
119 Th. Petchkasem
Tel: 0-3253 3540
www.baanbayan.com
Set in a century-old beach-front residence, this place is a real gem, evoking a bygone era yet with all the mod cons of a boutique resort. The lovely wooden house is surrounded by a large gar-

den. Both sea- and garden-view rooms, plus a pool and bar. Popular for weddings and private parties. (21 rooms) $$$

Baan Talay Dao
2/10 Soi Takiab
Tel: 0-3253 6024
www.baantalaydao.com
Centred round a 90-year old teak beach house, this resort lies on a nice stretch of Hua Hin beach towards Khao Takiab. Mainly studio rooms but there are also several nice villas and suites that are arranged around the pool and jacuzzi area. (32 rooms) $$

Centara Grand Beach Resort & Villas
1 Th. Damneon Kasem
Tel: 0-3251 2021
www.centarahotelsresorts.com
Historic colonial-style hotel nestled in a tropical garden. Although in the heart of Hua Hin beach, it feels very private. As well as six swim-

ming pools, there's a spa and fitness centre, plus several international dining options. (207 rooms) $$

Chiva-Som
73/4 Th. Petchkasem
Tel: 0-3253 6536
www.chivasom.com
Chiva-Som resort harnesses the best of traditional Thai hospitality with a relaxing location beside Hua Hin beach. This multi-award winning spa resort has a superb range of spa facilities, including a floatation tank, Pilates room, gym, water therapy suites, indoor and outdoor pools and a t'ai-chi pavilion. Extensive spa treatments plus surprisingly tasty spa cuisine at its in-house restaurants. They sell packages of three-days upwards, rather than room nights. (57 rooms) $$$$

Hyatt Regency Hua Hin
91 Th. Hua Hin Khao Takiab

Tel: 0-3252 1234
www.huahin.regency.hyatt.com
This large resort is laid out in several three storey blocks within extensive landscaped gardens. The family-friendly amenities extend to a dedicated kids beach area and giant water slide in the huge freeform pool area. Five restaurants and bars serve Thai and Western food, there are several water sports activities and the beautiful Barai Spa has a full range of treatments. (213 rooms) $$$

Let's Sea
83/188 Soi Talay 12, Th. Hua

PRICE CATEGORIES

Price categories show the starting price for a double room without breakfast and taxes:

$ = under US$70
$$ = US$70–130
$$$ = US$130–250
$$$$ = over US$250

Hin Khao Takiab
Tel: 0-3253 6888
www.letussea.com
This narrow resort running down to the sea was refurbished at the end of 2012. Accommodation is in two double storey blocks, on either side of a long pool, like canal bank houses. Rooms have a modern minimalist feel, each with its own terrace or adjacent deck with direct access to the water. Upper rooms also have roof decks. There's a Thai and Western restaurant on the beachfront and a rooftop spa. No kids under 12. (40 rooms) **$$**

PRANBURI

Aleenta
Pak Nam Pran
Tel: 0-2519 2044
www.aleenta.com
This luxurious resort

with simple, clean lines is one of the best along this stretch of coast. Private and intimate, it occasionally hosts A-list celebrities, who no doubt enjoy activities including yoga, t'ai chi and cooking classes. There's a pool, restaurant, bar and spa, and romantic dinners can also be set up on the beach. (22 rooms, suites and villas) **$$$**

Evason Hua Hin
Pak Nam Pran
Tel: 0-3263 2111
www.evason.com
Evason is a contemporary retreat with tastefully designed Asian-accented rooms. Its Earth spa is set in thatched huts amid lily ponds with an outdoor pavilion. There is a large pool, while dining options include two beach-front restaurants serving Mediterranean and Thai food, plus a quick-fix noodle bar. (185 rooms) **$$**

Huaplee Lazy Beach
Pak Nam Pran
Tel: 0-3263 0555
www.huapleelazybeach.com
This small boutique-style resort has six funky maritime-accented rooms and a couple of two-bedroom villas and a house. It has another nearby resort (called **Brassiere Beach** – no kidding) with which contains a clutch of six villas near Sam Roi Yot National Park (9 rooms) **$$**

Villa Maroc
Pak Nam Pran
Tel: 0-3263 0771
www.villamarocresort.com
Every room at this Moroccan themed resort has a sea view, iPods and a sophisticated sound system. Some villas have private pools. As well as a spa, there's an all day restaurant and a rooftop bar, and there are shops and restaurants nearby if you want options away from the resort. (15 rooms) **$$$$**

SAM ROI YOT N P

Dolphin Bay Resort
227 Moo 4, Hat Phu Noi,
Sam Roi Yot
Tel: 0-3255 9333
www.dolphinbayresort.com
Located north of Sam Roi Yot National Park, this well-managed children-friendly resort lies on a beach whose waters are a breeding ground for dolphins. There are regular rooms, bungalows and 1–3-bedroom apartments, a Thai and international restaurant and two swimming pools. (72 rooms) **$**

PRICE CATEGORIES

Price categories show the starting price for a double room without breakfast and taxes:
$ = under US$70
$$ = US$70–130
$$$ = US$130–250
$$$$ = over US$250

PETCHABURI

The eating-out scene in Petchaburi is uninspiring. Most of the better restaurants are confined to the area's small hotels and there are few independent eateries.

Thai

Rabieng Rim Nam Guesthouse
1 Th. Chisa-In

Tel: 0-3242 5707
Open: daily B, L and D .
There are few eateries with English-language menus in Petchaburi town, so this rustic wooden restaurant that juts out over the Petchaburi River is a real find. Part of a guesthouse popular with backpackers, this simple eatery attracts a mix of foreigners as well as locals.

There is a broad menu of Thai cuisine, and art displays line the walls of the restaurant. **$**

Thai and Western

Fisherman's Village
170 Moo 1, Hat Chao Samran
Tel: 0-3244 1370
www.thefishermansvillage.net
Open: daily B, L and D.
A rare find for this part of Thailand, this beach-

front restaurant (on nearby Hat Chao Samran) is part of a boutique resort, with dining on the breezy wooden deck or within the warmly lit interior. As well as all the major Thai favourites, the menu has a selection of pastas, steaks and several Western dishes. A good-value wine list is available, too. **$$**

CHA-AM

Like Petchaburi, the eating-out scene in Cha-am is disappointing and most of the better restaurants are confined to the hotels.

International

Cha-am Pub & Restaurant
252/6 Th. Jai Lai.
Tel: 08-2251 0871
www.chaampub.com
Open: daily B, L and D.
An Aussie run bar and restaurant tucked down a road parallel to Cha-am beachfront. The bar is part of the patio garden, while upstairs is a dining room with a piano. The food is the usual international pub fare, plus some Thai dishes. **$$**

i sea
Veranda Resort & Spa, 737/12 Th. Mung Talay
Tel: 0-3270 9000
www.verandaresortandspa.com
Open: daily L and D.
One of Cha-am's most stylish beach front eateries is a crisp, white minimalist affair with design-orientated furniture and both terrace and indoor seating. It specialises in fusion seafood and has a popular bar mixing up tropical cocktails and innovative smoothies. Also has a good wine list. The restaurant is part of the Veranda resort and therefore mainly frequented by hotel guests. Best to book a table if you're not staying here. **$$$**

Thai

Poom
274/1 Th. Ruamchit
Tel: 0-3247 1036
Open: daily B, L and D.
With a sea-view patio, this simple outdoor restaurant has been serving some of Cha-am's best Thai-style seafood for over a decade. It is very popular with the locals so advance bookings are essential, especially on weekends. **$$**

HUA HIN AND PRANBURI

International

Le Bistro Hua Hin
214 Th. Phetkasem
Tel: 0-3290 0143
Open: daily L and D.
This 2015 newcomer has a menu full of well presented, tasty French offerings like lobster bisque, duck leg confit, with possibly chocolate fudge cappucino for dessert. The lunch sets, from B350 for two courses, are a good deal. There's a small terrace, too. **$$$**

Brasserie de Paris
3 Th. Naresdamri
Tel: 0-3253 0637
Open: daily L and D.
This European flavoured bistro has excellent steaks and other meats at reasonable prices. A great pick is the *assiette royale* with shrimp, crab, scallops and lobster for two. Spread over two floors, the upstairs looks out to sea. The set meals are a great-value option. **$$$**

Crêpes & Co
37/103 Soi Moobaan Khao Noi
Tel: 0-3202 7240
www.cropoonoo.com
Open: 11am to 11pm.
This long standing, family oriented Bangkok favourite has expanded to Hua Hin with an open plan room, garden seating and an outdoor bar. Their crêpes, both savoury and sweet, have traditional French fillings, as well as other styles. They feature a wide menu including items drawn from Greece and Morocco, such as moussaka and tagines. **$$–$$$**

Gianni Italian Restaurant
42-2/3 Th. Dechanuchit
Tel: 08-1645 3744
www.gianni-italianrestaurant.com
Open: daily L and D.
Gianni Favro, who has a big reputation in Bangkok for his reliable, well-priced trattoria fare, opened this outlet in late 2012. Along with regional favourites like *saltimbocca alla romanna*, the kitchen plates pizzas, homemade pasta and ice cream or tiramisu for dessert. **$$$**

Thai

Chao Lay
15 Th. Naresdamri
Tel: 0-3251 3436
Open: daily L and D.
One of the most popular of Hua Hin's wooden plank seafood eateries, Chao Lay is always busy with local diners. Set on a jetty over the sea, it sells all kinds of fresh Thai-style seafood served grilled, deep-fried or steamed. **$$–$$$**

Let's Sea
83/188 Soi Talay 12, Th. Takiab
Tel: 0-3253 6888
www.letussea.com
Open: daily L and D.
Located on the less busy beach south of town, Let's Sea has tables in two *salas* and on the beach. The food is mainly well crafted by Thai standards with lots of seafood and a commitment to organic produce. The 20 percent Western dishes include steaks and roast chicken. **$$–$$$**

La Mer
111/2 Khao Takiab
Tel: 0-3253 6205
Open: daily L and D.
On the side of Khao Takiab hill at the southern end of the beach, this is Hua Hin's best positioned restaurant for dramatic evening views. A huge establishment spread over several platforms, it's seafood all the way on its large menu. Not par-

PRICE CATEGORIES

Price per person for a three-course meal without drinks:
$ = under US$10
$$ = US$10–25
$$$ = US$25–50
$$$$ = over US$50

ticularly glam, but it's the food and view that packs them in. **$$–$$$**

Mini Farm
5/240 Th. Liab Tang Rodfai, Soi Hua Hin 88
Tel: 0-3251 6383
www.minifarmgroup.com
Open: daily L and D.
Eat truly local at this open-air restaurant, with fresh produce coming from its attached organic farm. The menu has both Thai stalwarts like *tom yum goong*, soft shell crab salad and red curry, plus Western dishes, from spaghetti to steak. **$$**

Onn Onn Corner
Th. Poonsuk
Tel: 08-7999 4786
Open: daily D.

This small and very popular family-run diner with indoor and street-side tables is mainly good for its Thai dishes, although they also have some Western. Good things to try are Penang curry, the spicy chicken *laab*, prawns with mango and spare ribs with pepper and garlic. **$–$$**

Supatra-by-the-Sea
122/63 Th. Takiab
Tel: 0-3253 6561
www.supatra-bythesea.com
Open: daily L and D.
Located right at the end of Hua Hin beach, this lovely restaurant overlooks Khao Takiab hill. A sister of Bangkok's Supatra River House

restaurant, they serve contemporary and traditional Thai dishes on the torchlit garden terrace or up in the main pavilion. There are two small pavilions which can be reserved for private parties. **$$–$$$**

You Yen
29 Th. Naeb Kehardt
Tel: 0-3253 1191
Open: daily L and D.
Run by a local family, this beautiful, old wooden Thai house on the seafront has restaurant seating both in the garden next to the beach or in the house itself. The extensive menu is Thai-based with an obvious emphasis on seafood. **$$–$$$**

ABOVE: Tab Tim Grob.

PRICE CATEGORIES

Price per person for a three-course meal without drinks:
$ = under US$10
$$ = US$10–25
$$$ = US$25–50
$$$$ = over US$50

ACTIVITIES

HUA HIN AND PRANBURI

Nightlife

Dance Bars and Clubs

Hua Hin Brewing Company:
Hilton Hua Hin Resort & Spa, 33 Th. Naresdamri; tel: 0-3253 8999. This microbrewery separate from the hotel is crammed with tourists and cruising bar girls every night. The house band provides the main entertainment. Open late every night with free entry before 11pm.

Bars and Pubs

Ed Murphy's: 25, Th. Sela Kam; tel: 0-3251 1525; www.edmurphys.com. A busy Irish themed bar with all the usual beers, Brit style pub food and sport on TV. A live band bangs out pop and rock covers every night from 9pm. They have cheap rooms, too.

Elephant Bar: Centara Grand Beach Resort & Villas, 1 Th. Damneon Kasem; tel: 0-3251 2021. The resident band takes centrestage at Sofitel's plush colonial-style lounge bar, playing easy-listening sounds throughout the night.

Hi-4: 41/48 Th. Phetkasem; tel: 08-5299 2903. This large, well-established club has DJs and a nightly house band, usually playing rock, sometimes by well-known Thai bands from Bangkok. There's also an outdoor space for quieter moments. Relaxed atmosphere.

Retrophilia: 72/17 Dechanuchit; tel: 08-5996 4193. As the name suggests, these guys love old stuff, from the Beatles and Elvis soundtrack to vintage looking decor, much of which is for sale. It's close to the Night Bazaar and has cheap Thai food and alcohol. Downstairs is a vintage clothes shop.

Shopping

Cicada Night Market: Th. Khao Takiab; tel: 0-3253 6606; www.cicadamarket.com. Open from 4pm on Fri, Sat and Sun, Cicada draws the crowds with hand crafted clothes and accessories, and art market in white wooden buildings, buskers and mini concerts in a small amphitheatre. Take a snack break in the food court.

The Family Tree: 7 Th. Naresdamri; tel: 0-3251 1716; www.familytree-huahin.com. A small shop dealing in fair trade products sourced from community groups including ethnic minorities and artists with special needs. It's small and laid out like a clutter sale.

Rashnee Thai Silk Village: 18/1 Th. Naeb Kehardt; tel: 0-3253 1155. Set up as a workshop and village, a guided tour will show how silk is extracted from cocoons and then transformed into cloth.

Hua Hin Night Bazaar: Th. Petch-kasem (corner of Soi 72). Open from early until around midnight, this large market is packed with souvenir stalls, tailoring shops and eateries.

Market Village: 234/1 Th. Petch-kasem; tel: 0-3261 8888. Hua Hin's main downtown shopping mall has all the usual shop and fast food restaurant styles and a cineplex.

Outdoor Activities

Adventure Tours

Hua Hin Adventure Tour: 69/7 Th. Neadkehab; tel: 0-3253 0014; www.huahinadventuretour.com. Offers a variety of adventure tours into Kaeng Krachan and Sam Roi Yot national parks. Trips range from 1-day excursions to 3-day camping, trekking, kayaking and rock-climbing tours.

Boat Cruises and Fishing

Mermaid Cruises: 77/5 Moo 1, Pak Nam Pran, Pranburi; tel: 08-4800 7400; www.huahincruises. oom. Board its tonk pleasure boat, wind- and solar-powered catamaran or electric longtail boat for one of several trips including evening squid fishing, all-day fishing, and cruises to Monkey Island and Sam Roi Yot National Park.

Muay Thai

Grand Sport Stadium: Th. Petch-kasem (next to Grand Hotel); tel: 08-1269 6746. Usually has five to six bouts every Friday from 9pm, with Thai and international boxers (including women). Also has a martial arts school.

Golf

Royal Hua Hin Golf Club: tel: 0-3251 2475. Opened in 1924, this is Thailand's oldest golf course and is located close to the centre of town. The course follows the undulating topography and is fringed by large mature trees.

Black Mountain Golf Club: 565 Moo 7, Th. Nong Hieng; tel:

0-3261 8666; www.blackmountainhuahin.com. A highly ranked 18-hole course with lots of water and a separate nine hole par three option. Nearby is the **Black Mountain Water Park** with lots of fun for the family (www.blackmountainwaterpark.com). Attractions include water slides, bouncy castle and a giant wave pool.

Kite-boarding

Hua Hin Kite Centre: Soi 75/1; tel: 08-1591 4593; www.kiteboardingasia.com. Offers 1- to 3-day training on Hua Hin beach, which has a long windy season (Nov– Apr), making it perfect for both wind-surfing and kite-boarding.

Para Motoring

Sky Club Thailand: 136/351 Soi 102, Nong Kae; tel: 08-7401 1113; www.skyclubthailand.com. Certified pilots offer two-up tandem flights lasting 10, 20 or 30 mins, over Hua Hin in motorised paragliders. They also organise tours if you want to fly over places like Kanchanburi or Ko Samui.

Spas

Anantara Spa: Anantara Resort & Spa, 43/1 Th. Phetchkasem; tel: 0-3252 0250. Housed within the tropical luxury resort, the Mandara Spa is a chain of spas in Asia with a well-deserved reputation

The Barai Spa: Hyatt Regency, 91 Hua Hin-Khao Takiab Rd; tel: 0-3252 1234; www.huahin.regency. hyatt.com. Named after a reservoir created by the ancient Khmers, this sprawling facility offers every conceivable treatment to pamper you.

Chiva-Som: 73/4 Th. Petch-kasem; tel: 0-3253 6536; www.chivasom.com. Comprehensive range of facilities and a qualified team of holistic experts, homeopaths and personal trainers who can recommend tailor-made programmes for specific goals, such as detoxifying, improved fitness and stress relief.

Cookery School

Thai Cooking Course: 19/95 Th. Petchkasem; tel: 08-1572 3805; www.thai-cookingcourse.com. Day long courses include a market trip to purchase local ingredients you will need for the day, and hands on cooking of dishes such as green curry. Minimum of four people, maximum of 10. The course starts at 9am and finishes around 3pm.

BELOW: Som Tam.

KO SAMUI, KO PHANGAN AND KO TAO

Ko Samui conjures up images of an idyllic island paradise, and Ko Phangan is equally paradisiacal, except that it's often overshadowed by wild, anything-goes, all-night Full Moon Parties. If you prefer to dive or snorkel, head to the pristine haven of Ko Tao.

Bangkok

L ocated some 80km (50 miles) from the mainland town of Surat Thani in the southern Gulf of Thailand, palm-fringed **Ko Samui** is the biggest of 80 islands that make up the Samui Archipelago, an island chain including the party island of **Ko Phangan**, the dive mecca of **Ko Tao** and pristine **Ang Thong Marine National Park**. With only a handful of the islands featuring any significant settlement, much of the area remains unspoilt, with perfect white-sand beaches ringed by colourful coral reefs, and rugged forested interiors.

The coconut islands

For over a century, the immigrant Chinese from Hainan and the Muslim fishermen on these islands derived their incomes from coconut plantations and fishing. While tourism dominates today, many of Ko Samui's poorer islanders still make their living from the coconut plantations.

Ko Samui is an hour's flight from Bangkok, 644km (400 miles) away. The Samui Archipelago's three largest islands are firmly entrenched on the tourist map. While Ko Samui increasingly tailors itself to the higher-end market, Ko Phangan and Ko Tao still gear themselves to backpackers, the

first of whom arrived on these shores in the 1970s. This might soon change, however, as plans have been tabled to open an airport on Ko Phangan by 2015. Convenient ferry connections between the three islands make it easy to sample the unique pleasures of each on a single holiday.

The Samui Archipelago saw a significant jump in tourists in 2005, as holiday-makers scrambled to find alternative destinations away from the tsunami-hit resorts along the Andaman coast. Development boomed,

Main attractions
HAT CHAWENG
ANG THONG MARINE NATIONAL PARK
FULL MOON PARTY
HIN BAI (SAIL ROCK)
KO NANG YUAN
CHUMPHON PINNACLE

LEFT: the pier at Ko Tao. **RIGHT:** Coconut Palm tree on the beach at Ko Samui

Ko Samui is sometimes called the "Coconut Island", thanks to its vast coconut plantations.

particularly on Ko Samui, during the following years and the island remains a very popular holiday spot.

KO SAMUI

When globetrotting backpackers first began travelling to Ko Samui in the 1970s, travellers' tales of this island paradise soon surfaced, and it was only a matter of time before Samui's secret was out. The simple A-frame huts that once sheltered budget travellers can still be spotted on the island's peripheral beaches, but nowadays the most scenic bays have been taken over by luxury resorts that blend in with the palm-lined beach fronts.

However, Ko Samui's raw beauty is still largely intact, and its laid-back vibe is one reason the island attracts so many repeat visitors. Many have secured their own piece of this 247-sq-km (95-sq-mile) tropical paradise by buying holiday houses or condos on the island, which are more affordable than those in Phuket.

Ko Samui has rapidly established itself as Thailand's hottest spa destination, offering a wide variety of extravagant hotel-based pampering spas as well as independent day spas and retreat centres that claim to

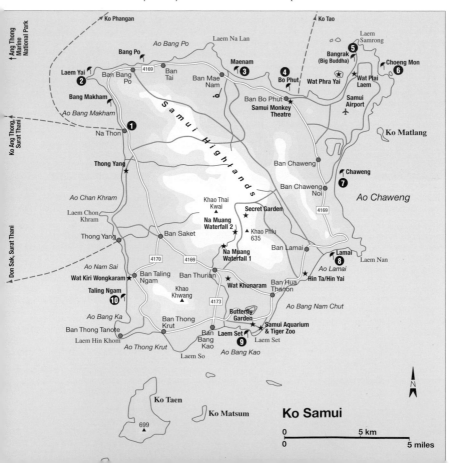

Ko Samui

0   5 km

0   5 miles

restore both physical and spiritual health. For those who tire quickly of the soft sandy beaches, the jungle treks and waterfalls of Samui's interior offer a different kind of escape.

Ko Samui still has some way to go before matching the yachting marinas and theme parks of Phuket, but as it now has an 18-hole golf course and large supermarket chains added to its list of amenities, it looks destined to follow in the same footsteps. The island's rapid rise, however, has not been without consequence. Severe water shortages are becoming a regular occurrence during the driest months, while the rainy season sometimes brings flood waters rushing down from deforested hills to many road and beach-front properties.

For better or worse, Ko Samui is becoming increasingly cosmopolitan. Dining choices are varied and moving more upscale, with more design-conscious eateries independent of hotels opening regularly. The nightlife scene is always busy, and the island has gained more atmospheric bars and clubs to join the dingy "beer bars", British-style pubs and meat-market clubs.

Some long-term repeat visitors to Samui complain that the island's idyllic charms are fraying at the edges. Aside from the obvious upsurge in construction, the behaviour and attitude of the locals have come under rap. While most of Samui's population still exudes the famous southern hospitality, there are increasingly disturbing reports of opportunistic rip-offs and a seemingly uncaring attitude that borders on rudeness. Road rage and assault have also been reported, along with unsympathetic, and at times compliant, responses by the local police.

Getting to Ko Samui

It is possible to fly direct to Ko Samui's airport (located in the north-eastern tip of the island) from Bangkok, Phuket and Krabi. The tropical escape begins the minute you touch down at the island's international airport. With its quaint open-plan buildings and manicured gardens, this is one of Thailand's most picturesque arrival points. Many people also travel by boat from mainland Surat Thani (Ban Don pier) to the

TIP

The southwest monsoon brings light, intermittent rains to the Samui archipelago from June to Oct. From Nov to Jan, the northeast monsoon takes over: the heaviest rains fall during this period, with Nov being the wettest month. Given the rather unpredictable wet-weather pattern, the best time to visit the islands is from Feb to May – although there are plenty of fine days right through to Sept.

BELOW: a beautiful beach in Ko Samui.

TIP

A popular pastime for Samui locals is to watch and gamble on buffalo fighting at one of the island's several stadiums. In front of an animated crowd hanging around the edge of the ring, the head-to-head duel involves two beasts locking horns and battling it out until one runs away with its tail between its legs. Check with your hotel on forthcoming events.

busy port town of **Na Thon** ❶ on Ko Samui's northwest coast.

Na Thon, which is also the island's administrative centre, has little of interest to visitors, save for a few Chinese-influenced old wooden shophouses, souvenir shops, banks, restaurants, travel agents, a few faceless hotels, and an immigration office for visa extensions.

Ko Samui's roads are generally well paved and the ring road, Route 4169, that loops the island is eminently driveable. Yet, accidents are frequent (mainly caused by intoxicated drivers) and great care should still be taken if driving your own car or riding a motorbike.

Hat Laem Yai/Hat Maenam

The secluded **Hat Laem Yai** ❷ beach, located on a headland with a steep hillside rising behind it, is home to one of Ko Samui's most expensive resorts, the all-villa **Four Seasons Koh Samui**. Laem Yai has magnificent orange-tinted sunset vistas, though it is thin on hotel and restaurant options.

The second beach of note on the north coast is **Hat Maenam** ❸,

about 13km (8 miles) from Na Thon and 6km (4 miles) from the airport. The 4km (2½-mile)-long stretch of beach is fairly isolated and quiet. The golden sand underfoot is a little coarse and the beach is pleasant but quite narrow. Numerous budget hotels have sprung up here in addition to the de-luxe **Santiburi Beach Resort, Golf & Spa**. Nights can be quiet in Maenam due to the near absence of bars and clubs; for them you have to head south to Bo Phut and Chaweng.

Hat Bo Phut

East of Maenam is **Hat Bo Phut** ❹. While the beach is nice enough and of similar standard to Maenam, the 2km (1-mile)-long Bo Phut is better known for the quaint seafront lane of old wooden shophouses known as **Ban Bo Phut** or **Fisherman's Village**. The old timber shacks have been tastefully converted into restaurants, bars and shops, making this one of the nicest places on the island to wander around. A number of resorts are found at Bo Phut, among them the luxurious **Anantara Bophut Ko Samui**.

BELOW: Fisherman's Village, Bo Phut.

Of all the islands in the gulf, Ko Samui has the most off-beach attractions, many of which can be enjoyed by the whole family. Largely set up for tourists, but also a mark of the island's coconut-plantation heritage, the trained "monkey work coconut" shows at **Samui Monkey Theatre** in Bo Phut (daily 10.30am, 2pm, 4pm; charge; tel: 08-7265 6662) reveal how southern Thais use simian labour to assist them in harvesting coconuts from towering palms. These shows will appeal or appal, depending on your view of animal welfare.

Hat Bangrak

Northeast of Bo Phut and part of a headland is **Hat Bangrak ❺**, better known locally as **Big Buddha Beach**, which takes its name from **Wat Phra Yai**, or Big Buddha Temple (daily 8am–5pm; free). The 12-metre (39ft)-high seated golden image is across the bay on a small islet linked by a causeway to the end of the beach. At low tide, the water can retreat quite far out, exposing a swathe of mud. There is some budget and mid-range accommodation set behind the beach.

A short hike and a left turn from the temple entrance in the middle of a large fish filled pond is **Wat Plai Laem**, an interesting little temple with a base shaped like a giant lotus flower. Above the pond is a giant pink statue of the multi-armed Chinese Goddess of Mercy, Kwan Im.

Hat Choeng Mon

On the other side of the headland is **Hat Choeng Mon ❻**, a small but serene white-sand bay backed by casuarina trees. It has a relatively undeveloped ambience, except for a couple of upmarket resorts. There is hardly any nightlife here, but then busy Chaweng beach is only a short drive away. Several of the island's premier beach resorts, such as the **Imperial Boathouse, Tongsai Bay**, and the all-villa **Sala Samui Resort**

& **Spa** occupy prime positions along this idyllic stretch of beach.

Hat Chaweng

The island's busiest beach by far, and arguably still the prettiest, is the 6km (4-mile)-long **Hat Chaweng ❼** on the east coast. The beach is roughly divided into three sections: North Chaweng, Central Chaweng and Chaweng Noi, in the south. The stunning powdery white-sand beach facing clear turquoise waters follows the shore from the headland in the north near the small island of **Ko Matlang**, all the way down to the curving bay and rocky end point of Chaweng Noi.

North Chaweng beach is sheltered by a coral reef, which means that while the sea is protected from strong winds during the monsoon season, the waters can also be still as a millpond at other times of the year. It is also less crowded than **Central Chaweng**, which has the highest concentration of development. Behind the rather cramped line of beach resorts, Chaweng Beach Road is a largely faceless sprawl of somewhat

Wat Phra Yai in Ko Samui.

BELOW: giant Buddha statue at Wat Phra Yai, Hat Bangrak.

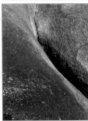

It's obvious how these boulders – Grandfather Rock and Grandmother Rock – in Hat Lamai got their quirky names.

BELOW: Hat Chaweng is Ko Samui's most popular beach.

tacky tourist-orientated shops, restaurants and bars. However, upmarket shopping arcades such as **Iyara Plaza**, **Central Shopping Arcade**, **Living Square Plaza** and **Central Festival**, due to open in 2014, are a sign of gentrification.

Past a tiny spit of land is the relatively quiet beach enclave of **Chaweng Noi**, which is thinner on accommodation and restaurants.

Hat Lamai

South of Chaweng, over a rocky ridge that has stunning viewpoints back towards the Chaweng shoreline, is Samui's second-most populous beach, **Hat Lamai 8**. The beach is lovely and far less hectic compared with Chaweng, with better accommodation choices for budget travellers, although there are also several boutique resorts. Lamai is also the home of the island's original "wellness" centres, namely **The Spa Resort** and **Tamarind Springs**.

A little beyond the beach's southern tip are two naturally hewn suggestive rock formations known as **Hin Ta** (Grandfather Rock) and **Hin**

Yai (Grandmother Rock). As they resemble male and female genitalia, the rocks are the subject of much photo-taking (and sniggering).

Dining at Lamai isn't a patch on Chaweng's variety and quality, and unfortunately, Lamai gets a bad rap for its slightly lascivious nightlife scene, with its slew of raunchy girly bars and the sex workers who prop them up.

Inland attractions near Lamai

Taking Route 4169 inland from Hat Lamai leads to one of the temples featured on most island tours, **Wat Khunaram** (daily 8am–5pm; free). The temple is famous as the home of mummified monk Luang Phor Daeng. His body is still seated in the same meditating position he held when he died over 20 years ago.

Continuing past the village of Ban Thurian is **Na Muang Waterfall 1**, where, in the wet season, a cascade of water plunges some 20 metres (66ft) into a large pool. Getting to **Na Muang Waterfall 2** involves a fairly strenuous 1½km (1-mile) trek; a more novel way would be an ele-

phant ride offered near the entrance to Na Muang Waterfall 1.

Another of Lamai's attractions is the **Samui Aquarium & Tiger Zoo**, located within the Samui Orchid Resort in south Lamai (daily 9am–6pm; daily show at 1pm; charge; tel: 0-7742 4017; www.samuiaquariumandtigerzoo.com). The aquarium exhibits are nothing to write home about; more entertaining is the daily bird and Bengal tiger show. Visitors also have the opportunity to become a sea-lion trainer for a day with the guidance of professional trainers.

South and west coasts

The south- and west-coast beaches aren't as pretty, although a few beautiful resorts have nestled along these shores. Some visitors intent on a more secluded holiday much prefer the beach at **Hat Laem Set ❾** (also sometimes referred to as **Hat Na Thian**) along the south. The stylish **Centara Villas Samui**, with its elegant rooms, is a popular accommodation choice here. Not far around the bay from Centara Villas you come to the **Butterfly Garden** (daily 8.30am–5.30pm; charge; tel: 0 7742 4020), where the rainbow-coloured wings of a variety of butterflies can be viewed within its net-covered compound.

Rounding the southern coast and heading to the west is **Hat Taling Ngam ❿**, the site of the spectacular **Intercontinental Samui Baan Taling Ngam**, where the views from a vantage point on a steep hill make up for the rather ordinary beach resting at the bottom.

Activities

Ko Samui's waters offer the typical gamut of water sports – jet-skiing, kayaking, windsurfing, water-skiing, parasailing, deep-sea fishing and sailing. The **Ko Samui International Regatta** (www.samuiregatta.com), which celebrated its 12th year in 2013, has helped to establish the island as a yachting base and a few companies now charter luxury boats.

Although Ko Samui has numerous dive shops, the waters around the island are not particularly good for diving and snorkelling. Most dive trips head out to **Ang Thong Marine National Park**, **Hin Bai** and **Ko Tao** (*see below and pages 178 and 179*).

For land-based action, hire a four-wheel-drive jeep and embark on an island safari exploring the winding dirt trails that lead up into the mountainous hills. The more adventurous can rent a mountain bike and explore the interior of the island.

ANG THONG N P

Although Ko Phi Phi's Maya Bay (*see page 251*) was the chosen location setting for the film *The Beach*, it was the dramatic scenery of **Ang Thong Marine National Park**, near Ko Samui, that was Alex Garland's original inspiration for his bestselling novel. Lying some 31km (19 miles) west of Ko Samui, the 42 islands that make up the Ang Thong archipelago stretch over a 100-sq-km (39-sq-mile) expanse of land and sea.

The famous mummified monk Luang Phor Daeng at Ko Samui's Wat Khunaram.

BELOW: Ko Samui's jungle-filled interior invites exploration.

Getting to Talay Nai lake on the island of Ko Mae Ko involves a 20-minute trek, but the vistas of the blue-green waters encircled by towering limestone cliffs is well worth the effort.

BELOW: sea-canoeing among the limestone formations of Ang Thong Marine National Park.

Virtually uninhabited by humans, the islands are home to a diversity of flora and fauna, including macaques, langurs and monitor lizards. Pods of dolphins are known to shelter in the waters late in the year.

Meaning "Golden Bowl", Ang Thong Marine National Park takes its name from the **Talay Nai** (inland sea), an emerald-green saltwater lagoon encircled by sheer limestone walls that are covered with vegetation. A principal stop on any day trip to the island chain, the picturesque lake can be reached by a trail from the beach on the island of **Ko Mae Ko**.

Several tour companies on Ko Samui operate day trips, including kayaking expeditions to the archipelago, which usually include a stop on the largest island of **Ko Wua Talab**, or Sleeping Cow Island. Aside from a beach and the park's headquarters, there is a steep climb 400 metres (1,312ft) up to a lookout point with unrivalled views of the surroundings, with Ko Samui and Ko Phangan in the distance. Also involving an arduous climb is Ko Wua Talab's other highlight, **Tham Bua Bok**, or Waving

Lotus Cave. It is named after lotus-shaped rock formations.

Diving and snorkelling at Ang Thong Marine National Park is usually best experienced at the northern tip of the island chain, around the islet of Ko Yippon. Although visibility isn't crystal-clear, the shallow depths make it easy to view the colourful coral beds, inhabited by sea snakes, fusiliers and stingrays. There are also shallow caves and archways to swim through.

KO PHANGAN

The second-largest island in the Samui archipelago, **Ko Phangan** is blessed with numerous seductive white-sand beaches and rich forest topography, yet the island's current international reputation stems almost exclusively from the infamous Full Moon Party *(see page 176)*, which takes place at Hat Rin on the island's southern tip. With an infamy rivalling that of Ibiza and Goa, the lunar gathering has steadily grown since the first party back in the late 1980s. Nowadays, the monthly beach party is a point of hedonistic pilgrimage for an estimated 30,000 revellers from all over the world.

Lying around 20km (12 miles) north of Ko Samui, or a 40-minute boat journey, Ko Phangan became an outpost on the shoestring traveller's map in the 1980s, around the same time as Ko Samui. But while the latter rapidly developed into a hub for package holiday-makers and flashy beach homes for the wealthy, Ko Phangan has largely remained an enclave of backpackers, drug-craving revellers and New Age nirvana-seekers. However, there are increasingly more upmarket accommodation choices, and pockets of the 193-sq-km (75-sq-mile) island are becoming built up, particularly Hat Rin and its vicinity, which now looks and feels like a separate resort when compared with the rest of the island.

While most revellers confine themselves to the southern-cape beaches of Hat Rin Nok (Sunrise Beach), Hat Rin Nai (Sunset Beach) and nearby Leela Beach, there are plenty of other more isolated bays that skirt the mountainous interior. Increasingly better roads have made the furthest reaches of the island more accessible, but even so, a couple of coves, such as Hat Kuat (Bottle Beach), can be reached only by boat.

The island's administrative centre and main arrival point is the small town of **Thong Sala ①**, located around halfway up the west coast. Apart from fishing boats unloading their daily haul, the port is usually busy with ferries, catamarans and speedboats travelling to and from Ko Samui, Ko Tao and Surat Thani. Accommodation touts pounce on new arrivals as soon as they set foot on the pier, which can be helpful if no reservations have been made and it is close to the full moon. The town has all the usual tourist-friendly services – internet cafés, banks, shops, and a few restaurants and bars. There are also several Thai-boxing camps, plus morning and night markets.

Ban Khai and Ban Tai

East of Thong Sala, the south coast is endowed with a continuous stretch of beach running all the way up to the Hat Rin cape, though the shallow reefs make the water often impossible to swim in. The most popular beaches here are between the villages of **Ban Tai ②** and **Ban Khai ③**; the former is a small fishing village with boats clogging up part of the seafront. Both basic and more comfortable family-run bungalow accommodation are found along the length to Thong Sala, with Ban Khai, the closest to Hat Rin, the only spot with any night activity.

Hat Rin

The original appeal of **Hat Rin**, east of Ban Khai, was that it had two beaches within easy walking distance – across a flat headland – where both sunrise and sunset views could be enjoyed. But this is now where all the action takes place, and these are certainly no longer Ko Phangan's most serene beaches.

Hat Rin Nok ④, or Sunrise Beach, is the wider, more popular bay, and

TIP

There are no official tourism offices in Ko Phangan. A good source for information is the website managed by the Phangan Batik shop in Thong Sala: www.koh phangan.com. The site has a wealth of information and useful tips, including Full Moon Party dates. There is also an official tourism website at www.koh-phangan tourism.com with details on tours and packages.

BELOW: verdant Ko Phangan.

Hat Rin beach.

is where the main nightlife cranks up, climaxed by the monthly Full Moon Party. Hat Rin attracts a global melting pot of young clubbers and alternative-lifestyle devotees, who find this tiny pocket of Thailand the perfect place to express their inner selves (fuelled, of course, by booze and drugs). This is the lure for many, though more jaded travellers will regard the scene as one big cliché.

The less attractive of the two beaches is **Hat Rin Nai ❺**, or Sunset Beach, a thinner stretch of sand lined with beach huts that offer at least a tad of respite from the late-night cacophony over at Hat Rin Nok. There is a pier towards the southern end of this beach for boats shuttling to Ko Samui. The walk between the two beaches is jam-packed with accommodation, shops, restaurants, internet cafés, travel agents and the like.

Further towards the island's southern tip is pretty **Leela** beach. It is around a 15-minute walk to Hat

Rin Nai, and has a more peaceful atmosphere, removed from the main Hat Rin mayhem.

East-coast beaches

There are several small but fine bays that run north up the east coast from Hat Rin, but a lack of roads makes boat transportation (from Hat Rin) the only way to venture there. Development is therefore patchy along this coast. **Hat Yuan ❻** and **Hat Yao** (not to be confused with the longer Hat Yao on the west coast), and particularly **Hat Thian ❼** are a draw with visitors who seek isolated and undisturbed beaches.

At the top of the east coast are the increasingly popular twin bays of **Ao Thong Nai Pan Noi ❽** and **Ao Thong Nai Pan Yai ❾**, described by many as the island's most beautiful coves. There is a good choice of accommodation at both bays, separated by a headland that can be traversed in about 20 minutes. Get-

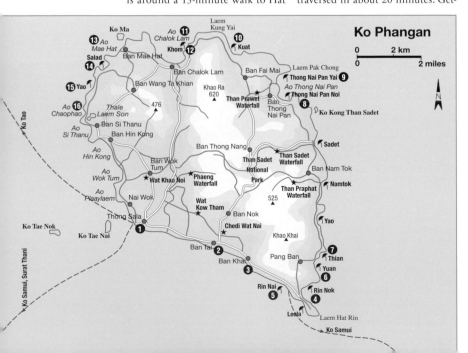

Ko Phangan

ting to these beaches is a nightmare, however, as the first stretch of the 12km (8-mile) road from Ban Tai in the south, as far as Sadet, is actually a dirt track, riddled with potholes. It's tricky to navigate on a motorbike, particularly after heavy rain. A good alternative is to take a pick-up truck taxi from Thong Sala.

North-coast beaches

Hat Kuat ⑩, or Bottle Beach, is the first of two bays that are worth seeking out on the north coast. There is a decent road from Thong Sala up to Ao Chalok Lam (see below), from where you can take a boat to Bottle Beach. It is one of Ko Phangan's best bays and has its own insular scene that attracts lots of repeat visitors. The splendid white-sand beach is backed by steep hills and, like elsewhere in Ko Phangan, most accommodation is at the budget end.

The second bay to the west, Ao Chalok Lam ⑪, holds a large fishing village. Ban Chalok Lam is the island's second port, with a pier in the centre of the large curving bay that is usually busy with fishermen

who supply the seafood restaurants here with fresh catches. The small white-sand cove of Hat Khom ⑫ along this stretch, and closer to the headland east, is the best bit of beach here, ringed by a coral reef offshore. The 10km (6-mile) road from Thong Sala in the south to Ao Chalok Lam is one of the island's best roads, so getting there is not a problem.

West-coast beaches

The west-coast beaches stretching from Ao Mae Hat all the way to Thong Sala in the south are considered more attractive than those along the southeast shores, but somehow they see fewer visitors compared with the Hat Rin area.

Starting from the northwest corner is Ao Mae Hat ⑬, which has a sandbank at low tide that connects to the reef-fringed tiny island of Ko Ma (Horse Island). The reef that runs up the coast from Ao Chaophao (see page 177) all the way to Ko Ma is considered by some to be the island's best snorkelling and diving site.

Further down the coast is scenic Hat Salad ⑭, with good snorkel-

TIP

The advantage of staying on any of the west-coast beaches is fewer crowds and beautiful sunset views, with the islands of the Ang Thong Marine National Park framed against the horizon.

BELOW: a rowing boat at Ao Thong Nai Pan Noi.

Full Moon Party

An essential stop on any back-packer's tour of Southeast Asia, the Full Moon Party on Hat Rin Nok is dubbed the "world's biggest beach party"

The raucous Full Moon Party (or F-M) on Hat Rin Nok, or Sunrise Beach draws hundreds of thousands of global visitors throughout the year. Estimates claim 10 million baht is added to the island's economy on one single party day alone, so the government's intermittent calls for the event to be scrapped are unlikely to materialise for a while at least.

The event builds in momentum from sunset to sunrise. Paradise Bungalows, at the southern end of the beach, was the original venue. It is where the most popular DJs spin their tunes, although others vie for attention at the main bars all along the beach. As each leans towards a different groove, the dance hotspots shift periodically.

Some 30,000 visitors attend each party, with the wildest events in December and January. Guesthouses inevitably fill up as the day approaches, with some only taking bookings for a minimum of four or five nights. Those craving beauty sleep should choose accommodation well away from Hat Rin Nok, which can be loud on most nights, rising to deafening on full moon. Transport to the party from other beaches is plentiful. And if you prefer to nurse a hangover within the confines of a luxury hotel in Ko Samui, numerous boats make the night-time crossing between the two islands.

Generally, people spend the night wasted on concoctions of cheap booze, getting painted in fluorescent ink, dancing and passing out on the sand. Aside from this and the fleeting romances (mostly of the one-night stand variety), a lot of party-goers are there to sample what first gave F-M its notoriety – the taking of illicit substances. Popular still are magic-mushroom omelettes and teas, Speed and Ecstasy punches, and ganja cookies. But beware, plain-clothed and uniformed police are on patrol and road blocks on routes to the party are set up to search for drugs. Penalties for possession of or being under the influence of illegal drugs are extremely harsh in Thailand.

Precautions

The party is great fun, but given the nature of the event and the potential for getting completely smashed it should be obvious that some precautions are needed. Pickpockets are on the prowl; thefts and muggings do happen, so it's best not to carry valuables. And don't take drugs from strangers or leave your drinks lying around; they are sometimes spiked. So too the drinks buckets that are available to fill up from.

Sunrise is met by triumphant cheers, and the incentive to raise the tempo once more for anyone who might be thinking about collapsing into bed. The beach party winds up late morning, but for those who still have their brain cells and eardrums intact, the traditional after-party kicks off at Backyard Bar up the hill. For upcoming F-M dates and other party details check out www.phanganist.com. ❑

LEFT: Full Moon party animals at Hat Rin Nok.

ling just off the northern edge of the beach. Next is an attractive 1km (½-mile)-long sandy stretch called **Hat Yao ⑮**, or Long Beach. It has become very popular in recent years and is giving Hat Rin a run for its money with its range of accommodation, bars, restaurants and other facilities. Further south is a nice small bay called **Ao Chaophao ⑯**, which has a decent range of facilities. The inland **Laem Son Lake** demarcates Ao Chaophao from the next beach, **Ao Si Thanu**. Further down the coast are three more beaches of note: **Ao Hin Kong** and **Ao Wok Tum**, both of which are divided by a small stream that empties into the sea, followed by **Ao Plaaylaem**.

Inland attractions

The beach at Ao Thong Nai Pan Yai was a favourite stop-off for King Chulalongkorn, who made numerous visits to Ko Phangan between 1888 and 1909. Another of the king's haunts was **Than Sadet Waterfall**, which flows out to **Hat Sadet** beach in the next cove down the east coast from Ao Thong Nai Pan Yai, or some 12km (7 miles) up from Hat Rin.

The island's largest falls, Than Sadet, meaning Royal Stream, has boulders carved with inscriptions by King Chulalongkorn, King Rama VII and the present monarch, Rama IX.

The island's other cascades are **Than Praphat Waterfall**, on the way to the east-coast beach of Hat Namtok, **Than Prawet Waterfall**, located near Ao Thong Nai Pan Noi, and **Phaeng Waterfall** halfway across the island en route from Thong Sala to Ban Chalok Lam village. All these falls come under the umbrella of **Than Sadet National Park**, a 65-sq-km (25-sq-mile) reserve that aims to protect the biodiversity of Ko Phangan's forested interior as well as the small outlying islands that are within the park's boundaries.

If the soul also needs centring, then the cave monastery at **Wat Kow Tham**, at the top of a hill near the village of Ban Tai, has a meditation centre called Nunamornpun. Its 10- and seven-day retreats, including some that are silent, are designed for Western visitors and place emphasis on the key principle of compassionate understanding. Early registration is advised

Wat Khao Tham is popular as a meditation retreat.

BELOW: Thong Nai Pan Yai beach on Koh Phangan.

as places fill up quickly. For more information and registration check www.nunamornpun-kohphangan.com.

Diving and snorkelling

As with Ko Samui, the majority of Ko Phangan's diving is conducted at a handful of dive sites some distance from the island, at **Ang Thong Marine National Park** *(see page 171)*, **Hin Bai** (Sail Rock) and around **Ko Tao** *(see page 179)*. Snorkelling and diving closest to Ko Phangan is best experienced along the reefs on the northwest tip of the island, around **Ko Ma, Ao Mae Ha**t and **Hat Yao**. Ko Ma is Ko Phangan's best dive site, with fairly shallow depths of up to 20 metres (66ft) and various types of coral, including a multicoloured anemone garden. The area is frequented by blue-spotted stingrays, giant grouper and reef sharks.

Located about halfway between Ko Phangan and Ko Tao, **Hin Bai** is regarded as one of the best dive sites in the Samui archipelago and is suitable for all levels of diver. The rugged rock emerges like an iceberg from the water; most of its bulk is hidden below the surface, reaching depths of 30-plus metres (98ft). The granite pinnacle is circled by large schools of pelagic fish, but the highlight is a dramatic vertical chimney that can be entered at 19 metres (62ft) below, with an exit at 6 metres (20ft) from the surface.

Nightlife and entertainment

Apart from the notorious Full Moon parties, Ko Phangan has plenty of other regular weekly and monthly party nights to keep extreme party animals bouncing until that ultimate night arrives again. **Half Moon** parties shape up twice a month, a week before and after full moon, held at a hypnotically-lit outdoor venue in Ban Tai. Unlike the free Full Moon parties, the Half Moons and all other parties on the island have an entry fee. The lovely waterfall setting for the pre-full moon **Paradise Party** attracts a large party contingent to the waterfalls that are found off the road to Ban Chalok Lam.

Famous for its post-full moon all-day recovery session, the funky

BELOW: diving among the coral reefs off Hin Bai (Sail Rock).

two-floor **Backyard Bar**, up the hill behind Hat Rin Nok on the way to Leela beach, also holds regular party nights, with differing musical slants. Hat Rin's bars tend to be ephemeral, but mainstays include **Pirate's Bar**, along with **Cactus Club** and **Drop-In Club**. For more information on the island's entertainment scene, check out www.phanganist.com, or see page 191 for nightlife listings. Sadly, safety concerns around the parties are increasing and some governments now issue warnings about attacks on tourists on the island. For tips on staying safe see Full Moon Party *(page 176)*.

KO TAO

Some say **Ko Tao**, or Turtle Island, is named after its rather loose geographical shape of a diving turtle; others have attributed its name to the turtles that were once prevalent swimmers in these waters. Today, the laid back island might just as well be called "aqualung island" for the density of affordable dive schools that operate expeditions to the coral-abundant waters. This is one of the world's best places to learn how to mine the pleasures of the deep.

Just a decade ago, Ko Tao, a rugged rock, topped with tropical forest and fringed with some picturesque secluded bays, consisted solely of rustic backpacker bungalows. It had little appeal for non-divers, who would quickly tire of listening to endless divers' tales in the bars and restaurants each night. Since then, development has brought better facilities, accommodation options and entertainment venues, with plenty more activities to occupy landlubbers. And the bonus of having a large percentage of visitors studying in dive schools or out on dive trips is that the island's beaches can be relatively peaceful and relaxing during the day.

The tiny 21-sq-km (8-sq-mile) island, located around 40km (25 miles) northwest of Ko Phangan and 60km (37 miles) from Ko Samui, is the northernmost inhabited island in the Samui archipelago. Due to its remoteness, it was seldom visited in the past, and there are few historical sites for visitors to explore, save for the initials of King Rama V (Chulalongkorn) carved into a large boulder at the southern end of Hat Sai Ree beach. The king visited the island in 1899, and the spot has become a place where locals pay their respects. In the 1930s and 1940s, the island was used as a political prison, but since the 1980s, Ko Tao has been welcoming increasing numbers of overseas visitors, who now arrive by ferries and speedboats from the mainland port of Chumphon *(see page 156)*, some 80km (50 miles) to the east; or from Ko Samui, Ko Phangan or Surat Thani to the south.

West-coast beaches

The island's main arrival point is the small but lively village of **Ban Mae Hat ❶** on the west coast. It is little more than a one-street village lined with a post office, banks, cafés, bars and other tourist-related facilities.

TIP

Ko Tao is too tiny and undeveloped to have a tourism office. A good bet for information and tips on the island is the website: www.kohtao today.com.

BELOW: a fire-eater performing at Ko Phangan's Full Moon Party.

There are plenty of dive shops on Ko Tao, but as most offer more or less the same services, it's best to shop around and ask for recommendations.

BELOW: taking the plunge at Ko Tao.

There are bays at **Hat Sai Nuan** and **Ao Jansom** south of the village, while to the north is the small, shallow bay of **Ao Hat Mae**. There is some accommodation here but it may be too close for comfort to the village for some. Much nicer is the 2km (1-mile)-long **Hat Sai Ree ②**, the island's longest and most popular curve of white-sand beach. Sai Ree is lined with hotels to suit most budgets, getting gradually quieter further north, with the ever-growing **Ban Hat Sai Ree** village backing on to the beach just over the halfway mark. Beyond Sai Ree, the road makes an incline up towards the northern tip of the island, with several more out-of-the-way cliff-top resorts, including the attractive **Thipwimarn**, from whose restaurant you can experience stunning sunset views.

South-coast beaches

Ko Tao's southern shores have quite a few small but nevertheless pretty beaches that are found in either direction from the island's second-busiest beach of **Ao Chalok Ban Kao ③**, a well-protected bay that is jammed with multiple resorts, dive shops, eateries and bars. The large headland at the eastern end of Ao Chalok Ban Kao has a fantastic viewpoint on top of the **John Suwan Rock**, with lovely vistas in either direction. To the east of the promontory is the long, yet quiet, **Ao Thian Ok ④**, and further still is **Hat Sai Daeng**.

Within walking distance, to the west of Ao Chalok Ban Kao, is the small and scenic bay of **Ao Jun Jeua**. Unfortunately, the monsoon season from June to October brings high winds and heavy seas here, causing disruption to ferry schedules and resulting in a lot of flotsam being-washed up on these beaches.

East-coast beaches

The east coast of the island has several isolated inlets. There are scant

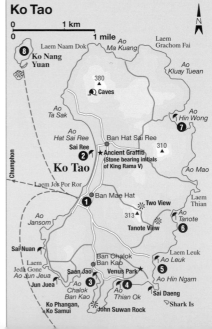

sleeping options (although Ao Tan-ote is expanding), and none have outstanding beaches, but there is plenty of good snorkelling and diving to be experienced. The dirt trails to the eastern shores can be treacherous (the only other way is by boat) and once you are there, it can be awkward and expensive to venture back west. Most resorts along this coast offer basic facilities, with some generating electricity only between sunset and sunrise. Heading north from Hat Sai Daeng, the bays include lovely **Ao Leuk ❺**, the scenic horseshoe-shaped **Ao Tanote ❻**, the tiny cape of **Laem Thian**, and, eventually, the remote **Ao Hin Wong ❼**.

North coast

A short boat ride off the island's northern tip is the picture-perfect **Ko Nang Yuan ❽**, a gathering of three islets joined together by mere wisps of sand that can be walked across at low tide. The setting is incredible, both above and below sea level, so much so that dive trips and boat tours from around the island, as well as Ko Samui and Ko Phangan,

all converge here, somewhat spoiling the idyll. With simple bungalows spread across the three outcrops, only the **Nangyuan Island Dive Resort** (tel: 0-7745 6088; www.nangyuan.com) has the rights to operate here, with outside visitors charged B100 just to step foot on the island.

Diving and snorkelling

As a premier dive destination, Ko Tao's reputation has diminished slightly in the last decade, mainly due to the hefty increase in the number of divers; at the more popular sites, the undersea human traffic can be annoying. Even so, visibility in the warm water is usually very clear – sometimes over 30 metres (98ft) – and there is a variety of dive sites to choose from. While sightings of giant groupers and turtles are not uncommon, and territorial disputes with triggerfish best avoided, an encounter with an underwater giant such as a whale shark is still a special event.

Unlike the lengthy journey times to dive sites from Ko Samui and Ko Phangan, Ko Tao is fortunate to have more than 25 chartered dive sites

A sign on Ko Tao.

BELOW: stunning Ko Nang Yuan is a must-see.

A man and his canoe at Ko Nang Yuan.

BELOW: taking a break at Ko Tao.

close by that can be reached in less than 30 minutes. The close proximity and favourable conditions (outside the Nov–Dec monsoon) make the island's waters an ideal place to learn how to dive.

Some of the best dive sites are found off Ko Nang Yuan, including the granite boulder and swim-throughs of **Nang Yuan Pinnacle**, the pair of coral-coated rock formations known as the **Twins**, and **Green Rock**, with its tunnels and swim-throughs. Some 5km (3 miles) northwest of Ko Tao, the **Chumphon Pinnacle** is arguably the best dive site in the Gulf of Thailand, suitable for advanced divers only, who may encounter grey reef sharks and sizeable fish. In the opposite direction, the **Southwest Pinnacle**, 7km (4 miles) from Ko Tao, is rated as one of the best soft-coral reefs in the region; its currents attract large schools of pelagic fish. Other frequently visited sites are **White Rock**, **Hin Wong Pinnacle** and **Shark Island**.

With nearly 50 dive schools and competitive dive packages that include accommodation, a few resorts

refuse to take in non-divers during the peak season. Advance reservations are advised. The majority of schools offer PADI open-water certification, with rates averaging from B8,500 to B10,000. Qualified divers can expect to pay B1,000 for fun dives, which are discounted if you bring your own equipment.

Activities

Ko Tao's compact size makes the island an ideal place for walking, with the reward of panoramic hilltop views or a hidden pristine cove at the end of your journey. If hiking the rugged coast is too strenuous, day-long boat trips around the island can be chartered independently with longtail-boat operators at beaches and piers, or through your guesthouse. A round-island tour will cost around B1,000 for the boat, but operators may ask for more depending on how many people are aboard.

Water sports such as kayaking, wakeboarding and water-skiing can be done on Ao Tanote or Hat Sai Ree. And on land there are increasing options like **Flying Trapeze Adventures** at Hat Sai Ree.

Entertainment

Some of the healthy diving camaraderie on Ko Tao spills over into its lively nightlife scene. The island is also an escape for Ko Phangan visitors who seek a reprieve from that island's party-town atmosphere, although Ko Tao has its own regular party nights with guest DJs (fliers and posters notify fresh-faced arrivals of the latest place to shake their booty). As the island develops, the nightlife on offer is starting to move from basic beach bars blaring loud trance and techno to the dreaded fire-jugglers and cheap-Thai-whiskey scene of Ko Phangan. But cooler venues, such as **MOOV Restaurant, Club and Art Garden**, also exist (*see page 193*). ❏

Ko Samui, Ko Phangan and Ko Tao

TRANSPORT

KO SAMUI

Getting There

By Air

Bangkok Airways owns the airport at Ko Samui and enjoyed a long monopoly on flights; although that has now ended, ticket prices are still among the highest in the country. From Bangkok, there are some 20 daily flights to Ko Samui operated by **Bangkok Airways** and **Thai Airways** (flight time is 65 minutes). Bangkok Airways also connects Ko Samui with Phuket, Krabi, U-Tapao (Pattaya), Trat (Ko Chang), Chiang Mai and Sukhothai.

Bangkok Airways also flies from Ko Samui direct to several regional cities, including Luang Prabang, Phnom Penh, Singapore and Hong Kong.

If you haven't made arrangements with your hotel for an airport pick-up, you can take a taxi. The driver will quote B400 for a ride to Chaweng, but B300 is more realistic. Private minivans also take passengers to the different beaches, though they usually wait until the van is full before leaving. Typical minivan fares are B70 to Bo Phut, B100 to Chaweng and Maenam, and B120 to Nathon and Lamai.

By Bus

Private tour companies along Bangkok's Thanon Khao San run bus services from there to Surat Thani (the jump-off point for Ko Samui). The ride takes about 10 to 11 hours and costs B450 to B850, depending on the type of bus and whether the ferry ticket to Ko Samui is included. Air conditioned buses leave daily from Bangkok's **Southern Bus Terminal** as well, from 7am to 8.30pm. The cost and duration are about the same as that of private companies.

Much quicker is the **Lomprayah** VIP bus (tel: 0-2629 2569; www.lomprayah.com) from Bangkok (departs 6am or 9pm) or Hua Hin (departs 8.30am or 11.30am) to Chumphon, which connects with the Lomprayah catamaran (departs 1.20pm or 7am) to Ko Samui (via Ko Tao and Ko Phangan). The entire trip to the island takes about 10½ hours during the day or just over 15 hours overnight. A one-way ticket costs B1,350, including catamaran.

By Train

There are a dozen daily train departures to Surat Thani from Bangkok's **Hualamphong Station**, running from 8.05am to 10.50pm. The journey takes approximately 9 to 12 hours (depending on the train service).

The station is in Phunpin, which is 13km (8 miles) from Surat Thani Town.

By Boat

If you don't fly direct to Ko Samui, most land transport will deposit you at Surat Thani. Here, several companies operate passenger and car ferries to Ko Samui from Don Sak, Ban Don and Pak Nam Tapi piers. Boats leave approximately every 1 to 2 hours' from 5am to 7pm, and take around 1½ to 2½ hours (depending on the boat). There is also a slow 6½-hour night ferry from Ban Don pier. Depending on the operator, tickets cost B120 to B350. Most ferries arrive at Ko Samui's main pier at Na Thon, which is around 40 minutes by songthaew to Chaweng beach. Some ferries carry on to Ko Phangan from Na Thon pier.

Getting Around

Songthaew trucks are the island's principal mode of public transport. Drivers always try to overcharge so make sure you hand over the correct fare. A journey down the length of Chaweng beach is B20, from Na Thon to Chaweng B60, with no journey costing more than B60. Late at night they operate more like taxis and the fare should be agreed on beforehand.

Metered taxis are becoming prevalent on the island but drivers rarely turn on the meter, preferring to quote extortionate rates for relatively short distances.

Motorcycle taxis are cheaper, with fares ranging from B20 to B30 for a short journey, and B150 to B200 for a longer ride from, say, Chaweng to Na Thon.

A variety of motorcycles, from mopeds to choppers (B200–500), as well as jeeps (B800–2,000), can be hired at all the main beaches. Motorcycle accidents are frequent, so make sure you wear a helmet.

KO PHANGAN

Getting There
By Air

It is possible to fly from Bangkok to Ko Samui and then take a ferry to Ko Phangan. A slightly cheaper, though more time-consuming option, is to fly to the mainland Surat Thani Airport, transfer to a connecting bus to the pier and then connect by ferry to Ko Phangan.

By Bus and Train

Surat Thani is the jump-off point for Ko Phangan, so the bus and train transportation is the same as Ko Samui's *(see page 183).*

By Boat

From **Surat Thani**, there are six daily ferries departing from either Don Sak, Ban Don or Pak Nam Tapi piers to Thong Sala pier on Ko Phangan. The boats take around 2–3 hours. A night ferry from Ban Don takes about 7 hours. Tickets cost B350–450 (depending on the service).

From **Ko Samui**, there are four daily ferries from Na Thon pier to Thong Sala pier on Ko Phangan. The ride takes 30–45 minutes and tickets cost from B250. Additionally there are several daily ferries and speedboats from MaeNam and Bangrak (Big Bud-

dha) beaches in Ko Samui bound for Hat Rin on Ko Phangan. Lomprayah *(see page 183)* also have quick catamaran services.

Getting Around

Songthaew trucks traverse the main roads, with the average fare around B50 from Thong Sala town to anywhere on the island, except Ban Khai (B30) or further-flung places such as Ao Thong Nai Pan (B80). Motorcycle-taxi fares range from B20–30 for a short journey, to B150–200 from Thong Sala to Hat Rin. Note: *songthaews* don't move until they are full, so if you wish to charter one, expect to pay about B250 or more for a trip.

Motorcycles (B150–500) and jeeps (B800–1,500) can be hired at the island's main centres. The roads are tricky and accidents common, so exercise caution.

KO TAO

Getting There
By Bus, Train and Air

Surat Thani is the jump-off point for Ko Tao, so the plane, bus and train transportation is the same as Ko Phangan's *(see left).*

Alternatively, you can use Chumphon as a base to get to Ko Tao. Buses travel regularly from Bangkok's **Southern Bus Terminal** to Chumphon (7 hours), where you can take a ferry to Ko Tao. There are also regular train departures to Chumphon from Bangkok's **Hualamphong Station**.

By Boat

From **Chumphon**, the boat ride to Ko Tao takes about 1½–3 hours. There are at least six daily boat departures from the pier at Pak Nam port in Chumphon to Ban Mae pier on Ko Tao. Depending on the operator, tickets cost around B350 to B700 one way.

From **Surat Thani**, the boat to Ban Mae pier on Ko Tao takes about 6½ hours (once daily); the

ABOVE: boats near Ko Phangan.

night boat takes about 9 hours. From **Ko Phangan**, it takes about 1½ hours (5 times daily); and from **Ko Samui** the ride takes 2–3 hours (5 times daily). These varying travel times reflect the different type of boats used, ranging from catamarans and speedboats to ferries.

Getting Around

Songthaew trucks run along the island's main road from Hat Sai Ree to Ao Chalok Ban Kao in the south. The average fare from the main village of Mae Hat to either Hat Sai Ree or Ao Chalok Ban Kao is B30; travel to further beaches such as Ao Leuk will cost B80. Motorcycle taxis run the same routes for around the same price and they can also access some of the dirt tracks. Rates rise considerably later at night. Motorcycles (B150–500 per day) and jeeps (B800–1,500 per day) can be hired, but most of the island's tracks are still not sealed so caution is advised. Depending on sea conditions, longtail boats carry passengers to the island's less-accessible beaches, with fares from Mae Hat to Ao Chalok Ban Kao costing B150; to Ko Nang Yuan B100; and to Ao Tanote B300. Some boats will only leave with a minimum number of people; otherwise the boat can be chartered.

ACCOMMODATION LISTINGS

KO SAMUI

HAT CHAWENG

Amari Palm Reef Resort
North Chaweng
Tel: 0-7742 2015
www.amari.com/palmreef
On the quieter northern end of popular Chaweng beach, this resort has a delightful seaside restaurant and two free-form pools. The stylishly outfitted rooms either face the beach or the verdant gardens. Italian and Thai/Asian restaurants are on site, plus the highly regarded Breeze Spa. (187 rooms) $$$

Ark Bar Beach Resort
Central Chaweng
Tel: 0-7796 1333
www.ark-bar.com
Party animals often stay here to enjoy the lively beach restaurant and happening bar. Glass-fronted rooms are well maintained, though the closer to the beach you are, the less peace and quiet you will get. (60 rooms) $

Buri Rasa Village
Hat Chaweng
Tel: 0-7723 0222
www.burirasa.com
This lovely boutique resort, just south of Chaweng's busiest stretch, is tastefully designed with a Thai village ambience. The rooms and suites have DVD players and Wi-fi internet access but retain an old-world charm, with four-poster beds. The stylish pool is perfect for lazing at, and

there's a restaurant, beach bar and spa. (32 rooms) $$$

Penzy Guesthouse
37/75 Moo. 3, Soi Alibaba
Tel: 08-7055 7048
Good value here, with a central location five minutes from the beach, but still quiet. There's free internet and rooms have TV and DVD players with a wide choice to borrow from. (8 rooms) $

HAT LAMAI

Pavilion Samui
Hat Lamai
Tel: 0-7742 4030
www.pavilionsamui.com
The Pavilion Samui has been on Lamai for years but was upgraded a few years ago into an upmarket resort, with prices and facilities to match. Lovely pool, spa and an attractive beach front. More expensive rooms have bathtubs on the balcony. (70 rooms) $$$

Rocky's Boutique Resort
Hat Lamai
Tel: 0-7723 3020
www.rockyresort.com
The basic rooms are just 30 metres from the private beach, while top end villas come with gas stoves if you don't want to trek to the two restaurants, including modern French on the beach. (50 rooms) $$

Rummana Boutique Resort
Hat Lamai
Tel: 0-7741 8418

www.rummanaresort.com
These stylish seafront suites and villas are arranged on a headland at the end of Lamai Beach. The open-air Horapa restaurant serves an international menu and there is also a spa for pampering. $$

Silavadee Pool Spa Resort
Hat Lamai
Tel: 0-7796 0555
www.silavadeeresort.com
The stunning contemporary Asian design in these rooms and villas, plus panoramic sea views, mark this as one of the island's top accommodation choices. Also on site are a "wellness" spa and The Height restaurant, which serves international and Thai food, either indoors or outside. (56 rooms and villas) $$$

The Spa Resort
Hat Lamai, Ko Samui
Tel: 0-7723 0855
www.thesparesorts.net
One of the island's most affordable health-spa resorts, with yoga, meditation and detox cleansing as options. The rooms, surrounding a pool, vary in standard and rate. They have another resort in the jungle. $

HAT CHOENG MON

Imperial Boat House
83 Moo 5, Hat Choeng Mon

Tel: 0-7742 5041
www.imperialboathouse.com
Almost everything is boat-shaped (or boat-inspired) in this hotel, including its swimming pool. Luxury rooms and suites are set in two-storey converted rice barges as well as in the main building. Extensive use of wood gives this hotel an interesting tropical feel. (210 rooms) $$

Sala Samui Resort & Spa
Hat Choeng Mon
Tel: 0-7724 5888
www.salasamui.com
Nearly all of these sleek, modern villas and suites have their own private pool. All have open-air bathrooms, DVD players and Wi-fi access. The Sala Spa also offers beauty treatments and yoga classes. There is also a beach bar and two restaurants with international and Thai food on offer. (69 rooms) $$$

HAT BO PHUT

Anantara Ko Samui
Hat Bo Phut

PRICE CATEGORIES

Price categories show the starting price for a double room without breakfast and taxes:
$$$$ = over US$250
$$$ = US$130–250
$$ = US$70–130
$ = under US$70

Tel: 0-7742 8300–9
www.anantara.com
Plush boutique resort along a quiet stretch of Bo Phut beach, with Fisherman's Village a short walk away. Rooms and suites either overlook the landscaped gardens or beach. The oversized bathrooms come with terrazzo tubs for two. There's also an infinity pool, spa, fitness centre plus Italian and Thai restaurants. (126 rooms and villas) **$$$**

The Lodge
Hat Bo Phut
Tel: 0-7742 5337
www.lodgesamui.com
Right in the heart of Fisherman's Village, this place has comfortable rooms with hardwood floors and balconies with sea views. (10 rooms) **$**

Peace Resort
Hat Bo Phut
Tel: 0-7742 5357
www.peaceresort.com
This long-standing resort on Bo Phut beach has a relaxed family vibe and, despite being fairly large, still retains an intimate atmosphere. There's a relaxing pool and all the bungalows have their own balconies. (102 rooms) **$$$**

Zazen Boutique Resort & Spa
Hat Bo Phut
Tel: 0-7742 5085
www.samuizazen.com
This boutique resort has a very tropical, modern-Thai feel, with its lush gardens and local accents in architecture and decor. The villas are spacious and well appointed and have flat-screen TVs and Wi-fi access (many have iPods). The in-house east-west fusion restaurant is widely acclaimed. (28 villas) **$$$**

LAEM YAI

Four Seasons Resort
Hat Laem Yai
Tel: 0-7724 3000
www.fourseasons.com/kohsamui
On the secluded beach of Hat Laem Yai, this hotel offers various (very expensive) options: from a one-bedroom villa nestled in the hillside to a five-bedroom beach residence, all with indulgent outdoor rain showers and private infinity pools. Teak and rosewood furnishings add to this resort's southern-Thai charm. (74 villas) **$$$$**

HAT MAENAM

Santiburi Beach Resort Golf & Spa
Hat Maenam
Tel: 0-7742 5031
www.santiburi.com
The Santiburi touts itself as the island's first golf resort, but even if the rolling greens don't entice you, the luxury resort has plenty more to offer. Located on quiet Maenam beach, it has a huge oval-shaped pool, with suites in the main building and lovely villas set in the large gardens or facing the beach. (71 rooms and villas) **$$$$**

W Retreat
Hat Maenam
Tel: 0-7791 5999
www.starwoodhotels.com
A spectacular modern resort with funky design edges throughout. The room facilities include widescreen TVs, Wi-fi sound docking, free internet, private decks and pools and sea views throughout. There's a stunning infinity pool and several restaurants, including modern Japanese. (73 rooms) **$$$$**

KO PHANGAN

Cocohut Beach Resort & Spa
Ban Tai (Leela Beach)
Tel: 0-7737 5368
www.cocohut.com
Located on Leela beach, yet still within walking distance of Hat Rin's main action, this popular resort sprawls over 100 metres (328ft) of prime beach-front land. It has several different types of room, ranging from the simple guesthouse to the more expensive pool-facing executive suites. All have balconies. There's also an internet café and a restaurant with huge video screen. (67 rooms) **$$**

Green Papaya Resort
Hat Salad
Tel: 0-7737 4230
www.greenpapayaresort.com
This resort has a mere 20 rooms to ensure privacy and a personalised touch. Set around a pool, the wooden bungalows come in five price ranges, with the executive suites featuring private terraces and outdoor jacuzzis. The beachside restaurant is built like a boat and has a Thai and Western menu. (20 rooms) **$$**

Haad Son Resort & Restaurant
Hat Son
Tel: 0-7734 9103.
www.haadson.net
Occupying the rocky headland at the end of an uninhabited, pristine white-sand beach, this is one of the best value resorts on the west coast. A variety of rooms, from simple huts to poolside villas and executive penthouse suites with private pools. There are two restaurants and sunset views to die for. (47 rooms) **$**

Panviman Resort
Ao Thong Nai Pan Noi
Tel: 0-7744 5101
www.panviman.com/kohphangan
This is a rather upscale sleeping option considering some of the room prices. It's perched on the headland that divides the pretty northeastern bays of Thong Nai Pan Yai and Thong Nai Pan Noi. Clustered around the pool, the stylish cottages and hotel rooms have modern amenities including air conditioning, minibar, satellite TV, and DVD players. (72 rooms) **$$**

Santhiya Resort & Spa
Ao Thong Nai Pan Noi
Tel: 0-7742 8999
www.santhiya.com
A smart resort on idyllic Thong Nai Pan Noi bay. Decorated in a blend of traditional and modern Thai style with teak

details, the rooms have ceiling-to-floor windows as well as verandahs with great views of the pool and gardens or the sea. They have a restaurant and a spa. (99 rooms and villas) **$$**

Sarikantang
Ban Tai (Leela Beach)
Tel: 0-7737 5055
www.sarikantang.com
Situated on the tip of Hat Rin at pleasant Leela beach, this small, boutique resort has a modern-Asian minimalist feel to it. Like most of the island's newer and more upscale resorts, it offers several types of room to suit different budgets, including an ocean-view suite with separate living room, DVD player and outdoor bathtub. Facilities include a spa and res-

Above: signage in Ko Phangan.

taurant and there are free kayaks available. (37 rooms) **$$**

Sunset Cove
78/11 Moo 8, Ao Chaophao
Tel: 0-7734 9211

www.thaisunsetcove.com
Though the wooden bungalows are packed tight, rooms are spotless and come with comfy beds, DVD play-

ers (with free movies) and open-air showers as standard. The sea front restaurant serves Western and Thai cuisine. (34 rooms) **$**

KO TAO

Ban's Diving Resort
Hat Sai Ree
Tel: 08-9980 7840
www.kohtaobansdiving.com
A range of clean, smart rooms at the top end (from B1,500), with hilltop, garden or pool views. They are mainly used by divers coming for the in-house PADI dive lessons, but are good value for non-divers, too. Very basic fan rooms start at B500. **$**

Charm Churee Villa
Ao Jansom
Tel: 0-7745 6394
www.charmchureevilla.com
Perched on pretty Ao Jansom, this cute resort has a traditional tropical feel. A variety of hillside cottages runs up to a very expensive five

bedroom villa. One of the two restaurants has great views, the other is on the beach. (30 rooms) **$$**

Chintakiri Resort
Ao Chalok Ban Kao
Tel: 0-7745 6391
www.chintakiriresort.com
This pleasing resort has Thai style bungalows located on a hillside with excellent views over the sea. There's free Wi-fi, a pool and restaurant. (19 rooms) **$$**

In Touch Resort
Hat Sai Ree
Tel: 0-7745 6514
www.intouchresort.com
Located at the quieter end of the beach, it's still not far to reach the action. The rooms are a mix of fan only bunga-

lows and slightly more expensive studios with air conditioning. The restaurant has Wi-fi. (11 rooms) **$**

Jamahkiri Boutique Resort & Spa
Ao Thian Ok
Tel: 0-7745 6400
www.jamahkiri.com
This resort, perched on a small hill, houses a highly pampering spa and four room sizes decorated in dark woods and silks. There's a terrace restaurant and a pool, plus fitness and PADI diving centres. Over the Christmas and New Year period there's a minimum 3-night stay. (12 rooms) **$$$**

The Place
Hat Sai Ree

Tel: 08-7887 5066
www.theplacekohtao.com
With only five villas, each with infinity pool and great views, and prices just nudging into the top range, you need to book months ahead here. The villas have kitchenettes, Bluetooth audio, movie and TV libraries and PCs with iTunes libraries. Ten minutes walk to Sairee if you want to get away. (5 rooms) **$$$$**

PRICE CATEGORIES

Price categories show the starting price for a double room without breakfast and taxes:
$$$$ = over US$250
$$$ = US$130–250
$$ = US$70–130
$ = under US$70

KO SAMUI

HAT CHAWENG

Thai and Western

Budsaba
Muang Kulaypan Hotel, 100 Moo 2, Hat Chaweng
Tel: 0-7723 0849/51
www.kulaypan.com
Open: daily B, L and D
This lovely Thai restaurant sits on the beach at the front of the stylish Muang Kulaypan hotel. Relax under intimate, rustic grass-roof pavilions with floor cushions and order classic Thai dishes while being entertained by live classical Thai music and dance performances. **$$**

Dr Frogs
Chaweng Noi
Tel: 0-7741 3797
www.drfrogssamui.com
Open: daily L and D.
Located in a prime spot overlooking Chaweng Bay, Dr Frogs is stylishly decked out in cream and olive tones with water-hyacinth sofas and plenty of teak and bamboo. The food is Thai, Italian and fusion fare, but, if you want what the good doctor ordered, go for buttered frogs' legs with garlic and parsley. **$$$**

Mitra Samui Restaurant
Chaweng Seafood Centre
Tel: 08-9727 2034
Open: daily B, L and D.
This is a large and not very pretty diner, but the cooks deliver extremely reliable Thai dishes at great value in a town that is getting relentlessly more pricey. The speciality seafood is on display for you to choose, but there are lots of other standards available, from spicy pork *laab* to mild chicken massaman. Very popular, so it tends to get crowded. **$**

The Page
14/1 Moo 2 Chaweng Beach
Tel: 0-7742 2767
www.thelibrary.co.th
Open: daily B, L and D.
This smart restaurant with a beautiful beachside location, attached to The Library resort, serves both Thai and Western dishes. Presentation is artful and the cooking is good, whether you're eating breakfast, mixed Thai appetisers or the multi-course tasting menu at dinner. **$$$**

Poppies
South Chaweng
Tel: 0-7742 2419
www.poppiessamui.com
Open: daily L and D.
This enduring beachfront restaurant has long been an island favourite. Sit under the stars beside the boutique resort's pool or in the authentic Ayutthaya-style teak pavilion as you dine on well-presented and refined Thai and Western dishes. **$$$**

International

The Cliff
Between Hat Chaweng and

ABOVE: Tom Yam Thai soup.

Hat Lamai
Tel: 0-7744 8508
www.thecliffsamui.com
Open: daily L and D.
An airy and modern clifftop restaurant set between the island's two busiest beaches. The view from this vantage point is its main appeal, but the Mediterranean fare is also very good. The menu includes dishes cooked in zesty and spicy piri piri sauce, as well as pastas, steaks and burgers. **$$$**

The Larder
9/144 Moo 2, Hat Chaweng
Tel: 0-7760 1259
www.thelardersamui.com
Open: Mon–Sat L and D.
The Larder brings some British-European gastropub finesse to the table with starters like foie gras miso and black truffle broth, moving through mains such as pan fried scallops and prawns, miso dijon sauce, roasted fennel and soused radish. There's a good wine and cocktail list and a relaxed atmosphere. **$$$**

Prego
North Chaweng
Tel: 0-7742 2015
www.prego-samui.com
Open: daily L and D.
Situated on the quieter north end of Chaweng, and managed by the Amari Palm Reef Resort opposite, this stylish Italian restaurant is open and airy, with soothing water features that add to the mood. The menu, which includes wood-fired oven pizza and fresh seafood, is reasonably priced given the quality of the food and the ambience. **$$$**

Red Snapper Restaurant & Bar
Chaweng Regent Hotel
Tel: 0-7730 0200
www.redsnappersamui.com

Open: daily D.
Located within the Chaweng Regent Hotel, this tastefully designed eatery combines a comfy lounge bar with live Latin music nightly. The food has a Mediterranean leaning, with juicy steaks and grilled seafood providing the backbone. All main dishes give you access to the large salad buffet. **$$$**

Rice
91/1 Moo 2, Hat Chaweng
Tel: 0-7723 1934
www.ricesamui.com
Open: daily L and D.
Smack in the heart of Chaweng's evening entertainment scene, this fine-dining Italian restaurant has a contemporary Asian look to its split-level interior, complete with a large lily pond at the front. Along with pastas and pizzas from the wood-fired oven, there are tempting mains such as tenderloin with gorgonzola. A glass elevator carries guests up to the third level for cocktails at the rooftop lounge bar. **$$$**

Zico's
38/2 Moo 3, Hat Chaweng (opposite Central Samui Beach Resort)
Tel: 0-7723 1560
www.zicossamui.com
Open: daily D.
Rio comes to Thailand at this Brazilian-style barbecue restaurant. Diners, especially meat-loving types, will salivate over the array of meats on offer – B850 per person allows you to eat as much as you want (including soup and the salad bar). Carnival dancing queens and samba rhythms create an upbeat vibe. **$$**

ELSEWHERE

Thai and Western

Barracuda Restaurant
Hat Maenam
Tel: 0-7792 1663
www.barracuda-restaurant.com
Open: Tue–Sun D.
This modest German run restaurant concentrates on European cuisine with Asian touches in

dishes like tea infused tuna served with wasabi and chocolate mousse with chilli. It's a popular place and there are only 20 seats, so it's best to book ahead. **$$$**

The Patio
Pavilion Samui Boutique Resort, Hat Lamai
Tel: 0-7742 4030
www.pavilionsamui.com
Open: daily B and D.
Part of the plush Pavilion boutique hotel, this lovely open-air beachfront eatery on Lamai is surrounded by ponds and fountains. Dine to live entertainment while enjoying spectacular views. The extensive menu has Italian and Thai dishes, plus some enticing desserts and potent cocktails. **$$$**

The Shack
Fisherman's Village, Hat Bo Phut
Tel: 0-7724 6041
www.theshackgrillsamui.com
Open: daily 3–11pm.
It may look like little more than a humble shack, but this American-owned establishment is a firm

favourite with the island's expats. Photographs of blues legends hang on the wall, and blues is the music of choice here. The chalkboard menu has a selection of local seafood and imported Australian meats, but make sure that you save room for the home-made icecream and New York cheesecake. **$$$**

Zazen
177 Moo 1, Zazen Boutique Resort & Spa, Hat Bo Phut
Tel: 0-7742 5085
www.samuizazen.com
Open: daily B, L and D.
Stylish and romantic, this restaurant looks out to the sea with Ko Phangan as a backdrop. Sit in an open-sided area with its Balinesestyle roof or on the candlelit terrace. The European chef serves up a blend of Asian and European cuisine using healthy organic ingredients. You can order dishes à la carte or choose from one of the four set menus available. **$$$–$$$$**

KO PHANGAN

Outside of Hat Rin and Thong Sala, there are fewer independant restaurants. Most eateries are contained within guesthouses, and while the food is passable, don't have too high expectations. Most menus present the familiar Thai and Western staples.

Thai and Western

Again and Again
Moo 5, Had Nai Pan Noi

No phone
Open: daily L and D.
This small family run joint serves very consistent Thai food along the well trodden lines of pad Thai, somtam, red curry and mango sticky rice for dessert. The friendly service extends to picking up a bottle from the shop If you want one. **$**

Fisherman's Restaurant & Bar
Ban Tai
Tel: 08-4454 7240

Open: daily L and D.
This small restaurant and bar serves mainly Thai food, but also has some Asian fusion dishes. The stress is on seafood, from simple grilled fish with salad, to mixed seafood platters, to the house speciality of yellow crab curry. **$$**

Luna Lounge
Ban Tai
Tel: 0-7744 5035
www.luna-restaurant-phangan.com
Open: daily L and D.

This mainly international menu has starters including a tapas selection and is big on barbecues, with lots of freshly caught local fish in a variety of sauces,

PRICE CATEGORIES

Price per person for a three-course meal without drinks:
$ = under US$10
$$ = US$10–25
$$$ = US$25–50
$$$$ = over US$50

from lemongrass to cognac. There are also some Thai dishes. **$$**

International

A's Coffee Shop
Thong Sala
Tel: 0-7737 7226
Open: Mon–Sat 10am–9pm.
Located within the Buakao Inn Guest House, this is a long-time favourite with visitors. It has a great variety of dishes, from traditional Thai to Pacific Rim cuisine, with specialities such as pizza baguettes, German, English and American breakfasts, and excellent pastas, all washed down by espresso, cappuccino and large margaritas. It occasionally hosts live gigs on weekends.
$–$$

Fabio's
Moo 2 10/1 Ban Tai
tel: 08-3389 5732
Open: daily B, L and D.
Home-made pastas and pizzas cooked in a wood fired oven are the favourite choices at this Italian. It has a casual atmosphere and a design conscious interior, but not very big, so booking is essential. **$$**

Om Ganesh
Hat Rin Nai
Tel: 0-7737 5123
Open: daily B, L and D.
Om Ganesh is a relaxing two-storey restaurant located near the Hat Rin pier. The restaurant serves excellent curries and Indian breads prepared by a cook with over two decades' experience in New Delhi.
$–$$

Restaurant Peppercorn
Hat Salad
Tel: 08-7896 4363

www.restaurantpeppercorn.com
Open: Mon–Sat 2–11pm.
Dining to a good view over the bay on a broad range of steak dishes, plus wide Euro influenced mains like lasagne, stroganoff and schnitzel. They also have a decent choice for vegetarians. **$$$**

The Mason's Arms
145/5 Thong Sala

Tel: 0-7723 8526
www.themasonsarms.in.th
Open: daily B, L and D.
This looks every bit like an English country pub and the food plays the part just fine. If you don't fancy fish and chips, there's always bangers and mash, Irish stew or Fisherman's pie. And a choice of cider and beer on tap to wash it all down. **$$**

BELOW: grilled fish.

KO TAO

Thai and Western

Barracuda
9/9 Moo 1 Hat Sairee
Tel: 08-0146 3267
www.barracudakohtao.com
Open: daily L and D.
The English chef/owner is big on fresh caught local seafood dishes, with the seafood platter a speciality. Look out for rack of ribs with Thai fusion barbecue sauce and seared tuna with Thai couscous. **$$**

Bizarro Tapas Bar and Restaurant
Ao Chalok Ban Kao
Tel: 09-0565 5434
www.bizarrokohtao.com
This cheap and cheerful Spanish-Argentinian run diner does specialities

like Cubana rice and ceviche, plus paella every Saturday, alongside pastas, barbecue ribs and baguettes. There are some Thai dishes, too, and a good list of cocktails. **$–$$**

The Gallery Restaurant
Hat Sai Ree
Tel: 0-7745 6547
www.thegallerykohtao.com
Open: daily D only.
There's an arty vibe here, with the owner's photos also on display next door to the well designed restaurant. The all Thai menu features chicken satay, green curry, plus some inventive cocktails. Only six tables, so book in advance. **$$**

International

Café del Sol
Mae Hat
Tel: 0-7745 6578
www.cafedelsol.ws
Open: daily B, L and D.
This pleasant little eatery serves a broad selection of authentic French, Italian and other international fare, cooked up by a Gallic chef. Tuck into big breakfasts, home-made pastas, bruschettas, tender steaks and smoked salmon. Good wines, coffee and free Wi-fi. **$$**

Reef Sports Bar & Restaurant
Mae Hat
Tel: 08-7101 3240
www.reefbarkohtao.com

Open: daily B, L and D.
This place fills the gap for people who need a no-nonsense plate of food. The large menu has pork chops and salmon steak, chilli con carne, fajitas, chicken madras, burgers, pizzas and pastas, plus a wide choice of Western breakfasts. There's free Wi-fi, a free pool table and sport on TV. **$$**

PRICE CATEGORIES

Price per person for a three-course meal without drinks:
$ = under US$10
$$ = US$10–25
$$$ = US$25–50
$$$$ = over US$50

ACTIVITIES

KO SAMUI

Nightlife
Dance Bars and Clubs

Green Mango: Soi Green Mango, Chaweng; tel: 0-7742 2148; www. thegreenmangoclub.com. Long-running outdoor venue with a rustic feel and multiple dance floors. It gets packed and runs very late.

Q Bar: Opposite Chaweng Lake View Hotel, mobile tel: 0-7796 2420; www.qbarsamui.com. Samui's version of Bangkok's famous Q Bar is a swish two-storey New York-style lounge, with indoor and outdoor areas and a creative drinks list to go with the hip-hop and house beats.

Reggae Pub: Chaweng Lagoon; tel: 0-7742 2331. A Samui mainstay, it's become more tired than trendy, but still stays busy with cruising single men and the working girls they hope to meet. Mainstream dance sounds with a touch of Bob Marley.

Sound Club: Chaweng; tel: 0-2240 3700; www.soundclubsamui. com. There are two dancefloors for different music styles at this outdoor club, which plays mainly R&B, hip hop and house. It starts around 11pm and runs very late.

Sweet Soul Cafe: Soi Green Mango, Chaweng; tel:0-7741 3358. Owned by Green Mango, opposite, and possibly even more popular. The music is a mix of R&B and hip hop with the pop hits.

Bars and Pubs

Ark Bar Beach Resort: Central Chaweng: tel: 0-7796 1333; www. ark-bar.com. Located on the sands of the central stretch of Chaweng beach, this bar and restaurant has several DJ nights with house sounds picking up from early evening.

The Frog & Gecko Pub: Bo Phut; tel: 08-9866 8657; www.frogand-

gecko.com. Owned by a British-American couple, there is international and Thai food and a long cocktail list to go with the beers. There's a pool table, occasional live music and quiz nights.

Tropical Murphys: Chaweng; tel: 0-7741 3614; www.tropicalmurphys. com. This premier Gaelic haunt is a two-level pub and restaurant with appetising dishes, local and imported beers on tap and live band music.

Wave Samui: Chaweng; tel: 0-7723 0803; www.thewavesamui. com. With its library of guidebooks and friendly staff, Samui Wave dispenses travel advice, cheap beers and free movie screenings, mostly to a backpacker crowd.

Kathoey Cabaret

Starz Cabaret: Chaweng; tel: 08-4744 9074. Packing them in every night for free shows at 8.30, 9.30 and 10.30pm. Starz is Samui's most popular (but not the only) kathoey, or transsexual, cabaret act.

Shopping

As Samui's development continues unabated, shops geared to both tourists and residents are beginning to spring up all over the island. By far the greatest concentration is in and around Chaweng, with at least two major supermarket chains (Tesco Lotus and Tops) having set up shop, as well as small boutique arcades such as Iyara Plaza, Living Square Plaza and the huge Central Festival. In addition, market stalls and shops along Chaweng's main drag peddle the same counterfeit clothing, bags, sports shoes, CDs and DVDs you find in Bangkok. Also commonly found in Chaweng are artists' studios where you can purchase replicas of your favourite masterpieces, as well as handicraft and home-furnishing stores.

Outdoor Activities
Diving

CSI Samui: 101/20 Moo 1, Bophut; tel: 08-4843 8934; www. csisamui.com. This PADI dive centre has a range of courses for beginners through to PADI Divemaster certification. Dive sites cover the whole Gulf, and there are snorkelling and kayaking options for non-divers.

Discovery Dive Centre: Amari Palm Reef Resort, Chaweng; tel: 0-7731 0761; www.discoverydivers. com. A small but well-equipped dive centre with its own speedboat. As well as offering courses and fun dives, it also rents out underwater video and photography equipment, in addition to kayaks, windsurfing boards and catamarans.

Searobin: 24/3 Moo 5 Bophut; tel. 08-1535 7768; www.divesearobin.com. This dive shop offers a full range of PADI scuba courses and fun dive tours. Staffed by friendly, multicultural instructors, it now offers theory courses online, so you can maximise your time in the water. There's another branch at Chaweng.

Go-karting

Samui Go-Kart: 101/2 Moo 1, Bo Phut; tel: 0-7742 5097. Open from 9am till late, this jungle-fringed track has three types of karts, the slowest of which are suitable for kids.

Cable Ride

Canopy Adventures: Secret Falls, Maenam; tel: 0-7743 0811; www.canopyadventuresthailand. com. Suspended from the trees above, you will glide through the forest canopy in Ko Samui's lush interior at this site. The 2- to 3-hour trip includes six exhilarating treetop rides (no experience necessary), a swim in a waterfall and a refreshing drink at their jungle bar.

Golf

Santiburi Beach Resort Golf & Spa: 12/15 Moo 4 Maenam; tel: 0-7742 5031; www.santiburi.com. This lush 18-hole (par 72) course lies on the hills behind quiet Maenam beach on Samui's northern coast. They also have a nine hole course.

Kayaking

Blue Stars: Chaweng; tel: 0-7730 0615; www.bluestars.info. This outfit runs 1- and 2-day kayak trips around Ang Thong Marine National Park. The 2-night trips feature a barbecue dinner and overnight camping on a desolate beach. The departure point on Ko Samui is Na Thon pier.

Sailing

Samui Boat Charters: Fisherman's Village, Bo Phut; tel: 08-7276 7598; www.samuiboatcharter.com. Offers a fleet of speedboats and yachts for trips to the islands, deep-sea fishing or diving. Professionally crewed and full waiter service if you need it.
Samui Ocean Sports: Chaweng Regent Beach Resort; tel:0-81940 1999; www.sailing-in-samui.com. This established German-run sailing company offers private yacht charters – plus a management training programme for boat owners.

Sightseeing Tours

Mr Ung's Magical Safari: Moo 3, Chaweng; tel: 0-7723 0114; www.ungsafari.com. Mr Ung runs three tours – a full- and half-day "safari", as well as a day of deep-sea fishing. The full-day safari includes an optional elephant ride, plus four-wheel-drive jeep tours into the lush jungled interior and a waterfall swim.

Spas

Breeze Spa: Bophut; tel: 0-7742 2015; www.amari.com/palmreef. Set in a beautiful private garden with just four split-level suites, this spa offers an array of indulgent massages, scrubs, treatments and facials. The signature "Head Over Heels" treatment takes 4 hours.
The Spa Resort: Lamai; tel: 0-7723 0855; www.sparesorts.net. One of Thailand's longest-running spas, this no-frills resort is well-known for its fasting and cleansing programmes. Often booked up in advance. Also has yoga, Reiki and traditional Thaimassage classes.
Tamarind Springs Forest Spa: 205/7 Moo 4, Samui Ring Rd; tel: 0-7742 4221; www.tamarindsprings.com. A truly inspired setting, this well-regarded spa has rustic timber pavilions under which you can enjoy its range of therapeutic massages. Also offers classes in yoga, t'ai chi and *qigong*.

Cookery School

Samui Institute of Thai Culinary Arts (sitca): Chaweng; tel: 0-7741 3172; www.sitca.net. A professionally run cookery school, this institute has been featured widely in the media. It conducts hands-on morning and late-afternoon/dinner courses (both B2,250). Budding chefs learn to cook three or four dishes, and finish by eating them. The school also runs 3-day fruit- and vegetable-carving courses.

KO PHANGAN

Nightlife
Bars and Dance Clubs

Backyard Bar: Hat Rin Nok; tel: 0-7737 5244. A long-established Ko Phangan favourite and the home of the Full Moon Party afterbash, this bar is located up the hill behind Hat Rin Nok. Generally quiet outside its regular parties.
Cactus Club: Hat Rin Nok. Popular mainstay on this beach. It also organises fun day trips to interior waterfalls and nearby beaches.
Drop-In Club: Hat Rin Nok; tel: 0-7737 5444. Located between Cactus Club and Paradise, this long-established bar has the usual beach-mat and cushion set-up on the sand, and plays more listener-friendly commercial music.
Pirate's Bar: Ao Chaophao. This imaginatively designed bar takes the form of a boat built into the rock face at the end of the beach. To cash in on the Full Moon Party phenomenon, it hosts the monthly Moon-Set Party a few days before and after the real McCoy.
Zoom Bar: Hat Rin Nok, tel; 0-7737 4161; www.sheesha-bar.com. A large bar with a loud, loud sound system that makes it a favourite during the various parties, F-M and otherwise. The line up depends on who's playing, but favours diverse forms of trance.

Outdoor Activities
Diving

Chaloklum Diving: Ao Chalok Lam; tel: 0-7737 4025; www.chaloklum-diving.com. Located on the north coast, this outfit has been operating for a decade now. It has its own boat and a policy of running courses for small groups, ensuring maximum attention. Courses are taught in both English and German.
Haad Yao Divers: 84/31 Moo 8, Hat Yao, mobile tel: 08-6279 3085; www.haadyaodivers.com.

BELOW: Tamarind Springs Spa.

Located on the island's west coast, this reputable European-run outfit offers all the main PADI and speciality courses, including lessons for children and snorkelling.

Phangan Divers: Hat Rin; tel: 0-7737 5117; www.phangandivers. com. This is one of the island's first and most comprehensive dive schools. As well as PADI courses, fun dives and snorkelling-equipment rental, it also operates a stress and rescue programme to help you deal with emergency situations and an Instructor Development Centre for professional certification.

Health and Fitness Centres

Blooming Lotus Yoga: Hat Yuan; tel: 08-6086 0336; www.thailand yoga.net. Qualified expat instructors offer daily yoga classes and yoga retreats, plus yoga teaching courses should you want to go into business yourself.

Adventure and Tours

Phangan Safari Boat: Thong Sala; tel: 0-7723 8232; www.safari boat.info. Daily trips by boat stop at beaches and coves around the island. Snorkelling gear is provided, along with breakfast, lunch and snacks. Alternatively, explore the caves, lagoons and coral of Ang Thong Marine Park, or head inland on the Rainforest Adventure, which takes in an elephant camp, zip-lines above the jungle canopy, archery and more.

SL2K Adventure: Baan Manali Resort, Thong Sala; tel: 08-3390 3125; www.sl2kadventure.com. Tour the island on the adventurous "multisport discovery" activity, through trekking, cycling, snorkelling and kayaking. Or stick to the water with catamaran sailing and diving. Lessons are available and there are facilities for groups, couples or single people.

Wake Up: 71/3 Moo 7, Chaloklum; tel: 08-7283 6755; www.jungl-egym.co.th. The specially built boat creates waves for you to jump as

ABOVE: dive shop.

you speed along behind on a wakeboard attached behind, like water skiing. They also organise boat trips of the region.

Spas

When the neurons are shot after a heavy dose of partying, Ko Phangan has a few establishments to detoxify the body and purify the mind. For a holistic-retreat experience, consider **The Sanctuary** (mobile tel: 08-1271 3614; www.thesanctuarythailand.com) on Hat Thian, a centre offering fasting, colonic cleansing and yoga. Or else try the **Monte Vista** (mobile tel: 08-1747 7329; www. montevistathailand.com) near Thong Sala, which provides similar services. They also provide a working holiday programme in which you get shared accommodation and access to several daily courses in return for working at the centre.

Nightlife

Choppers Bar & Grill: Hat Sai Ree; tel. 0-7745 6641. A friendly, beery Australian-run bar with pool table and on-screen films and sport.
Fizz: Hat Sai Ree; tel: 08-7887 9495. This relaxed lounge bar-restaurant offers beachside ambi-

ence and bean bags to sprawl on.
Lotus Bar: Hat Sai Ree, tel: 08-7069 6078; www.tonylotusbar. com. A popular party bar with fire shows and dancing on the beach.
MOOV Restaurant, Club and Art Garden: Mae Hat. This cool club and bar has DJs, cocktails and tapas style food to enjoy in a garden with its own tree house and bottle igloo.
Maya Beach Club: Hat Sai Ree; tel: 08-0578 2225. Open-sided wooden bar spills the crowd on to the beach for the nightly DJ sounds.

Outdoor Activities

Adventure

Goodtime Adventures: Hat Sai Ree; tel: 08-7275 3604; www.gt adventures.com. GT runs a series of activities, from pub crawls to cliff jumping, boating and wakeboarding. Not necessarily in that order.

Diving

Big Blue Diving: Hat Sai Ree and Mae Hat; tel: 0-7745 6179; www. bigbluediving.com. One of Thailand's best dive companies, with a well-deserved reputation.
Easy Divers: Mae Hat; tel: 0-7745 6010; www.kohtaoeasydivers com. With a branch on Mae Hat and Ko Nang Yuan, Easy Divers runs regular, speciality courses and live-aboard trips.
Planet Scuba: Mae Hat; tel: 0-7745 6110; www.planetscuba.com. One of Thailand's most reputable dive outfits with over two decades of experience.
Scuba Junction: Hat Sai Ree; tel: 0-7745 6164; www.scuba-junction.com. Located halfway up Hat Sai Ree beach, this outfit has its own boat and runs a wide range of courses.

Sailing

Island Cruises Sailing: Mae Hat; tel: 0-7745 7002, www.island-cruises. org. Enjoy sailing cruises around the islands in one of the company's two yachts or take an extended course to learn the ropes yourself.

NORTHERN ANDAMAN COAST

This region is well known for its pristine diving and snorkelling hotspots – the famed Similan and Surin islands – as well as the awesome limestone formations at Phang Nga Bay. Also worth exploring are land-based attractions such as waterfalls, hot springs and jungle trails.

The Andaman Coast, along western Thailand, stretches from Ranong on the Isthmus of Kra all the way south to Satun near the Malaysian border. This chapter only covers the land and sea attractions as far south as Phang Nga. The region provides easy access to the renowned scuba and snorkelling hotspots of Similan and Surin islands, as well as to the dramatic limestone formations towering out of the waters around Phang Nga Bay.

RANONG

Located 600km (370 miles) from Bangkok and 300km (185 miles) from Phuket, **Ranong** is relatively far from major centres. The province has the highest annual rainfall in Thailand, and while it has a coastal location, it is not blessed with beautiful beaches. It's home to a large port, with numerous fishing boats and fish-processing factories.

What Ranong does offer, however, is easy access to a number of inland attractions, as well as to the undeveloped islands of Ko Chang and Ko Phayam, both reached in about 2 to 3 hours. Its proximity to **Myanmar** (25 minutes by boat) also makes it

handy for foreigners in South Thailand who have to leave the country to renew their visas. With the easing of the political situation in Burma and the opening up of tourism there, Ranong could become far more popular than it currently is.

Ranong Town

The run-down **Ranong Town** ① offers a limited choice of accommodation and even the most expensive hotels need a good lick of paint. Good places to eat are few and far between

Main attractions
SURIN ISLANDS
BURMA BANKS
KHAO LAK
SIMILAN ISLANDS
AO PHANG NGA

LEFT: the Similan Islands in the Andaman Sea are a diver's haven. **RIGHT:** Punyaban Waterfall in Ranong.

Pool at the Jansom Hot Spa hotel in Ranong (see page 206).

BELOW: Wat Hat Som Paen at dusk.

and nightlife is limited, but it is a good base from which to explore the inland attractions.

Outside Ranong Town

The **Punyaban Waterfall**, about 15km (9 miles) north of Ranong Town and off Highway 4, is frequently overshadowed by the larger Ngao Waterfall *(see below)*, but is no less beautiful. Punyaban's cascading waters can be witnessed from a few levels. Access to its base is possible by scaling a few boulders, while a 300-metre (985ft) nature trail leads to an elevated lookout. From here the water below hits the rocks spectacularly and disperses into a fine mist.

About 2km (1½ miles) southeast of town is **Raksawarin Park ❷**, where Ranong's most famous attraction, the natural **Hot Springs** (daily 8am–5pm; free), is found. Heated to around 65 degrees C (150 degrees F), the water is too hot to bathe in, but there are concrete pools circled by stone seats

where people can stop, sit and inhale the reviving steam.

The dirt road through Raksawarin Park, past the Hot Springs, leads to a junction that forks one way to the village of **Hat Som Paen**. This one-time tin-mining village has a creek running though the temple, **Wat Hat Som Paen** (daily 8am–5pm; free), where giant carp swim freely and can be fed with locally sold fish food. Superstitious locals believe the carp to be angels who should be treated with respect.

Ranong's only beach, **Hat Chan Damri ❸**, which overlooks the British-named **Victoria Point** in Myanmar, is approximately 9km (6 miles) from town. It is a small but pleasant beach when the sun is shining, but the monsoon rains frequently litter its sands with broken palm leaves, twigs and fallen coconuts.

The large **Ngao Waterfall**, 13km (8 miles) south of Ranong, is situated within **Khlong Phrao National**

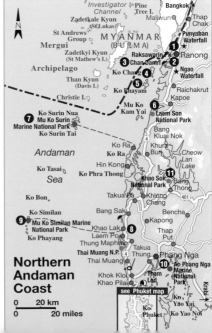

Northern Andaman Coast

0   20 km
0   20 miles

Park (daily 8am–4.30pm; charge). Originating deep within the dense forest, water pours down the cliff and can be seen from a distance.

Directly across Highway 4 from Ngao Waterfall are the so-called **Ghost Mountains**, so named because of their complete lack of trees. This series of grass-covered hills changes its colour to golden brown during the hot summer months.

Ko Chang

The quiet and undeveloped island of **Ko Chang ❶**, in Ranong Province, could not be further removed from the other Ko Chang found along the Eastern Seaboard *(see page 129)*. There are no ATMs here or on Ko Phayam, so take cash with you or be prepared to trek back to Ranong for a top up.

The island is part of the **Mu Ko Phayam National Park**, and home to small fishing communities of people who moved from Surat Thani and Ko Phangan decades ago.

Leaving from both Ranong (2½ hours) and Laem Son National Park (1 hour), the boat ride to Ko Chang is particularly scenic, even in bad weather. During the monsoon season, from May to October, boats stop running altogether as the seas are too dangerous to cross, and accommodation on the islands shuts down. The limited availability of electricity has deterred large resorts, and the available basic beach bungalows use generators for five or six hours from 5pm. Calm waters and shallow coral reefs allow safe swimming and snorkelling, although the water is largely unclear, and there are no cars on the island. Ko Chang is largely a place to lie around and chill out.

Most of the island's golden-sand beaches stretch along the west coast, the longest being **Ao Yai**, where there is no pier, so access is only possible by longtail boat and then a wade through the water. The beach spans 4km (3 miles), and has the majority of the island's accommodation. Two concrete tracks lead to Ko Chang's only village. As the paths are flat and there is plenty of shade, it is easily reached in 30 minutes on foot, but all you will find is a a small restaurant.

There are several smaller beaches, such as **Ao Lek** on the east coast, but

TIP

From May to Oct, the southwest monsoon brings heavy rain to the entire Andaman Coast. While this means that some of the islands further away cannot be accessed because of rough seas, it's not unusual to get days of intermittent sunshine, even during the peak rainy-season months.

BELOW LEFT: hot springs at Ranong. **BELOW RIGHT:** playful young monks.

The waters around Laem Son National Park are prime game-fishing locations.

they are at least a 5km (3 mile) trudge from the village and have very little accommodation or facilities. On the other hand, the seclusion and privacy may appeal to some.

Ko Phayam

Smaller than Ko Chang, but more developed and gaining in popularity is **Ko Phayam** ❺, 15 minutes away by boat. The pier is fairly quiet, apart from a handful of convenience stores, an internet café and hordes of motorcycle taxis and touts trying to entice guests to their bungalows.

Along with monkeys, boars and sea birds, Ko Phayam has a population of around 500 people, who mainly eke a living by growing cashew nuts and coconuts. The two main white sandy beaches are on opposite sides of the island, shadowed by forested hills shadows. Like Ko Chang, the roads are small, many going from concrete to dirt trails as they progress inland, and also like Ko Chang, there are no cars. As the walk to the other side of the island can take a good hour, motorcycle taxis on the island do a brisk trade. There are no restaurants

on either of the beaches, so meals are confined to the hotel you stay at.

The longest and most popular beach, with the most accommodation, is **Ao Yai** on the southwest coast. Most bungalows (some with 24-hour electricity) are set slightly back from the white-sand beach-front behind a border of palm and pine trees, which allow for uninterrupted views from anywhere along the sand.

Ao Khao Khwai, on the northwest coast, is the second base for visitors, but being smaller and having fewer bungalows makes it a less popular choice. Nonetheless, it has a fine stretch of sand and clear water, providing snorkelling opportunities at the plentiful coral near the shore, although poor fishing practices have destroyed much of it. Its nickname, Buffalo Bay, comes from the curvature of its two sides, resembling a pair of buffalo horns.

Laem Son National Park

Reaching into both Ranong and Phang Nga provinces, **Laem Son National Park** ❻ covers an area of 315 sq km (120 sq miles), of which

roughly 85 percent is sea. Offshore from its 60km (37 miles) of coastline are a number of small islands that are considered prime locations for game fishing. Birdwatchers often visit in the hope of spotting a few of the park's 130 bird species, while nature lovers can observe animals such as common tree shrews, Malayan flying lemurs, slow loris, macaques, civets and mouse deer. With the exception of the abundant wildlife, the park is generally quiet all year round.

Fringed by casuarinas, the beach at **Hat Bang Ben** is home to the park's headquarters and the main entry point for visitors. From massive stretches of beach to vast open sea and towering trees, everything here is super-sized; only the waves are small, making Bang Ben safe for swimming throughout the year. A scattering of islands offshore make for a picturesque view from virtually anywhere along the shore, and its flat, compacted sand is easy to walk on.

A number of the islands in Laem Son National Park are easily reached by excursions organised at local guesthouses or by chartering a long-tail boat. A 40-minute trip leads to the dramatic boulder formations at **Ko Khang Khao**, where the smooth white sand and colourful pebbles are as popular with sunbathers as the coral and marine life is with snorkellers and scuba divers. It is **Ko Kam Yai**, however, which is just over an hour away by boat, that is considered the most beautiful island in the national park area. Its pristine reefs hover very close to shore, making for excellent snorkelling and scuba diving.

SURIN ISLANDS

The five islands that make up the **Surin Islands Marine National Park 7** (Nov–May; charge) lie some 55km (34 miles) from the coast and are renowned for their superlative diving and snorkelling spots. Not surprisingly, they are mainly visited by divers on live-aboard boats. The scenery above water is equally spectacular, with numerous sandy bays and coves backed by verdant jungle. The Surin Islands were uninhabited until World War II, and today, have only a few hundred permanent residents. The ecology of the islands has suffered badly over the years due to fishermen using dynamite to blast fish up to the water's surface. Mooring posts to prevent anchor damage have helped coral regrowth in recent years, while dynamite fishing has been banned.

The two main islands of **Ko Surin Nua** and **Ko Surin Tai** are separated by a 200-metre (655ft) narrow channel of small beaches and pockets of mangroves that can be waded across at low tide. These islands are virtually uninhabited, although Ko Surin Tai is home to a small community of *chao lay* or "sea gypsies", and Ko Surin Nua is home to the park's headquarters and the island's only accommodation – rustic bungalows and a campsite. The other three islands, **Ko Ri**, **Ko Khai** and **Ko Klang**, are just small, rocky islets covered with sparse vegetation and are not worth exploring.

TIP

The boat trip from Ranong to the islands off its coast is unbearably slow. Occasionally, there is a speedboat service, which takes less-than-half the time for only a little extra *(see also page 205)*.

BELOW: a Surin islander taking a break.

Muslim men outside the mosque at Khao Lak. Muslims form a significant percentage of the local population in these parts.

BELOW: Khao Lak's beaches have now recovered after the 2004 tsunami.

Diving in the Surin Islands

The Surin Islands' most popular dive site, **Richelieu Rock**, is only just exposed at low tide. It is one of the world's top locations for sightings of whale sharks, with February to April being the best time. On average, 10 percent of all dives in a year at Richelieu result in an encounter with this 20-metre (65ft) behemoth.

Around 60km (37 miles) northwest of the Surin Islands are the renowned **Burma Banks**, where the three submerged peaks of **Silvertip**, **Roe** and **Rainbow** rise to within 15 metres (50ft) of the sea's surface, the remainder dissappearing into the 300-metre (980ft)-deep waters. Encounters with silvertip, nurse and, occasionally, grey reef sharks, are a near certainty. The only way to dive these sites is on a live-aboard dive charter arranged out of Khao Lak, Phuket or Ranong.

KHAO LAK

Frequented primarily by diving enthusiasts, the sleepy beach resort of **Khao Lak** ❽ is the closest access point to the marine-life saturated **Similan Islands** that lie some 60km (37 miles) offshore. Khao Lak was steadily emerging as an upmarket alternative destination to neighbouring Phuket until the colossal tsunami struck in December 2004. Khao Lak was one of the two areas in Thailand – the other being Ko Phi Phi – where the earthquake-generated waves caused the most substantial damage and loss of life.

It is seen by many as a pleasant, less frenetic alternative to Phuket, although development is increasing rapidly, with hotels, shops and restaurants spreading back on the side roads leading from the beach to the main Highway 4 to Phuket. But the beach is beautiful and local bye-laws that restrict building to below tree level help maintain the overall charm of the area. The beaches extend in a very long, shallow arc along the bay, offering many places of relative seclusion, even in the peak season.

Khao Lak's beaches

The view over Khao Lak when arriving from Phuket, located 80km (50 miles) to the south, is quite stunning. As the narrow mountain road winds

down to the beaches below, turquoise waters lapping against the sand give an impression of an unspoilt haven. Khao Lak is in fact made up of a string of beaches, each separated by rocky outcrops, keeping them quiet and secluded while also appearing to merge into one and another.

From north to south, the beaches are **Bang Sak**, **Pakarang Cape**, **Khuk Khak**, **Bang Niang**, **Nang Thong** and, finally, **Khao Lak**. The last is a relatively small beach stretching 800 metres (2,625ft). Most of the development is centred on Bang Niang, Nang Thong and Khao Lak beaches. Swimming conditions in the high season are excellent on all, but during the monsoon season, it is better to keep to the north, towards the rocky headland, where the currents are not so strong.

SIMILAN ISLANDS

Promoted in nearly every dive shop and diving website, and mentioned in countless brochures throughout Thailand, is the beautiful **Similan Islands National Park ❶** (Nov–May; charge), situated 100km (62 miles) northwest of Phuket but most easily accessible from Khao Lak, the nearest mainland point, 60km (37 miles) away.

Similan, derived from the Malay word *sembilan*, means nine, in reference to the nine small islands that make up this 128-sq-km (50-sq-mile) marine national park. For easy reference, the islands are numbered from north to south in descending order, starting with **Ko Bon** (No. 9), **Ko Ba Ngu** (No. 8), **Ko Similan** (No. 7), **Ko Payoo** (No. 6), **Ko Miang** (collective name for islands Nos 4 and 5), **Ko Pahyan** (No. 3), **Ko Phayang** (No. 2) and **Ko Hu Yong** (No. 1).

With the exception of Ko Ba Ngu and Ko Miang, the islands are uninhabited and for years, prior to their rise in popularity among the diving fraternity, were visited only by sea gypsies. Today, the islands are

an attraction for day-trippers from Phuket and Khao Lak and divers on multi-day live-aboard boats.

Like most places in Thailand, the reefs suffered greatly in the past thanks to dynamite fishing and indiscriminate anchoring of boats and trawlers. Since 1987, fishing has been banned and boundaries set for mooring, allowing the reefs to return to their former state. The authorities are now also closing many dive sites for a period each year to attempt some recuperation of resources, so be sure to check the situation beforehand.

Diving the Similans

There are more than 20 dive sites around the Similan Islands. Trips from Phuket and Khao Lak take in any number of these, depending on the dive operator and length of expedition. The eastern side of the islands feature hard coral gardens where the most popular activity is drift diving along slopes that lean dramatically from the surface down to depths of 30–40 metres (100–130ft). Popular sites include **Christmas Point** and **Breakfast Bend**, both at Ko Ba Ngu,

TIP

Because the famous Burma Banks dive site is located within the territorial waters of Burma (Myanmar), the only way to visit it is by travelling on a live-aboard dive cruise boat that would have the required papers to be granted access.

BELOW: snorkelling in the clear waters around the Similan Islands.

Snorkelling is a worthwhile activity around the Similan Islands, even if most visitors tend to be divers.

BELOW: powder-like sand and clear aquamarine waters are the hallmarks of the Similan Islands.

where soft-coral growth and colourful sea fans are among the largest found in Thailand. The napoleon wrasse, a rare sight in Thailand, is occasionally seen at Breakfast Bend, along with leopard sharks resting on the sands below.

The western side of the Similan Islands offers faster-paced and more exhilarating diving, with currents swirling around huge granite-boulder formations and dramatic holes and overhangs. Colourful soft corals grow so thick on many of these boulders that the rock is no longer visible. Most dive sites on the west coast are best seen with a guide, since navigation can be tricky. Popular sites include **Fantasy Reef** and **Elephant Head** at Ko Similan, where clown fish, lionfish and the occasional turtle visit.

AO PHANG NGA

Under an hour by road from huket airport, 65km (40 miles) away, is the mainland town of **Phang Nga**. The town has little attraction for tourists and the few caves and waterfalls nearby are not overly impressive, with the exception of the most famous, **Tham Phung Chang** (Elephant Belly Cave). Located about 3km (2 miles) from the town, the hill that the 1,200-metre (3,937ft) tunnel burrows into resembles a crouching elephant of sorts. Phang Nga tour operators organise trips that take people through the cave by means of wading in and rafting and canoeing on the water before finally emerging on the other side of the hill.

The main attraction of this area is **Ao Phang Nga**, the site of Thailand's most striking jungle-clad limestone rock formations, monoliths and cliffs. Spread over a coastal area of 400 sq km (155 sq miles) between Phuket and Krabi, the islands are part of the **Ao Phang Nga National Park ⑩**. While impressive by day and evocative of a Chinese brush painting, the spectacular vistas of towering karsts are most captivating at night when the moon casts haunting shadows off the eerie rock structures into the watery depths around them. Sheltered from both northeast and southwest monsoon seasons, the blue-green waters around the bay are calm all year round.

Trips to the bay are mostly arranged from either Phuket or Krabi, but they can also be booked in Phang Nga Town itself. A more interesting way of exploring Phang Nga is by sea canoe. These low-lying craft allow access under the jagged edges of the karsts, which shelter hidden lagoons within. The karsts support their own mini ecosystem, including small troops of monkeys that have been reported to swim from island to island.

Ko Ping Kan and Ko Panyi

Thailand has long been sought after as an exotic film locale, and in 1974, one of the rocky pinnacles of Phang Nga was featured in the film *The Man with the Golden Gun*. **Ko Ping Kan** is better known today as **James**

Bond Island. The small beach here is perpetually crowded with day-trippers, who pose for pictures with the geological oddity called **Ko Tapu** behind them. Rising from a precariously thin base 200 metres (650ft) out of the water, the rocky outcrop seems destined to tip into the water at some point. Bond fans are smitten though, and there is something undeniably cool about standing at the very location where 007 once stood.

All tours of Ao Phang Nga also make a stop at nearby **Ko Panyi**, a Muslim village built entirely over the water and nestled against towering cliffs. Come lunchtime each day, it transforms from a quiet fishing community into a bustling hive of restaurants and souvenir shops with the arrival of 3,000 or so tourists on their way to or back from James Bond Island. Overnight tours of Ao Phang Nga stop here for the night, but the accommodation is very basic.

Apart from stopping off at James Bond and Ko Panyi islands, most tours pass by a number of rocks and uninhabited islands whose names take after the strange shapes they

resemble. Another popular stop is **Khao Khien** (Painting Rock) to see ancient cave art painted on to its inner walls. An array of animals, including monkeys, elephants, fish and crabs, are depicted alongside human stick figures.

KHAO SOK NATIONAL PARK

Easily accessible from Phuket on the east and Surat Thani on the west, **Khao Sok National Park ⓫** (daily; charge) is often thought of as simply another national park. However, alongside the usual flora, fauna, rivers and forests are some features that make Khao Sok unique. It is home to the world's oldest evergreen rainforest, 160 million years or thereabouts, and its location at the mountain ridge between the east and west coasts makes it the wettest area in Thailand (rains from both the Gulf of Thailand and the Andaman Sea coasts deposit as much as 3,500mm/138ins of rainfall annually).

Within the park's dense rainforest lies the world's second-largest flower, *Rafflesia Kerrii*, measuring 80cm

If in the Phang Nga area, a worthwhile detour is the Tham Suwankhuha cave temple, located 10km (6 miles) south of Phang Nga Town.

BELOW: exploring Ao Phang Nga's James Bond Island (Ko Tapu is on the left).

(31ins) in diameter when in bloom. The flower is endangered, so should be photographed from a distance to avoid damage.

Geographically, much of the 740-sq-km (285-sq-mile) park comprises limestone mountains, most in the 400–600 metre (1,300–2,000ft) range, although the highest is 960 metres (3,150ft). Lowland rainforest dominates, but there are also many towering trees, some reaching heights of around 65 metres (215ft). Mammals including elephants and leopards roam free (though are rarely spotted), while cobras, tarantulas and scorpions make frequent appearances.

Jungle trails

Of the nine trails in the park, eight follow the same route for the first 5km (3 miles) along the **Sok River**, after which they split. One continues a further 2km (1 mile) to the **Ton Gloy Waterfall**, where swimming is possible, and another to the **Bang Leap Nam Waterfall**, which is not as large but easier to reach. **Tan Sawan Waterfall** is the hardest trek, involving a clamber over slippery and sometimes steep rocks to cross the river. The ninth trail leads in a different direction altogether, following the **Bang Laen River** all the way to **Sip-et Chan Waterfall**.

You can tackle these jungle trails yourself, but half-day tours booked from Phuket or Krabi have experienced guides who will point out rare flora and signs of animal life that the untrained eye could easily miss.

Another popular day trip is to **Cheow Lan Lake**, some 60km (37 miles) from the main accommodation area. It is home to over 100 small islands and was formed in the 1980s when the **Ratchprabha Dam** was built to provide water for a hydroelectric power plant. Mountains and cliffs surrounding the river can be explored, but only on a guided trek. Activities on the lake include boat trips, fishing and canoeing, as well as walks around it to locations such as **Nam Talu Cave**. The lake is at its most beautiful in the early morning when the hooting of gibbons can be heard from deep within the mists hanging over the lakes and mountains.   ❑

BELOW: Floating village on Cheow Lan Lake. Khao Sok National Park.

N ORTHERN ANDAMAN COAST

TRANSPORT

RANONG AND SURROUNDINGS

Getting There
By Air
Ranong Airport is situated 24km (15 miles) north of Ranong Town. Ranong is not the most lucrative route in the country, and several airlines that started scheduled flights to the town have later stopped. Nok Air and Ranong Air both started flights at the end of 2013, but check ahead to see the latest situation. Alternatively, travellers can fly into Phuket, Krabi

BELOW: beach-side *tuk-tuk* drivers.

(see pages 230 and 260) or Surat Thani and then take a bus journey (see below) to Ranong.

By Road
All the air-conditioned buses that travel daily from Bangkok's **Southern Bus Terminal** to Phuket and Krabi pass the Ranong bus station just off Highway 4. The 600km (373-mile) journey takes around 9–10 hours. It is also possible to get to Ranong from either Phuket or Krabi, some 300km (185 miles) away by bus (the ride takes about 4–5 hours) or Surat Thani (3 hours). Alternatively, take a train to Chumphon and a bus to Ranong (2 hours).

Getting Around
Ranong
Songthaew trucks and motorcycle taxis are the primary mode of transport on Ranong. These run frequently from Thanon Ruangrat in the town centre to locations near the town and to Laem Son National Park, 60km (37 miles) south of Ranong.

Ko Chang and Ko Phayam
The islands of Ko Chang and Ko Phayam can be reached by boats departing from the Ranong port area. Timetables frequently change and getting a straight

answer is difficult. One solution is to pre-arrange a boat pick-up with your chosen resort; the trip is B200 and takes just under 3 hours (despite claims of 1–2 hours). A quicker speedboat service occasionally operates, which takes only 40 minutes, but tickets cost as much as B500. Note: boats only make the trip if there is enough demand. The only form of transport on Ko Chang and Ko Phayam is motorcycle taxis.

Surin Islands
The closest mainland base to the Surin Islands is Khura Buri pier, about 110km (68 miles) south of Ranong Town. Boats depart daily at 9am and take between 4 and 5 hours to reach the islands. It is also possible to take a boat from Amphoe Kapoe pier in Ranong Town. Trips leave daily during the November to April high season and take around 7 hours to get there. Note: most people who travel to the Surin Islands are divers on live-aboard boats.

KHAO LAK AND SIMILAN ISLANDS

Getting There
By Air and Road
Khao Lak is situated just off

Highway 4, some 780km (485 miles) south of Bangkok and 80km (50 miles) north of Phuket. The easiest way to get there is to fly to Phuket *(see page 230)* and take one of the airport mini-buses (B2,200) or taxis (B1,300) from there. The journey time from Phuket airport to Khao Lak is just over an hour. By regular bus it takes around two hours and costs B60.

Getting Around
Khao Lak

Motorcycle taxis and *songthaew* are the primary mode of transport along Khao Lak's several beaches. *Songthaew*s can be hailed from the road, and fares range from B20 to B40 for anywhere within Khao Lak. They can also be chartered like taxis, but make sure that you agree on the price before you get in.

Alternatively, motorcycles and cars can be hired. Inquire at your hotel reception desk for more information.

Similan Islands

The easiest departure point for the Similan Islands is Khao Lak, but Phuket is also a jump-off point for a large number of Similan-bound diving and snorkelling excursions. Boats only operate from Nov–Apr, after which time the waters are deemed too rough and dangerous to cross.

Thap Lamu pier, located about 8km (5 miles) south of Khao Lak, is where boats depart on the 3-hour journey to the Similan Islands. Most tours from Phuket travel by road to Thap Lamu pier and then make the connection to the islands by boat.

AO PHANG NGA AND KHAO SOK NATIONAL PARK

Getting There
By Air and Road

Phang Nga is 790km (490 miles) south of Bangkok and 90km (55

miles) north of Phuket. The easiest and the most common ways to get to Phang Nga are to fly to first either to Phuket *(see page 230)* or to Krabi *(see page 260)* and from there take an airport minibus (B1,800) or taxi (B900). Phang Nga is midway between Phuket and Krabi on Highway 4. If you're travelling alone it's worth trying to find travelling companions to share a taxi with at the airport.

Getting Around

Motorcycle taxis and *songthaew* trucks are the primary mode of transport in Phang Nga. But the town is also small enough to get around on foot.

Tours of Phang Nga Bay and Khao Sok National Park are best handled by travel agencies in Phang Nga. Generally, however, more people tend to visit these places from their base in Khao Lak, Phuket or Krabi. Enquire with travel agents at these places for more information.

ACCOMMODATION LISTINGS

RANONG AND SURROUNDINGS

RANONG

Jansom Hot Spa Ranong
2/10 Th. Petchkasem
Tel: 0-7781 1510
www.jansomhotsparanong.net
Although it is perhaps the best known, this hotel is by no means the best. The rooms are large, but from the paintwork to the lifts, this 1960s throwback appears old and run-down and in need of

updating and renovation. The hotel justifies its prices, however, due to the hot-spring-water baths on the site. (182 rooms) **$$**

Numsai Khaosuay
14/19 Th. Poemphon
Tel: 0-7783 4888
www.numsaikhaosuay.com
This low rise resort located just out of town off Highway 4 is quite smartly designed compared to what else is currently avaiable in the area. They have free Wi-fi, a swimming pool

and the Leela restaurant has Thai and Western food. (28 rooms) **$$**

Pathu Resort
29/5 Th. Phetkasem
Tel: 08-1894 7343
www.pathuresort.com
Set in a verdant private tropical garden with its own swimming pool, this is one of the area's better budget options. The rooms, all of which have balconies, are bright, clean and well-appointed, with wireless internet, a mini-bar and cable television. The

resort staff are very friendly and helpful. (28 rooms) **$**

Tinidee Hotel
41/144 Th Tamuang
Tel: 0-7783 5240
www.tinidehotels.com/ranong
Easily the best hotel in Ranong Town. Rooms are clean and decently appointed and the hotel staff are friendly. Hot-spring water is provided in all of the guest rooms as well as in the swimming pool, spa and jacuzzi areas. (138 rooms) **$$**

LAEM SON N P

Andaman Peace Resort

Hat Bang Ben
Mobile tel: 0-7782 0239
Rooms have direct sea views, making it far more scenic than its main competitor, Wasana Resort, but the food at the attached restaurant is not great and staff have trouble speaking English. (12 rooms) $

Wasana Resort

Hat Bang Ben
Tel: 0-7786 1434
www.wasanaresort.org
This seems to be the best-equipped resort, offering tours and renting canoes. Staff are friendly, speak good English and are more than happy to give advice. The food served at the restaurant is as good as it gets within the park. There is no sea view, but the beach is within walking distance. (8 rooms) $

KO CHANG

Cashew Resort

Ao Yai
Tel: 08-1485 6002
Ko Chang's first and largest resort has a variety of bungalows made from wood and bamboo to solid stone. There are more facilities here than at many other resorts, including a dive school and a beach bar with pool table. Open only from mid-October to May. (25 rooms) $

Hornbill Bungalows

206/1 Mu 4 Tambon Ban Pu Noi
Tel: 0-3255 9218
Only open from November–May, on its own beach on the island's northern tip, this resort offers eight variously styled en-suite bungalows. Owner Mr Oo takes guests on fishing trips, while his wife Mrs Jib cooks up some mean curries. (5 rooms) $

Sunset Resort

Ao Yai
Tel: 0-7782 0171
Shaded beach bungalows with a pleasant attached restaurant. Beach volleyball is played daily at sunset in front of the resort and the staff are happy to advise on fishing and other nearby activities. Open mid-October to May only. (15 rooms) $

KO PHAYAM

Bamboo Bungalows

Ko Phayam
Tel: 0 7782 0012
www.bamboo-bungalows.com
This popular cluster of bungalows open year-round, is one of the livelier places in the evenings, when guests from nearby hotels come to enjoy the restaurant and music on the beach. Free Wi-fi and free kayaks. Nestled about 100 metres (330ft) back

from the beach front. (25 rooms) $

Payam Cottage Resort

69/1 Moo 1 Ko Phayam
Tel: 08-047 0999
www.payamcottage.com
These cottages have large balconies with ocean views, and the open-air restaurant is set in a pretty beach-facing garden and serves both Thai and international dishes. Diving, snorkelling and mountain biking are organised here and there is 24-hour electricity on site. (31 rooms) $

Sabai Sabai Beach Bungalows

Ko Phayam
Mobile tel. 00-7095 4053
www.sabai-bungalows.com
This resort has fan only beach huts, bungalows and some camping space. There's free Wi-fi and on water there's a sailing boat and tree kayaks. The beachside bar, lounge and restaurant has music jam sessions at night. (15 rooms) $

KHAO LAK AND SIMILAN ISLANDS

KHAO LAK

Casa de La Flora

67/213 Moo5, Khuk Khak
Tel: 0-7642 8999
www.casadelaflora.com.
This 2011 newcomer is a cluster of featureless grey-cube villas shaped like valve TVs. It claims to offer a cutting-edge "neoteric lifestyle". It's situated right on the beach and has sleek, minimalist and very modern interiors with blond wood and large windows. Swimming

pool, spa, restaurant and Wi-fi are all-in. (36 rooms) $$$$

JW Marriott Khao Lak Resort & Spa

41/12 Moo 3, Khuk Khak
Tel: 0-7658 4888
www.marriott.com
This beach front chain resort is located within large gardens and has a kids club and many water features in the extensive pool areas. There's free Wi-fi, all the usual spa treats and several restaurants serving Thai, Japanese and international food. (297 rooms) $$$

Khaolak Bhandari Resort

26/25 Moo 7, Nang Thong
Tel: 0-7648 5751
www.khaolakbhandari.com
Set slightly back from the beach amid tropical gardens, the romantic Thai-style pavilions that form this resort twist around palm trees and a large, curved swimming pool. Has a good restaurant serving Thai and Western options, and an open-air bar. (77 rooms) $$$

Khao Lak Merlin Resort

7/7 Th. Petchkasem

Tel: 0-7642 8300
www.merlinphuket.com/khaolak_merlin
With three swimming pools, a fitness room, spa and tennis courts, this resort caters to more than just the sedentary sun-worshipper.

PRICE CATEGORIES

Price categories show the starting price for a double room without breakfast and taxes:
$ = under US$70
$$ = US$70–130
$$$ = US$130–250
$$$$ = over US$250

There's a kids' club and playground, a pool bar, beach bar and lounge. Rooms are large yet homely, many with high ceilings that add to the sense of spaciousness. (209 rooms) **$$$**

Le Méridien Khao Lak Beach and Spa Resort
9/9 Moo 1, Khuk Khak
Tel: 0-7642 7500
www.lemeridienkhaolak.com
Set within 20 hectares (50 acres) of sandy beach and tropical garden. Rooms are luxurious and large, with

lounge areas and 29-inch flat-screen TVs. Bathrooms have separate baths and rain-showers with glass panelling that allows an unobstructed view of the living and balcony areas. Three restaurants, two bars and one excellent spa. (243 rooms) **$$$**

Mukdara Beach Villa and Spa
67/179, Moo 5, Khuk Khak
Tel: 0-7642 9999
www.mukdarabeach.com
Mukdara is spread over 32 sq km (12 sq miles),

with luxury accommodation split into two types – Royal Wing, with rooms on the top floors getting ocean views, and villas set around an enormous pool. There is also a library, tennis court and beach-side bar by a second pool. (148 rooms) **$$**

The Sarojin
60 Moo 2, Khuk Khak
Tel: 0-7642 7900
www.thesarojin.com
Arguably Khao Lak's most luxurious resort, The Sarojin is the ulti-

mate in indulgence, with direct access to a secluded 11km (7-mile) stretch of private beach. Rooms are situated in low-rise buildings and each is appointed luxuriously with strong Thai accents. Ground-floor rooms have access to private gardens, while the ones upstairs have capacious terraces. Two restaurants, a bar, spa and an exquisite infinity pool complete the picture of elegance. (56 rooms) **$$$$**

AO PHANG NGA AND KHAO SOK NATIONAL PARK

PHANG NGA TOWN

Phang Nga Inn
2/2 Soi Lohakit
Tel: 0-7641 1963
Lovely converted house with rooms in different styles, all with comfy beds and clean linen. Free internet offered. **$**

AO PHANG NGA

Note: options listed here are on the island of Ko Yao Noi, which is ideally located to enjoy the panoramas of Phang Nga Bay.

Lom Lae Beach Resort
Moo 4, Ko Yao Noi
Tel: 0-7659 7486
www.lomlae.com
Entering via a wooden walkway over a swamp doesn't raise expectations. But this resort is actually quite pretty. The bungalows are imaginatively conceived, with sliding doors, sunken

stone bathrooms and quirky features. A variety of outdoor activities are organised. (11 rooms) **$$**

The Paradise Koh Yao
Ko Yao Noi
Tel: 0-7658 4450
www.theparadise.biz
This beautiful resort is nestled in a secluded spot adjacent to a stretch of private beach. Rooms have semi-outdoor bathrooms, open living areas and air conditioning. Some have postcard-perfect views of lovely Phang Nga Bay. The resort can arrange transfers from either Phuket or Krabi. (70 rooms) **$$$**

Six Senses Hideaway
Ko Yao Noi
Tel: 0-7641 8500
www.sixsenses.com
This is the ultimate romantic getaway. Live like Robinson Crusoe but with every conceivable comfort at hand at your villa with infinity pool, including a personal butler to cater to your every whim. The

gorgeous views of ethereal Ao Phang Nga will keep you spellbound but when you tire of that, there are other diversions – two restaurants, spa, gym and a variety of activities, including dive trips and tours of Ao Phang Nga. (54 villas) **$$$$**

KHAO SOK N P

Budget

Bamboo House
Khao Sok
Tel: 0-1787 7484
www.krabidir.com/bamboohouse
Basic but clean and comfortable stilted wood bungalows with separate bathroom and hot showers, and there's now a tree house option. The restaurant serves Thai and Western food. In high season there is a monthly full-moon barbecue by the Sok River, and they organise treks of Khao Sok and other activities. (17 rooms). **$**

Khao Sok Las Orquideas Resort
Khao Sok
Tel: 0-7739 5009
www.khao-sok-resort.com
A lovely resort in the village, close to the national park. The rooms, which are located in four villas in extensive tropical gardens, include some family options for four people. All have air conditioning and free Wi-fi. Breakfast is provided in the price, but there's no restaurant, although there are plenty of dining options nearby. There are free bicycles, and motorbikes are available for hire. Various tours can be arranged. (6 rooms). **$**

PRICE CATEGORIES

Price categories show the starting price for a double room without breakfast and taxes:
$ = under US$70
$$ = US$70–130
$$$ = US$130–250
$$$$ = over US$250

RANONG AND SURROUNDINGS

ABOVE: coconut rice is popular in Thailand.

RANONG TOWN

There are a few good eateries in Ranong, but outside of this town, in places such as Ko Chang and Ko Phayam, the main options are those restaurants attached to the small hotels (see page 207), where the fare will be generally simple but, in some cases, decent enough.

Thai and Western

Buono@Ranong
1/12 Th. Chonraru
Tel: 08-3632 9844
Open: daily 10am–10pm.
This friendly Thai-run place serves decent Western food, much of it in the Italian café style. Seating available both inside and out. **$**

Cafenidee
Tinidee Hotel. 41/144 Th. Tamuang
Tel: 0-7783 5240
Open: daily B, L and D.
The comfortable and relaxed environment of this café-restaurant provides one of the most refined place to eat in Ranong. While the international menu is not fantastic, the Thai and Chinese choices are good and there is a bit of a garden view on show. A house band and singer perform here every night from 6pm. **$$**

Coffee House
173 Th. Ruangrat
Tel: 0-7782 2447
Open: daily B, L and D.
This unassuming little roadside restaurant looks basic from both the inside and out, but don't be deterred as the food is fantastic and

good value for money. There is a large selection of freshly made breads with a wide choice of fillings on offer; the chicken and cheese baguettes are delicious. **$**

DD Coffee
299/1 Th. Ruangrat
Tel: 0-7783 0111
Open: daily B, L and D.
The canvas-teepee entrance announces Ranong's Wild West image as you step into this restaurant. Inside, pizza, pasta, some Thai and DD's pride and joy – its ice cream – are served. Look out for the strong iced coffee melt – it is highly recommended. **$**

Kay Kai Internet and Café
293/6 Th. Ruangrat
Tel: 0-7781 2967
Open: daily B, L and D.
This cosy café is still one of the quieter internet joints in town. Try the inexpensive pasta and great fruit shakes for some relaxed and unassuming refreshment. **$**

Pon's Place
Th. Ruangrat
Mobile tel: 0-7782 3344
www.ponplace-ranong.com
Open: daily B, L and D.
This is actually a travel agency, but it has a sideline café with a mix of Thai and Western food. The pizzas, sandwiches and snacks are basic, but there's free Wi-fi, and it's a handy place to grab a bite when organising trips around the region. **$**

Ranong Hideaway Sophon's Bistro
Th. Ruangrat
Tel: 0-7783 2730
www.ranonghideaway.com
Open: daily L and D.
Very popular restaurant serving everything from Thai to German to Italian. Dishes include crispy shrimp and cashew nut salad, green curry and pork rib stew, plus pastas, sandwiches and all day breakfasts. **$–$$**

KOH PHAYAM

Thai and Western

The Beachside Restaurant
Blue Sky Resort, Mae Mai, Koh Phayam
Mobile tel: 08-1489 2881
Open: daily B, L and D.
This restaurant boasts a truly idyllic location set in a thatched sala alongside the beach. It is attached to a relatively new upmarket resort, and the food it serves up to customers is as good as it gets on the island. There's a choice of filling burgers, pastas, steaks and a range of standard Thai dishes. **$$**

PRICE CATEGORIES

Price per person for a three-course meal without drinks:
$ = under US$10
$$ = US$10–25
$$$ = US$25–50
$$$$ = over US$50

KHAO LAK AND SIMILAN ISLANDS

KHAO LAK

International

Fizz Bistro n Bar
26/34 Th. Petchkasem Khuk Khak
Tel: 08-6277 9080
www.facebook.com/fizzbistrokhaolak.
Open: daily L and D.
Fizz's modern, slightly arty interior design – unusual for the area – is an attraction here as much as the pretty good Thai and Western food and friendly service. Customers have a choice of à la carte, with dishes such as *laab*, Penang curry, pastas and tuna tartar, or set menus. **$$**
Khao Lak Seafood
19/1 Moo 7, Khuk Khak
Tel: 0-7648 5318

www.khaolakseafood.com.
Open: daily L and D.
Favoured by residents for some of the best fresh seafood in Khao Lak, this unassuming little restaurant is busy throughout the year and well worth a visit. They also rent out budget rooms. **$-$$**
Rusty Pelican
67/139 Moo 5 Soi Jerung Plaza, Hat Bang Niang
Tel: 08-7192 1085
Open: daily L and D.
An atmospherically rustic Mexican diner complete with a small bar and pool table. All the usual Mexican fare is served here, from quesadillas to burritos and tacos, and, of course, lashings of tequila and mojito. **$$**
Smile Khao Lak
5/15 Moo 7, Th. Phetkasem,

Khuk Khak
Tel: 08-3391 2600
www.smilekhaolak.com
Open daily L and D.
This roadside café has a mainly Thai menu with a couple of Western dishes, too. It includes lots of visitor-friendly milder choices such as spring rolls, chicken satay and massaman curry, and there's also a good list of vegetarian options. **$-$$**

Thai

Baan Thai
Le Méridien Beach Resort and Spa, 9/9 Moo 1, Khuk Khak
Tel: 0-7642 7500
www.lemeridienkhaolak.com
Open: daily D only.
This simple yet elegant restaurant overlooks a natural lagoon and offers a healthier range

of Thai dishes than the usual deep-fried options and dishes doused in coconut milk. **$$$**
Hill Tribe Restaurant
13/22 Moo 6, Khuk Khak
Tel: 08-6283 0933
www.hilltribe-restaurant.com
Open: daily L and D.
Run by a couple from Chiang Rai, this serves northern specialities like Duck Hill Tribe style, with tofu, cashew nuts, mushrooms and snow beans, along with standards such as Tom Yam goong. **$-$$**

PRICE CATEGORIES

Price per person for a three-course meal without drinks:
$ = under US$10
$$ = US$10–25
$$$ = US$25–50
$$$$ = over US$50

ACTIVITIES

RANONG AND SURROUNDINGS

Nightlife

The limited nightlife options in Ranong are mainly found on Thanons Ruangrat and Phetkasem. You might want to check out watering holes such as the **Sir Pol Pub** or the live music at **Jammy Bar**. The nightlife scene on the offshore islands of Ko Chang and Ko Phayam is, at best, negligible and, at worst, non existent. Ko Chang, with its lack of electricity, all but shuts down in the evenings. Although Ko

Phayam is a little busier than Ko Chang at night, there are still no bars to frequent as such, but rather just extensions to the guesthouses that play music and serve cold alcohol.

Shopping

There is a large market, open both during the day and at night, on Thanon Ruangrat in Ranong Town. The stalls here sell a varied selection of items, including Thai food, handicrafts and household decorations, such as silk flowers. With the exception of this market, however, the retail options in Ranong are rather limited.

Outdoor Activities
Diving

Ranong's two leading dive operators offer day trips and live-aboards to the Surin Islands, as well as to nearby Ko Phayam.
A-One Diving: 256 Th. Ruengrad; tel: 08-1891 5510; www.a-one-diving.com. This multilingual dive company has been in operation since 1999. Catering to both scuba divers and snorkellers, the company specialises in live-aboards, but can also arrange PADI courses for customers, with most of the theoretical and practical training for these conducted at Ko Phayam.
The Smiling Seahorse: 170 Th. Ruangrat; tel: 08-6011 0614;

www.thesmilingseahorse.com. This French run outfit takes groups of no more than 12 people and conducts regular expeditions to sites in Thailand and Burma, including Richelieu Rock, Black Rock and Shark Cave. PADI dive courses can be completed for beginners or advanced divers.

Spas

Spas around Ranong focus on one thing and one thing only – the natural mineral waters of the nearby Raksawarin Hot Springs. The selling point for any Ranong spa is the therapeutic natural baths in which visitors can relax and soak away any lingering stress and tension.

Jansom Hot Spa Ranong: tel: 0-7782 2516; www.jansomhotspa ranong.net. Mineral water is pumped directly into the men's and women's communal baths This is the best known of the town's spas, but overcrowding at certain times of day can become a source of annoyance. It is generally quieter later in the evening, so aim to visit at this time if you are more in search of some peace and quiet.

Siam Hot Spa: 73/3 Moo 2, Th. Petchkasem; tel: 0-7781 3551; www.siamhotsparanong.com. Open: daily 10am–10pm. Probably the nicest of Ranong's spas, and surprisingly, also reasonably priced. A separate men's and women's jacuzzi pool, sauna and steamroom are available for customers to use. There is also a café/bakery on site. Located directly opposite the Raksawarin Hot Springs.

Tinidee Hotel Spa: 41/144 Th. Tamuang; tel: 0-7783 5240; www. tinideehotels.com/ranong. This hotel spa welcomes non-guests in addition to those staying at the hotel to use its swimming pool, gym, massage and spa facilities as well as the hot-spring-water jacuzzi that is replenished daily. The facilities here are cleaner and less crowded than alternative hotels in the area.

KHAO LAK AND SIMILAN ISLANDS

Nightlife

Khao Lak has few thriving nightspots. Bars are mainly dotted round Bang Niang and Nang Thong beaches. Many of the latter's restaurants and bars tend to close during the low season.

Degree Bar: Th. Khao Niau, Bang Niang. A wooden cowboy-themed music bar, the likes of which are found all over the country. They serve Thai food and have live bands playing local and international pop and rock tunes.

Happy Snapper Bar: 5/2 Moo 7, Khuk Khak; tel:0-7648 5500; www.happysnapperbar.com. This lively multi-level bar, run by the bass player from one of Thailand's top rock bands, has a live band or DJ performing nightly and Wednesday jam sessions.

Tarzan Bar: 21/1 Moo 7, Khuk Khak; mobile tel: 0-1089 1412. Laid-back bar that is popular with both locals and expats. Small and intimate, with a pub-type atmosphere and music that plays late into the night.

BELOW: snorkelling in the area.

Outdoor Activities

Golf

Thap Lamu: 38 Moo 5, Tumbol Lumgain; tel: 0-7644 3288. An 18-hole, 6,825 yard, par-72 course at the Thai Navy Sport Development Centre, a couple of kilometres south of Khao Lak. Five fairways run beside the beach and there's also a pro shop, driving range and café on site.

Diving

Several dive sites are easily reached from Khao Lak, making it a major haven for scuba enthusiasts.

In addition to being the main gateway to the Similan Islands, the wreck-diving site of *Boonsong*, where an old tin-mining boat sank in 1984, is easily accessible from there. So, too, is the tin-mining boat called *Premchal*, which in August 2001 sank to its watery grave at a depth of 21 metres (69ft).

Divers Land: 26/3 Moo 7, Khuk Kak; tel: 0-7648 5420. www.divers land.com. This was Khao Lak's first integrated diving resort, with accommodation, restaurant, fitness and training centres, as well as dive-equipment sales and service centres. Both diving and snorkelling trips can be organised by this company.

IQ Dive: 4/42 Moo 7, Khao Lak, tel: 0-7648 5614; www.iq-dive.com. A Swiss-Thai dive outfit offering daily and overnight excursions to many islands, including the Similans. They have a range of PADI dive courses and accommodation is available.

Sea Dragon Dive Center: 5/51 Mu 7, T. Khuk Khak; tel: 0-7648 5420; www.seadragondivecenter.com. Established in 1993, this friendly and informal outfit was the first dive centre in Khao Lak. Operating at the northern, quieter end of Khao Lak and open all year round, the instructors here can speak English, German, French, Dutch, Swedish, Afrikaans and Thai.

PHUKET

Thailand's largest resort island is a base for trips to several world-famous dive sites. If brash Patong proves overwhelming, you can escape to any one of the 16 natural coves, carpeted with blinding white sand, that are strung along the island's western coastline, or head to Phuket Town to see its temples and market.

Phuket, which is marketed as the "Pearl of the Andaman" reflecting its shape as well as its physical beauty, has been transformed over the past three decades from a sleepy little island into the country's most popular beach destination. It receives an escalating volume of visitors currently standing at around four and a half million each year. It is Thailand's smallest province but largest island, at 587 sq km (225 sq miles), and has hotels to suit all budgets, including huge luxury resorts, expensive boutique properties, and upmarket villa-style houses. There has also been a condominium boom, along with shops, schools and hospitals of international standard, which unsurprisingly has encouraged many foreigners to take up permanent residence here.

The stunning white-sand beaches along the 48km (30-mile)-long west coast are separated by picturesque headlands. Some are small and pristine with intimate hidden coves, while others teem with noisy jet-skis, crowds of sun-worshippers, and vendors trawling the sands selling colourful sarongs and souvenirs.

Phuket is a base for trips to several renowned dive sites in the surrounding seas, and the number of operators offering courses, organised excursions and live aboards is astounding. Phuket is also an excellent base for the exploration of islands, national parks and mainland beaches such as Khao Lak and Krabi.

People and economy

Of the approximately 300,000 people living on Phuket, the majority are Buddhist, with Muslims comprising around 35 percent. Many locals make

Main attractions
PHUKET BUTTERFLY GARDEN AND INSECT WORLD
PHUKET FANTASEA
KATA HILL VIEWPOINT
PHUKET SEASHELL MUSEUM
WAT CHALONG
KO RACHA YAI

LEFT: Laem Promthep.
RIGHT: plantation worker extracting latex from a rubber tree.

Phuket

0 _____ 5 km

0 _____ 5 miles

their living from the island's rubber and pineapple plantations, but since the 1980s, tourism has overtaken agriculture as the main source of income. There are several tourist-related theme parks and activity centres, such as Siam Niramit and the Phuket Butterfly Garden and Insect World (*for both, see below*), and visitors enjoy a good choice of international and Thai restaurants. And the shopping scene has never been better, with malls such as Central Festival Phuket bringing chic brands to the island.

One downside to Phuket's continuing popularity is its shrinking capacity to handle what may now be perceived as overload. Emerging tourism markets, notably Russian and Chinese, the latter of whom have recently overtaken Malaysians as the island's most numerous visitors, have pushed airport arrivals and departures past the eight million mark. The longer the airport queues the more intense the development, which places pressure on Phuket's natural resources – the very springs of its popularity. Commentators are now talking of the dangers of Phuket

becoming an island city that feeds neighbouring attractions such as Krabi and Phang Nga. Care will be needed to maintain the allure of the Pearl of the Andaman.

PHUKET TOWN

On arrival, many people head straight for the beaches and give **Phuket Town** a miss. But, only 20 minutes drive from Patong, the place is worth at least a day trip as there are some sights that are rich in culture and tradition. The town can seem busy and unattractive, with an impossible-to-follow one-way traffic system, but, while by car it's easy to get lost, on foot and with the aid of a good map, it's not difficult to navigate.

Siam Niramit and Simon Star Show

Not quite in Phuket Town but in Rassaada on the outskirts, there's a Phuket version of Bangkok's cultural attraction **Siam Niramit ❶** (Wed–Mon 5.30–10pm; tel: 0-7633 5000). As well as facilities such as a floating market, restaurants and tableaux of village life, a spectacular one-hour

BELOW: colonial buildings in Phuket town centre.

TIP

Inside Put Jaw Temple are two cans filled with numbered sticks. Speak your problem aloud and then shake the cans, picking up the first stick that falls out. The number on the stick will correspond to a pigeon hole in the adjacent hall. Inside you will find a piece of paper with your fortune written on it (you need an interpreter). Fortunes are told free, but you are expected to leave a donation.

show starts at 8.30pm highlighting aspects of Thailand's history and culture. Another Rassada attraction is the **Simon Star Show ❷** (charge; tel: 0-7652 3192) in a purpose built B130-million theatre. Its ladyboy lip-synching cabaret shows daily at 6pm, 7.45pm and 9.30pm include an underwater sequence.

Phuket Butterfly Garden and Insect World

At the start of Thanon Yaowaraj, heading towards Phuket Town centre, is the **Phuket Butterfly Garden and Insect World ❸** (daily 9am–5.30pm; charge; tel: 0-7621 0861; www.phuket butterfly.com). Inside are over 40 species of butterfly in a natural rainforest environment and an enclosure full of rare and native birds of Thailand. It's an ideal outing for children. Information boards point out the differences between butterflies and moths, and there are educational exhibits of live eggs, larvae and pupae.

A large pond brimming with koi carp is a reminder that until 2004 there was also an aquarium here. This has since been replaced with Insect World, where stick insects, tarantulas, scorpions and other notorious creepy crawlies go about their daily business, unaware of watchful eyes marvelling at them.

Khao Rang

Just south of the Butterfly Garden is **Khao Rang**; a spiralling road leads to a summit revealing (according to most brochures) panoramic views over Phuket town. The leafy surrounds and solitude makes it a peaceful place to have a picnic. The park is popular with locals, and is a favourite escape for young courting couples. **Tung-Ka Café** (tel: 0-7621 1500), at the peak of the hill, serves delicious and cheap Thai food.

Chinatown

In the heart of Phuket Town, between Thanon Thalang and Thanon Deebuk, is the **Chinatown** area, where old colonial houses and Sino-Portuguese-style mansions dominate, recognised by tiled roofs, artistically chiselled exteriors and tall pillars. Many are privately owned, but some are open to the public. Phra Pitak Chinpracha Mansion on Krabi Road, regarded as Phuket's most beautiful home, now contains a branch of the international Thai restaurant chain **The Blue Elephant** (*see page 235*). Many shophouses have been restored into art galleries, coffee shops and outlets for traditional Chinese herbal medicines. **The Thai Hua Museum** (daily 9am–5pm; tel: 0-7621 1224) on Krabi Road has wide ranging exhibits and the **Thavorn Hotel Lobby Museum** on Rassada Road (tel: 0-7621 1333) has items ranging from tin mining paraphernalia to toy trains and opium beds.

On Thalang Road, the popular **China Inn** is a colourful and artistic antiques store, restaurant and garden café decorated in rich Chinese red and gold. Other cultural artefacts are found at the 80 year-old former post

BELOW: a butterfly at the Butterfly Garden and Insect World.

office on Montri Road, which is now the **Phuket Philatelic Museum** (tel: 0-7621 1020).

Chinese temples

Due to the strong Chinese presence in Phuket, a number of local temples are Taoist in character. A few in particular stand out. **Sanjao Sam San** (daily 8am–6pm; free) at Thanon Krabi, erected in 1853 in dedication to Tien Sang Sung Moo, the Goddess of the Sea and patron saint of sailors, is recognisable by the gold statues which stand proudly outside. Inside, intricate carvings adorn the walls.

Also worth a visit is the **Put Jaw Temple** (daily 8am–6pm; free) on Thanon Ranong, dedicated to Kwan Im, the Chinese Goddess of Mercy. At a little over 200 years old, this is the oldest Chinese Taoist temple in Phuket. Not overly impressive from the outside, it is better known for what happens within. In the middle hall, resting before an image of Kuan Im, are a number of fortune-telling devices, including a pair of wooden divining blocks, which when dropped to the floor imply a "yes" or "no"

answer to a question – depending on which side they fall on. Your fortune can also be told by the aid of divining sticks *(see margin tip on page 216)*.

Jui Tui Temple (daily 8am–6pm; free), just next to Put Jaw, is much more ornate. On the altar inside is the red-faced statue of Kiu Ong Ya, one of the Nine Emperor Gods to whom the temple is dedicated. This temple is the main location for the annual Vegetarian Festival *(see page 35)*, when the streets come alive with the thousands who flock here to witness devotees perform grotesque acts of self-mutilation.

Across from Jui Tui Temple, on the corner of Thanon Ranong, is the **Central Market**, where you can watch housewives as they banter with the merchants among piles of vegetables, fruit and fish. The uninitiated, however, may find the pungent scents overpowering.

PHUKET'S INTERIOR

Most visitors confine themselves to Phuket's beaches and see little else of the island. This is a real pity as the lush interior is filled with verdant

BELOW: the Jui Tui Temple in Phuket Town.

TIP

The southwest monsoon brings heavy rain from May to Oct to the Andaman Coast, including Phuket. Nov is the start of the dry season but Dec to Feb is best. Apr and May are the hottest months and Sep the wettest. Hotel rates in Phuket are the lowest from May to Oct and many people take advantage of this as there can be intermittent days of sunshine in between rainy spells.

BELOW LEFT AND RIGHT: Wat Phra Thong and its half-buried Buddha statue.

jungle-covered hills interspersed with rubber and pineapple plantations. Phuket's compact size and relatively good roads allow you to access trails that lead through primary rainforest, take a dip at hidden waterfalls and still be back at your beach-side hotel come nightfall.

Thalang area

About 12km (7 miles) north of Phuket Town is a large roundabout that dominates Thanon Thepkrasat-tri (Route 402). It is known both for its ability annoyingly to halt free-flowing traffic and for the striking statues of two women encircled by flags. Called the **Heroines' Monument**, these female figures stand proud with drawn swords and honour Lady Chan and Lady Muk, the widow of the governor of Phuket and her sister, who led the successful defence of the island against the invading Burmese in 1785.

The statues mark the entry into the **Thalang** district. Thalang Town itself is rather run-down, but it is steeped in history, having moved to several different locations before taking up its current position in the geographical centre of Phuket in 1894.

A short distance northeast of the monument is the **Thalang Museum** (Wed–Sun 9am–4pm; charge; tel: 0-7631 1426; www.nationalmuseums.finearts.go.th). The museum contains a few interesting artefacts and displays on Phuket's past. Everything from Phuket's prehistoric cave dwellers to the island's invasion by the Burmese and the great tin-mining boom of the 19th century are recounted here, along with displays of its ethnic diversity as a maritime crossroads.

Return to Route 402 and continue to **Thalang Town** to see one of Phuket's most famous temples, **Wat Phra Thong ❹** (daily 8am–6pm; free), a little north beyond the main crossroads. Inside the main hall is the statue of a golden Buddha half-buried in the ground. From the chest up it measures about 2 metres (7ft). Over the years, thanks to stories circulating that the Buddha image was cast in gold, many people, including an invading Burmese army, have tried to dig it out of the ground. To date, none have succeeded in unearthing

it, and most have met with grisly deaths, or so the story goes, as a result of a curse associated with the image. The statue is in fact made of brick and plaster, with a thin layer of gold covering it.

Khao Phra Taew National Park

East of Thalang Town is **Khao Phra Taew National Park ❺** (daily 6am–6pm; charge), a pretty but hardly spectacular protected reserve. This is Phuket's largest tract of virgin rainforest, covering 22 sq km (8½ sq miles). A leisurely 20-minute walk from the park entrance, over some steep rocks, leads to **Bang Bae Waterfall**. It's a nice spot for lunch and a swim, but is not overly remarkable as it's neither high nor carries much water, and at certain times of year is totally dry. A further 3km (2 miles) along the same route is **Ton Sai Waterfall**, which, although more impressive, is also at risk of drying up during the summer months.

The rainforest is particularly lush during the May to October monsoon season, when flowers bloom and the greenery is more vibrant. Guides are available at the information centre at the park entrance and should be used for treks. Unless you are an expert, the rare fan-shaped *lang khao* palms and telltale signs of wildlife are easy to miss. Tigers and bears once roamed the park, but today it is far more common to see monkeys, civets and other small animals.

Gibbon Rehabilitation Centre

A 15–20 minute walk from Bang Pae Waterfall leads to the **Gibbon Rehabilitation Centre ❻** (daily 10am–4pm; free; tel: 0 7626 0491; www.gibbonproject.org). This is a non-profit organisation that aims to stop the poaching of Thailand's gibbons for tourist attractions and the pet trade. The gibbons are kept in large enclosures but as the whole purpose is to reintroduce them to the wild, it's not possible to see them up close. Although located within the national park, the Gibbon Rehabilitation Centre receives none of the money from park fees and relies solely on donations from visitors.

WEST COAST

Phuket's western coastline is its main claim to fame. Over centuries, the coast has been sculpted by pounding waves into 16 coves stretching from north to south and carpeted in powdery white sand.

Sirinat National Park

A large chunk of the northwest cape is given over to **Sirinat National Park ❼**. Formerly called Nai Yang National Park, it was renamed in 1992 in commemoration of Her Majesty Queen Sirikit's 60th birthday. The 90-sq-km (35-sq-mile) park, of which 75 percent comprises the surrounding seas, encompasses the beaches at **Hat Nai Yang** and **Hat Nai Thon**, as well as the northern mangrove area at **Hat Mai Khao**.

Gibbons kept as pets are reintroduced to the wild at Phuket's Gibbon Rehabilitation Centre.

Below: water buffalo at Khao Phra Taew National Park.

Endangered turtle species lay their eggs at Hat Mai Khao between Nov and Feb each year.

Casuarinas are the most common trees found in the park, and many species of bird, mammal and insect live within its mangrove forests. The park's marine environment is diverse and its coral reefs are among the most pristine found around Phuket. Located in water between 4–7 metres (12–23ft) deep are extensive plate and tree corals, as well as sea fans and sea anemones. The 600-metre (1,970ft)-long **Thachatchai Nature Trail** at the northern end of the park follows signs along a wooden walkway highlighting various species of flora and fauna common to this region.

Hat Mai Khao

Despite being the longest of Phuket's beaches, at over 17km (11 miles) long, the secluded location of **Hat Mai Khao** ❽ at the top north of the island also makes it one of the quietest. The sands are more golden than white and a little coarse underfoot, but the waters are very clean. There is little to do at Hat Mai Khao other than soak up the sun. As the beach is part of the protected Sirinat National Park, development is virtually nonex-

istent, which is perhaps why hundreds of olive ridley sea turtles, as well as the odd giant leatherback turtle, come ashore to lay their eggs here between November and February each year.

There are several hotels on this beach, with notable names being the **JW Marriott Resort & Spa** and the sleek and very stylish all-villa **Anantara Phuket** resort located next door. The JW resort, the first to open, was initially criticised for encroaching on national-park property, but the hotel managed to change public perception by initiating the **Marine Turtle Foundation**. All guests who stay at the JW resort are encouraged to donate US$1 a day to support local conservation efforts that help ensure the turtles' yearly return to Mai Khao's pristine shores.

Hat Nai Yang

Despite housing the headquarters of Sirinat National Park and being a protected area, **Hat Nai Yang** ❾ has a few hotels. Still, it is very laid-back and quiet compared with the beaches further down the coast. In the low season it is virtually deserted, but high season sees a strip of thatched wooden beach huts serving cold beer and seafood. The beach itself is a beautiful curving bay lined with evergreen trees that provide both visual relief and shade. A large coral reef around 1km (½ mile) offshore is home to many different species of fish, and Mai Khao's nesting turtles sometimes stray on to the shores of Nai Yang as well.

Hat Nai Thon

The smallest of Sirinat National Park's three beaches, and one of the most isolated on the island, is **Hat Nai Thon** ❿, which, due to its position at the foot of a series of high hills, is harder to reach and requires a journey on a long and winding road passing jungle and rubber plantations. The beach is not totally deserted, how-

BELOW: JW Marriott Resort & Spa on Hat Mai Khao.

ever, and a few sun beds are available for hire. Nai Ton is sheltered from the wind and waves and offers good swimming and snorkelling along its rocky headlands, which attract rich marine life year round. Offshore are the remains of a wrecked tin dredger; found at a depth of 16 metres (52ft), a favourite spot with divers.

Ao Bang Thao

The 8km (5 mile) stretch of beach at gently curving **Ao Bang Thao ⓫** is dominated by the Laguna Resort, an integrated development of five luxury hotels, the most exclusive being the **Banyan Tree Phuket**, with its 18 hole golf course and multi-award-winning spa. With its Family Fun Zone and Camp Quest activities for children aged 8–12 years, Laguna is a popular option for family holidays. The sand on Bang Tao beach is among the whitest on the island, and the water is crystal-clear. Beware of the strong undertow, however, during the monsoon season. Accommodation runs the length of this beach, all of it thankfully low-rise, and there are several restaurants and antique shops.

Ao Pansea and Hat Surin

One of Phuket's most exclusive resorts, the luxury **Amanpuri** occupies prime position at **Ao Pansea ⓬**, with Thai-style pavilions interspersed in a coconut plantation. This hotel is the preserve of both the mega-rich and a host of A-list celebrities.

Although the law in Thailand states that all beaches in the country are public, Pansea seems to be one of several exceptions, helped by the fact that it is closed off by headlands at each end. The other end of Ao Pansea is anchored by the 5-star **The Surin Phuket** resort, which is much more affordable, but still beyond the reach of many.

Beyond the resort, the beach becomes **Hat Surin ⓭**, where the sand is more of a golden hue than white. There are many luxury private villas here, while the Twin Palms resort dominates the beach and charges exhorbitant prices for loungers. However, there is still a local feel to the place, with vendors at makeshift stalls selling freshly grilled prawns and barbecued mackerel, but there are now several restaurants,

TIP

Even if you can't afford to stay at the famed Amanpuri resort (by far Phuket's most expensive), go there for lunch or a drink to soak in the ambience, architecture and views from its lofty perch at the top of a cliff.

BELOW: Hat Surin is pretty, but be careful of the undertow during the monsoon season.

Having been through the catastrophic tsunami in Dec 2004, Phuket now has an early warning system and clearly marked evacuation routes, if ever a tsunami should hit its shores again.

BELOW: Hat Patong is by far Phuket's busiest beach.

too. Again, beware of the undertow during the monsoon season.

Hat Kamala

High-profile Patong received the most coverage when the tsunami hit Phuket in December 2004, but it was the quieter **Hat Kamala** that took the brunt of the killer waves. Damage to this area of mostly Muslim villages was severe and the area took longer to recover than any other in Phuket. Kamala is only a few minutes away from the hustle and bustle of Patong yet could not be more different in character; the beach is calm, relaxed and peaceful, with few vendors touting for business. Headlands to the north and south shelter the beach, and with forested hills rising inland, the overall effect is a very picturesque bay. Kamala retains something of a village atmosphere.

In the heart of Kamala is the **Phuket Fantasea** (daily Fri–Wed 5.30–11.30pm, show time 9pm; tel: 0-7638 5111; www.phuket-fantasea. com). The 57-hectare (140-acre) complex, which cost a massive US$60 million to construct, touts itself as

a night-time cultural theme park. Visitors can pose for photos while riding elephants and cuddling tiger cubs, although the latter are quickly taken from you after the flash goes off and passed on to the next paying customer. The show itself combines high-wire trapeze acts, acrobatics, pyrotechnics and illusions, traditional dance, and a whole menagerie of performing animals, including at one point over 40 elephants on stage all at the same time.

Hat Patong

For every person drawn to **Hat Patong** . there is another who can't escape quickly enough. But, love it or hate it, Phuket would not be the tourist magnet it is without its multitude of shops, restaurants, street stalls, neon lights, flashy bars and discos. The beach is crowded with sunburnt bodies sheltered under rows of beach umbrellas – even in the low season it is virtually impossible to find a quiet spot on the sand – and the constant barrage of hawkers gets annoying, with touts from restaurants and tailors going overboard to entice you

into their shops. On the plus side, the location is naturally beautiful: the sea is crystal-clear outside of the monsoon season, and is good for swimming or snorkelling (although care should be taken not to get too close to the jet-skis and banana boats whizzing by close to the shore). Also beware the scams associated with hiring these craft (see Crime and Safety, page 288).

There is plenty to spend your money on, with lots of variety. The range of cuisines on offer is immense and caters for every palate. While the nightlife in certain areas is seedy and the prostitution blatant, you can have a fun and entertaining night if you don't take it all too seriously. There are transsexual cabaret shows, plenty of bars, running from Thai-style to the ubiquitous Irish-themed pubs, and a few decent dance venues.

As Patong was developed early into a more commercial centre, it doesn't have the benefit of the beach-side resorts found in other locations, and only one hotel, **Impiana Resort Patong**, is right on the beach. All other properties are tucked behind the beach-side Thanon Thaveewong.

Patong nightlife

In the heart of Patong is **Soi Bangla**, the epicentre of the seedy sex trade with bar after bar of young Thai prostitutes, *kathoey*, or "lady-boy" transsexuals, and the explicit "ping-pong" sex shows. Despite the blatant commercial trade, the atmosphere is relaxed and feels surprisingly safe. While single men may get hassled to buy drinks for the bar girls, women, couples and even families can amble down the street, stop in a bar or two and be treated no differently than they would elsewhere on the island. Patong also has a fairly large gay district, featuring everything from sex-orientated places to gay-friendly hotels, bars and cafés, that mainly centres around the network of lanes

that make up the **Paradise Complex** near the Royal Paradise Hotel on Thanon Raja Uthit.

Patong's version of Thailand's popular transsexual cabaret shows is **Simon Cabaret** (show nightly at 6pm, 7.45pm and 9.30pm; charge; tel: 0-7634 2114; www.phuket-simoncabaret.com), located on Thanon Sirirat heading south out of Patong. While some people find the show rather dull, with the performing "lady-boys", or *kathoey*, miming the lyrics and acting and dancing flamboyantly, it has a Vegas-style glitz that draws people in every night.

Hat Karon Noi and Hat Karon

Past Hat Patong is **Hat Karon Noi**, sometimes referred to as Relax Bay. Although it is a public beach, this crescent of sand is dominated by a single hotel, **Le Méridien Phuket**, making access to it a little difficult.

Further south is the 4km (3 mile) long beach at **Hat Karon ⑰**, which, despite being Phuket's second-most popular beach after Hat Patong, is rarely packed. The sand is golden in

TIP

To see the "lady-boys" at Simon Cabaret without watching the show, head to the car park around 11pm when they all come out and line up for photos. This is a better opportunity to see them up close and personal.

BELOW: Patong's Soi Bangla comes alive at night.

Waitresses in Flintstone costume at Karon's Dino Park and Mini Golf Course.

BELOW: it is easy to see why Hat Kata Yai is one of Phuket's best beaches.

colour and its beauty is only slightly tarnished by the ugly sand dunes and grassy embankment leading up to the road backing it. It was this elevated position that spared Karon from the same degree of tsunami devastation that Patong suffered. During the rainy season, large waves make Hat Karon excellent for surfing but unsafe for swimming. There is a good range of hotels, most of which, like in Patong, are tucked behind the beach-side Thanon Karon.

One of Karon's most prominent attractions is the kitsch **Dino Park and Mini Golf** (daily 10am–10pm; charge; tel: 0-7633 0625; www.dino park.com). It is impossible to miss this sight with its huge dinosaur statue towering outside and staff dressed in Flintstone costumes. At night, an elephant stands at the entrance, waiting to be fed bananas. The tables are carved out of stone and set among pretty waterfalls and jungle vines, but the food is overpriced and tastes bland. More impressive is the mini golf course (18 holes), which trails over rocks and across rivers, passing screeching

dinosaurs with smoking nostrils and clusters of half-hatched eggs.

Hat Kata Yai and Hat Kata Noi

Just past the headland from Karon is **Hat Kata Yai** ⑱ (mostly referred to only as Kata), arguably one of the most scenic of Phuket's beaches and the reason why Club Med chose to open its resort here. This lovely beach is blessed with white sand and clear waters good for swimming and snorkelling. As a result, it is very popular and, being relatively small, can get busy. At night, it is quiet and romantic, and there are a number of seafood restaurants lit by fairy lights overlooking the waves lapping the shore. The southern end of the beach is home to **The Boathouse** hotel, which has a well-known fine-dining restaurant.

Separated by a rocky headland is **Hat Kata Noi** ⑲, which shares the same white sand and clear blue-green waters as the preceding beach but is even prettier and more peaceful. The sprawling but unattractive **Katathani Phuket Beach Resort** has almost complete run of this beach. At the southern end of the beach are some decent corals for snorkelling.

Kata Hill Viewpoint

Cars sometimes struggle and motorbikes splutter trying to crest the sharp, steep mountain road that leads out of Kata. On a sunny day, the view from this road is breathtaking. There are a couple of small bar-restaurants here that play reggae and soft rock music. Built on simple wooden platforms over the hillside looking towards the sea, both are good for watching the setting sun.

A little further along on the opposite side of the road is **Kok Chang Elephant Camp** (tel: 08-9591 9413). Visitors can arrange to go on elephant treks (20, 30 or 50 minute rides are available), or just feed the

elephants bananas or pineapples, and stop for a refreshing drink at the bamboo bar at the front of the park, where they will often be joined by two resident monkeys.

At the peak is the **Kata Hill Viewpoint ㉒**, from which the three stunning bays of Kata, Karon and Patong can be seen in one fell swoop. This famous scene appears on postcards island-wide; photography conditions are better in the morning, as even on a seemingly perfect day, the clouds can roll in by mid-afternoon and block the view.

Hat Nai Harn

South of Kata and lying between two ridges is stunning white-sand **Hat Nai Harn ㉑**, the epitome of a chilled and laid back Thai beach. For this it can thank the **Samnak Song Nai Harn Monastery**, which occupies a large portion of the seafront land, and has therefore thwarted development. Nai Harn, backed by an open lagoon, is a quieter alternative to the island's other beaches and is popular with expats, who are frequently seen exercising their dogs

on Sunday mornings. It offers some conveniences in the form of a few small bars, restaurants and shops. An open lagoon, the cause of much controversy when the trees bordering it were ripped out in early 2005, backs the beach. The trees were cleared to make way for what is now a jogging track, and the surrounding grounds re-landscaped.

SOUTH COAST

The south-coast beaches from Laem Promthep onwards are largely mediocre at best and mainly used as a staging point for explorations of the islands off the southern coast.

Laem Promthep

Leading up the mountain from Nai Harn is another viewpoint that features on many a postcard of Phuket, **Laem Promthep ㉒** (Promthep Cape). This busy point overlooking a splendid headland stretching into the blue Andaman Sea is packed every evening throughout the year when hordes of tourists flock to see the sun sink slowly over the horizon. When the conditions are right, the sunset

EAT

The views at Promthep Cape Restaurant (tel: 0-7628 8656; daily lunch and dinner) are much better than the mostly mediocre food, of which the most impressive are the fresh oysters, reared in the owner's farm. Service is slow, but the staff are friendly and the prices reasonable.

BELOW: aerial view of Kata, Karon and Patong beaches from the Kata Hill Viewpoint.

TIP

Phuket is the sailing centre of Thailand, with several regattas throughout the year, including the King's Cup, held every December around the king's birthday. Ao Chalong is where most boats dock and the Ao Chalong Yacht Club (tel: 08-5249 0823; www. acyc.asia) holds regular races. The clubhouse is a good place to meet people and find out about crewing opportunities.

vistas here are wonderful. **Promthep Cape Restaurant** *(see margin tip)*, overlooking the cape and serving cheap Thai food, is surprisingly quiet considering the number of visitors.

Hat Rawai

A base for the vast majority of Phuket's foreign residents, **Hat Rawai** ㉓ offers all the attractions of island life but without the intrusive tourist facilities of Kata, Karon and Patong. Rawai is often picturesque, with its rows of small fishing and long-tail boats waiting to journey to the nearby islands, but at low tide, the exposed rocks make it unsuitable for swimming and snorkelling. Rawai is famous for its street vendors who barbecue freshly caught seafood along the beach road throughout the day and the fresh seafood restaurants that open in the evenings. To the south of the beach is a small *chao lay* (sea gypsy) village that can be visited.

Nearby, on Thanon Viset, is the **Phuket Seashell Museum** (daily 8am–6pm; charge; tel: 0-7661 3666; www.phuketseashell.com), with an interesting display of over 2,000 different species of shell and fossil; some of the latter are reputedly over 380 million years old.

Ao Chalong

North of Rawai is **Ao Chalong**, which is known mainly for a temple, a huge Buddha statue, and a pier, from which many scuba expeditions and boat trips to nearby islands depart. The massive 45-metre (150ft) Buddha statue dominates the area from atop Nakkerd Hill, and is worth visiting for vistas across the sea and southern tip of Phuket. The new Chalong Bay Marina is scheduled to launch in 2015.

Wat Chalong ㉔ (daily 7am–5pm; free), located inland of Rawai on Route 4021, is Phuket's most important Buddhist temple and the largest of the island's 29 Buddhist monasteries. Architecturally, it's not that different from other Thai temples, but it is one of Phuket's most ornate and among the most visited by both Thais and foreigners. The temple is associated with the revered monks Luang Pro Chaem and Luang Pho Chuang, famous herbal doctors and bone-setters who tended to the people of Phuket during

BELOW: Ko Hae, also known as Coral Island.

the tin miners' rebellion of 1876. Far from being just physical healers, they also mediated in the conflict, bringing both parties together to resolve disputes. Today, many Thais visit the temple to pay homage to the two statues that honour the monks.

SOUTHERN ISLANDS

The waters around Phuket's southernmost tip are dotted with a number of islands. All can be reached by the longtail boats lining Hat Rawai beach or the pier at Ao Chalong. If staying overnight at islands such as Ko Racha, the resort there will arrange the boat transfer for you.

Ko Bon

Nearest to shore is the small but pretty **Ko Bon** ㉕, which can be reached in just 10 minutes. One side of the island is owned by a private resort company due to open on the mainland and is intended for the private use of its guests, possibly with accommodation. Unfortunately, Ko Bon has no other rooms for rent and no fresh water or electricity.

Most day-trippers head for diving and snorkelling on the other side of the island, where the **Bon Island Restaurant**, a small Thai seafood place, is all that rests on the sandy beachfront. Some of the coral close to shore was damaged by the 2004 tsunami, and larger fragments are still strewn on the beach, too heavy to be moved (but actually look quite pretty). Coral in the deeper waters remains undamaged, and the water in front of the Bon Island Restaurant is particularly good for snorkelling.

Ko Hae

About 20 minutes from mainland Phuket, and often combined on a day trip with Ko Bon, is **Ko Hae** ㉖ (Coral Island). Amenities are better than at Ko Bon, with a number of restaurants, a few small shops and a choice of water sports. Overnight

stays are possible at the **Coral Island Resort** (tel: 0-7628 1060), the island's only accommodation; nights are generally very quiet when all the day-trippers have returned to Phuket. The crystal-clear turquoise waters around the island make it particularly good for both swimming and snorkelling, and there is a shallow coral reef within easy swimming distance of the beach.

Ko Kaeo

Despite being only a 10-minute boat ride from mainland Phuket, **Ko Kaeo** ㉗ is by far the least-visited by day-trippers due to its lack of facilities, giving them the chance to have their own private beach for the day. The pretty island is home to a number of Buddha statues and shrines, hence it's name, which translates as Buddha Island.

Ko Racha

Around 20km (12 miles) off the coast of Rawai are **Ko Racha Noi**, a small uninhabited island with more rocks than beaches, and the larger **Ko Racha Yai** ㉘. Of the many islands within close proximity of Phuket, Ko

Ko Kaeo island has numerous Buddha statues and shrines.

BELOW: pristine Ao Batok on Ko Racha Yai.

Spectacular marine life awaits divers in the waters around Ko Racha Yai and Noi.

Racha Yai is one of the most exclusive, as it's the site of a luxury resort known simply as **The Racha**, on the northeast coast along **Ao Batok**. High season sees Ko Racha Yai transform into a bustling hotspot, with day-trippers arriving on longtail boats and filling the beaches. The shoreline of the beach in front of The Racha is picturesque, the sand almost talcum powder-like and the waters crystal-clear turquoise. Watch out for the small corals and rocks, however, when you wade into the waters.

Ko Racha offers some of the best diving in the Phuket area, and as the going is generally free of hazard, it's suitable for all levels. The islands are often compared to the waters around the Similan Islands. The **Bungalow Bay** reef offshore of Ao Batok has clear waters and soft coral gardens, with good visibility and currents that allow gentle drift diving along sloping reefs. Elsewhere on the island are more white-sand beaches and snorkelling spots. Resting at the bottom of a grassy slope on the eastern coast is **Ao Kon Kare**, a small sandy beach with **Lucy's Reef** within swimming distance, a

nickname given to the staghorn coral found here. Further up the east coast, a submerged wreck is found off **Ao Ter** at depths of 25–35 metres (80–115ft); it is popular with more advanced divers. On the northern coast is **Ao Siam**, where shallow waters not only make for good snorkelling but also prevent boats from docking, keeping this beach less busy than those in other parts of the island.

The smaller **Ko Racha Noi** also has a few good dive sites for experienced divers; depths here are generally greater and currents stronger. On the southwest side of the island, lots of interesting reef fish are drawn to a 27-metre (88ft) shipwreck, while a large pinnacle at the northern tip attracts stingrays and reef sharks.

Phuket's other dive sites are scattered around the Andaman Coast (*see pages 200–1, 254 and 258–9*).

EAST COAST

The east coast of Phuket was once the bank of a flooded river. Unlike the west, this side of the coastline comprises mainly limestone shoals and virtually no sandy beaches.

BELOW: poolside at dusk, The Racha resort.

Laem Panwa

The only real beach spot on the eastern coast of Phuket is **Laem Panwa**, 10km (6 miles) southeast from Phuket Town. This quiet cape is frequently filled with yachts sailing around **Ao Yon ㉙**, where a totally unspoilt stretch of sand sheltered by headlands on both sides makes it a good spot for swimming all year round. Only a handful of hotels and restaurants stand in the Laem Panwa area, and as *tuk-tuks* and motorcycle taxis rarely journey over the winding mountain road to get here, the beach is often deserted.

Khao Khad Viewpoint (reached by following signs along Thanon Sakdidej, which lead through Muang Tong village) is a beautiful spot from which to gaze out to the sea. From this elevated point, Phuket Town lies to one side, Chalong Bay to the other, and the shadowy outline of Ko Phi Phi *(see page 250)* island can be seen in the distance.

On the southernmost tip of Laem Panwa, on Route 4129, is the **Phuket Aquarium & Marine Biological Research Centre** (daily 8.30am–4.30pm; charge; tel: 0-7639 1126). The impressive display of sharks, tropical fish, reefs and a touch pool with starfish and sea cucumbers makes an excellent primer before taking that first diving or snorkelling trip. There's also a nature trail to learn about coastal habitats.

Ko Sirey

To the east of Phuket Town, and separated from the mainland by a small bridge, is the tiny island of **Ko Sirey ㉚**, home to a small *chao lay* (sea gypsy) fishing community. The area is poor in terms of material wealth but rich in cultural appeal. Be sure to ask permission if taking photographs. It was planned to make the island's life more accessible with a Sea Gypsy Cultural Centre. The building has been erected, but the fate of the cen-

tre is unclear as other development on the island is slated to increase.

There is a small beach on the eastern side of Ko Sirey, known as **Hat Teum Suk**. It is not really a swimming beach, however, and is visited mostly by Thai families.

Naga Pearl Farm

The jetty at Ao Po, north of Phuket Town, is the departure point for the 30-minute boat ride to the island of **Ko Nakha Noi ㉛**. This is where you will find the **Naga Pearl Farm** (daily 9am–3.30pm; charge; tel: 0-7742 3272), where full-sized South Sea pearls worth thousands of pounds are cultivated. Also on display here is a replica of the world's largest pearl, the original of which is currently housed at the Mikimoto Pearl Museum in Japan. Visitors can wander round and see pearls at various stages of cultivation, from the nurturing of the baby oysters to the extraction of pearls from their shells years later. Longtail-boat operators at Ao Po can arrange a boat ride to the island (about B300 per person for a return trip) or else book a guided tour directly with the farm. ❑

TIP

Visits to minority communities have become very much a part of the tourist experience, and many villages adapt well. But this is not always the case. If visiting Ko Sirey sea-gypsy village, please consider the inhabitants, who may not be in the mood to be a photo opportunity.

BELOW: "sea gypsy" children.

PHUKET

TRANSPORT

Getting There

By Air

Phuket International Airport
(tel: 0-7632 7230/5) is located in
the north of the island. Though
most visitors to Phuket stop off in
Bangkok first for a few days, many
also fly directly to Phuket from
Hong Kong (Dragonair, Thai Airways), Kuala Lumpur (Malaysia
Airlines, AirAsia, Qatar Airways),
Shanghai (Shanghai Airlines, Jun-
yao), Sydney (Jetstar) and Singapore (SilkAir, Jetstar Asia, Tiger
Airways, Air Asia). Internally, Thai
Airways offers daily flights from
Bangkok, while Bangkok Airways
flies daily from Bangkok and Ko
Samui. Several budget airlines fly
to Phuket from Bangkok, including Orient Thai Airlines, AirAsia
and Nok Air *(see page 103 for
details)*.

By Road

Air-conditioned buses from the
Southern Bus Terminal in
Bangkok make the 14-hour overnight trip to Phuket. But with so
many cheap flights there, this
uncomfortable option is even
less appealing. Air-conditioned
buses depart daily for nearby
Krabi, Phang Nga, Ranong, Surat
Thani, Satun, Hat Yai and Trang
from Bus Terminal 2, in Phuket
Town (Th. Thepkrasattri; tel:
0-7621 1977).

ABOVE: outside Jui Tui temple.

By Boat

Boats from Krabi and Ko Phi Phi
to Phuket normally drop passengers off at Rassada pier in Phuket
Town. It takes roughly 2½ hours
from Ko Phi Phi and 3 hours from
Krabi. Boats from Ko Lanta travel
via Krabi or Ko Phi Phi. Between
May and October, boats may stop
operating due to wet weather.

The islands south of Phuket,
such as Ko Bon, Ko Hae, Ko Kaeo
(Buddha Island) and Ko Racha,
can be visited by chartering a
longtail boat from Rawai beach,
and, except for Ko Racha, can be
reached in 10–20 minutes. Visi-

tors to further-flung Ko Racha
usually join a day trip on a larger,
quicker boat from Chalong pier.
Depending on sea conditions,
transfer time is 45–60 minutes to
Ko Racha. The Racha resort on
the island can also arrange both
the land transfer from the airport
and the boat trip for hotel guests
– albeit at inflated rates.

Getting Around

From the Airport

Travelling to Phuket Town or
Patong from the airport generally
takes about 30 minutes. Even
during the high season, traffic
flows freely. If you plan to drive,
Hertz and Avis *(see page 231)*
both have car-rental counters at
the airport.

Taxi: In the Arrival Hall, airport
taxis and limousines can be
hired at set rates displayed on a
board. After paying the fare, a
coupon is issued that is then
given to the driver. Prices are
B200–400 for the nearby northern beaches, rising to B550 to
B750 for different locations in
Patong. Trips to hotels on Kata
and Karon have a flat fare of
B650. Alternatively, there are red
and yellow metered taxis outside
the airport (you may need to
insist that they turn on the
meter). The price is around B400
to Phuket Town.

Minivans: Shared minivans (around B100 to Phuket Town, B150 to Patong) have ticket counters in the arrival hall. If you are part of a large group, book a quicker 8-seater minibus. The fares are around B900 to Phuket Town, B1,200–1,500 to Patong and B1,300 to Kata and Karon. Tickets are sold next to the limousine booths.

Airport Bus: Tickets for the airport bus can be bought on boarding or from booths in the arrival hall. At the time of writing, the bus only travels to Phuket Town, with several stops along the main route only. It takes at least 45 minutes. The full fare is B90.

Taxis and Tuk-tuks

Public transport in Phuket is notoriously poor. There are few metered taxis and those that have meters will never use them. Taxi fares have to be negotiated, except for taxis boarded from taxi stands at major shopping centres and some beaches, where prices are fixed.

Tuk-tuks are plentiful, but prices are among the highest in Thailand, costing nearly as much as taxis. Agree on a price before getting in a tuk-tuk, and be aware that it will be more expensive at night and during rainy spells. Unlike those in Bangkok, Phuket's tuk-tuks have four wheels instead of three and are painted bright red. These converted open-air vans have two benches in the back, and are not very comfortable on long journeys. Expect to pay from B300 for a trip between Phuket Town and Patong, and about B200–250 between Patong and Kata or Karon, although it ultimately comes down to what you can negotiate in the end.

Motorcycle taxis are a cheaper but more dangerous way to travel, with at least one death per week resulting from road collisions occurring during the high season.

Songthaew

Small, blue public buses called songthaew shuttle passengers from the market on Th. Ranong in Phuket Town to the main beaches. They leave every half-hour between 6am and 6pm (return journeys end at 4pm). The songthaew to Rawai and Nai Harn depart from Th. Bangkok. There are no songthaew connections between beaches. Songthaews move very slowly and stop frequently to cram in as many local passengers as possible, but the fare is only B30–40.

Rented Cars

Driving in Phuket can certainly be challenging. Motorists frequently resist giving way, and exceed the speed limit. It is not uncommon to see trucks overtaking on blind corners. As a result, road accidents are shockingly common, most involving motorcyclists. An alarming number of people also drink and drive, in part because of limited public transport.

The roads outside the centre of town are less busy, making driving almost pleasurable. Note, however, that scenic roads during the day become pitch black and hazardous to navigate come nightfall.

Standard car rental ranges from B700 to B2,500 a day. Use a reputable company because many of the independent beachfront businesses will not provide insurance.

Avis, Phuket Airport; tel: 08 9969 8674; www.avisworld.com.
Budget, Phuket Airport (also in Phuket Town and Patong); tel: 0-7632 7744; www.budget.co.th.
Phuket Car Rent, tel: 08-9724 2823; www.phuketcarrent.com.

BELOW: a customised taxi in Patong.

PHUKET

PHUKET TOWN

Chinotel
133–135 Th. Ranong
Tel: 0-7621 4455
www.chinotelphuket.com
This new hotel is centrally located and has a striking modern Chinese design. All rooms are ensuite, with free Wi-fi and cable TV. There's no restaurant, but eating options are aplenty nearby. (24 rooms) **$**

Royal Phuket City Hotel
154 Th. Phang Nga
Tel: 0-7623 3333
www.royalphuketcity.com
This centrally located hotel is large yet welcoming. Facilities include Tien Kung Chinese restaurant and the Rattan Box café, which has international food and live music at night, plus fitness centre and swimming pool. (251 rooms) **$$**

HAT MAI KHAO

JW Marriott Phuket Resort & Spa
Moo 3, Mai Khao
Tel: 0-7633 8000
www.marriott.com
Located a few minutes from the airport, this self-contained sanctuary has extensive facilities including six restaurants, fitness centre, spa and water sports. Set in sprawling landscaped grounds

with lovely water features, the resort sits just adjacent to a national park and a turtle-nesting sanctuary. Some people like the isolation while others feel it's too far away from the town and the main beaches. (246 rooms and 13 suites) **$$$**

HAT NAI YANG

Indigo Pearl
Nai Yang
Tel: 0-7632 7006
www.indigo-pearl.com
Located within Sirinat National Park and by the beach, the hotel has a design of wood, stone and metal, using contemporary and traditional Thai accents inspired by Phuket's tin-mining past. Rooms have satellite TV and Wi-fi access. (292 rooms) **$$$$**

AO BANG TAO

Angsana Laguna Phuket
10 Moo 4, Th. Srisoonthorn
Tel: 0-7632 4101
www.angsana.com
This large and luxurious resort sits on its own small island in the centre of a lagoon, with Bang Tao beach at the front and forests at the back. Lagoon-style pools wind through the property, while facilities incude seven restau-

rants and bars and Xana beach club, hosting top DJs. (409 rooms) **$$$**

Banyan Tree Phuket
33 Moo 4, Th. Srisoonthorn
Tel: 0-7637 2400
www.banyantreephuket.com
The most exclusive of the seven hotels within the Laguna Phuket complex, the award-winning Banyan Tree has luxurious Thai-style villas with landscaped gardens and private outdoor pools. Excellent spa on site. Guests here, and at the hotels below, can access the Laguna Complex facilities, including golf course. (108 rooms) **$$$$**

Dusit Laguna
390 Th. Srisoonthorn
Tel: 0-7636 2999
www.dusit.com
Low-rise, modern Thai-style buildings contain bright and airy rooms with wooden floors. Part of the Thai-owned luxury Dusit group, it's located right on Bang Thao beach. All rooms have balconies, and there are six restaurants to chose from. (226 rooms) **$$$**

AO PANSEA

Amanpuri
118/1 Moo 3, Pansea
Tel: 0-7632 4333
www.amanpuri.com
One of Phuket's most exclusive retreats, this is situated on a headland with its own private beach and a fleet of lux-

urious boats. The Amanpuri is all about understated elegance in its very traditional Thai-style villas. A-list celebrities are drawn here by the seclusion. The beach is located at the bottom of a long flight of steps. (40 rooms and 31 villas) **$$$$**

The Surin Phuket
118 Moo 3, Pansea
Tel: 0-7662 1580
www.thesurinphuket.com
The rooms here are among coconut trees, each with private verandah and teak floors. As the cottages hug a cliff, expect to climb a lot of stairs that sometimes take a circuitous route. It has one of Phuket's most inviting swimming pools, a spa, tennis courts and a gorgeous beach front. (103 rooms) **$$$**

HAT SURIN

Manathai Resort
121 Th. Srisunthorn
Tel: 0-7627 0900
www.manathai.com
This boutique resort is very stylish at the price, with modern Asian accents throughout the design. The rooms have flat-screen satellite TV, DVD players and free Wi-fi. There's a small but well-landscaped pool, a spa and Weaves restaurant, which serves international food. Poolside rooms are great value. (52 rooms) **$$**

Above: Le Méridien.

Twin Palms Phuket
106/46 Moo 3, Surin
Tel: 0-7631 6500
www.twinpalms phuket.com
Modern and stylish resort only a 5-minute walk from Surin beach. Contemporary decor with white walls and bed linen contrasting with dark wooden floors and furniture. All the usual amenities expected from a luxury resort plus the hip Oriental Spoon restaurant serving innovative Western and Thai dishes. (76 rooms) $$$$

HAT PATONG

Amari Phuket
2 Th. Meun-Ngern
Tel: 0-7634 0106-14
www.amari.com
Perched on a headland at the quiet end of the beach, all the rooms here have a private balcony and sea views. Three restaurants cover Thai, Italian and international foods, while the Breeze Spa offers pampering treatments. (197 rooms) $$

Ban Thai Beach Resort
94 Th. Thawiwong
Tel: 0-7634 0850
www.banthaiphuket.com
From its minimalist foyer bordered by pools to its well appointed, modern Thai-style rooms and suites, Ban Thai is extremely easy on the eye. Central location in Patong close to restaurants and shops. It has three swimming pools, all with bars. (290 rooms) $$$

Burasari Resort
18/110 Soi Ruamjai
Tel: 0-7629 2929
www.burasari.com
Burasari is a maze of exotic plants, flowers and waterfalls set around a swimming pool. The decor is a blend of contemporary and Thai, and the resort itself is well located: just a minute's walk down a quiet street off the main beach road – keeping it secluded yet in the midst of the action. (90 rooms) $$

Expat Hotel
163/17 Th. Ratutit
Tel: 0-7634 2143
www.expathotel.com
Situated on the back road near the central street of Soi Bangla and a 5-minute walk from the beach, the Expat Hotel is a favourite with return guests. Its old-style decor keeps prices lower than many other Patong hotels in the same price range. Clean rooms, friendly service and large swimming pool make it great value for money. (46 rooms) $

La Flora Patong
39 Th. Thaweewong
Tel: 0-7634 4241
www.laflorapatong.com
Modern resort with clean lines and a white-walled Mediterranean feel. The rooms are pool or sea view, with private balconies, free Wi-fi, LCD screens with satellite TV, plus DVD, CD and MP3 players. The Current of the Sea restaurant serves seafood fusion dishes and there's a spa with all the usual treatments. (67 rooms) $$$

HAT KARON

Centara Villas Phuket
701 Th. Patak
Tel: 0-7628 6300
www.centralhotelsresorts.com
Perched on a hill with sweeping views of the sea, the trade-off is a five-minute walk to Karon beach. However, as the hotel is located at the northern end of Karon, it is also close to Patong beach. Rooms take a contemporary slant on traditional motifs, with patios or terraces as standard. (72 rooms) $$$

Hilton Phuket Arcadia Resort & Spa
333 Th. Patak
Tel: 0-7639 6433
www.hilton.com
This huge resort stretches over 75 acres in a prime location at the centre of Karon, with the beach located a short walk across the road. There are four restaurants and excellent facilities including pool and spa, tennis and squash courts, jogging and walking tracks, a playground and a putting green. Free scuba-diving lessons are another draw. (679 rooms) $$$

Le Méridien Phuket Beach Resort
Karon Noi
Tel: 0-7637 0100
www.starwoodhotels.com
Located in a sheltered bay with a private beach on its doorstep. Facilities are top rate: two massive adjoining swimming pools, spa, numerous restaurants, bars and shops, golf driving range and one of the island's largest and most modern gyms. Rooms are spacious and tastefully furnished. (407 rooms) $$$

HAT KATA

Katathani Hotel and Beach Resort
Kata Noi
Tel: 0-7633 0124
www.katathani.com

PRICE CATEGORIES
Price categories show the starting price for a double room without breakfast and taxes:
$ = under US$70
$$ = US$70–130
$$$ = US$130–250
$$$$ = over US$250

Located on quiet Kata Noi, where guests have pretty much the run of the stunning beach. The resort is large and spread out so it never seems overcrowded with tourists. Rooms (the standard ones feel cramped) have been given a makeover in teak and sandstone but the star attraction here is the beach. (479 rooms) **$$$**

Mom Tri's Boathouse
Kata Yai
Tel: 0-7633 0015
www.boathousephuket.com
Prime beach-front location along the broad Kata Yai beach. Rooms are smallish but have sunset-facing sea views and were recently renovated. Award-winning Boathouse Wine & Grill on site. (33 rooms and 3 suites). Note: south of the Boathouse, on the cliff just above the headland, is the luxury **Villa Royale** (tel: 0-7633 3658; www.villaroyale.com), which operates under the same management as Mom Tri's Boathouse. Many of its Thai-style villas have stunning sea views and are only a short walk to the smaller and more intimate Kata Noi beach. (27 villas) **$$$$**

Peach Hill Hotel & Resort
2 Th. Laemsai
Tel: 0-7637 1600
www.peach-hill.com
This hilltop resort looks deceptively small. But once inside, the verdant grounds open out to reveal three swimming pools. The service and level of English spoken here is impressive. The de-luxe rooms that are on

offer here are particularly nice. (211 rooms) **$$**

HAT NAI HARN

The Royal Phuket Yacht Club
23/3 Moo 1, Th. Vises
Tel: 0-7638 0200
www.theroyalphuketyachtclub.com
With direct access to Nai Harn beach, the Royal Phuket Yacht Club has the sparkling sea to its front and a lagoon at its back, and is in high demand year-round. Rooms, all with private terraces, are spacious and tastefully furnished. All have sea views, most overlooking the bay and nearby Promthep Cape. Popular with those seeking a quiet beach away from the hustle and bustle further up the island. (110 rooms) **$$$**

HAT RAWAI

Friendship Beach Resort & Spa by iCheck Inn
27/1 Soi Mittrapap, Rawai
Tel: 0-7628 8996
www.friendshipbeach.com
This place fits the bill for a quiet beachfront location. There's a spa on site with all the usual relaxing treatments, plus cleansing and detox, and the open fronted beach bar and restaurant has a broad range of international dishes. It is popular with kite surfers for the good winds and kite surfing school located next door. (260 rooms) **$**

Mangosteen Resort & Ayurveda Spa
99/4 Moo 7, Soi Mangosteen

Tel: 0-7628 9399
www.mangosteen-phuket.com
Intimate resort with a sea view to one side and mountains to the other. Rooms have free Wi-fi and DVDs, flat-screen TVs and many have private jacuzzi baths. The saltwater swimming pool bends and twists its way around the resort's buildings and restaurant. There is no direct beach access, unfortunately; however, a shuttle bus is offered to Nai Harn beach and the journey takes only 5 minutes. (40 rooms) **$$**

LAEM PANWA

Cape Panwa Hotel
27 Moo 8, Th. Sakdidet
Tel: 0-7639 1123
www.capepanwa.com
Located among palm trees and set slightly to the back of a quiet beach, the large, comfortable rooms in this hotel are sea-facing. Classes in cooking, painting and the Thai language are on offer, and there are five bars and five restaurants to ensure a wide choice of entertainment. (246 rooms) **$$$**

Sri Panwa
88 Moo 8, Th. Sakdidet
Tel: 0-7637 1000
www.sripanwa.com
Accommodation at this beautiful hillside retreat overlooking Cape Panwa starts with 100-sq-metre (1076-sq-foot) pool suites, each with sea views and its own infinity pool, rising to larger suites and villas. The Baba Pool Club has Thai, Japanese and Western dining options,

a dance venue and a 25-metre pool. (78 rooms) **$$$$**

KO RACHA YAI

The Racha
Ko Racha Yai
Tel: 0-7635 5455
www.theracha.com
One of the island's most exclusive resorts, The Racha has a chic, modern style with its minimalist white-on-white villas and luxurious open-air garden bathrooms with rain-showers. If the budget allows, plump for the villas with private pools, or at the very least, the large deluxe villas. A dramatic rooftop glass-edged infinity swimming pool overlooks the turquoise bay. (70 villas) **$$$$**

KO HAE

Coral Island Resort
Ko Hae (Coral Island)
Tel: 0-7628 1060
www.coralislandresort.com
The only choice for an overnight stay on this island. All cottages are air conditioned, with jacuzzi and terraces overlooking the sea. Has the island's only swimming pool. Offers diving and snorkelling trips. (40 cottages) **$**

PRICE CATEGORIES

Price categories show the starting price for a double room without breakfast and taxes:
$ = under US$70
$$ = US$70–130
$$$ = US$130–250
$$$$ = over US$250

PHUKET

PHUKET TOWN

International

Salvatore's
15-17 Th. Rasada
Tel: 0-7622 5958
Open: Mon–Sat L and D,
Sun D.
The portly Salvatore
looks the part as he
oversees this generous
Italian menu that starts
with appetisers such as
lobster Catalan-style and
moves through pastas
and risotto to main
courses. Try gnocchi with
lamb sauce, followed by
home-made ice cream
and round off with
freshly ground Italian
coffee. The tables in the
rustic interior are fully
booked most nights so
reservations are strongly
recommended. **$$–$$$**

**Watermark Bar and
Restaurant**
22/1 Moo 2, Th. Thopkacattri
Tel: 0-7623 9730
www.watermarkphuket.com
Open: daily L and D.
Overlooking the yachts
at the Boat Lagoon
Marina, there's a chic
atmosphere here for
"multiethnic" choices
such as honey-and-gin-
ger duck breast and
grilled white snapper in
pistachio crust. There
are Thai dishes, too, and
everything on the menu
is well executed. **$$$**

Thai

The Blue Elephant
96 Th. Krabi

Tel 0 7635 4355
www.blueelephant.com.
Open: daily L and D.
Located in the glorious
former governor's man-
sion this worldwide
chain presents Thai food
with foreigner-friendly
flavours. It's mainly tra-
ditional but with some
successful interchange
of product and tech
nique in dishes such as
salmon *laab* and seared
duck breast with sweet
tamarind sauce accom-
panied with fried shal-
lots and crispy kale.
They also offer cooking
lessons. **$$$$**

**Siam Indigo Exotique
Bar and Restaurant**
8 Th. Phang Nga
Tel: 0 7625 6697
www.siamindigo.com
Open: Wed–Mon
11am–11pm.
This French-owned eat-
ery in an 80-year-old
building has tall win-
dows, thick-beamed
ceilings and colourful
local art on the walls.
The menu predomi-
nantly features exquisite
Thai, plus a few fusion
dishes, although they're
pleased to grill up some
meat if you prefer. The
patisserie-style baked
selections are outstand-
ing. **$$$$**

AO BANG TAO

International

360 Degrees
31/1 Moo 6,
Cherngtalay Thalang

Tel: 0-7631 7651
www.pavilions-resorts.com
Part of the luxury Phuket
Pavilions resort, this
chic timber-floored res-
taurant's hilltop vista is
a romantic spot from
which to view gorgeous
sunsets. Bills its well-
presented fare as "gour-
met café food" – and
delivers. **$$$**

The Red Room
293/25-26 Th. Srisoonthorn
Tel: 0-7627 1136
www.theresidenceresort.com
Open: daily L and D.
The red walls and can-
dles create a seductive
ambience at this restau-
rant owned by the luxury
Residence Resort. From
the European menu, try
starters like Caesar's
salad, followed by a
choice of pastas and
mains including roasted
lamb rack. Alternatively,
take a spicy seafood
salad and chicken mas-
saman from the selec-
tion of Thai. **$$–$$$**

Siam Supper Club
36-40 Lagoon Rd
Tel: 0-7627 0936
www.siamsupperclub.com
Open: daily 6pm–1am.
Chic ambience with mel-
low jazz and lounge
sounds. The perfect
place to enjoy a cocktail
or two. Serves mouth-
watering meat dishes
including grilled tender
loin of beef, rack of lamb
spare ribs, as well as
tasty vegetarian options.
The grilled goat's cheese
with pesto balsamic
dressing is simply
divine. **$$$–$$$$**

HAT KAMALA

International

Rockfish
33/6 Hat Kamala
Tel: 0-7627 9732
www.rockfishrestaurant.com
Open: daily 8am–late.
They have trendy food
and Thai dishes at this
three-storey open-sided
house. Choices include
goat's cheese fritter with
red-onion marmalade,
and beef tenderloin
wrapped with bacon,
served with grilled rock
lobster. The atmosphere
is casual and the sunset
beach views are lovely.
$$$–$$$$

HAT PATONG

International

Da Maurizio
223/2 Th. Prabaramee
Tel: 0-7634 4079
www.damaurizio.com
Open: daily noon–
midnight.
One of the finest of
Phuket's restaurants,
with waves breaking on
rocks close to tables and
flickering candlelight

PRICE CATEGORIES

Price per person for a
three-course meal
without drinks:
$ = under US$10
$$ = US$10–25
$$$ = US$25–50
$$$$ = over US$50

bouncing off the interior walls. The delicious Italian food includes dishes like parmigiana with aubergine and scamorza cheese, home-made pastas and the classic beef Rossini. Advance booking is essential. **$$$$**

Royale Nam Tok
Soi Nam Tok, 116/102 Kathu, Patong Beach
Tel: 08-7263 7327
www.royalenamtok.com
Open: daily D, except Sun.
Run by a Belgian couple, this posh, traditional French restaurant is located near a waterfall 10 minutes from Patong Beach. All the classics are there, from lobster bisque, through pan-fried *foie gras de Strasbourg*, to steak tartare. **$$$$**

Indian

Baluchi
Horizon Beach Resort, Soi Kep Sap
Tel: 0-7629 2526
www.horizonbeach.com
Open: daily L and D.
This restaurant serves authentic North Indian and a few Thai and international dishes. Set menus available for lunch and dinner as well as extensive à la carte selection. Mutton *rogangosh* is the house speciality, although the *tandoori nisa* (barbecued tiger prawns) is also very impressive. **$$**

Thai

Baan Rim Pa
223 Th. Prabaramee
Tel: 0-7634 0789
www.baanrimpa.com
Open: daily noon–midnight.

Famous cliff-hugging restaurant in the style of an old teak house. Known for its ambience and quality food. Serves outstanding Royal Thai cuisine, retaining all the flavour but without the chilli kick. Arrive early and have a drink on the terrace while enjoying the sea views. Reservations are essential. **$$$–$$$$**

Savoey Seafood
136 Th. Thaweewong
Tel: 0-7634 1171
www.savoeyseafood.com
Open: daily L and D.
Impossible to miss with its prime beach-front location and elaborate outdoor displays of fresh fish and ridiculously huge "Phuket lobsters". Selected seafood is whisked away and returned cooked to your liking, whether deep fried, grilled or steamed with Thai herbs. **$$**

HAT KARON

International

Las Margaritas
528/7 Th. Patak
Tel: 0-7639 8350
www.las-margaritas.net
Open: daily L and D.
A mix of cuisines from across the globe, including Mexico, India, Hawaii, the Mediterranean and, of course, Thailand. Of the extensive selection of dishes, the Mexican offerings are the best. The sizzling chicken fajitas go down well with a bottle of Corona. **$$**

El Gaucho
Mövenpick Resort & Spa, 509 Th. Patak
Tel: 0-7639 6139
www.moevenpick-hotels.com

Open: daily B, L and D.
A split-level restaurant with an outdoor terrace serving a Brazilian-style churrasco grill, in which waiters tour the tables with various meats on skewers. You choose what you want and eat till you drop. Visits to the salad bar are included. **$$**

Thai and Western

Ging Restaurant
192/36 Th. Karon
Tel: 08-1271 2446
Open: daily L and D.
This well-run place is very busy mainly for its friendly service and good Thai food, although it also has some Western choices. The menu runs the gamut of local specialities such as pepper garlic duck and massaman curry. Finish with ice cream. They also have free Wi-Fi. **$$**

On The Rock
Marina Phuket Resort, 47 Th. Karon
Tel: 0-7633 0625
www.marinaphuket.com
Open: daily B, L and D.
Cosy little restaurant within the Marina Phuket Resort, aptly named after the sea-facing rocks on which its elevated deck rests. Menu is predominantly Thai with a few Western dishes. Reservations recommended. **$$**

HAT KATA

International

Capannina
30/9 Moo 2, Th. Kata
Tel: 0-7628 4318
www.capannina-phuket.com
Open: daily noon–11pm.

Italian-managed terracotta-and-mustard-coloured eatery serving the usual Italian fare: antipasti, fresh breads, home-made pasta and risotto. The real draws, though, are the huge stone-fired oven pizzas. The large pizza measures a whopping 60cm (24ins) in diameter! **$$**

Mali Seafood
20/10 Th. Kata
Tel: 0-7628 4404
www.mali-seafood.com
Meaning "jasmine" in Thai, this informal, open-sided, 100-seater eatery has pine floors and an off-white colour scheme. A soundtrack of frothy Top 40s music accompanies signature dishes such as grilled grouper with mango salsa. **$$$**

Mom Tri's Boathouse Wine and Grill
182 Th. Kata
Tel: 0-7633 0015
www.boathousephuket.com
Open: daily D only.
This is an internationally acclaimed restaurant with a panoramic view of Kata Bay. Has a fine, if pricey, wine list, although its zesty vodka sorbet is a good alternative. Serves a selection of well-prepared Thai, European and seafood dishes – try the exquisite Rock Lobster Trilogy. **$$$–$$$$**

Thai

Kata Mama
40 Th. Kata
Tel: 0-7628 4006
Open: daily 8am–midnight.
This popular family-run operation serving home-style Thai dishes and seafood has been around for over 35 years. Serves favourites

such as fried fish with garlic and pepper, and barbecued prawns with chilli sauce. They also have a place in Karon. **$**

HAT NAI HARN

International

L'Orfeo
95/13 Soi Saiyuan
Tel: 0-7628 8935
www.orfeo-phuket.com
Open: daily high season, Mon–Sat low season, D only
A wonderfully romantic spot if you manage to get a table. Sirloin tips are a house speciality, served on wooden chop-

ping boards with a choice of sauce. Desserts change regularly, but keep an eye out for the zesty lemon mascarpone mousse and the crêpe flambée with Calvados. **$$**

Quarterdeck Restaurant
The Royal Phuket Yacht Club
Tel: 0-7638 0200
www.theroyalphuketyachtclub.com
Casual but smart dining at an open-sided restaurant overlooking the bay. The cuisine is a mix of Asian and international, with seafood specialities featuring strongly, and there are regular good-value sets. Arrive early for sunset cocktails at the lounge. **$$$**

AO CHALONG

International

Vset Restaurant
44/1 Th. Vset
Tel: 0-7638 1212
Open: daily 11.30am–11pm.
This semi-open-air restaurant at Chalong Pier has a chic café interior, with smart wood tables, Perspex chairs and an open kitchen. The "modern Western" menu has high end product such as foie gras and wagyu beef and neat touches such as red snapper with quail-egg salad. **$$$**

Thai

Kan Eang 2
9/3 Th. Chaofa
Tel: 0-7638 1323
Open: daily 10am–10pm.
Seafood restaurant directly overlooking the sea where a small fireworks display erupts at 8pm nightly, making it the perfect place for a celebration. **$**

PRICE CATEGORIES

Price per person for a three-course meal without drinks:
$ = under US$10
$$ = US$10–25
$$$ = US$25–50
$$$$ = over US$50

ACTIVITIES

The Arts

Dinner, Dance and Drama

Palazzo Theatre and Restaurant: 86/3 Moo 6, Th. Vichidsongkram, Kathu; tel: 0-7620 2277; www.phuket-palazzo.com. Sample a five course European meal in this dinner-theatre venue as a series of artistes entertain in a show that includes singing, dancing, magicians and aerial acrobats. The 2-hr show starts at 7.30pm from Tuesday to Friday and includes a free drink.
Phuket Fantasea: 99 Moo 3, Hat Kamala; tel: 0-7638 5000; www.phuket-fantasea.com. This huge award-winning theme park hosts a show that is more Las Vegas than traditional Thai entertainment. It features acrobatics, dance, drama and trained animals. Daily shows except Thursday, 5.30–11.30pm; showtime at 9pm.

Art Galleries

Talented artists make quality reproduction paintings based on customers' photographs at a number of galleries on Phrachanukhro Road in Hat Patong. Original works are more expensive, but emerging artists frequently hold exhibitions. Check local newspapers for details.
    Elsewhere on the island, original pieces in various styles can be found at many price levels.
Soul of Asia: 5/50 Moo 3, Cherngtalay; tel: 0-7627 1629; www.soulofasia.com. Owned by a Dutch collector, this gallery shows Asian and international artists, including Warhol prints and Dalí sculptures.

Nightlife

Phuket nightlife in significant areas has the high-profile energy you might expect from a holiday destination, although bars at

some of the quieter beaches close early. Patong in particular always has more than its fair share of all-night offerings. There's a small scene in Phuket Town, Karon and Kata beaches, too, but more subdued, and while some parts of the island see a slow nightlife expansion, in many places it is almost nonexistent.

Hat Patong

The choice of entertainment in Patong is diverse, with heaving clubs and sex shows on one street contrasting with chic and trendy cocktail bars on the next. Most of the scene in Patong takes place along **Th. Bangla** and the tiny streets that radiate off it (such as Soi Eric, Soi Easy etc) all the way past the **Th. Rat-U-Thit** junction and also **Soi Sunset**. Most common are the raucous "beer bars", simple open-air bars with wooden tables and stools, and hordes of young women in skimpy dress beckoning customers. Listed here are less sleazy spots that couples would be more comfortable in.

Dance Bars and Clubs
Banana Disco: Th. Thawiwong; tel: 0-7634 0301. Basement disco on the beach road, just before Soi Bangla. This busy venue is air conditioned and so never uncomfortable despite the heaving crowds. Plays Top 40 hits and has a large dance floor.
Seduction Beach Club & Disco: Soi Happy, Th. Bangla; tel: 08-1188 1230; www.seductiondisco. com. A hot club on three floors playing different music styles through excellent sound systems. As well as the house DJs they have regular imported acts such as Paul Oakenfold and Hed Kandi and regular crews from Bangkok.

Bars and Pubs
Joe's Downstairs: 223/3 Th. Prabaramee; tel: 0-7634 4254. The contemporary all-white design, with its long bar and white tables, chairs and silk cushions, contributes to the popularity of Joe's. There's a great view for sunset cocktails and a tapas menu.
Molly Malone's: 68 Th. Thaweewong; tel:0-7629 2771; www.molly malonesphuket.com. Popular Irish pub at the centre of Patong with both an indoor bar and outside drinking and dining area.
Scruffy Murphy's: 5 Th. Bangla; tel: 0-7629 2590; www.scruffymurphys phuket.com. Another popular Irish pub with a nice party atmosphere and Celtic Rock bands playing nightly. Serves standard but tasty range of pub grub.

Kathoey Cabaret
Simon Cabaret: 8 Th. Sirirat, Patong; tel: 0-7634 2011; www. phuket-simoncabaret.com. Popular show that draws in crowds both for its exaggerated theatrical performances and for the chance to have photos taken with Phuket's most convincing kathoey or transsexual "lady-boys".

ABOVE: Simon Cabaret.

Phuket Town

Lost Legends of Phuket: Underwood Art Factory, 49/6 Moo. 5, Th. Chalermphrakiat Ror 9; tel: 08-8762 5110; www.lostlegend sphuket.com. This concert space cum-restaurant-cum-art gallery located in an old warehouse has a variety of imaginative live music shows such as *Phantom of the Popera*, mixing rock, soul and R & B.
Timber Rock: 118/1 Th. Yaowarat; tel: 0-7621 1839. Relatively quiet until around 11pm, after which the place goes wild with live rock'n'roll and dancing until the early hours.
Watermark Bar: Boat Lagoon Marina, 22/1 Moo 2, Th. Thepkasattri; tel: 0-7623 9730; www.water markphuket.com. People either love or hate the recently renovated Watermark, seeing it as pompous and pretentious or modern and trendy. Either way, this harbour-side bar is undeniably sophisticated.

Hat Karon

Angus & Arfur O'Tool's: 516/20 Th. Patak, Karon; tel: 08-3390 4351; www.otools-phuket.com. Popular Irish bar located at the end of a plaza, slightly off the main road. Shows live sports matches, serves cold draught Guinness and an excellent Irish-style breakfast.
Harry's Restaurant & Pub: 15/5 Th. Luangpohchuan; tel: 0-7639 8258. This family-friendly pub restaurant has kid's activities and

quiz nights as well as live music and weekend all-you-can-eat buffets to help the beer go down.

Hat Kata

The Boathouse: Kata Yai; tel: 0-7633 0015. This elegant beachfront bar is the perfect location to sip a few cocktails and watch the sunset. Live music every evening and jazz on Sat from 8pm.
Ska Bar: next to Kata BBQ; tel: 0-7893 4831. A rickety wooden reggae music bar open till late, sometimes performing fire shows for a diverse mix of locals, expats and couples.

Ao Chalong

Skippers Bar & Restaurant: Royal Phuket Marina; tel: 0-7636 0890; www.skippersphuket.com. Overlooking the main marina at one of the islands top sailing centres, it's no surprise to find a nautical theme in the design here. In addition to a full international menu and bar snacks, they have live music, pub quizzes and a large screen showing a full range of sporting events.

Hat Nai Harn

Yoonique Stone Music Café: Th. Nai Harn, mobile tel: 08-0903 0717. Located right opposite the lake, Yoonique is run by musician Yoon, hence the place is busy with bands. The stage is usually open for people to jam and they have dedicated open-mic nights on Tuesdays. Unusually for a Thai bar, they don't serve food.

Gay Venues

Phuket's gay scene isn't as hot and happening as Bangkok's or Pattaya's, with most of it taking place around the **Paradise Complex** along Th. Rat-U-Thit. Here, bars, clubs and saunas cater to a colourful gay clientele. Phuket also has its very own gay festival (see www.gaypatong.com) that takes place usually in April each year and a gay Full Moon Festival touted to happen annually was launched in October 2013 (www.glowphuket.com).

Boat Bar: Soi 5, Paradise Complex, Patong; tel: 0-7634 1237; www.boatbar.com. Located near the main entrance of the Royal Paradise Hotel. Popular and trendy gay club with outdoor bar, DJs and nightly cabaret.

Kiss Bar: 123/7-8 Paraside Complex, Patong; tel: 0-7634 1804. Kiss relocated to a new venue across the street in 2013. It's a popular club and they have an outside bar with a DJ and another inside where they host two nightly dance and ladyboy shows starting from 11.45pm.

Shopping

While Bangkok offers a greater variety of shops, the emergence of large shopping malls such as Central Festival on the outskirts of Phuket Town has increased the opportunities to go on a spending spree in Phuket. These malls often have small stalls displaying local goods such as jewellery and beachwear, while the larger shops within sell international brand names such as Levi's and Nike.

All the beaches are lined with stalls selling designer knock-off T-shirts and handbags as well as bootleg CDs and DVDs. DVD prices are usually fixed at B100, but be sure to ask to see the quality first.

Generally, prices can double or even triple during the high season

so always bargain and never accept the first price you hear. A huge open-air clothing and souvenir market facing Karon beach is one of the few places that indicate prices on their goods. While you may end up paying a little bit extra, some people are glad to avoid the hassle of bargaining for better deals.

Shopping Malls

Central Festival: 74–75 Moo 5, Th. Vichit; tel: 0-7629 1111; www.centralfestivalphuket.com. This 800,000-sq-metre mall on the outskirts of Phuket Town has a department store, restaurants, seven-screen cinema, bowling alley and shops selling chic fashion, beauty products, home decor, electronics, and anything else you can imagine.

Jungceylon: 181 Th. Rat-U-Thit 200 Pee, Patong; tel: 0-7660 0111; www.jungceylon.com. A cavernous lifestyle mall in the heart of Patong housing the upscale department store Robinson's, a supermarket chain, a cinema and almost 200 other stores, including a range of restaurants, bars and spas.

Ocean Shopping Mall: 38/1-15 Th. Tilok-U-Thit, Phuket Town; tel: 0-7622 3057; www.phuketocean group.com. This mall has a supermarket, cheap clothes, cosmetics and many craft stalls. It has two branches in Patong.

Antiques

Chan's Antiques: 99/42 Moo 5, Th. Chalermprakit; tel: 0-7626 1416. Home to Phuket's largest collection of antiques from Thailand and neighbouring countries. Even if not shopping, with so many displays, it is fascinating to walk around this old Thai-style building on the outskirts of Phuket Town.

Fashion and Clothing

The best and widest range of clothing is found at the **Central Festival Department Store** (in Phuket Town) and **Jungceylon** mall in Patong. Local brands are

excellent value for money should you be able to squeeze into them, and international labels such as Nike and Levi's are considerably cheaper here than in Europe and the US. Cheaper clothes are best bargained for at streetside stalls and markets. **EXPO Market**, in Phuket Town, on Tilok Utit 2 Road, is one of the better ones, and bargains can always be found at the weekend night market, where jewellery often sells for as little as B20. The French-owned boutique within Siam Indigo Exotique Bar and Restaurant on Phang Nga Road, Phuket Town, is well worth checking out for unique items of clothing, jewellery and accessories.

Tailors

The majority of Phuket's tailors are situated around Patong and Kata beaches. Many have overbearing touts who try to cajole you into going inside, which unfortunately often acts as a deterrent to doing just that. Prices are competitive, so it is best to look at the quality and design of the garments in shop windows. The following shops are just a sample:

King's Fashion: 146 Th. Thawiwong, Patong; tel: 0-7634 0192.
Mr Singh's Fashion Gallery: 26/2 Th. Rat-U-Thit, Patong; tel: 0-7634 5038.

Handicrafts and Home Decor

Jim Thompson: Canal Village Laguna, 390/12-15 Moo 1, Th. Srisontorn; tel: 0-7603 4534; www.jimthompson.com. This brand, which is synonymous with quality Thai silk, has several stores in Phuket alone. It stocks a wide range of fabrics, clothing, accessories and home-decor items.
Lotus Arts de Vivre: Amanpuri Resort, Hat Pansea; tel: 0-7632 4333; www.lotusartsdevivre.com. Collections of exquisitely designed high-priced items, particularly strong on jewellery, objets d'art and lacquerware.
Siam Ceramic Handmade: 104/17-18 Soi Post Office, Th.

Thawiwong, Patong, mobile tel: 08 1537 6071; www.thaibenjarong.com. The traditional Thai porcelain ware here, painted in five trademark colours and called Benjarong, has won both local and overseas fans.

Outdoor Activities

Bungee Jumping

Jungle Bungy: Th. Vichitsongkram; tel: 0-7632 1351; www.phuketbungy.com. Daredevils leap from a crane overlooking a beautiful wooded area towards the waters of Kathu Lake below. A breathtaking site – if you can keep your eyes open long enough to enjoy it! Fully licensed and insured.

Deep-sea Fishing

Phuket Fishing Charters: Chalong, mobile tel: 08-1370 3181; www.phuketfishingcharters.com. This Canadian-Thai company accepts online credit-card bookings for its day and night fishing trips. There's a good choice of boats and a strict catch-and-release policy for big-game fish. **Wahoo:** 48/20 Moo 9, Chalong ; tel:0-7628 1510; www.wahoo.ws. An experienced company, with a fleet extending to luxury boats all fully equipped with first-class fishing gear.

Diving and Snorkelling

Phuket's only notable snorkelling spots are around the headlands at Kata Yai and Kata Noi beaches. Shacks along the sand rent snorkelling gear by the day or hour. Better snorkelling can be found on trips to nearby islands and most dive operators offer a cheaper snorkelling-only option. Phuket is a popular base for many day trips and live-aboard excursions. Conditions are best during the December–April dry season when seas are calm and the water at its clearest.

Most dive shops offer everything from introductory dives to advanced dive-master certification. Prices vary, but so, too, does the condition of boats and equipment. The following is a selection:
Dive Asia: 24 Th. Karon, Kata; tel: 0-7633 0598; www.diveasia.com. Has a full range of multilingual dive courses and runs trips to most surrounding dive spots, including Phi Phi, Shark Point and the Similans.
Oceanic Dive Centre: 30 Th. Karon; tel: 0-7633 3043; www.oceanicdivecenter.com. This Scandinavian/Thai-managed PADI outfit runs scuba-diving live-aboards to the Similan Islands, Burma Banks and Hin Muang, plus day trips.
Scuba Cat Diving: 94 Th. Thaweewong, Patong; tel: 0-7629 3121; www.scubacat.com. Phuket's first National Geographic dive centre is Canadian-owned and English-managed. The most prominent on Patong due to its central location and outdoor training pool.

Golf

Blue Canyon Country Club: 165 Moo 1, Th. Thepkasattri; tel: 0-7632 8088; www.bluecanyonclub.com. Beautifully landscaped on a 720-acre (290-hectare) green with two award-winning 18-hole courses. First golf course ever to hold the Johnny Walker Classic twice and has played host to such greats as Nick Faldo and Tiger Woods.
Red Mountain: 119 Moo 4 Th. Vichitsongkram Rd, Kathu; tel: 0-7632 2001; www.redmountainphuket.com. A stunning course with beautiful views amid the rolling hills of a former tin mine. It's well maintained with fast greens and provides a challenge for good handicappers. There's a spa on site.

Go-karting

Patong Go Kart Speedway: 118/5 Th. Vichitsongkram; tel: 0-7632 1949; www.gokartthailand.com. Formed in 1990, this 750-metre (2,460ft) racetrack has various karts with top speeds between 40km (24 miles) and 110km (70 miles) per hour. Open daily and floodlit to enable night rides. Situated at the foot of Patong Hill in the Kathu district, next to Jungle Bungy.

Horse Riding

Phuket Riding Club: 95 Th. Viset, Rawai; tel:0-7628 8213; www.phuketridingclub.com. All levels are welcome to join either of two tours along the beach or through the forest. Experienced guides lead the way. They also have dressage rings available for all levels.

Sailing

The Phuket Raceweek regatta (www.phuketraceweek.com) at Rawai each July and the King's Cup Regatta (www.kingscup.com) at Nai Harn Beach every December attract international sailors and offer chances to crew.
SY Stressbreaker: mobile tel: 0-1894 3966; www.thailand-sail.com. Offers adventure sailing in the Mergui Archipelago, either aboard the 19-metre (63ft) ketch *Stressbreaker*, which comfortably sleeps eight, or one of four other boats. Activities available on trips include diving, windsurfing and kayaking. Food and drink is supplied.
Topper Sail Phuket: Ao Yon; tel:08-5215 9185; www.toppersailphuket.com. Run by two expert sailors from the UK, Topper has a range of dinghies either for fun sailing or lessons at all levels up to regatta training. They also rent out and sell dinghies.

Shooting

Phuket Shooting Range: 82/2 Th. Patak; tel: 0-7638 1667. Deafening shooting range with choice of gun. Also offers paintballing, archery, karting and several other activities. Open: daily 9am–6pm.

Sea Canoeing

Phuket is the best base to book tours to see the magnificent karsts of Ao Phang Nga (see page 202). Cruises are the usual way of visiting Phang Nga Bay. The **June Bahtra**, an old Chinese junk, offers day and evening sunset cruises with dining options and can be booked through any tour company in Phuket. Or check its website at www.asian-oasis.com.

The more novel way to explore Ao Phang Nga, however, is by sea canoe. These low-lying craft enable you to enter the area's karsts when the tide is low enough to explore hidden islands. The following is a selection.

Andaman Sea Kayak: tel: 0-7623 5353; www.andamanseakayak.com. Tours by inflatable canoe start in the early morning, from Monday to Friday, visiting a number of caves and lagoons as well as Naka and James Bond islands. Lunch is also included. They occasionally offer overnight trips that might include camping on the beach.

John Gray's Sea Canoe: 124 Th. Yaowarat Soi 1; tel: 0-7625 4505; www.johngray-seacanoe.com. Run by an environmentalist, these trips around the karsts, caves and lagoons include a starlight trip during which you can launch krathongs (candles on banana leaf floats) into the water. They also organise trips to islands further afield.

Thai Boxing

Bangla Boxing Stadium: 198/4 Th. Ratha-utit; tel: 08 9726

BELOW: Phuket is a good base to pick up diving in Thailand.

1112; www.banglaboxingstadiumpatong. com. Fights can be seen at 9pm every Wed, Fri and Sun involving both Thai and visiting fighters, many of whom will have graduated from training programmes on the island.

Tiger Muay Thai: 7/6 Moo 5 Soi Tad-ied, Ao Chalong; tel: 0-7636 7071; www.tigermuaythai.com. This well run training camp has various programmes for men and women of all levels. As well as Muay Thai they have other disciplines, including mixed martial arts, wrestling and yoga.

Spas

All across Thailand there have long been small, streetside shophouses offering cheap Thai massages, and the majority of hotels have taken this one step further, with on-site spas offering a range of traditional and New Age treatments. More recently, a clutch of day spas have emerged on the scene, generally offering the same range of treatments but at more reasonable prices. Many will arrange transfers to and from your hotel.

Atsumi Healing Centre: 34/18 Soi Pattana, Rawai; tel: 08-1272 0571; www.atsumihealing.com. Natural therapy centre with a choice of three detox programmes, from four to 30 days (they encourage at least 10). Complementing it are morning yoga sessions followed by daily colonic irrigation. Weight loss is claimed to be guaranteed and minor infections often disappear during the process.

Banyan Tree Spa: Banyan Tree Resort and Spa, 33 Moo 4 Th. Srisoonthorn; tel: 0-7632 4374; www.banyantreespa.com. The spa has won numerous accolades (including World's Best Spa Resort by readers of Condé Nast Traveller). Surroundings are elegant, with open-air spa pavilions containing Thai artefacts and even fish ponds. Highly skilled therapists are trained in rare and unique treatments. Expect to pay highly for such indulgence.

Kata Day Spa: 100/7 Th. Kata, Hat Karon; tel: 08-1476 8080; www.katadayspaphuket.com. A simple day spa that offers all the usual massage options plus a variety of body wraps, scrubs, facials, manicures and pedicures. Treatments last from 30-minute massages to a mix of everything running at over four hours. They have a pick up service.

Lemongrass House: 0/2 Moo 1, Th. Srisoonthorn, Cherng Talay, (Surin Beach); tel: 0-7632 5501; www.lemongrasshouse.com. This is not a spa but a spa-products shop (opposite Surin beach) filled with all sorts of aromatic natural scents, oils, lotions and potions. They now have outlets around the region, including Australia. They promise to use no animal ingredients and that no products have been tested on animals.

Oasis Spa Phuket: 26 Soi Plukjao, Hat Karon; www.oasisspa.net. Open daily 10am–10pm, this outfit has three centres on the island, with others in Cherngtalay and Hat Kamala. This Karon hilltop location has views of the sea and the Big Buddha statue and has a rooftop pool and herbal steam room. Four-handed massages are a popular choice, along with the expected scrubs and body wraps.

Sightseeing Tours

Most generic sightseeing tours are operated by independent travel or tour agents, located in Phuket Town and at the beaches. They will advise and book tours and transport at very short notice. Inquire at your hotel reception. For specialist nature tours of Phuket and surroundings, contact:

Siam Safari: 17/2 Soi Yodsanae, Th. Chaofa, Chalong; tel: 0-7638 4456; www.siamsafari.com. This is one of the longest-running tour companies in Phuket, offering a range of land-based tours incorporating jeep safaris, elephant trekking, canoeing and visits to Thai villages, local Buddhist temples and national parks.

KRABI, KO PHI PHI AND KO LANTA

This region is dominated by a geographical wonder that attracts rock-climbing enthusiasts: sheer limestone peaks that rise dramatically out of the water. And if the pristine beaches of Krabi do not impress you, head to the legendary Ko Phi Phi and other nearby islands.

The lush and sprawling 4,708 sq-km (1,818-sq-mile) **Krabi Province**, just east of Phuket, is famous for sheer-sided limestone outcrops known as karsts. Their formation began millions of years ago as a result of limestone created by seashell deposits when parts of mainland Krabi were submerged with water. Subsequent continental shifts bulldozed the limestone into the towering peaks that are now scattered in the waters of the Andaman Sea, including at Ao Phang Nga (see page 202). Krabi is a popular destination with climbers, who come to scale these challenging rock faces.

Many of the islands around Krabi Province are tiny or uninhabited, although the best known, **Ko Phi Phi** and **Ko Lanta**, are both inhabited and extremely attractive to tourists for their legendary beaches.

The Krabi mainland is also blessed with a string of white-sand beaches that attract thousands during the dry season from November to April (see margin tip page 245). Inland on Krabi are lush rainforests that harbour rare species of bird and wildlife. Camera crews often travel miles to take advantage of Krabi and the idyllic surroundings for commercials, television shows and even movies, including the blockbusters The Beach, Around the World in 80 Days and Star Wars III.

KRABI PROVINCE

Krabi Town

Located some 180km (112 miles) from Phuket, **Krabi Town ①** is the main jump off point for travellers en route to the beaches and islands of Krabi Province. Thanon Maharat, which is the central point in the busy

Main attractions
PEE HUAKALOK
KHAO NOR CHU CHI WILDLIFE SANCTUARY
RAILAY BAY
KO PHI PHI
KO LANTA
HIN DAENG AND HIN MUANG

LEFT: sea canoeing along the Krabi coast.
RIGHT: Krabi Town children.

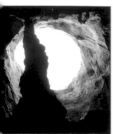

The limestone pinnacles of Khao Khanab Nam.

and compact town, is where the main market and most of the restaurants and shops are found. A concentration of guesthouses and hotels is located on Thanon Chao Fa, a few minutes from **Chao Fa Pier**. The pavements around Chao Fa Pier become a hub of bustling activity in the evenings when grills are fired up and saucepans and woks clatter in unison to whip up a feast of freshly caught grilled seafood and various stir-fries.

At the bottom of Krabi Town is **Thara Park**, an attractively landscaped and shaded spot overlooking **Krabi River**. On the river's opposite bank are dense mangroves and a small but thriving fishing community living in wooden huts raised on stilts. Longtail boats can be hired at Chao Fa pier to explore these mangrove forests, which shelter many types of fish, crab, shrimp and shellfish, and are important nesting grounds for hundreds of bird species.

Most tours of the mangroves will

BELOW: Buddha statue at Wat Tham Seua.

include a stop at the limestone pinnacles of **Khao Khanab Nam ②**. The two 100-metre (328ft) pinnacles that rise dramatically from the side of Krabi River have come to represent the town. Legend has it that two ceremonial *krabi* (swords) were discovered here in ancient times. Inside one of the peaks is a series of caves with impressive formations of stalactites and stalagmites. In one of the caves, skeletons have been found, thought to belong to people who took refuge here before being cut off and trapped by a massive flood.

KRABI'S INTERIOR

Wat Tham Seua

More commonly referred to as "Tiger Cave Temple", **Wat Tham Seua ❸** (daily 8am–6pm; charge) was founded by Jamnien Silasettho, a monk and teacher of meditation. The temple is set amid forests and cliffs 9km (6 miles) from Krabi

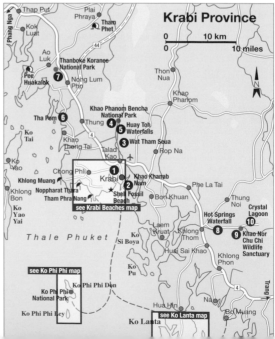

Town and is easily reached by car or motorbike. At the rear of the temple is a concrete staircase; clambering up the 1,272 steps to the 600-metre (1,970ft) peak brings you to a small shrine and a footprint of the Buddha in a flat rock. The hour-long ascent is exhausting, but the fantastic view of the surrounding area from the top makes up for it. A second staircase, next to a large statue of Kwan Im, the Chinese Goddess of Mercy, takes you on a different route up 1,237 steps.

Scattered around this forest are towering limestone rock faces and a large cave with a Buddha image. Flanking the sides of the statue are a human skeleton encased in glass and several ticking clocks, intended to serve as poignant reminders of the fragility of time and life.

Khao Phanom Bencha N P

Khao Phanom Bencha National Park ❹ (daily 8am–6pm; charge), about 20km (12 miles) to the north of Krabi Town, is the site of a dramatic 1,397-metre (4,583ft) karst called **Khao Phanon Bencha**, or "Five-Point Prostration Mountain". Other attractions include leopards and Asiatic black bears among the reserve's official list of 32 species of mammals and 218 of birds. Even tigers have been spotted, although sightings of these are extremely rare. The cascading waterfalls flowing down the mountain slopes are other features in the 50 sq km (19 sq miles) park, but are best seen in or just after the rainy season when the waters are full. The main waterfall, the 11-tiered **Huay Toh Falls** ❺, is a 350 metre (1,150ft) walk from the park headquarters, and the tiers are at varying heights of up to 80 metres (262ft).

Tha Pom

There is an unusual canal some 34km (21 miles) north of Krabi Town that most locals refer to as **Tha Pom** ❻ (daily 8am–6pm; charge), although on signs leading to it the name appears as **Tha Pom Khlong Song Nam**, which translates as "Canal of Two Waters". A 700 metre (2,300ft) boardwalk takes you on a trail past mangrove and forest, eventually leading to the main attraction, a

TIP

The southwest monsoon brings heavy rain from May to Oct to the Andaman Coast, including Krabi, Ko Phi Phi and Ko Lanta islands. Room rates can drop as much as half during the wet months, so some people take advantage of this and hope for the best. There can be intermittent days of sunshine in between rainy spells.

BELOW: Wat Tham Seua, Krabi.

stream of clear water with two distinct colours. The water will appear colourless in poor weather, but on a good day, when the sun's rays penetrate the water, turquoise-blue and emerald-green layers appear. This phenomenon apparently happens during high tide when tidal seawater meets fresh spring water running off the mountainside.

Thanboke Koranee N P

Numerous caves and waterfalls are among the charms of **Thanboke Koranee National Park ❼** (daily 8am–6pm; charge), located about 45km (28 miles) northwest of Krabi Town. One of the highlights is **Pee Huakalok**, a cave where an oversized human skull was found over half a century ago. Superstitious locals believe that the ghost of this head dwells within the cave and they have immortalised their fear with its name: *pee* is Thai for ghost, *hua* means head and *kalok* is skull. The walls of the cave are embellished with hundreds of colourful cave paintings and prehistoric drawings, estimated by archaeologists to

be between 2,000 and 3,000 years old. The cave burrows deep into a hill surrounded by water and mangroves, but is accessible by boat from **Bor Tor Pier**, 7km (4 miles) south of Ao Luk.

Hot Springs Waterfall

Beyond the town of Khlong Thom, around 55km (34 miles) southeast of Krabi Town on Highway 4, there is an unusual phenomenon at the **Hot Springs Waterfall ❽** (daily 8am–5pm; charge). An underground hot spring here leaks water through the earth's surface and cascades down smooth boulders. It is quite an experience to let the soothing warm water wash over you before you take a dip in the cool waters of the stream, a sort of natural hydrotherapy in the middle of the jungle. This picturesque waterfall is a popular place to relax in but is relatively small and can get crowded around lunchtime when large tour groups arrive. If travelling on your own, early morning is the best time to get here.

Khao Nor Chu Chi Wildlife Sanctuary

A 10-minute drive east of the Hot Springs Waterfall is the **Khao Nor Chu Chi Wildlife Sanctuary ❾** (daily 8am–5pm; charge), also known as Khao Pra Bang Khram Wildlife Sanctuary. This is said to be the last patch of lowland rainforest in Thailand and one of the few locations in the world where the endangered bird species known as Gurney's Pitta can be found.

A 3km (2-mile) trail from the park leads through a shaded path to the **Crystal Lagoon ❿**. Bacteria and algae living in this emerald-coloured pond cause a variation of colours ranging from pale green where the temperature is cooler to a greenish blue where the temperature peaks at around 50°C (122°F). It's safe to swim in but the calcium carbonates in the

BELOW: Hot Springs Waterfall at Thanboke Koranee National Park.

water make it unsuitable for drinking, and a sign at the entrance asks you to refrain from using shampoo or soap. Be cautious of slippery moss at the water's edge – the best way in is to sit first and slowly inch your way into the pond to avoid a painful and ungraceful splash.

KRABI'S BEACHES

Hat Khlong Muang and Hat Noppharat Thara

Several hotels are fortunate enough to share the secluded white sands at **Hat Khlong Muang A**. Backed by lush vegetation, this lovely beach is extremely quiet and has a nice ambience. Set away from Krabi Town (but only a 30-minute drive away), it has clean waters that are pleasant to swim in year-round. The accommodation at Hat Khlong Muang is now going more upmarket, joining the long standing 5-star **Sheraton Krabi** and the stylish **Nakamanda** resort.

An extended finger of land called Hang Nak Cape separates Khlong Muang from the next beach, **Hat Noppharat Thara B**, which has beautiful, uninterrupted views out towards a cluster of limestone islands. Shady casuarinas back this 2km (1-mile)-long beach and seafood vendors congregate around the car park. The western end of the beach is quiet and because it is separated by a canal, can only be accessed by longtail boat. The middle section is similarly quiet, with a visitors centre and the park headquarters, while the eastern section is the busiest.

Ao Nang

A few minutes' drive from Hat Noppharat Thara, and sharing the same view of the limestone cliffs in the distance, albeit obstructed by a line of longtail boats, is **Ao Nang C**, the most commercial and developed beach on mainland Krabi.

A free back massage at Krabi's Hot Springs Waterfall.

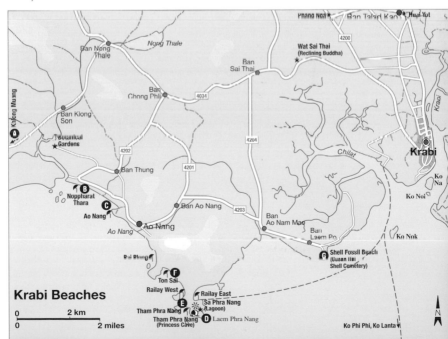

Krabi Beaches

0 ____ 2 km
0 ____ 2 miles

The Krabi coastline is strewn with islands, which make for fun exploration. Most tour agencies sell the well-known 'Krabi Four Islands' tour, covering Ko Poda, Ko Tup, Ko Kai and Phra Nang Cave.

BELOW: view of Hat Railay East and Hat Railay West beaches.

Located 22km (14 miles) east of Krabi Town, Ao Nang gets somewhat crowded in the high season but is not yet so built up as to be completely ruined, and the development at least means that facilities such as bars and restaurants will be provided for those who prefer a little action.

Ao Nang beach would be nicer were it not for the longtail boats congesting its shore; at high tide there is very little space to relax. The quiet is also shattered by the loud and piercing drone from the engines of these longtail boats. The splendid backdrop of the limestone cliff-studded Andaman Sea, however, makes up for it. At the north of the beach is a cluster of open-air seafood restaurants, usually owned by the small hotels behind them. With displays of snapper, barracuda and shellfish, these restaurants fill up rapidly in the evenings. Other restaurants serving mostly Thai and Italian food are found along the main beach road.

Laem Phra Nang (Railay Bay)

Surrounded by sheer limestone cliffs on three sides and only accessible by boat, the peninsula of **Laem Phra Nang** , better known as **Railay Bay**, feels more like an island paradise than the mainland beach that it actually is. This stunning peninsula has four beaches, each with crystal-clear turquoise waters, powdery white sands and the aforementioned limestone cliffs that seemingly melt into the waters below, making it one of the world's leading rock-climbing destinations.

Hat Railay West and Hat Railay East

Most arriving boats head straight to the western side of the peninsula, to **Hat Railay West**. The absence of a pier demands a short wade to the shore, but this has fortunately also prevented ferry-loads of day-trippers landing on its pristine white sands. Although developing, Railay West is a world away from nearby Ao Nang. Its tastefully designed resorts (no ramshackle guesthouses here) along with nice landscaping has prevented it from turning into a busy backpacker haunt. Accommodation is more expensive than on the other

Krabi beaches, but that is the premium to be paid for direct access to such a lovely beach.

On the opposite side of the peninsula is **Hat Railay East**. Backed by dense mangroves, this is a less scenic beach and is unsuitable for swimming due to the incredibly low tides and the jagged rocks along the foreshore. Still, the lower-priced bungalows here get their fair share of trade. Access between the two Railay beaches is easy – a 5-minute walk along a flat, paved pathway takes you from one beach to the other. The same people appreciating the mango-streaked sunsets on Railay West are often seen a few hours later enjoying fire shows and all-night parties at Railay East.

Hat Tham Phra Nang

Undeniably, the prettiest beach in Railay Bay, if not the whole of Thailand, is **Hat Tham Phra Nang** **E**, where the extravagant and ultra-expensive **Rayavadee Resort** occupies prime position (there is no other accommodation here). Set amid 11 hectares (26 acres) of coconut groves and surrounded by limestone cliffs,

Tham Phra Nang is endowed with the softest of white sands, limpid turquoise-blue waters and beautiful coral reefs offshore. Although staying at the Rayavadee gives you the most direct access to this beach, many daytrippers from Railay West and Railay East flock to Tham Phra Nang to sunbathe, swim and snorkel.

Hat Tham Phra Nang is named after a princess (*phra nang*) whom locals believe resides in the area. Near the Rayavadee Resort, at the beach's eastern end, is **Tham Phra Nang** (Princess Cave), where a collection of wooden phallic objects sit as an offering to her, the supplicants hoping that she will bestow the surrounding mountains and sea with fertility. The cave is not as spectacular as it's made out to be and is little more than a series of small overhangs, but a map at its base highlights the way towards a **viewpoint** *(see margin tip)* and **Sa Phra Nang** (Princess Lagoon), which are both far more impressive.

The route to both sights is straightforward but neither is suitable for the very young, elderly or unfit, and good shoes are a must. The most

TIP

Check the tide before scaling the cliff towards the viewpoint high above Hat Tham Phra Nang. When the tide is at Hat Railay East, it makes for much more stunning views from the top.

BELOW: a longtail boat in Railay.

The Shell Fossil Beach at Krabi, also known as the Susan Hoi Shell Cemetery.

challenging part of the walk is at the beginning, which involves clinging to ropes to clamber up a fairly steep incline; after this, the pathway becomes easier to follow. Veering to the left as the pathway splits leads to a viewpoint with spectacular vistas of the east and west bays of Railay. Continuing straight leads to a sharp rock face with yet more ropes, this time used to almost abseil down into the Princess Lagoon. The lagoon is suitable for swimming, but is not crystal-clear and does have some rocks.

Hat Ton Sai

From Hat Railay West, it is possible at low tide to walk to the nearby **Hat Ton Sai ⑨**. Longtail boats can also be hired to make the 5-minute journey, or if feeling energetic, you may simply swim to the beach. Budget travellers are attracted to Ton Sai by its cheaper accommodation and more convivial atmosphere. Of all the beaches on the Laem Phra Nang headland, Ton Sai has the most vibrant nightlife, with beach bars open until the early hours and hosting monthly full-moon parties. The

BELOW: longtail boats moored at Hat Ton Sai.

view out to sea is as beautiful as that of Railay's, with limestone monoliths in the foreground and to the sides, but the sand is not as white, and at low tide the beach becomes muddy which makes swimming difficult.

Rock climbing

Sheer limestone cliffs facing mile upon mile of tranquil sea make Railay Bay a favoured spot for rock climbers. Most of the roughly 650 routes that have developed since Krabi's cliffs were first scaled in the late 1980s are located in this peninsula. Among the most popular climbs is the challenging yet phenomenal **Thaiwand Wall** on the southern end. There are a range of other climbs suited to beginners right through to professionals, involving limestone crags, steep pocketed walls, overhangs and stalactites. Any of the climbing operations around Railay will advise on the best climbs, some of which are accessed by a combination of boat and a hike through the jungle.

Shell Fossil Beach

Some 17km (11 miles) from Krabi Town, with its entrance marked by a small Chinese temple, is the **Shell Fossil Beach ⑩** (also known as Susan Hoi Shell Cemetery). Extending right to the edge of the sea are the remnants of a 75-million-year accumulation of shell deposits – which look like large concrete slabs from afar. This phenomenon can only be seen at two other locations worldwide, one in Japan and the other in the US – the one in Krabi is the only coastal site. Visitors either love or hate this sight but some people appreciate the enormity of witnessing evidence of life that existed millions of years before humans.

KO PHI PHI

Lying in the Andaman Sea between Phuket and Krabi (about two hours

by boat from either location) are the twin islands that together make up **Ko Phi Phi** – the larger **Ko Phi Phi Don** and the smaller **Ko Phi Phi Ley**. The islands are part of the protected **Mu Ko Phi Phi National Park**, but somehow, development, especially on Ko Phi Phi Don, seems to have escalated over the years, ruining its natural beauty. From afar, though, they are still stunning with their mountains and lovely arcs of soft white sand washed by crystal-clear waters. Ko Phi Phi Don is where all the accommodation and facilities are while Ko Phi Phi Ley is uninhabited and mainly visited on day trips.

The islands' rise to fame is characterised by both fortune and tragedy. Until 1999, Ko Phi Phi was still considered a quiet, idyllic retreat. Turquoise waters bordering limestone cliffs and palm tree-filled interiors made it a postcard-perfect location, and visitors would leave feeling that they had seen a truly idyllic tropical island. Then came the hit film *The Beach*, which was shot mainly at Ao **Maya** (Maya Bay) in 1998 on Ko Phi Phi Ley. Within one year, thousands were flocking to Ao Maya in the hope of seeing this utopian image of the perfect unspoilt beach up close. While Ko Phi Phi Ley was spared development, it suffered from over-crowding and this took its toll on the ecology. The larger Ko Phi Phi Don also saw a rash of construction – resorts, restaurants and bars built quickly to cater for the relentless onslaught of tourists.

The December 2004 tsunami hit Ko Phi Phi at its busiest time. Its popularity coupled with the peak tourist season meant that hotels on Ko Phi Phi Don were fully booked and every tourist facility was at its maximum capacity. When the tsunami waves hit the narrow centre of Ko Phi Phi Don, the damage that they caused was immense; numerous shops, restaurants and hotels were reduced to rubble and thousands of lives were lost. The most evident damage was opposite the main **Ton Sai village** at **Ao Lo Dalam**, where entire resorts were washed away. Given the scale of the disaster, Ko Phi Phi's recovery was a lot swifter than predicted – although some lament the govern-

Close-up view of rock-climbing winches and hooks.

BELOW LEFT: rock climbing at Railay Bay. **BELOW RIGHT:** Maya Bay on Phi Phi Lei.

TIP

Several companies operate regular ferry services to Ko Phi Phi Don from Phuket and Krabi. The more expensive ones justify their higher prices with indoor air-conditioned areas. However, if the seas are rough, it's better to be on deck with the bracing salty air blowing against you.

ment's failure to assign national-park status to the area in the aftermath of the catastrophe.

There are no roads on the island, so walking from one place to another is generally the only way to get around. Most dive sites around Ko Phi Phi were unaffected by the tsunami, and it remains one of Thailand's most popular diving locations.

Ko Phi Phi Don

Ko Phi Phi Don is made up of two elongated islands joined together by an isthmus to create what looks like, from the air, a giant high-backed chair. Most development is concentrated on the bays found on either side of the isthmus – Ao Ton Sai and Ao Lo Dalam.

Boats to the island dock at the main pier at **Ao Ton Sai ❶**, a bay that would be far prettier were it not for the ferries and longtail boats lining it from one end to the other. An entrance fee of B20 to stay on the

island is payable on disembarking. There are a few information booths at the end of the pier, beyond which is **Ton Sai village**, a compact area of restaurants, bars, dive shops, internet cafés and stalls selling everything from sarongs and beaded jewellery to sandwiches and banana pancakes.

Opposite Ao Ton Sai, and only a few minutes walk away, is **Ao Lo Dalam ❷**, a quieter and prettier bay with a lovely curve of white sand skimming clear blue waters. What makes it even nicer is that post-tsunami reconstruction along this beach was slower and thus less ramshackle than Ao Ton Sai.

Much of the island's accommodation is today located on **Hat Hin Khom ❸**, at the western end of Ao Ton Sai, and on **Hat Yao ❹** (Long Beach) at the southwestern tip of the island. Access to Hat Yao is either by longtail boat (10 minutes) from Ton Sai or a 40-minute walk. Prices are typically higher than elsewhere

BELOW: approaching the pier at Ko Phi Phi Don.

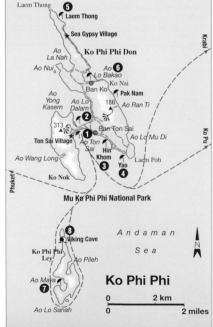

in Thailand and although rooms are generally of above-average standard, the elevated prices do not usually reflect the actual quality.

The best snorkelling and the most exclusive resorts are found to the north of the island on **Hat Laem Thong ❺**, where the majority of visitors are either honeymooners or those seeking a more isolated beach. There is a morning ferry between here and Ton Sai, otherwise all transport is by hired longtail boat. Hat Laem Thong is also the home of a small community of *chao lay*, or "sea gypsies". These folk mainly make their living by fishing or ferrying tourists around the islands.

South of Hat Laem Thong, along the same northeastern coastline, is **Ao Lo Bakao ❻**, which has mainly upmarket accommodation on its quiet beach. Both Hat Laem Thong and Ao Lo Bakao were spared the worst of the huge waves of the tsunami as they are located on the east side of the island.

Inland attractions are limited but many people take the 30-minute hike over to the **viewpoint** located high on a bluff at the southern end of Ao Lo Dalam. To get there, follow the path eastwards towards Hat Hin Khom and turn left when it forks inland. Understandably, the scenic point is at its busiest around sunrise and sunset; from here the vista of the twin bays of Ao Ton Sai and Ao Lo Dalam, separated by a thin band of land with the mountain behind, is breathtaking.

Ko Phi Phi Ley

The uninhabited **Ko Phi Phi Ley** is a mere speck at 6½ sq km (2½ sq miles). It lies about 4km (2 miles) south of Ko Phi Phi Don. Formed entirely from limestone, the island is surrounded by steep karsts rising out of the sea that circle it almost completely. Of the picturesque bays around the island, the most visited are **Ao Pileh** to the east and the aforementioned **Ao Maya ❼** on the west coast. Ao Maya would be a more beautiful spot were it not for the daytrippers who descend here in droves and frequently leave their litter behind.

Also at Ko Phi Phi Ley is the **Viking Cave ❽**, at the northeastern

Longtail fishing boats, commonly found at the beaches and islands of South Thailand, are a cheap means of transport but the incessant droning noise the engines make is annoying.

BELOW: from the viewpoint on Ko Phi Phi Don.

Harvesting prized birds' nests at the Viking Cave.

end of the island. Inscribed on the cave walls are coloured chalk drawings of various boats, believed to have been sketched hundreds of years ago by pirates who used the cave as a shelter. Today, the pirates have been replaced by hundreds of swifts that build their nests in crevices high up in the steep cave walls. These nests are collected by local villagers who climb the tall rickety ladders, risking life and limb, to collect the birds' nests so highly prized by Chinese gourmets for their claimed health-giving properties. Swarms of swifts descend on the caves of Ko Phi Phi Ley every year between January and April and build nests using their saliva as a bonding material.

Diving and snorkelling

Many of the dive sites around Ko Phi Phi can also be accessed from Phuket, Krabi and Ko Lanta. Around Ko Phi Phi itself, the best diving and snorkelling sites are **Hin Bida** (Phi Phi Shark Point), **Ko Pai** (Bamboo Island), **Ko Yung** (Mosquito Island) and **Ao Maya**, on the western side of Ko Phi Phi Ley. The **King Cruiser**

BELOW: magnificent Maya Bay.

wreck between the waters of Phuket and Ko Phi Phi is another favourite dive site.

KO LANTA YAI

The term Ko Lanta is generally used to refer to **Ko Lanta Yai**, the largest of only three inhabited islands in an archipelago of over 50. Originally named Pulao Satak, meaning "Island with Long Beaches", by the *chao lay* (sea gypsies) who first settled on the island, Ko Lanta Yai stretches 27km (17 miles) in length and 12km (7 miles) in width.

Most visitors to Ko Lanta travel direct from Krabi, from which ferries set off twice daily on a journey that takes about 2 hours and terminates at **Ban Sala Dan** village on Ko Lanta's northernmost tip. Due to strong winds and rough seas, boats do not operate between May and October. The island's one main road loops around the island, while a few smaller roads lead inland towards the southeastern coast, where there are small settlements of sea gypsies. Development has been mainly confined to the west coast, where spec-

tacular sunsets viewed from along a number of striking white-sand beaches are a near-daily certainty. The east coast is fringed by long stretches of mangroves and swimming is not possible. Ko Lanta has developed rapidly over the past few years, although much of the island still shuts down during the quiet low season. Most of the new hotel developments have been of the upscale variety, but Ko Lanta still manages to maintain its sleepy island feel, with beach bungalows out-numbering high-rise hotel developments.

The development also means there is now a greater range of accommodation available, as well as an increase in activities. Many resorts have in-house spa treatments to offer, some have Thai cooking lessons, and there are some with on-site dive operations.

Dan Sala Dan

Whether arriving by passenger or car ferry, the first stop for most visitors is the compact main village of **Ban Sala Dan ❶**. Guests at the more exclusive resorts on Ko Lanta have the luxury of being delivered right to the doorstep, or rather shorestep, of their hotel by private boat transfers.

Concrete posts and overhead hanging cables make Ban Sala Dan village a rather unsightly place, but for a relatively small island it is well equipped with a police post, clinic, tour agents and Internet facilities. There are also a few small but well-stocked local convenience stores. Along the pier are a number of seafood restaurants where fresh daily catches are displayed on beds of ice.

Hat Khlong Dao

A few kilometres south of Ban Sala Dan is the first of the island's westerly beaches, **Hat Khlong Dao ❷**. Shallow waters and safe swimming conditions make this 3km (2-mile) stretch of beach a popular choice with families. Its close proximity to

the pier at Ban Sala Dan also appeals to scuba divers seeking easy access to the nearby dive sites. Despite its attractions – white sand, picturesque hilly backdrop and some of the most dramatic sunsets along the western coast – Khlong Dao rarely seems crowded. The beach is wide enough that, even in the peak season, it's often possible to find a relatively secluded spot.

Ao Phra Ae

Almost, if not equally, as popular as Khlong Dao is the neighbouring **Ao Phra Ae ❸** (Long Beach), which is slightly longer at 4km (3 miles) and shaded by vast stretches of coconut and pine trees. Phra Ae is good for swimmers and sunbathers, although parts of the seabed are steep and the water not as calm, so families with small children should consider alternative options. There are lots of accommodation choices and an ample variety of restaurants.

Hat Khlong Khong

Just south of Ao Phra Ae is laid-back **Hat Khlong Khong ❹**, which,

TIP

If you plan to rent a jeep or a motorbike and explore Ko Lanta yourself, be sure to fill up with enough petrol before leaving the main village of Ban Sala Dan. The few petrol stations on Ko Lanta are expensive, difficult to find and shut early.

BELOW: Muslim islanders on Ko Lanta.

A Thai salad in Ko Lanta.

Below: Ko Lanta fisherman.

although not great for swimming, is one of the island's best beaches for snorkelling; at low tide the rocky underlay reveals an assortment of fish and other marine life. Accommodation is generally cheaper than on the more northerly beaches, with an emphasis on clean but basic beach-front bungalows. Most have attached restaurants and beach bars that spring to life in the evenings, enticing customers with tables on the sand and colourful performances by fire-eaters.

Inland diversions

There are limited attractions on Ko Lanta, apart from its stunning beaches. Some 4km (2½ miles) south of Hat Khlong Khong, the road splits into two. The left fork leads all the way to the east coast of the island, where few tourists venture. A turn-off at the 3km (2-miles) mark to the right leads to the **Tham Mai Kaeo** ❺ caves. It is best to get your hotel to

organise this trip as finding the caves on your own is a bit of a challenge – you need to clamber up a steep hill, often with the help of tree branches. The combination of slippery paths, rickety bamboo ladders and confined spaces make this an inadvisable activity for the less physically fit. The expedition leads through a labyrinth of winding tunnels and caverns, past dramatic rock formations. At the end, after negotiating a steep slope with the aid of a rope, is a deep pool, where you can cool off.

A sunrise trip to the central peak referred to simply as **Viewpoint Hill** ❻ is worth the effort. To get there, continue on the road that heads east (signs along the way will guide you towards this attraction).

As the early-morning sky changes from pitch-black to soft blue, the haunting, gravestone-like profiles of limestone cliffs will appear almost magically, one by one, until the sea seems filled with them. The near

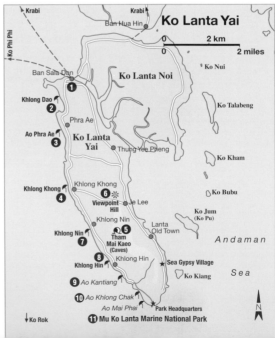

360-degree panoramic vista in the crisp morning air is truly breathtaking. The experience can be enjoyed over a sunrise breakfast at the café on the hill. If the thought of rising before dawn fills you with dread, you can go at sunset and have cocktails at the romantic **Noon Restaurant**, which has good Thai food and a few Western dishes.

Hat Khlong Nin and Hat Khlong Hin

Turning right about 4km (2 miles) from Hat Khlong Khong leads past a few convenience stores and wooden restaurants before emerging at **Hat Khlong Nin ❼**. This lovely beach has a relaxed feel and is imbued with the atmosphere of a small, intimate village. The powdery white sands of Hat Khlong Nin stretch about 2km (1 mile), and calm waters outside of the monsoon season make it excellent for swimming. Accommodation consists primarily of stylish resorts such as **SriLanta** and the **Rawi warin**, most with in-house restaurants and beach bars. At the start of Hat Khlong Nin is the popular

reggae-style **Rasta Baby Bar**. A stroll along the beach front reveals more of the same; at night-time, the next bamboo beach bar is never more than a short walk away.

At its southern end, Hat Khlong Nin merges with the similar-sounding but much smaller and secluded **Hat Khlong Hin ❽**. Separated from the former by a cluster of trees, the waves here are rough during the monsoon season. It is quite empty at the moment and awaits further development.

Ao Kantiang

About 6km (4 miles) from Hat Khlong Hin is the lovely and picturesque bay of **Ao Kantiang ❾**. This bay has a secluded and private feel to it as it's framed on both sides and to the back by jungle-covered hills. To the north and high up on the hill are a handful of small resorts; there are lovely views from the top but it also means climbing up a considerable number of steps to reach it. The southern end of this bay is anchored by the luxury **Pimalai Resort and Spa**. This five-star resort is set in 40

Typical beach bar along Hat Khlong Nin.

BELOW: picturesque Ao Kantiang is anchored by Pimalai Resort and Spa at one end.

Lighting hot-air balloons in Ko Lanta.

hectares (100 acres) of natural tropical surroundings and has direct access to the 1km (½-mile)-long stretch of pure white-sand beach.

Ao Khlong Chak and Ao Mai Phai

Beyond Ao Kantiang, the further south one ventures, the more remote and isolated the beaches become. But persevere and you will be rewarded with a cluster of the most scenic and sparsely developed beaches on the entire island, including **Ao Khlong Chak** ⑩, one of the smallest, at just 400 metres (1,310ft) long. Only a handful of resorts are found here. Ao Khlong Chak is most famous for its impressive waterfall, found 1½km (1 mile) inland, that flows throughout the year.

Beyond this is a short but steep drive through the jungle leading to the lovely cove of **Ao Mai Phai** (Bamboo Bay). This is the last and southernmost beach before reaching the headquarters of the Mu Ko Lanta Marine National Park on the southern tip. Ao Mai Phai is backed by mountains on three sides, and

BELOW: snorkelling near Ko Rok.

the relative difficulty of access and geography give this bay a real sense of remoteness and tranquillity. It's a quiet haven with little development. The beach is only 500 metres (1,640ft) in length, but is ideal for swimming; a shallow boulder-strewn stretch at the northern edge is more suited to snorkelling. As you head south from here, look out for monkeys foraging in the area (but be careful not to approach them, even if they appear tame).

Mu Ko Lanta Marine N P

Declared Thailand's 62nd official National Park in 1990, **Mu Ko Lanta Marine National Park** ⑪ comprises the southern tip of Ko Lanta Yai and 15 small surrounding islands. The southernmost tip of Ko Lanta comprises two beaches: **Laem Tanode** and the rocky **Hat Hin Ngam**; the latter is where the park headquarters is situated. A 2½km (1½-mile) hiking trail leading along a cliff begins here and offers the chance of spotting a range of fauna such as fruit bats, deer, wild pigs and reptiles, including monitor lizards, cobras and green snakes. Also here is a small white lighthouse, from which there are scenic views out to the sea and mountains.

Snorkelling and diving

Some of Thailand's finest spots for snorkelling and scuba diving are found in the waters off Ko Lanta. The most visited site for snorkelling, and considered by many to be one of Thailand's best for such activity, is **Ko Rok**, about 47km (29 miles) south of Ko Lanta. There are actually two islands here, **Ko Rok Nai** and **Ko Rok Nok**, both graced with powdery white-sand beaches with an extensive patch of brightly coloured coral in between. Visibility is very good, and many interesting types of reef fish can be found in these waters.

Approximately 20km (12 miles) from Ko Rok are the twin peaks of **Hin Daeng** and **Hin Muang**, frequently rated as one of the world's top-10 dive sites. An incredible variety of marine life thrives around this site. As the only outcrops in this area of deep, open sea, they also attract many pelagics, as well as large tuna and barracuda. Schools of grey reef sharks often approach divers and the area has one of the highest incidences of whale-shark sightings in the world.

OTHER ISLANDS

Ko Bubu

Those seeking an even quieter retreat than Ko Lanta may wish to visit the smaller and more peaceful islands nearby. At 7km (4 miles) off the east coast of Ko Lanta, the tiny island of **Ko Bubu** takes just 30 minutes to circumnavigate by foot. This uninhabited island only has a basic restaurant and a few simple bungalows on the western coast, where the small but stunning gently-sloping beach is fringed by turquoise waters ideal

for swimming. Boat transfers can be arranged for guests of **Bubu Island Resort** (tel: 0-7561 8066), the only resort on the island; there is no other regular service. Longtail boats at Krabi and Ko Lanta can, however, be chartered for the journey.

Ko Jum (Ko Pu)

Larger than Ko Bubu is **Ko Jum** (Ko Pu), to the northwest of Ko Lanta. While facilities are steadily increasing here, it has yet to sustain much impact from tourism and is still pleasantly underdeveloped. The flat southern part is covered in palms and casuarinas, and the mountainous northern tip reaches a height of 395 metres (1,296ft). The island is gifted with powdery white-sand beaches and clear waters with plenty of healthy and colourful coral reefs. Some 3,000 permanent islanders reside on Ko Jum, earning a living mainly from fishing and the rubber plantations that are found here. Accommodation now runs from budget to expensive at resorts such as the stylish **Koh Jum Beach Villas** (tel: 08-6184 0505; www.kohjumbeachvillas.com). ❏

Sea-gypsy (*chao lay*) fisherman on Ko Jum mending his net.

BELOW: Ko Bubu at dusk.

KRABI, KO PHI PHI AND KO LANTA

TRANSPORT

Getting There

By Air

Krabi International Airport (tel: 0-7563 6541/2; www.krabiairport. org) is about 18km (11 miles) east of Krabi Town. Although most visitors to Krabi and its surrounding islands stop off in Bangkok first, several airlines have international routes, such as **Air Asia** (www.airasia.com), including Australia, Hong Kong, India and mainland China; and **Bangkok Airways** (www.bangkokair.com) from Cambodia and Singapore. Domestically, airlines flying from Bangkok to Krabi are **Bangkok Airways** (also from Chiang Mai and Ko Samui), **Air Asia** (also from Chiang Mai) and **Thai Airways** (www.thaiairways.com), who also fly from Phuket and Chiang Mai.

If you haven't made arrangements with your hotel for pick-up at the airport, use one of the airport taxis. Fares are about B400 to Krabi Town and approximately B650 to B750 to Krabi's beaches. Travel time from Krabi Airport to the town centre takes around 30 minutes, with Ao Nang beach taking slightly less time. Pay the posted fare at the counter in the Arrival Hall and avoid the touts that hover outside the terminal. Minivans from the airport are slower but cost only B150 to Krabi Town.

By Bus and Taxi

Air-conditioned buses depart from Bangkok's **Southern Bus Terminal** daily for Krabi on the 12-hour overnight journey. Tickets range in price, as do levels of comfort. There are also direct buses from Phuket (3½ hours), Hat Yai (6 hours) and Ko Samui (2½ hours via Surat Thani on the mainland). Travel agents in any of these areas will advise on buying tickets. Note: in Krabi Town, the public buses terminate at Talat Kao, about 5km (3 miles) north of town, while private tour buses end up at Andaman Wave Master station in the town centre. Local buses and taxis run from both stations to the beaches and the pier.

Taking a taxi from Phuket, Hat Yai or Ko Samui is quicker. From Phuket Airport, for instance, a taxi to Krabi will cost B2,500 and make the trip in 2½ hours. If you can get a cheap air ticket to Phuket *(see page 230)*, you could fly to Phuket and then take a taxi to Krabi.

By Boat

During the high season, it's possible to take a boat from Phuket via Ko Phi Phi to Krabi. The journey from Ko Phi Phi is approximately 2 hours; from Phuket it's just under 3 hours. Boats from Phuket and Ko Phi Phi arrive at Krabi Passenger Pier on Th. Tharua. Enquire with travel agents at either of these destinations as there are boats of varying quality and speeds available.

Getting Around

Non-metered taxis, motorcycle taxis and *tuk-tuks* can be hired from Krabi Town and the beaches. The drivers in town often speak limited English, although those who operate around the beaches are more than adept at negotiating prices. Expect to pay between B200 and B400 for a short half-hour ride in a taxi or *tuk-tuk* (both charge about the same rates). Local bus services are provided by *songthaew* – converted pick-up trucks with two wooden benches in the back.

Krabi Town and the beach road are full of car-rental companies, many offering cheap deals but often without the security of full insurance. Check on this before renting. **Budget** (tel: 0-7563 6171) is one of several options at Krabi Airport. Motorcycles are available for hire along Ao Nang beach road but be sure to wear a safety helmet.

Railay Bay

Longtail boats make the 45-minute trip from Krabi Town (or 15 minutes from Ao Nang) to the Railay beaches throughout the day. They charge a fixed rate of B100 (B60 from Ao Nang) per person each way, but only leave once they have six people. Prices rise after 7pm. There is a stone walkway from the boat at Railay beach, which will be partially under water at low tide, so prepare for a short (and possibly slippery) wade. You can also hire boats for the day at a negotiated rate.

KO PHI PHI

Getting There

Although Ko Phi Phi is, administratively speaking, within Krabi Province, it is located about the same distance from both mainland Krabi and Phuket, roughly 2 hours by boat. **Advance Aviation** runs helicopter trips, including transfers to Ko Phi Phi, from Phuket (www.advanceaviation.co. th). The price is around B78,000 per hour, but the machine holds six people.

Ferries from Krabi depart from the **Passenger Ferry Terminal** on Th. Tharua in Krabi Town; those in Phuket leave from Phuket Town's **Rassada Pier**. All boats land on Ao Ton Sai on the larger island of Ko Phi Phi Don. Tickets can be purchased at travel agents in both Phuket and Krabi, but ask around as they charge vastly different fees for the same boats. If you've booked accomodation on Ko Phi Phi, get your hotel to arrange the boat transfers for you. There is now an entry fee, of about B20, for people staying on Phi Phi, payable on disembarkation.

Note: many people do Ko Phi Phi as a day trip from Phuket or Krabi; packages with round-trip transfers, lunch and snorkelling cost anything from B1,200 to B1,800, depending on the type of boat used.

Between the months of May and October, ferries may not run due to bad weather, in which case private transfers can be arranged through travel agents.

Getting Around

There are no roads on Ko Phi Phi, so the main way to get around is on foot. Distances between some of the main beaches are short and pathways flat. Longtail boats will make the journey from the Laem Thong beach at the north of the island to Ton Sai in the south for about B400 or more, but may be reluctant to make the 1-hour journey back once darkness falls. Shorter rides to closer beaches will cost from B50 to B100.

KO LANTA

Getting There

It is not possible to fly directly to Ko Lanta. You will have to get to Krabi *(see page 260)* first and then make the transfer by boat (some airlines will include a boat transfer in the ticket price). Ferries from Krabi depart from the **Passenger Ferry Terminal**, located 3km (2 miles) west of the town centre on Th. Tharua. Boats leave at 11am daily and dock at Ban Sala Dan pier on the northern tip of Ko Lanta. The journey takes around 2 hours, but note that boats do not operate during the

May–Oct monsoon season. Alternatively, if you have booked accomodation on Ko Lanta, get your hotel to arrange the land and boat transfers.

There is no direct ferry from Phuket to Ko Lanta. You will need to catch the ferry to Ko Phi Phi from Phuket's Rassada Pier (8.30am, 11am and 2.30pm) and then take a connecting ferry (11.30am and 3pm) to Ko Lanta.

Getting Around

The road surfaces on Koh Lanta have undergone development works recently and are much improved, although island transportation remains difficult as there are no taxis available. Some guesthouses and higher-end resorts offer transfer services to the beaches and to Sala Dan village where there are motorcycle taxis, which here are very like small *tuk-tuks*.

Jeeps can be hired from rental agencies in Ban Sala Dan, and the majority of guesthouses can arrange motorbike rental for you. Be aware, though, that neither of these options is likely to include adequate, or in the case of motorbikes, any form of insurance. Safety helmets are strongly advised.

Some of the more upmarket resorts on Ko Lanta will arrange boat transfers directly to the beach they are located on for guests, dispensing with the need for any road travel.

BELOW: longtail boat in Ko Phi Phi.

Krabi Town and Beaches

Krabi Town

Ban To Guest House
22/6 Th. Chao Fa
Tel: 0-7561 2950
www.bantoguesthouse.com.
Set amid peaceful greenery on Krabi's outer limits, this guesthouse painted in bright orange is hard to miss. Inside, the rooms (all with spacious balconies) are clean, colourful and simply furnished. (20 rooms) $

Ao Nang

Ao Nang Villa Resort
113 Ao Nang
Tel: 0-7563 7270.
www.aonangvilla.com
Great location only a minute's walk from the beach front, with two large free-form swimming pools resting at the foot of Krabi's limestone mountains. The Villa Spa is located in a Thai-style house within the resort and two restaurants on site prepare Thai and international food for guests. (79 rooms) $$

Centara Grand Beach Resort & Villas
396-396/1 Moo 2, Ao Nang
Tel: 0-7563 7789
www.centarahotelsresorts.com
There are rooms and villas with garden or sea views in this beach-front resort. All have terraces or balconies, plus flat-screen TVs and internet

(extra charge). The three restaurants serve Japanese, Thai and international cuisines; there is also a spa, a dive centre and boats for hire. (192 rooms) $$$

Cliff Ao Nang Resort
85/2 Moo 2, Ao Nang
Tel: 0-7563 8117
www.thecliffkrabi.com
Small, elegant and located in the hills a 10-minute walk from the sea, the mountain views from this elevated position are stunning. The villas have a pleasing traditional design and if you are content to spend some relaxing time around the pool, this is one of Ao Nang's most peaceful retreats. (22 rooms) $$

Krabi Resort
232 Moo 2, Ao Nang
Tel: 0-7563 7030
www.krabiresort
A 5-minute walk from the beach, this resort sprawls over 7 hectares (18 acres) and offers a choice of bungalows or cheaper rooms in the main block. Huge swimming pool. $$

Hat Khlong Muang

Nakamanda Resort & Spa
126 Moo 3, Hat Khlong Muang
Tel: 0-7562 8200
www.nakamanda.com
Classy and elegant, the standard villas are 56 sq metres (603 sq ft), have Thai-style pointed

roofs and are linked by shaded wooden walkways. Sandstone sculptures are scattered around the grounds and the artistically designed pool is simply stunning. The Asian and Western restaurant has a poolside terrace and the spa has a variety of massage packages. A very romantic hotel. (36 rooms) $$$

Sheraton Krabi Beach Resort
155 Moo 2, Hat Khlong Muang
Tel: 0-7562 8000
www.sheratonkrabi.com
Set directly on Khlong Muang beach, this large resort is spread across a number of blocks but fits in so well with the natural surroundings that it actually appears smaller. There's a beautiful sea-facing pool, a Mandara Spa and a water sports centre with facilities for activities including sailing, kayaking and windsurfing. High-speed internet access is available in rooms. Dining options include Mediterranean, Indian and Thai. (246 rooms) $$

Sofitel Krabi Phokeethra Golf and Spa Resort
Hat Khlong Muang
Tel: 0-7562 7800
www.sofitel.com
Surrounded by pristine rainforest, this sprawling luxury resort has a vast, serpentine 7,000-sq-metre swimming pool. Most rooms have large ocean-facing bal-

conies with views of the limestone islands. There are three restaurants, a nine-hole golf course next door, a fitness centre and spa, and a children's playground. (299 rooms) $$

Hat Tham Phra Nang

Rayavadee
Hat Tham Phra Nang
Tel: 0-7562 0740
www.rayavadee.com
The most exclusive – and expensive – resort in the entire Krabi Province and hailed by many magazine surveys (including *Condé Nast Traveller*) as one of the world's best. Tucked away in a headland alongside spectacular Tham Phra Nang beach on one side and the more prosaic Railay East beach on the other. The well-designed villas all but melt into the surroundings. Includes several restaurants and a spa. This is a truly magical location. (102 rooms) $$$$

Hat Railay West

Railay Bay Resort & Spa
Hat Railay West
Tel: 0-7562 2998
www.railaybayresort.com
This resort sprawls from Railay West beach

inland all the way to Railay East beach. It features a variety of cottages, all equipped with cable TV and air conditioning. There's a beachside restaurant and swimming pool on site. (130 rooms) **$$**

Railay Village Resort
Hat Railay West
Tel: 0-7581 9412
www.railayvillagekrabi.com
This resort is perfectly situated for sunsets on scenic Railay West beach but be warned that the popular beach gets very crowded. The hotel offers a choice of

bungalows that are set close to the beach and among coconut groves. There is a swimming pool, restaurant and tour desk on site.(48 rooms) **$$**

Sand Sea Resort
Hat Railay West
Tel: 0-7581 9463
www.krabisandsea.com
A pleasant hotel with a variety of room styles (and prices). Restaurant serving Thai and Western food, beach-front swimming pool, minimart and internet facilities available on site. (42 rooms) **$**

HAT RAILAY EAST

Sunrise Tropical Resort
Hat Railay East
Tel: 0-7581 9418
www.sunrisetropical.com
Located on Railay East, this place is blessed with dramatic sunrises. Prettier Railay West beach is only a 5-minute walk away. Rooms have been stylishly executed with wooden floors, and the pool, which is surrounded by coconut palms, faces towering

limestone pinnacles. (28 rooms) **$**

AO TON SAI

Krabi Mountain View Resort
Ao Ton Sai
Tel: 0-7562 2610
www.krabimountainviewresort.com
Pleasant bungalow-style huts between the cliffs and waters of Ton Sai beach, with Railay West just a 10-minute walk at low tide. Rooms are clean and modern. (46 rooms) **$**

KO PHI PHI

AO TON SAI

Chao Ko Phi Phi Lodge
Ao Ton Sai
Tel: 0-7660 1083
www.chaokoresort.com
Set on the beach front just a 2-minute walk from the busiest part of Ao Ton Sai. Rooms are comfortable, with air conditioning and satellite TV. Facilities include a mini-mart and a small sea-facing swimming pool. (44 rooms) **$**

Phi Phi Banyan Villa
Ao Ton Sai
Tel: 08-1909 1333
Right in the centre of Ao Ton Sai, the beach, restaurants, shops and pier are just 5 minutes' walk away. Rooms are decent (the ones in the garden wing are slightly pricier) and have air conditioning, cable TV and hot water. (40 rooms) **$**

PP Palm Tree Resort
Ao Ton Sai

Tel: 0-2164 1001
(Bangkok office)
www.pppalmtreeresort.com
This centrally located three-storey hotel is arranged around a small swimming pool, so many rooms have pool view or pool access. There's an international restaurant and a bar. (48 rooms) **$**

HAT HIN KHOM

Bayview Resort
Hat Hin Khom
Tel: 0-7560 1127
www.phiphibayview.com
Split-level bungalows set on a hillside and encircled by a thick tree-filled grove. Restaurant and small pool on site. Rooms enjoy panoramic views across the sea towards Ko Phi Phi Ley. (70 rooms) **$$**

Phi Phi Andaman Resort
1 Moo 7, Hat Khin Khom
Tel: 0-7560 1111

www.phiphlandamanresort.com
Located a 10-minute walk from Ton Sai pier and set in a tropical garden backing onto the beach. Mix of bungalows with fan or air conditioning and basic white walls and tiled floors. All pleasant, bright and spotlessly clean. One of the better options for accommodation in this price range. (50 rooms) **$**

HAT YAO

Paradise Resort
Hat Yao
Mobile tel: 0-1968 3982
www.paradiseresort.co.th
Set on relatively quiet Hat Yao beach, this place is accessed by a 10-minute boat ride from Ao Ton Sai. There's a variety of rooms, all air conditioned, and some with sea views. Restaurant, bar and internet access. **$**

HAT LAEM THONG

Holiday Inn Resort
Hat Laem Thong
Tel: 0-7562 7300
www.phiphi.holidayinn.com
A nice resort where the seclusion is a popular draw for honeymooners. The range of rooms runs from garden villas to studios with direct access to the beach from private verandahs. They have a large free-form pool, tennis courts, a dive centre and water sports equipment such as kayaks and sailboards, and there's a good selection of restau-

PRICE CATEGORIES

Price categories show the starting price for a double room without breakfast and taxes:
$ = under US$70
$$ = US$70–130
$$$ = US$130–250
$$$$ = over US$250

rants and bars on site. (97 rooms) **$$**

Zeavola Resort
Hat Laem Thong
Tel: 0-7562 7000
www.zeavola.com
Ko Phi Phi Don's only luxury all-suite resort is situated on the island's far northern tip. The oversized suites – ranging from the cheaper Village Suites to the mid-range Garden and Hillside ones to the more expensive Beachfront Suites – are in the style of thatched bungalows, each with separate bedroom and living room. Completely made of teak wood, they replicate local island houses. Two restaurants, a spa and pool. (52 rooms) **$$$$**

AO LO BAKAO

Outrigger Phi Phi Island Resort & Spa
Ao Lo Bakao
Tel: 0-7562 8900 (Krabi office)
www.outriggerthailand.com
This attractive resort is situated on 800 metres (2,500ft) of private beach. The villas use lots of wood and thatched roofing and are spread among the trees, with options on the hillside or beach front. The rooms are tastefully designed but it is the idyllic location that keeps guests coming back. Good range of facilities – four restau-

ABOVE: Ko Phi Phi.

rants, two bars, an internet café, fitness centre and a spa. There's also a children's pool and slide. (104 rooms) **$$$**

KO LANTA

HAT KHLONG DAO

Crown Lanta Resort & Spa
Hat Khlong Dao
Tel: 0-7562 6999
www.crownlanta.com
This slightly elevated property is on a peninsula, so enjoys two private beaches. The basic rooms have pool views and the top-of-the-range villa is 253 sq metres (2,723 sq feet) of pure luxury. There are two restaurants, a bar and a spa on site. (83 rooms) **$$$**

Holiday Villa
Hat Khlong Dao
Tel: 0-7568 4370
www.holidayvillalanta.com
At the beach's southern end, accommodation at this resort takes the form of rooms contained within Thai-style villas; some hillside villas are two-storey, with more expensive suites on the upper floor. Facilities on offer include a restaurant and a swimming pool. (27 rooms) **$**

AO PHRA AE

Lanta Sand Resort & Spa
Ao Phra Ae
Tel: 0-7568 4633
www.lantasand.com
There are local design touches everywhere at this lovely resort, with its swimming pool, spa and guest rooms tucked in between luscious greenery and coconut palms. All rooms have open-air, natural garden bathrooms. (78 rooms) **$$**

Layana Resort and Spa
Ao Phra Ae
Tel: 0-7560 7100
www.layanaresort.com
Warm and welcoming boutique resort more suited to couples than families. Both the swimming pool and oversized jacuzzi have the sea in front and a backdrop of forested hills behind. All rooms are equipped with broadband internet connections. (50 rooms) **$$$$**

HAT KHLONG NIN

The Narima
99 Moo 5, Hat Khlong Nin
Tel: 0-7566 2668.
www.narima-lanta.com
Three rows of sea-facing wooden huts with air conditioning. Good value for money in this price range, and very secluded, although this means a trek if you want to find alternative facilities. They have massage and a restaurant onsite. (32 rooms) **$**

Rawi Warin Resort & Spa
Hat Khlong Nin
Tel: 0-7560 7400
www.rawiwarin.com
This large resort (formerly Langham Place) is situated at the foot of a series of hills and overlooks a lovely beach, it has four swimming pools (including one that is built into the sea). Complete range of facilities. Claims to be committed to conservation principles, including the use of

renewable energy and recycling. Good value. (185 rooms) **$$**

SriLanta
Hat Khlong Nin
Tel: 0-7566 2688
www.srilanta.com
This charming beachside property has simple yet stylish thatched-roofed bungalows. Its Thai-Western restaurant, scattered with floor cushions, is built from wood and grass and is supported by tree trunks. There is also an onsite spa for guests to use. (49 rooms) **$$**

AO KAN TIANG

Costa Lanta
Moo 1, Saladan
Tel: 0-7561 8092
www.costalanta.com
This smart resort with a contemporary minimalist design has a massage service, pool and a Thai restaurant overlooking the sea. There's a secluded feel, but bars and restaurants are five

minutes walk away. A variety of day trips are also available. (22 rooms) **$$**

Pimalai Resort and Spa
Ao Kan Tiang
Tel: 0-7560 7999
www.pimalai.com
A luxurious five-star

resort that cleverly mixes Thai and contemporary styling. Highly rated spa, plus restaurants, dive centre, infinity pool and direct access to a stunningly beautiful 900-metre (2,950ft) beach front. Undeniably exclusive

but a downside is that it is a bit far out if you wish to be close to the busier beaches. If it's isolation you crave, however, then this is the ultimate place to chill out and experience true Thai relaxation. (79 rooms and 39 villas) **$$$$**

PRICE CATEGORIES

Price categories show the starting price for a double room without breakfast and taxes:
$ = under US$70
$$ = US$70–130
$$$ = US$130–250
$$$$ = over US$250

RESTAURANT LISTINGS

KRABI TOWN AND BEACHES

KRABI TOWN

International

Café Europa
1/9 Soi Ruamjit
Tel: 0-7562 0407
www.cafeeuropa-krabi.com
Open: Daily (closed Sun in low season) B, L and D. This cosy café is somewhat of an institution in Krabi Town. The limited menu is based around a few signature dishes, including pepper steak, meatballs and goulash, all with side salad and bread. Stacks of Thai and international newspapers and magazines make it a pleasant place to relax over a cuppa. **$–$$**

Thai

Night Market
Soi 10, Th. Maharat
Open: daily D only.
The best food in Krabi Town, not to mention the one least likely to burn a hole in your pocket. Absorb the atmosphere and sample

local delicacies at this local night market. Choices differ nightly, but the *kaab moo* (pork leg), a delicious meaty dish simmered for hours in soy sauce and accompanied with green vegetables and rice, is a good bet. **$**

Ruen Mai
Uttarakit Road, Khlong Chilat
Tel: 0-7563 1797
Open: daily 11am–9pm. In its new location, a tented bamboo structure a 15 minute taxi ride along the road to Ao Nang, the celebrated Ruen Mai still serves its wide selection of Southern Thai specialities. Neither strong flavours nor lashings of chilli are sacrificed to protect sensitive palates; this is the way the locals eat. The staff will prepare meatfree versions of any dish on request. **$–$$**

AO NANG

Only Ao Nang beach has enough independant restaurants to warrant

coverage here. Eating at Krabi's other beaches is mainly confined to hotel restaurants and guesthouse cafés.

Thai and Western

Azura Nova
142 Ao Nang
Tel: 0-7563 7848
Open: daily L and D, except Sun, D only. Italian restaurants dominate Ao Nang's beach road, and this one has a good reputation. Lovely Mediterranean ambience with tiled floors, marble tables and vines creeping up the walls. Owned by Italians, the food is as authentic as it can get. The pizzas, pastas and risottos are all delicious. **$$**

Bombay Palace
27/1, Moo2, Aonang
Tel: 08-6952 3829
www.bombaypalaceaonang.com
Open: daily L and D. Good filling plates of Indian food including all the international favourites like onion bhaji, samosas and chicken tikka, with heaps of basmati rice and nan bread.

They also serve Thai dishes, pizzas and pastas, but it's better to stick with the Indian. **$$**

Carnivore Steak and Grill
12/ Moo 3 Ao Nang
Tel: 0-7566 1061
www.carnivore-thailand.com
Open: daily 4–11pm. They use New Zealand beef and lamb for the hearty mains, and also have lighter options such as seafood and salads. All the usual French style items are available, from salad niçoise to lobster bisque and potato gratin, and there's a very good range of imported bottled beers. **$$–$$$**

Jeanette's Restaurant
245/8 Moo 2, Ao Nang
Tel: 08-9474 6178
Open: daily L and D. Located on a boardwalk,

PRICE CATEGORIES

Price per person for a three-course meal without drinks:
$ = under US$10
$$ = US$10–25
$$$ = US$25–50
$$$$ = over US$50

this down-to-earth Swedish-Thai joint may not be much to look at but don't overlook it. It has a convivial atmosphere and is popular with expats. Freshly-squeezed juices, shakes, beers, Swedish coffee and even vintage wines are available at the bar. **$$**

Thai

Lae Lay Grill
89 Moo 3 Ao Nang
Tel: 0-7566 1588
www.laelaygrill.com
Open: daily 11am–10pm.
The hillside location of this restaurant affords great views over the bay and gets you away from the main strip. They specialise in seafood served fresh from the tanks, whether in crab curry, steamed sea bass with chilli and lime, or wok-fried lobster with butter and ginger, to name but a few. They arrange *tuk-tuk* pick-ups from hotels. **$$–$$$**

KO PHI PHI

AO TON SAI

Only restaurants at this beach are listed here. Eating out at the other beaches is largely confined to the hotel restaurants.

Thai and Western

Anna's Restaurant
Ton Sai Village
Mobile tel: 08-5923 2596
Open: daily, B L and D.
Anna's tries to cover all the bases by serving a bit of everything, and they do it pretty well. There are full English breakfasts, German schnitzel, burgers, Italian meat balls and a wide choice of Thai. It's a clean, smart interior of faux wood beams and they have free Wi-fi. **$–$$**

Le Grand Bleu
Ton Sai Village
Tel: 08-1979 9739
Open: daily, D.
This French place, not far from the pier, has a pleasant wooden interior and very friendly service. The menu includes standards such as moules marinières, steaks and seafood with sauces and there's a small wine list. They also have some Thai dishes. **$$**

Italiano Bar & Restaurant
Ton Sai Village
Tel: 08-7560 1065
Open: daily L and D.
The pastas and good, thin and crispy wood-fired pizzas are satisfyingly filling after a hard day on the beach. The menu mixes all the usual Italian favourites with a select choice of Thai. **$$**

Unni's Restaurant
Ton Sai Village
Open: daily B, L and D.
There's a little twist of Mexican dishes among a menu of generally Thai and Western here. Take a crowd and share a table of burritos, fajitas, red curry and spaghetti carbonara, and wash it all down with cheap cocktails. Finish with cheesecake and chocolate brownies. **$$**

Thai

Pum Restaurant
Ton Sai Village
Tel: 08-1521 8904
www.pumthaifoodchain.com
Open: daily 11am–9pm
Stylish eatery, unlike most of the casual set-ups on the island. A large selection of well-presented Thai dishes, including the "Green Lipstick" and "Red Lipstick" (green and red curries). They also do cooking classes. **$$**

KO LANTA

BAN SALA DAN

Thai and Western

Lanta Seafood
73 Moo 1, Ban Sala Dan
Tel: 0-7568 4106
Open: daily L and D.
The seafood eateries along Sala Dan pier have dishes that look much the same. Locals, however, seem to favour this place, with its snapper, prawns and squid, all served at tables directly overlooking the sea. **$$**

AO PHRA AE

Thai and Western

The Irish Embassy Bar
233 Moo 2, Ao Prae Ae
Tel: 08-6905 7638
Open: daily B, L and D.
Home from home for pub lovers. This Irish pub is actually Irish run, and has the usual pub-style menu full of hearty drinking dishes like fish and chips, pie and mash and a roast on Sundays. There's imported beer and cider on draught for lubrication, a friendly atmosphere, pub quizzes and sport on TV. It's a must if you happen to be there on St Patrick's Day. **$$**

Red Snapper
Ao Phra Ae
Tel: 0-7885 6965
www.redsnapper-lanta.com
Open: daily L and D.
Alfresco restaurant with direct beach access from its leafy garden location. The short menu changes regularly, and is European, often with Asian flavours. There are tapas portions good for sharing as well main size plates, with popular items like mushroom risotto and BBQ ribs. They even have a cheese selection. **$$**

Tides
Layana Resort and Spa,

Ao Phra Ae
Tel: 0-7560 7100
www.layanaresort.com
Open: daily B, L and D.
This posh resort restaurant offers the chance of a splash-out meal just inches from the waves – they have white linen-clad tables set up on the beach overlooking the sea. Try steaks, seafood or traditional Thai, paired with something from the reasonable wine list. **$$$**

HAT KHLONG NIN

Thai

Roi Thai
75/1 Moo 6, Hat Khlong Nin
Tel: 0-7566 2549
www.myroithai.com
Open: daily 8am–late.
This is a romantic beach restaurant with good Thai food. Dishes include Thai-style pork spare rib cooked with honey, and

there are standards such as *laab* and pad Thai. **$$**

AO KAN TIANG

Thai

Same Same But Different
85 Moo 5, Ao Kan Tiang
Mobile tel: 0-1787 8670
Open: daily B, L and D.
Location is key to the popularity of this laid-

back beach restaurant. Menu contains a few sandwiches and salads but is predominantly Thai. A good range of dishes. **$–$$**

PRICE CATEGORIES

Price per person for a three-course meal without drinks:
$ = under US$10
$$ = US$10–25
$$$ = US$25–50
$$$$ = over US$50

ACTIVITIES

KRABI TOWN AND BEACHES

Nightlife

Ao Nang

Irish Rover Bar and Grill: 247/8 Moo 2, Ao Nang; tel: 0-7563 7607; www.irishpubaonang.com. Irish-style pub just off a side street from the main beach road. Convivial atmosphere, with Guinness flowing all evening and sports on overhead TVs.
Luna Beach Bar: Ao Nang. Nightly fire shows, pool tables and DJs is the mix that draws crowds to this busy beach bar. There's not much action, though, until late.

Railay West and East

Bobo's: Bobo Plaza, Hat Railay West. This quiet beach bar with its candlelit tables is the only purpose-built bar on Railay West to watch the setting sun. All other places are basically restaurants that happen to serve drinks.
Gecko Bar: Hat Railay East. Hip and happening beach bar set on the rocks of Railay East. Often has parties lasting late into the

night; a favourite spot to gather after all the other beach bars wind down.

Shopping

In Krabi Town, the **Vogue Department Store** (285–6 Th. Montri; tel: 0-7524 3589) has cosmetics and a supermarket on the first level, and clothing and sports gear on the upper levels.

BELOW: delicious food in Krabi.

Night markets in Krabi Town include a food market alongside **Chao Fa Pier**, which is mainly frequented by locals and has a variety of low-priced dishes on offer, and a more tourist-orientated place outside the **City Hotel** on Th. Srisawat that sells clothes and souvenirs. There's also a **Weekend Night Market** on Maharat Soi 8 selling all manner of goods on Fridays, Saturdays and Sundays

Outdoor Activities

Golf

Pakasai Country Club: Ban Lik Nai, Nua Klong; tel: 08-6810 3413; www.pakasaicountryclub.com. This course with lake views is currently Krabi's only 18-hole golf course. Games can be arranged with your hotel or online.
Krabi Driving Range: Th. Klong-kanan, Nua Klong. Just a few minutes' drive from Ao Nang, this driving range has a practice green and two chipping greens, one with a bunker. Bookings via www.krabigolftours.com or through tour agents.

Deep-sea Fishing

Me Mee Fishing Tours: 49/1 Moo 2 Ao Nang, tel: 08-1091 6091; www.memeeaonang.com. Offers full-day, half-day and night fishing trips with snorkelling on longtail or large boats. The price includes insurance and hotel transfer.

Sea Canoeing

Krabi's limestone cliffs and beautiful bays make it a favoured location for sea-canoeing enthusiasts. Tours from mainland Krabi usually depart from Ao Thalane or Ao Luk, where monkeys, otters and tropical birds are a common sight. Away from the main Krabi beaches, one of the prime canoeing areas is around the Railay peninsula (Ko Hong and Ko Bileh are favoured spots). The popularity of this site is not without good reason – aside from the cluster of rocky peaks and hidden caves, the peninsula is accessible only by longtail boat, meaning there are no large boats or noisy jet-skis sharing the water with you.

Mr. Kayak: 52/2 Ao Nang-Chongplee; tel: 0-7563 7165. Offers good equipment and has friendly, knowledgeable staff. A well-paced two-island visit takes in lagoons, mangrove swamps, monkey colonies, caves and more.

Phranang Full Moon Kayaking: Moo 5 Ao Nang; tel: 08-6593 3441. They have sunrise and sunset trips of the surrounding area. The night trip includes dinner on the beach.

Sea Kayak Krabi: 40 Th. Maharat Soi 2, Krabi Town; tel: 0-7563 0270. Offers both half- and full-day guided canoeing trips to Ao Thalane, Ao Luk and Ko Hong. Lunch is provided on the full-day tours.

Rock Climbing

Krabi is famous for its limestone cliffs and hosts the Krabi Rock & Fire International Contest each April. There are over 150 pegged routes both inland and offshore in the Phra Nang Bay area. Operators in Ao Nang and Railay can advise on the best courses to suit people of different ages and levels of skill and fitness. Most routes are challenging but there are also several beginner climbs.

Equipment rentals, instruction and guides are all available. The following companies are recommended.

Hot Rock Climbing School: Bobo Plaza, Hat Railay West; tel: 0-7562 2245; www.railayadventure. com. Half- and full-day courses and three-day sport climbing for the more experienced.

Railay Rock Climbing Shop: Hat Railay West; www.railayrockclimbing shop.com (contact through online email form). This team, run by Thailand's top female climber, offers courses from half- day upwards and includes deep water climbing.

Diving and Snorkelling

There are a number of outstanding dive sites close to Ao Nang and Railay beaches. Dive shops along the Ao Nang and Railay beach fronts offer day trips to these sites plus live-aboards to those further afield in the Andaman Sea. Snorkelling trips to nearby islands (such as Ko Poda and Ko Kai) can be booked with any one of several tour agents along the beach front.

Kon-Tiki: 161/1 Moo 2, Ao Nang; tel: 0-7563 7826; www.kontiki-thailand.com. This company of 30-years' experience has a full range of PADI courses available

plus daily snorkelling and dive trips and live-aboards that travel as far as the Similans. They also have centres in Phuket, Khao Lak and Ko Lanta.

Scuba Addicts: 245/5 Moo 2, Ao Nang; tel: 0-7563 7394; www. scuba-addicts.com. Reputable operator offering PADI courses as well as day trips and live-aboards.

Thai Boxing

Ao Nang Krabi Thai Boxing Stadium: 100 Moo 3, Ao Nang; tel: 08-1979 6482; www.aonang-thai boxing.com. One of the largest stadiums in the south, with seating for over 2,000 people (and ringside sofa seating for a closer view). Matches are held on Monday and Friday evenings. They also have a training camp if you want to give it a try.

Spas

Let's Sea, Let's Relax: 86/2 Moo 2, Ao Nang; tel: 08-7674 4005. There are several treatments at this spa, including Thai, aromatherapy, hand and foot reflexology and various scrubs. It's a clean, relaxing place a notch up in ambiance and price from the cheap beachside massages. Manicures and pedicures also available.

ABOVE: Texrock Climbing in Krabi.

Mandara Spa: Sheraton Krabi Beach Resort, 155 Moo 2, Hat Khlong Muang; tel: 0-7562 8000; www.sheratonkrabi.com. This luxury experience has massages combining elements of Japanese, Hawaiian, Thai, Swedish and Balinese and has several Arabic hammam treatments.

Villa Spa: Ao Nang Villa Resort, Ao Nang; tel: 0-7563 7271; www.aonangvilla.com. Located in a Thai-style house, the Villa Spa has specialised treatments such as a face-lift massage to tone skin and increase elasticity, and a hot-sand compress to relieve tired and stressed muscles.

KO PHI PHI

Nightlife
Ao Ton Sai

Nightlife on Ko Phi Phi is predictably concentrated on Ao Ton Sai, with mainly small open-air bars making up the scene.

Apache: This huge sea-facing bar is a popular place to relax and chat. Features money-off deals on "buckets" of whiskey, gin, vodka and cocktails throughout the night.

Carlitos: Small but very popular bar that goes quite insane after midnight, with crowds spilling out on to the beach. Great party atmosphere.

Reggae Bar: The island's biggest, and many would argue best, party venue with a huge Thai-boxing ring on the ground floor (you're welcome to get in and try it out) and a dance floor on the open-air upper level.

Outdoor Activities
Rock Climbing

Spider Monkey: tel: 08 9728 1608; www.spidermonkeyphiphi.com. Phi Phi doesn't have the climbing cachet of Krabi, but these guys run half- and full-day trips from fun climbs to solo open water, where you dive off the rock face into the sea.

ABOVE: beach restaurant.

Diving and Snorkelling

Ko Phi Phi seems to have a dive shop at every turn, all offering pretty much the same trips at very similar prices. The only obvious difference is in the attitude of the staff. With so much competition, there is a lot of pressure from street touts, who do go for the hard sell. Generally, the ones who don't try so hard for business are those who have better reputations.

The following is a selection of what is on offer:

PP Aquanauts Scuba: tel: 0-7560 1213; www.aquanauts-scuba.com. This was one of the first dive centres on the island and has friendly and experienced staff. Strong emphasis is placed on personal instruction, with a maximum of four divers per instructor.

Phi Phi Barakuda Diving Center: tel: 0-7560 1006; www.phiphibarakuda.com. Friendly and informative dive shop, although sometimes a little pushy.

Island Divers: mobile tel: 0-9873 2205; www.islanddiverspp.com. Friendly and professional staff at this centre offer PADI dive courses, day trips and live-aboard

diving, as well as snorkelling and kayaking tours.

KO LANTA

Nightlife

Most of the action takes place on Ao Phra Ae, centred around bars set up along the beach.

Cheeky Monkey Bar: Hat Klong Dao. Run by an Aussie guy supplying the usual bonhomie, with occasional live music and sport on TV.

Opium Bar: Ao Prae Ae. Settle into the relaxed scene at this bar/club, which is regularly one of the busiest in the area. They have DJs spinning at the decks every night.

Why Not Bar: Hat Kantiang; www.facebook.com/whynotbarkohlanta. Straw mats on the beach, fire shows and the chance to jam with the live band every night.

Outdoor Activities
Diving and Snorkelling

The waters around **Mu Ko Lanta Marine National Park** are home to some of Thailand's best snorkelling and diving sites (see page 258). Most dive operators are found at Ban Sala Dan, while upmarket resorts usually have a dive centre on their premises. The following is a selection of what is on offer:

Blue Planet Divers: Ban Sala Dan; tel: 0-7566 8165; www.blueplanetdivers.net. Qualified instructors offer extensive courses and dive trips aboard a modern air-conditioned boat. Multilingual staff are on hand.

Dive & Relax: 223 Moo 2, Ao Phra Ae; tel: 08-4842 2191; www.diveandrelax.com. There is a raft of choices here, whether you want a introductory dip into the underwater world or do your PADI qualification. They have a maximum of four divers per dive master and to save time offer practical training online.

TRANG, SATUN AND SONGKHLA

Thailand's **deep south** is where you will find picture-perfect beaches and get a taste of Thai-Muslim culture and cuisine. While Trang and Satun provinces shelter pristine isolated islands, Hat Yai in Songkhla province offers bullfighting and bargain shopping.

Bangkok

Misconceptions abound when it comes to Thailand's southernmost provinces. Many Thais regard the region's predominantly Muslim residents as rough and prone to violence. The region is also one of the country's poorest. Relatively few people visit the area due to its scant tourism infrastructure. The provinces of Narathiwat, Yala and Pattani should be expressly avoided as they are in the midst of a violent separatist insurgency, and, at the time of writing, most Western embassies were also advising against travel to Songkhla. Check for updates if you decide to travel to Hat Yai. Otherwise, Trang and Satun provinces, covered in this chapter, are perfectly safe to visit.

A vibrant melting pot

Sampling Thai-Muslim culture and cuisine is a particular attraction. Some of the most fascinating highlights of the entire southern region are found in the deep south. These include the pristine islands of Ko Tarutao Marine National Park (where one season of the TV series *Survivor* was filmed), the vibrant cultural melting pot that is Songkhla, and Trang's diverse island life. If you want to avoid the crowds and sample some of Thailand's unadulterated nature and culture, head for the deep south.

TRANG PROVINCE

Trang Province holds what is probably the greatest variety of attractions of any of the provinces in the deep south, as well as an interesting urban centre in Trang Town. North of the province, there are picture-perfect beaches and islands with ample accommodation, a wealth of outdoor activities and good food. To the south of Trang, the beaches and islands are

Main attractions

THAM LOD
THAM MORAKOT
KO KRADAN
KO TARUTAO MARINE NATIONAL PARK
KO LIPE
KU YU

LEFT: the village of Hua Laem on Ko Muk.
RIGHT: a coffee shop in Trang Town.

Shadow puppetry,
common in Thailand's
deep-south region, is an
art form that has its
roots in nearby
Malaysia.

BELOW: the Anantara Si
Kao resort on Hat
Chang Lang.

more isolated but they offer some fascinating wildlife and the chance to observe everyday life on an island.

Trang Town

Trang Town ❶ is a pleasant place with a predominantly Chinese population and enough attractions to warrant at least an overnight stay. While Trang is well known among Thais as the birthplace of Chuan Leekpai, a former prime minister, travellers will be more taken by another legacy – its food. From Chinese-style coffee shops to one of Thailand's best night markets – located along Thanon Ruenrom – the food in Trang is one of its highlights. Trang Town also has a very colourful morning market. Every morning, vendors sell a plethora of fresh produce on Thanon Ratchadamnoen and Thanon Sathani, while copious amounts of seafood line the streets behind the Ko Teng Hotel.

Thanks to its Chinese inhabitants, every October Trang plays host to a Vegetarian Festival that rivals the one celebrated in Phuket. During the week-long festival, the frenzied faithful, having abstained from meat, alcohol and sex for a week, walk over red-hot coals and skewer themselves with all sorts of sharp instruments.

Trang's beaches

A string of secluded beaches along the Trang coast and several islands off the coast are worth seeking out. Trang's formidably long 119km (74-mile)-long coastline from Hat Pak Meng to Hat Chao Mai, plus a number of lovely islands nearby, are part of the **Hat Chao Mai National Park**.

Some 40km (25 miles) west of Trang Town is **Hat Pak Meng**, a rather shallow beach that gets quite muddy at low tide. There are a few places to stay here, a string of seafood restaurants and a pier at the northern end where boats depart for trips to nearby islands. But apart from these, Pak Meng doesn't have much going for it. It's very much a local scene with Thais picnicking and having a good time on its shores at weekends.

South of Hat Pak Meng is **Hat Chang Lang ❷**, a lovely, isolated beach with greyish-white sands and backed by soaring casuarina trees. The beach is only swimmable at high

tide; when the tide is low it exposes large sand banks that are great to walk on. The only hotel of note here is the **Anantara Si Kao** (formerly the Amari Trang Beach Resort), right on the beach and unexpectedly luxurious for such a remote area. When the conditions are right, the sunsets can be truly spectacular here, bathing the horizon, studded with islands and limestone crags, in an orange glow.

Beyond Hat Chang Lang are more beaches – **Hat Yong Ling**, **Hat Yao** and **Hat Chao Mai** – but both facilities and accommodation becomes very sparse. Nearby Ban Chao Mai is where the harbour is located, a jump-off point for tours of various islands off the coast.

Inland of Hat Yao are the caves at **Tham Lod**, which make for an interesting day trip. Reached by kayak, the journey winds its way past mangrove forests and enters a cave through a tiny gap. A 10-minute paddle in darkness follows until you emerge into a

hidden lagoon surrounded by mangroves and towering limestone walls.

Trang's islands

About 16km (10 miles) southeast of Hat Pak Meng is **Ko Hai ③** (also known as Ko Ngai). It actually lies in Krabi Province, but is more accessible from Trang. Ringed by clear water and coral reefs, it has several low-key resorts and a near-perfect swimming beach on its eastern side.

Approximately 8km (5 miles) south of Ko Hai (and facing Hat Chang Lang) is **Ko Muk ④**. Boats to Ko Muk usually arrive at the small fishing village of Hua Laem, on the east side of the island, which is home to hundreds of permanent inhabitants and numerous rubber plantations, giving it a rural atmosphere. Ko Muk's finest beach is the secluded **Hat Farang** on the west coast, a cove-like inlet ringed by limestone cliffs not unlike Railay Bay in Krabi. The highlight of Ko Muk is the amazing

The streets of many towns in the region are lined with elaborate wooden birdcages holding doves. These birds are renowned for their cooing, with contests organised and awards given out.

The National Museum in Satun is housed in the former Kuden Mansion.

and popular **Tham Morakot**, "Emerald Cave", in the northern part of the island. During low-tide, it's possible to swim through this partially submerged cave, the last few metres of which is done in complete darkness, to emerge at a hidden beach surrounded by towering limestone cliffs and lush greenery.

Another must-see island is **Ko Kradan** ❺, about 6km (4 miles) southwest of Ko Muk, which some consider to be the most beautiful island in the area. The beaches are blinding-white and there are some nice reefs offshore. Most of the accommodation on the island is rather ramshackle, one exception being the luxury **Seven Seas Resort**, and is mainly visited by day-trippers who come to laze on its beaches, or to snorkel and dive. The Anantara resort on mainland Trang runs the plush **Anantara Beach Club** on Ko Kradan's stunning **Hat Na Ko**, with deckchairs, water-sports facilities and a restaurant but, unfortunately, only hotel guests are allowed access.

Southwest of Ko Kradan are two less-frequently visited islands. The first is **Ko Libong** ❻, the largest island in the group and known for its wildlife. The waters around the island are one of Thailand's remaining habitats of the dugong, a marine mammal also known as the manatee. **Libong Beach Resort** (tel: 0-7522 5205), one of only two resorts on the island, offers snorkelling trips that take visitors into the waters populated by the dugongs.

Southeast of Ko Libong is **Ko Sukorn** ❼, home to just four villages and very few cars. The island's beaches are concentrated on the western shore, the most attractive of these is **Hat Talo Yai**, home to some of the island's sprinkle of low-key resorts.

SATUN PROVINCE

Sharing a border with Malaysia in the far south of Thailand, remote **Satun Province** is a mountainous area, and is, in many ways, more Malay than Thai in terms of culture. Despite this, Satun has successfully managed to avoid the conflicts of its neighbouring provinces to the east, and is a safe area to travel to. Satun Town offers no real attractions, but nearby lies

what is possibly the highlight of the entire deep-south region, the pristine islands of Ko Tarutao Marine National Park.

Satun Town

Set in a lovely green valley walled by towering limestone cliffs, **Satun Town ❽** is a pleasant enough place, but in all aspects is more of a transit point than a destination in itself. The town's only real tourist attraction is the elegant Sino-Portuguese **Kuden Mansion**, a house originally built to accommodate King Rama V for a visit that never materialised. In 1902, the building became the governor's mansion before it was turned into Satun's **National Museum** (Wed–Sun 9am–4pm; charge). The restored building features mainly exhibits on southern-Thai life.

Ko Tarutao Marine N P

The **Ko Tarutao Marine National Park ❾** (mid-Nov–mid-May; charge) encompasses more than 1,400 sq km (541 sq miles) of the Andaman Sea and comprises 51 islands. Only three of the islands are inhabited, mainly by *chao lay* (sea gypsies). Established as a national park in 1974, the forests and seas that comprise Tarutao are home to Thailand's most pristine coral reefs – said to harbour 25 percent of the world's tropical fish species – and an incredible variety of fauna. The islands support creatures such as langurs, crab-eating macaques and wild pigs, as well as aquatic mammals such as whales, dolphins and dugongs (manatees). Several kinds of turtle lay their eggs on the largest island, Ko Tarutao, especially on Ao Sone beach on the west coast. This spectacle can be witnessed every January.

The marine park is divided into two distinct parts: **Tarutao Archipelago**, located 45km (28 miles) off the coast of mainland Satun, and the **Adang-Rawi Archipelago**, about 50km (30 miles) west of Ko Tarutao

itself. The islands of the latter group are known for their excellent dive spots, and include the park's most popular island, Ko Lipe. The park is only open during the dry season, typically mid-November to mid-May. Boat trips to the islands set off from the fishing town of **Pak Bara**, 60km (40 miles) north of Satun Town.

Ko Tarutao

Imposing **Ko Tarutao ❿**, the largest of the park's islands, is an excellent place for hiking and exploring caves, or simply relaxing on the wide beach. The 152-sq-km (59-sq-mile) island is home to the park headquarters (tel: 0-7478 3485), located behind the vast stretch of powdery white sand on the western shore known as **Ao Phante Malacca**. Behind the park office, at the end of a short path, is **Toe Boo Cliff**, which provides great views over the bay from its craggy summit after a 30-minute climb.

Daily longtail boat trips depart from the park headquarters for **Tham Jarakhe** (Crocodile Cave). Only accessible during low tide, the cave was once supposedly home to saltwater

Hornbills on the island of Ko Tarutao.

BELOW: view from Toe Boo Cliff, Ko Tarutao.

TIP

The southwest monsoon brings heavy rain from May to Oct to the Andaman Coast, including Trang and Satun. Songkhla, which sits on the Gulf of Thailand coast, experiences the worst rains from Nov to Feb.

crocodiles. To the south of Ao Phante Malacca are two scenic beaches, **Ao Jak** and **Ao Molae**. To get to the next beach, **Ao Sone**, an important nesting ground for endangered turtles from September to May (and especially January), requires a good 2-hour walk.

On the island's eastern side is **Ao Taloh Wow**. During the 1930s and 1940s, this was a place of exile for Thai prisoners, both criminal and political; at one point in 1941, more than 3,000 prisoners were held here. Ko Tarutao made the news again in 2002 when **Ao Rusi**, located on the northeast coast of the island, was used as a setting for the American reality television show *Survivor*. It gave rise to some controversy as Thai environmentalists feared that the virgin environment would be irrevocably harmed. In the end, hard business won out. But to its credit, CBS, the show's producers, left the area more or less in the pristine condition it was in when the film crew first arrived.

Ko Lipe and Ko Adang

BELOW: arriving by boat at Hat Na Ko on Ko Lipe.

Tiny **Ko Lipe** ⑪, 40km (25 miles) from Ko Tarutao, is the most popular

and also the most developed island in the park. Unlike on Ko Tarutao, some of the accommodation on Ko Lipe is open year-round, but access to the island greatly depends upon the state of the weather, which is generally best from October to May. Despite the fact that Ko Lipe lies within the national park boundaries, the approximately 1,000 *chao lay*, or sea gypsies, who inhabit the island have gained the right to develop sections of it. This accounts for the largely disorganised and often unattractive development that has taken root. Fortunately, there isn't enough of it to detract from the natural beauty of the island.

Boats from Pak Bara arrive at **Hat Na Ko** ("front of the island") in the north, where there is some accommodation. A short walk from Na Ko via a dirt path is **Sunset Beach**, probably the most beautiful of Ko Lipe's beaches. It harbours only a few small-scale resorts and offers views of the neighbouring islands. On the south side of Ko Lipe is **Ao Pattaya**, with its long sandy coastline and clear water, making it the most popular beach and home to most of the island's accommodation and bars.

For those interested in diving and snorkelling, Ko Lipe's prime position in the middle of the Adang-Rawi Archipelago makes for easy access to nearby dive sites. Popular spots in this area include the reefs surrounding **Ko Rawi**, **Ko Yang** and **Ko Hin Sorn**.

Visible from the shores of Sunset Beach, and less than 2km (1 mile) away, is towering **Ko Adang** ⑫, which has a densely forested interior, lovely white-sand beaches and basic national park accommodation. Popular with day-tripping snorkellers, jungle trails inland lead to waterfalls and scenic viewpoints.

SONGKHLA PROVINCE

Songkhla Province is an oft-overlooked destination. Although the flashy border city of Hat Yai draws thousands of Malaysian and Singaporean tourists each year, Western tourists typically give the entire province a wide berth. This is unfortunate as Hat Yai isn't nearly as seedy as it's thought to be, and offers great food, bargain shopping and the chance to see the southern-Thai pastime of bullfighting. Note: Hat Yai has been the victim of bomb attacks and at the time of writing most Western governments were advising against travel to Songkhla. Check for updates. Directly east of Hat Yai, the tiny provincial capital, Songkhla Town, is a fascinating melting pot of southern Thai culture, with decent beaches, interesting temples and what is perhaps the best of the deep south's famous night markets.

Songkhla Town

Little-visited **Songkhla Town** ⑬, 25km (16 miles) east of Hat Yai, is one of the deep south's most memorable towns. Essentially Chinese, but with a visible Muslim minority, Songkhla Town is located on a finger of land separating the Gulf of Thailand from the Thale Sap Songkhla, a large brackish lake. On the north coast of this promontory is **Hat Samila**, a long white-sand beach marked by a bronze mermaid statue, a popular photo spot. While not great for swimming, the beach is nice enough for a stroll to watch the sun set or for a meal at one of the many beach-side restaurants.

Songkhla Town's charming old enclave, located between Thanon Nakhorn Nok and Thanon Nang Ngaam, still possesses a number of Sino-Portuguese buildings and numerous Chinese-style restaurants and old coffee shops that haven't changed in decades.

Songkhla National Museum (Wed–Sun 9am–4pm; charge), housed in an elegant Sino-Portuguese mansion that was also at one time the city's poorhouse, is a good place to while away an hour or so if you're passing through town. Inside are exhibits of art, sculpture, pottery, ceramics and furniture from all the major periods of Thai history.

Songkhla's most famous temple, **Wat Matchimawat** (daily 8am–6pm; free), is located directly west of

Yaksha statue outside Wat Matchimawat.

BELOW LEFT: Songkhla night market. **BELOW RIGHT:** Songkhla National Museum.

Songkhla Town's Sino-Portuguese architecture.

BELOW: the view from Khao Tang Kuan.

the old town. Its highlights are the beautiful temple paintings, probably executed in the early Rattanakosin period more than 200 years ago.

Another worthwhile temple to visit is the hilltop compound of **Khao Tang Kuan** (daily 8am– 7pm; charge). Accessible by air-conditioned tram, construction of this temple complex, influenced by European style, was originally commissioned by King Rama V. It offers great views over Songkhla Town and Ko Yo island.

Around Songkhla

Directly east of Songkhla, in the salty waters of the Thale Sap, is the island of **Ko Yo** , an excellent day trip from Songkhla or Hat Yai. In recent years the island has become something of a cultural tourism spot. The island is famous for its hand-loomed cotton weaving called *phaa kaw yaw*. The best place to buy this fabric, either in lengths or as clothing, is at the central market.

Also on Ko Yo is the interesting **Thaksin Folklore Museum** (daily 8.30am–5pm; charge; tel: 0-7433 1184), which highlights the history, architecture, traditions and handicrafts of the people of South Thailand. One exhibit is dedicated to coconut-milk scrapers, de-huskers and grinders, emphasising the importance of coconuts as a cash crop in the south.

Another worthwhile sight is the **Khao Saen** Muslim fishing village, located about 5km (3 miles) from Songkhla Town. Look out for the rows of colourful prawn-fishing boats that are docked each evening along the beach. The intricately decorated boats, embellished with dragon prows, make for an interesting photo subject.

Hat Yai

The sprawling and featureless **Hat Yai** is one of the largest cities in the south, and is predominantly Chinese in character. Unfortunately, it has become a tourist destination for all the wrong reasons – it attracts busloads of Malaysians and Singaporeans who travel across the border from Malaysia to frequent the numerous sleazy massage parlours and nightclubs that seem to line every street in Hat Yai. There are no real draws in Hat Yai, but the shopping and great food plus ample accommodation options on offer will appeal to those who have just come from one of the islands.

If in Hat Yai during the beginning of the month, make sure to catch the particularly colourful southern-Thai spectacle of **bullfighting**. This is held on the first Saturday of the month at the **Noen Khum Thong Stadium** (charge; tel: 0-7438 8753), located about 10km (6 miles) west of Hat Yai. Unlike the Western version of the sport that involves a matador, as practised in Spain, Thai bullfights only involve two bulls going head to head with each other and locking horns, trying to force the opponent into submission.   ❑

TRANG, SATUN AND SONGKHLA

TRANSPORT

TRANG TOWN AND BEACHES

Getting There

By Air

Trang Airport (tel: 0-7521 8224) is located about 4km (2 miles) south of Trang Town. There are daily flights between Bangkok and Trang on **Nok Air**. From the airport, *tuk tuks* cost around B150 to Trang Town, and World Travel (tel: 0 7521 4010/1) operates minivans to Trang Town (B500) or to Trang's beaches (B1,000). Alternatively, resorts also arrange airport transportation for guests.

It is also possible to fly to Krabi, where there are more air connections (see page 260) and then take the taxi to either Trang Town or directly to its beaches for B1,800–2,000. The ride will take about 75 minutes.

By Train, Bus and Taxi

There are two overnight trains daily between Bangkok's **Hualamphong Station** and Trang, taking about 15 hours. Buses leave Bangkok's **Southern Bus Terminal** for Trang daily, taking about 12 hours. The bus terminal in Trang is at Th. Huay Yot. Ticket prices vary, depending on type of bus.

In addition, there are bus connections from nearby destinations such as Phuket (4 hour journey time), Krabi (2½ hours) and Hat Yai (4 hours).

Getting Around

Motorcycle taxi and *tuk-tuk* trips within Trang Town cost between B20–B30 for short rides. Taxis and minivans to Trang's beaches will cost between B300–400.

The jump-off point for Ko Hai and Ko Muk is Pak Meng pier, while the pier at Ban Chao Mai serves Ko Kradan, Ko Libong and Ko Sukorn; from these piers daily boats serve the islands. Or you can charter a longtail boat; be sure to negotiate the price (B200–400, depending on distance). Most island resorts will arrange transfers if you have booked a room with them.

SATUN AND KO TARUTAO NATIONAL PARK

Getting There

Getting to Satun isn't easy. The closest airport to Satun Town is in Hat Yai (see page 280), 130km (80 miles) away on the east coast. From Hat Yai, there are buses and taxis that make the trip to Satun Town. Or travel by road from Trang, 140km (87 miles) away.

From Bangkok's **Hualamphong Station**, there are five trains a day to Hat Yai, from where you can travel by road to Satun. The train journey alone will take 14 to 18 hours, and all are essentially overnight services. From Bangkok's **Southern Bus Terminal** there are several air-conditioned buses every day bound for Satun, taking at least 13 hours to cover the 973km (605 miles).

Getting Around

Downtown Satun Town is compact enough to walk to most destinations. Motorcycle taxis and *tuk-tuks* are also available, and should cost B20–30 between any point in town. For information on getting to Ko Tarutao National Park, see below.

Ko Tarutao N P

Boats to Ko Tarutao National Park leave from Pak Bara, 60km (40 miles) north of Satun Town. Although in Satun Province, Pak Bara is more easily accessible from Hat Yai and Trang than from Satun Town; both Hat Yai and Trang have direct bus services to the pier. From Satun Town you can hire a *songthaew* to take you to Pak Bara. At Pak Bara pier are numerous touts and agencies selling tickets to the islands. A round-trip ticket costs B900 and allows ticket-holders to disembark at any of the islands. There are twice-daily boats leaving Pak Bara, at noon and at 3.30pm. The trip to Ko Tarutao takes around 1 hour and Ko Adang or Ko Lipe 3 to 4 hours.

SONGKHLA AND HAT YAI

Getting There

Hat Yai Airport (tel: 0-7422 7000) is located 12km (8 miles) from the city and is a major hub for both international and domestic flights. It is serviced by several airlines, including Air-Asia, Nok Air, Tiger Airways, Malaysia Airlines, Orient Thai and Thai Airways.

From Bangkok, there are five trains a day to Hat Yai, 900km (560 miles) away. Travel time is 14 to 18 hours, depending on the type of train, so it is best to book a sleeper on the overnight train. Several air-conditioned buses depart daily from Bangkok's Southern Bus Terminal on the 14-hour trip to Hat Yai.

Hat Yai is less than 50km (30 miles) from the Malaysian border, and it's possible to travel between the two countries. There are countless tourist buses that run between Hat Yai and major cities in Malaysia, including Penang and Kuala Lumpur, and even as far as Singapore. Contact any of the travel agents in downtown Hat Yai for details and tickets. There are also local buses, taxis and a daily train that make the hour-long trip to Padang Besar, the nearest town on the Malaysian side of the border.

Getting Around

There are plenty of motorcycle taxis and *songthaew*s within Hat Yai and Songkhla. The latter is approximately 25km (16 miles) east of Hat Yai, and can easily be reached by either bus, minivan or taxi.

ACCOMMODATION LISTINGS

TRANG TOWN AND BEACHES

TRANG TOWN

Thumrin Thana Hotel
69/8 Th. Huay Yot
Tel: 0-7521 1211
www.thumrin.co.th
Largely orientated towards business travellers, this is an old style hotel. It has a convenient downtown location, a swimming pool, restaurant and a bar. Rooms are available at higher price levels, but for value for money the cheapest are best. (289 rooms) **$**

HAT CHANG LANG

Anantara Si Kao
Hat Chang Lang
Tel: 0-7520 5888
www.sikao.anantara.com
The only international-class hotel on Hat Chang Lang. Large, tastefully furnished rooms and capacious villas, excellent spa and fine restaurants. The beach, unfortunately, is shallow even at high tide and is better for long walks rather than swimming. To make up for this, the hotel has a private beach club on Ko Kradan island for its guests. (138 rooms) **$$$**

KO HAI

CoCo Cottage
Tel: 08-9724 9225
www.coco-cottage.com
Features Balinese-style wooden bungalows with open-air bathrooms, only a few steps from the beach. Air-conditioning only available at night. (28 rooms) **$$**

Fantasy Resort
Tel: 0-7521 5923
www.haifantasy.com
Spacious air-conditioned bungalows and suites at a range of prices. Also provides a decent variety of services, including a pool, internet access, a spa and movie nights at weekends. (40 rooms) **$**

KO MUK

Koh Mook Charlie Beach Resort
Tel: 0-7520 3281
www.kohmookcharlieresort.com
Located on Hat Farang, with a range of decent rooms including budget bamboo chalets with fans, plus internet access, kayaks, movie screenings, and a nice location among the cliffs and coconut trees. Good restaurant on site. (80 rooms) **$**

KO KRADAN

Seven Seas Resort
Tel: 0-7520 3389
www.sevenseasresorts.com
The island's first luxury resort, these designer villas offer a blend of indoor and outdoor living. Rooms have a back-to-nature theme, with terrazzo finishing and generous woodwork, while open-air bath-

rooms have rain-showers. (39 rooms and villas) $$$$

KO LIBONG

Libong Beach Resort
Tel: 0-7522 5205
www.libongbeachresort.com

The lovely white-sand beach here is a great viewpoint for the daily sunset. The resort has fan and aircon rooms, a family-friendly atmosphere and staff can organise snorkelling trips to other islands. Good dive centre on site. (22 rooms) $

KO SUKORN

Sukorn Beach Bungalows
Tel: 0-7520 7707
www.sukorn-island-trang.com
A low-key resort with a family atmosphere. Offers cheaper fan-

cooled as well as more expensive air-conditioned rooms. A range of tours is also available. The resort is well known for its efforts to work with the local community. No children under seven are permitted, however. (20 rooms) $

SATUN AND KO TARUTAO NATIONAL PARK

SATUN TOWN

Pinnacle Satun Wangmai Hotel
43 Th. Satun Thani
Tel: 0-7471 1607/8
www.pinnaclehotels.com
Satun's only "upmarket" hotel lies slightly outside the town centre, but is nevertheless a comfortable place to stay. The downtown hotels are really not worth considering. (108 rooms) $

KO TARUTAO NP

Ko Tarutao

Lodgings on Ao Phante Malacca and Ao Taloh Wow are available Nov to May. Book with the park authorities (tel: 0-7478 3485). Electricity only available 6pm to 6am.

Ko Lipe

Bundhaya Resort
Ao Pattaya, Koh Lipe

Tel. 0-7475 0248-9
www.bundhayaresort.com
This large operation on Pattaya beach has bungalows in six different styles (and prices). Beach-front restaurant and massage centre. (82 rooms) $
Green View Beach Resort
Hat Pattaya
Tel 08 2830 3843
www.greenviewkohlipe.com
Bamboo and thatch bungalows amid gardens right on the beach. This is the busiest

beach so noise levels are high. Boat trips available. $
Serendipity Beach Resort
Sunrise Beach
Tel: 08-8395 5158
www.serendipityresort-kohlipe.com
These well-crafted wooden bungalows with thatched roofs nestled in the hillside close to the beach have good sea views. The bar-restaurant serves good Thai, Western and fusion food. (12 rooms) $$$

SONGKHLA AND HAT YAI

SONGKHLA

BP Samila Beach Hotel & Resort
8 Th. Ratchadamnoen
Tel: 0-7444 0222
This well-located hotel is at the end of Hat Samila, near the famous mermaid statue. It offers large but dated rooms, the more expensive of which have views over the Gulf of Thailand. A range of facilities such as a pool, fitness centre, spa, coffee shop

and restaurants are available. (228 rooms) $
Pavilion Songkhla Hotel
17 Th. Platha
Tel: 0-7444 1850
www.pavilionhotels.com
One of the taller buildings in Songkhla, the Pavilion hotel is one of only two higher-end hotels in the town. Featuring the amenities one would expect in a hotel of this category, in addition to a snooker room, karaoke lounge and Thai massage facilities. (179 rooms) $

HAT YAI

Centara Hat Yai
3 Th. Sanehanusorn
Tel: 0-7435 2222
www.centarahotelsresorts.com
Located in the heart of Hat Yai, above the Central Department Store, this imposing hotel, one of the best in town, offers comfortable rooms plus a pan-Asian restaurant and a spa on site. (200 rooms) $
Sakura Grand View
186 Th. Niphat Uthit 3
Tel: 0-7435 5700

www.sakuragrandviewhotel.com
This popular hotel, close to the train station, boasts a central location, helpful staff and spotlessly clean and tidy rooms. There is also a large spa on site. (291 rooms) $

PRICE CATEGORIES

Price categories show the starting price for a double room without breakfast and taxes:
$ = under US$70
$$ = US$70–130
$$$ = US$130–250
$$$$ = over US$250

Trang Town and Beaches

Trang Town

Thai/Chinese

Trang is particularly well known for its old-world Chinese-style coffee shops, known locally as *raan kopi*. At these places, typically open from morning until afternoon, locally produced coffee (*kopi*) can be enjoyed on marble-topped tables along with Chinese steamed buns or Trang's famous barbecued pork. Try the longstanding **Yuchiang** on Th. Phraram VI (daily 7am–5pm; $); or the restaurant located below the **Ko Teng Hotel** (daily 8am–5pm; tel: 0-7521 8622; $), just a few blocks north.

Raan Khao Tom Phui
Th. Phraram IV
Tel: 0-7521 0127
Open daily 5pm–2am.
This unpretentious restaurant, popular with locals and open only in the evenings, is an excellent place to fill up on spicy Chinese-Thai favourites such as *khanaa fai daeng*, Chinese kale flash-fried with chillies and garlic, or *hoi lay phat phrik phao*, fresh clams fried with hot chilli paste. $

Trang Night Market
Cnr Th. Ratchadamnoen and Th. Phraram VI
Open daily 5pm–midnight.
Trang's night market is one of the culinary highlights of the deep-south region. Every evening, the small street at the corner of Ratchadamnoen and Phraram VI becomes an endless parade of *raan khao kaeng*, or rice-and-curry vendors, many of whom have roadside seating. It looks daunting but the food is mostly fresh. Try the local favourite, *khanom jeen*, rice noodles eaten with curry sauce and vegetables. $

Thai and Western

Trang Thana
Thumrin Thana Hotel, 69/8 Th. Huay Yot
Tel: 0-7521 1211
www.thumrin-thana.com
Open daily 6am–midnight.
Basic hotel coffee shop that serves a good selection of Thai dishes. The breakfast and lunchtime buffets, which mainly cater to large tour groups, are good value for money, but the à la carte selections are all very reasonably priced, too. $$

Hat Pak Meng

This sleepy beach by the Pak Meng pier is very much a local scene, swarming with mainly Thai picnickers at weekends. There is a string of seafood restaurants that come alive in the evenings, but most of them are quite basic and there is nothing that stands out, except perhaps the restaurant at **Lay Trang Resort** (tel: 0-7527 4027). Seafood cooked Thai-style is well prepared here.

Hat Chang Lang

Acqua Restaurant and Leelawadee

Anantara Si Kao,
Hat Chang Lang
Tel: 0-7520 5888
www.anantara.com
If staying at the Anantara Si Kao resort at Hat Chang Lang, you are virtually forced to eat at its restaurants as there are hardly any good eateries within walking distance of the hotel. So it's a good thing that the Anantara makes great efforts to serve some fine food (and at prices that won't break your wallet). **Acqua**, on the first floor serves Italian fare in elegant and stylish surroundings (reservations are advised). On the lower level is the **Leelewadee** restaurant. Decorated with a bright orange and marine theme, there is excellent Thai food on offer here, both à la carte and also some good-value sets. Massaman curry served in a clay pot is a favourite. $$$

BELOW: a selection of Thai fruit.

SATUN AND KO TARUTAO NATIONAL PARK

Food options for the tourist are predictably meagre in Satun Town. On the islands of Ko Tarutao National Park, eating out is largely confined to the guest houses that are situated there.

Thai and Western

Satun Night Market
Th. Satun Thani
Open: daily 5pm–midnight.
Satun's night market is one of the best in southern Thailand. The quality of the food is good, and the emphasis here is on rich curries. As Muslims are a majority in Satun, most of the food is *halal*. **$**

Time
43 Th. Satun Thani
Tel: 0-7471 2286
Open daily 11am–11pm.
Features very good Thai and decent Western-style food. Highlights from the menu include the sea bass, and the excellent but intimidating-sounding "fish-head noodles". **$**

ABOVE: cooking meat skewers.

SONGKHLA AND HAT YAI

SONGKHLA

Thai

Raan Tae Hiang Iw
85 Th. Nang Ngam
Tel: 0-7431 1505
Open: daily L and D.
Located in the heart of Songkhla's old district, this Chinese-Thai eatery, known to locals as "Tae", is a local legend. Highly recommended are the *yam mamuang*, a spicy salad of sour mangoes and dried shrimp, and *tom yam haeng*, a delicious "dry" version of the famous *tom yam* soup. **$**

Songkhla Night Market
Th. Wachira
Open: daily 5pm–midnight.
Songkhla's night market, probably the largest in the region, has Chinese, Thai and Muslim food, all at very low prices. To get there, tell the minivan or motorcycle driver to go to "Wachira", the name of the road where the market is held. **$**

HAT YAI

The lively strip downtown known as Th. Thammanoonvithi has a wide variety of restaurants to entice hungry customers.

Western and Thai

The Swan
129-131 Th. Thammanoonvithi
Tel: 0-7435 4310
Open: daily 11am–midnight.
This welcoming English-style pub is a great place to relax with a draught beer. Features a diverse selection of Thai and English dishes. **$$**

Thai

Hat Yai Night Market
Th. Montri 1 (near the Pakistan Mosque)
Open daily 5pm–midnight.
Hat Yai's night market has a mix of Muslim and seafood dishes. Though not as diverse as the offerings at Songkhla's night market, it is still a great place to sample local food, such as the Muslim influenced *khao mok kai*, or rice cooked with chicken and spices. **$**

Sky Buffet
Lee Gardens Plaza Hotel,
29 Th. Prachatipat
Tel: 0-7426 1111
www.leeplaza.com
Open: daily L and D.
This hotel, one of the tallest in Hat Yai, offers a Thai-style buffet lunch and dinner at its 33rd-storey restaurant with panoramic views. Enjoy all-you-can-eat Thai favourites such as *kaeng khiao waan*, or green curry, as well as the view over downtown Hat Yai. **$**

Sor Heung
79/16 Th. Thammanoonvithi
Mobile tel: 0-1890 3455
Open: daily L and D.
Expect good Thai-Chinese food at this restaurant, which has branches all over Hat Yai. Choose from a variety of fresh ingredients to be flash-fried or made into a Thai spicy salad called *yam*, or simply pick from the diverse pre-cooked Chinese-style dishes on offer. **$**

PRICE CATEGORIES

Price per person for a three-course meal without drinks:
$ = under US$10
$$ = US$10–25
$$$ = US$25–50
$$$$ = over US$50

ACTIVITIES

TRANG TOWN AND BEACHES

Outdoor Activities

Diving and Snorkelling

Princess Divers: tel: 0-7520 3281. Located at Charlie Beach Resort on Ko Muk, it offers PADI courses and diving and snorkelling tours.
Rainbow Divers: tel: 0-7520 6962; www.rainbow-diver.com. Based at Ko Hai's Fantasy Resort & Spa, this is a reputable German-run operation.

SATUN AND KO TARUTAO NATIONAL PARK

Outdoor Activities

Diving and Snorkelling

Scuba diving and snorkelling are the main reason many choose to visit Ko Tarutao National Park. Several dive operators can be found at Pak Bara pier and on Ko Lipe. In addition, many of the bungalows on Ko Lipe can arrange snorkelling trips.
Adang Sea Tour: Pak Bara; tel: 0-7478 3338; www.adangseatour. com. This reliable agency provides boat services for sightseeing as well as scuba diving and

UNDERWATER WEDDINGS

Every St Valentine's Day, the waters off Trang play host to the Underwater Wedding Ceremony, a unique way to tie the knot and a popular tourist draw. For more information, check: www.underwater wedding.com.

snorkelling opportunities.
Forra Dive Resort: tel: 08-0545 5012; www.forradiving.com. Two dive-based resorts on Ko Lipe with PADI courses and fun dives around Tarutao.
Sabye Sports: Sunset Beach, Ko Lipe, mobile tel: 08-9464 5884; www.sabyesports.com. Based on Ko Lipe, this centre offers equipment rental and a variety of PADI dive courses.

Kayaking

John Gray's Sea Canoe: tel: 0-7625 4505; www.johngray-sea canoe.com. This Phuket-based company has multi-day kayak tours of the Tarutao islands with jungle treks and beach camping.

SONGKHLA AND HAT YAI

Nightlife

In **Songkhla**, Th. Sisuda, near the Indonesian Consulate, is home to many of the bars frequented by expats. The more popular ones include **Auntie** and **Corner Bier**. A block north, along Th. Sadao, is a collection of raucous but friendly bars with Thai hostesses catering mostly to a clientele of expatriate oil workers.

Much of the nightlife in **Hat Yai** is sleazy, fuelled by thousands of Malaysians and Singaporeans looking for a good time. But there are some places worth checking out, including the following bars:
Post Laser Disc: 82/83 Th. Thammanoonvithi; tel: 0-7423 2027. This popular restaurant-bar is an expat hangout of sorts, and plays host to live music every Friday night.
Sugar Rock: 114 Th. Thammanoonvithi. Laid-back bar and café that has been a Hat Yai fixture for some time.

Shopping

Much of downtown **Hat Yai** resembles a large market, with products ranging from knock-off brand-name T-shirts to cashew nuts, all sold on the streets. Popular shopping areas include the maze-like **Kim Yong Market** and **Santisuk Market**. Be prepared to bargain at these markets. For more formal, air-conditioned shopping, visit the **Central** department store, or the **Lee Gardens Plaza**, opposite.

Outdoor Activities

Golf

Thong Yai Golf Course: Hat Samila, Songkhla; tel: 0-7432 3761. This nine-hole beach-side golf course is currently the only place that you can tee-off in Songkhla.

Spas

The streets of central Hat Yai are lined with numerous massage parlours; despite appearances, many do in fact offer legitimate massages. Below are some of the better ones.
Spa Cenvaree: Centara Hat Yai, 3 Th. Sanehanusorn; tel: 0-7435 2222; www.spacenvaree.com. Offers massage and treatments that use indigenous Thai products.
Garabuning Spa: 50/6 Th. Sripoowanat; tel: 0-7435 4140. Has a herbal steam sauna as well as offering herbal and salt-based body scrubs.
Sittara Spa: 78 Radyindee Soi 7; tel: 0-7423 8594; www.sittaraspa. com. This spa offers treatment packages with an emphasis on aromatherapy.
The Weenee Hatyai: 123 Th. Petkasem, Soi 10; tel: 0-7446 9222; www.theweenee.com. A popular and clean hotel spa.

RIGHT: enjoying the sea and sand.

A–Z

AN ALPHABETICAL SUMMARY OF PRACTICAL INFORMATION

A ddresses

Given Bangkok's size and twisting alleyways, and as most of it developed with little central planning, finding your way around can be a bit confusing. The city is mostly laid out using the *soi* system – smaller streets leading off a main road, with each *soi* having a number after the name of the main road. For example, Sukhumvit Road (or Thanon Sukhumvit) has numerous streets branching from it in sequence, such as Sukhumvit Soi 1, Sukhumvit Soi 3, etc (odd and even numbers on opposite sides). *Sois* may be subdivided using a slash after the number followed by another

number. The same system is used for shop and house addresses, a slash separating the block or building number from the shop. So an address might read 36/1 Sukhumvit 33/1. Most hotels provide business cards with the address written in Thai to show to taxi drivers. Fortunately, taxis are not expensive in Bangkok, so if you do get lost, it won't cost you too much to find your destination.

Thailand's island and beach destinations are a lot easier to work out. There are fewer roads, many of which are recent additions to the landscape. A typical address might be preceded by the word Moo (referring to the residential estate) before the name of

the road or *soi*, as in 23/3 Moo 1. But many places don't even have complete addresses and will just state the beach or general area in which they are located.

Admission Charges

Thailand has a two tier pricing system under which tourists are charged up to ten times what Thais pay. This applies to national parks, museums and some larger temples. At press time, the government was also debating whether to charge tourists for entering the country. Most temples are free to enter. Tickets to the Grand Palace complex in Bangkok also allow entry to some other sites in Dusit, but otherwise there are few concessions.

B udgeting for your Trip

By Western standards, Bangkok is a bargain. Five-star hotels cost half or a third of what they would in New York or London, and at the other end, budget (if a bit dingy) accommodation can be as cheap as B200 per night. Street food can be excellent and you can have a filling and tasty meal for B30 to B40. Transport is cheap, with bus fares priced from B7–B22, a ride on the Skytrain and metro from B16–B40. Taxis are inexpensive as well (see page 102). Drinks in bars cost from B60–B100 and in clubs from B180–B300. If you live frugally, you can get by on B500 a day, but the sky is the limit here if you want to live it up at luxury hotels and eat at fine restaurants.

As a general rule of thumb, prices are generally higher outside the capital. In fact, destinations that attract a lot of tourists will have higher costs of living. Phuket and Ko Samui, for instance, are the most expensive islands, while Ko Phangan, Ko Lanta and Ko Chang are gradually moving up the cost-of-living scale. On the other hand, largely untouched places such as Trang and Satun offer the best bargains.

C hildren

Travelling with children is not especially difficult in Thailand. Thais love kids, and those with blond hair will receive special attention. It can be a bit overwhelming, but people are just being friendly and it is part of the Thai sense of community.

Footpaths in Bangkok are not pedestrian-friendly. They are often in disrepair and, inevitably, something or somebody obstructs them: leave the pushchair at home and bring a back- or chest-mounted baby carrier. Many department stores and malls have play areas and baby changing facilities, and some upmarket

hotels offer babysitting services.

Children should never approach dogs, monkeys or other small animals; those wandering the streets are more feral than in the West, and rabies is still a risk.

The tropical sun is intense, so high-SPF lotion and hats are important. Make sure children keep their hands clean, as various bugs are more virulent in tropical climates.

Climate

There are three official seasons in Thailand: hot, rainy and cool. But to the tourist winging in from more temperate regions, Thailand has only one temperature: hot. To make things worse, the mercury drops only a few degrees during the night, and is accompanied 24 hours by humidity above 70 percent. Days and nights, however, during the cool season can be pleasant.

Here is what you can expect:
• Hot season (Mar to mid-June): 27–35°C (80–95°F)
• Rainy season (June to Oct/Nov): 24–32°C (75–90°F)
• Cool season (Nov to Feb): 18–32°C (65–90°F), with less humidity.

There are regional variations along Thailand's coastline, but generally the Eastern Seaboard and northern Gulf of Thailand

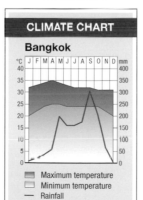

CLIMATE CHART

Bangkok

Maximum temperature
Minimum temperature
— Rainfall

coast have weather similar to that of Bangkok. The southern Gulf of Thailand coast around Ko Samui is a little different: it receives light, intermittent rain from June to October; in November, however, the northeast monsoon brings the heaviest rains. Phuket and the Andaman coast experience their wettest months from May to October. November can be a bit unstable.

What to Wear

Clothes should be light and loose; fabrics made from natural fibres are definitely more comfortable than synthetics. During the height of the rainy season, sandals are preferable to shoes. Sunglasses, hats and sunscreen are recommended for protection from the tropical sun, and it's best to carry an umbrella during the rainy season. Convenience stores sell them if you get caught out.

While Thailand does not have the formal dress code of Hong Kong or Tokyo, personal appearance is important. Suits are increasingly commonplace, and a shirt and tie is the bare minimum for business appointments.

Shorts are taboo for women and men who wish to enter some of the more revered temples. Women wearing sleeveless dresses and short skirts may also be barred from some temples and mosques.

In some parts of south Thailand, Muslims are in the majority so dress properly in deference to the religion and to Thai sensitivities. Although topless sunbathing is common at some beaches in Pattaya, Phuket and Ko Samui, it is illegal. It also makes locals uncomfortable.

Crime and Safety

Although Bangkok, like all cities, has an underbelly of violent crime, tourists rarely encounter it and the streets are generally very safe. The biggest risk to travellers is from scams and con artists. Beach destinations, including Pattaya, now have a major problem with claims that tourists have damaged jet skis, or other equipment. These disputes sometimes escalate into violence, and, with rampant corruption and bribery, the police response is usually unsatisfactory at best. Following travel warnings by several western embassies, in 2013 the government set up dedicated tourist courts at Suvarnabhum airport and in Pattaya and Phuket, with possibly more to come.

Thais tend to be non-confrontational, and the country is generally safe for women travellers in terms of both casual harassment and serious assault. That said, it is best to avoid walking alone at night on beaches.

If you do run into trouble, there are **Tourist Police** (TP) units at the major destinations that are specially assigned to assist travellers. However, much of the time, there is little they are able to do but record the details of the crime and provide a report (for insurance purposes). Most members of the force speak some English.

Tourist Police

TP National Hotline: 1155 (anywhere in Thailand); www.tourist. police.go.th.
Bangkok Tourist Assistance Centre: 4 Th. Rachadamnern Nok; tel: 0-2281 5051. In Bangkok, TP booths can also be found in tourist areas, including Lumphini Park (near the intersection of Th. Rama IV and Th. Silom) and Patpong (at the Th. Surawong intersection).

Drugs

Both hard and soft drugs are easy to procure in Thailand but it is illegal to possess, consume or trade in them. If caught, the penalties are harsh and the death sentence can apply. Stay clear of drug dealers. Police raids are common at tourist destinations and at the infamous full-moon parties at Ko Phangan *(see page 176)*, both plain-clothed and uniformed police will be on the prowl.

Insurgent Activity

Over the past three decades, a low-level insurgency has been brewing in the deep southern provinces of Pattani, Yala and Narathiwat, as well as in parts of Songkhla. Fuelled by foreign Muslim fundamentalists, this has given rise to violent separatist movements and constant unrest. Most governments advise against travel to these provinces, so check for updates.

Common Scams

• Touts at Bangkok's Patpong who offer live sex shows upstairs. Once inside, you are handed an exorbitant bill and threatened if you protest. Pay, take the receipt, and go immediately to the Tourist Police, who will usually take you back and demand a refund.
• Don't follow touts who offer to take you to a gem factory for a "special deal". The gems are usually synthetic or of substandard quality and there is no way to get your money back.
• *Tuk-tuk* drivers who offer to take you on a free tour and then stop at every gem, silver and tailor shop along the way where they will collect a commission for wasting your day. A common ruse they use to lure you is by pretending that the attraction you want to visit is closed for a special ceremony. Don't believe them.

Keep in mind that in Thai culture, strangers rarely approach and engage foreigners in conversation, so if you find yourself on the receiving end, be on guard, no matter how polite and innocent they appear to be. Feel free to be rude and walk away, even if it goes against the rules of polite behaviour. Also, remember that not all scam artists are Thai. Use normal levels of common sense and everything should be fine.

Women Travellers

Thailand is generally safe for women travellers, even those travelling alone. Thais tend to be non-confrontational, so violent and sexual crimes towards foreign

women are not common. That said, like anywhere, it isn't a great idea to be walking alone on quiet streets or beaches late at night.

Customs Regulations

The Thai government prohibits the import or export of drugs, dangerous chemicals, pornography, firearms and goods that display the Thai flag. Attempting to smuggle heroin or other hard drugs in or out may be punishable by death. Scores of foreigners are serving very long prison terms for this offence.

Foreign currency exceeding US$20,000 either entering or leaving the country should be declared. Thai currency leaving the country is restricted to B50,000. Foreign guests are allowed to bring in 200 cigarettes and 1 litre of wine or spirits without paying tax.

Buddha images, antiques and art objects cannot leave Thailand without a Department of Fine Arts permit *(see below)*.

For more details ,contact the

Export Permits

The Thai **Department of Fine Arts** prohibits the export of all Thai Buddha images, images of other deities and fragments (hands or heads) of images dating before the 18th century. All other antiques must be registered with the department. The shop will usually do this for you. If you decide to handle it yourself, take the piece to the office at Thanon Na Prathat (tel: 0-2628 5033), together with two postcard-sized photos of it. The export fee ranges from B100–200, depending on the antiquity of the piece. Fake antiques do not require export permits, but airport customs officials are not art experts and may mistake it for a genuine piece. If it looks authentic, clear it at the Department of Fine Arts to avoid problems later.

National Museum, Bangkok (tel: 0-2224 1333); or the Thai **Customs Department** (hotline: 1164; www.customs.go.th).

D isabled Travellers

Thailand falls short on accommodating the disabled, though this is slowly improving. Pavements are often uneven, studded with obstructions and there are no ramps. Few buildings have wheelchair ramps. In Bangkok, some major roads have textured brickwork on the paths for the blind. A few Skytrain stations have lifts, but not nearly enough; the metro has lifts at every station. Getting to many of Thailand's smaller islands often entails taking small boats that are moored at poorly designed piers. It would be a challenge for a disabled traveller on his/her own to get around Thailand – a companion is advisable. There are some online resources, such as www.accessiblethailand.com, that can help with things like hotels and local carers or assistants.

E lectricity

Electrical outlets are rated at 220 volts, 50 cycles and accept flat-pronged or round-pronged plugs. Adaptors can be purchased at department or hardware stores.

Embassies & Consulates

Australia: 37 Th. Sathorn Tai; tel: 0-2344 6300.
Canada: 15/F, Abdulrahim Place, Th. Rama IV; tel: 0-2636 0540.
New Zealand: 14/F, M Thai Tower, All Seasons Place, 87 Th. Withayu; tel: 0-2254 2530.
Singapore: 129 Th. Sathorn Tai; tel: 0-2286 1434.

EMERGENCIES

In case of emergency call the following numbers:
Fire, Police: **191**
Medical Emergency: **1669**
Tourist Police: **1155**

United Kingdom: 14 Th. Withayu; tel: 0-2305 8333.
United States: 120/22 Th. Withayu; tel: 0-2205 4000.

Etiquette

Thai people are remarkably tolerant and forgiving of foreigners' various eccentricities, but there are a handful of things that upset them that you should be aware of (see also Clothing, page 287).

The Royal Family

Thais have great reverence for the monarchy and disapprove of disrespect towards the institution. Lese-majesty laws, although usually invoked to settle business or political rivalries, can result in jail terms for defaming, insulting or threatening royalty. Standing for the national anthem is expected in cinemas.

Buddhism

A similar degree of respect is accorded to the second pillar of Thai society, Buddhism. Disrespect towards Buddha images, temples or monks is not taken lightly and, as with the monarchy, public expressions against the institution are illegal.

Monks observe vows of chastity that prohibit being touched by (or touching) women, even their mothers. When in the vicinity of a monk, a woman should try to stay clear to avoid accidental contact.

At temples, the scruffy and the underclad are frequently turned away, so dress appropriately.

Terms of Address

Thais are addressed by their first rather than their last names. The name is usually preceded by the word khun, a term of honour, a bit like Mr, Mrs or Ms. Following this to its logical conclusion, Silpachai Krishnamra would be addressed as Khun Silpachai.

Thai Greetings

The common greeting and farewell in Thailand is sawadee, (followed

by khrap when spoken by men and kha by women). In more formal settings this is accompanied by a wai – raising the hands in a prayer-like gesture, the fingertips touching the nose, and bowing the head slightly. However, don't make the mistake of giving a wai to all hotel staff, children or the people at the corner shop – it embarrasses them. In these cases, a nod is perfectly sufficient. Almost all Thais understand that this is not a part of Western cultures. In business meetings, the wai is often followed by a handshake.

Head and Feet

Thai Buddhism regards the head as the wellspring of wisdom and the feet as unclean. For this reason, it is insulting to touch another person on the head (children are an exception), to point one's feet at anything or step over another person. In formal situations, when wishing to pass someone who is seated on the floor, bow slightly while walking and point an arm down to indicate the path to be taken, and a path will be cleared.

Public Behaviour

Two decades ago, Thai couples showed no intimacy in public. That has changed due to modernisation and foreign influence on the young, but even these days, intimacy rarely extends beyond holding hands. As in many traditional societies, displaying open affection in public, such as kissing and passionate cuddling, is a sign of bad manners.

G ay & Lesbian Travellers

Gay people quickly discover that Thailand is one of the most tolerant countries in the world. The gay nightlife scene in Bangkok, Pattaya and Phuket is a thriving one. Bangkok also hosts the on-off annual Bangkok Gay Pride Festival (www.bangkokpride.org), with similar events in Pattaya (www.pattayagayfestival.com) and in Phuket (www.gay-patong.com).

Utopia, at www.utopia–asia.com, is Bangkok's major online resource for gays and lesbians. It's a good place to make contacts and to find out what's going on in Thailand and Asia.

Purple Dragon is a travel agency that caters exclusively to gay travellers. It is located at 942/58 Charn Issara Tower 1, Thanon Rama IV; tel: 0 2236 1776; www.purpledrag.com.

H ealth and Medical Care

Visitors entering Thailand are not required to show evidence of vaccination for smallpox or cholera. Check that your tetanus boosters are up to date. Immunisation against cholera is a good idea, as are hepatitis A and B innoculations. Malaria and dengue persist in remote and rural areas outside Bangkok. When in the countryside, especially in the monsoon season, apply mosquito repellent on exposed skin at all times – dengue mosquitoes are at their most active during the day.

Many first-time visitors take a while to adjust to the heat. It is important to drink plenty of water, especially if you've drunk alcohol. Avoid too much sun when out and about and use sunblock with a high SPF – the sun is far more powerful at this latitude than in temperate regions.

Tap water in Bangkok has been certified as potable, but take no chances and drink bottled water instead, which is widely available throughout Thailand. In Bangkok and at reputable hotels and restaurants at Thailand's major tourist centres, ice is clean and presents no health problems.

Stomach upsets are usually caused by overindulgence and rarely by contaminated food. Many stomachs react negatively to a sudden switch to a new cuisine. It's best to stick to freshly cooked food.

Buy travel insurance before travelling to Bangkok. Evacuation insurance is not really necessary since hospitals listed below are of international standard.

Hospitals

The level of medical care in Bangkok and some of Thailand's regional centres is excellent, particularly at the hospitals listed here, all of which also have specialised clinics.

Thailand is one of Asia's leading medical-tourism destinations; people are drawn to the country's world-class facilities and exceptional levels of customer service. Many procedures (including cosmetic surgery and sex changes) have shorter waiting times, and cost a fraction of what would be charged at home. Equipment is up to date and the doctors are usually trained overseas and speak English. By Thai standards, these international hospitals are considered expensive, but the fees are much lower compared with most Western countries. Note: the hospitals listed here also have dental clinics.

Bangkok

BNH Hospital: 9/1 Th. Convent, Silom; tel: 0-2686 2700; www.bnh hospital.com. This squeaky-clean hospital offers comfortable rooms, top-notch equipment and a large team of specialists. Service is efficient and English is widely spoken.

Bumrungrad Hospital: 33 Soi 3, Th. Sukhumvit; tel: 0-2667 1000; www.bumrungrad.com. This one is top of the range, and looks more like a five-star hotel than a hospital. Offers a huge range of specialised clinics, excellent staff, and a selection of rooms, from basic four-bed to luxury suites.

Ko Samui

Samui International Hospital: 90/2 Moo 2, Chaweng; tel: 0-7723 0781; www.sih.co.th. The best on the island and on a par with the best in Bangkok.

Pattaya

Bangkok Hospital Pattaya: 301 Moo 6, Th. Sukhumvit km 143; tel: 0-3825 9999; www.bph.co.th. Part of a network of well-equipped modern private hospitals, with a branch in Phuket.

Pattaya International Hospital: Pattaya Soi 4; tel: 0-3842 8374; www.pih-inter.com. This hospital is equipped to deal with emergencies and elective surgical procedures, including sex changes.

Phuket

Bangkok Hospital Phuket: 21 Th. Hongyok Utis, Phuket Town; tel: 0-7625 4425; www.phuket hospital.com. Popular with foreign tourists who come for health checks and surgical procedures.

Phuket International Hospital: 44 Th. Chalermprakiat; tel: 0-7624 9400; www.phuket internationalhospital.com. One of the best health-care facilities on the island and familiar with the needs of international patients.

Medical Clinics

In Bangkok, for minor problems, head to **MedConsult Clinic**, The Racquet Club, Sukhumvit Soi 49/9; tel: 0 2762 7855; www.med consultclinic.wordpress.com, is run by a native English speaking general practitioner who will make house calls. All the major hotels in Bangkok and in the major tourist centres also have doctors on call or clinics they can recommend.

Badalveda (www.badalveda.com) is a network of dive medicine centres, with branches in Phuket, Ko Tao, Pattaya, Ko Samui and Bangkok. They have hyperbaric chambers and are experienced in treating dive-related ailments.

Dental Clinics

Apart from the dental clinics at the international hospitals listed here, the **Dental Hospital** at 88/88 Soi 49 Th. Sukhumvit; tel: 0-2260 5000-15, is recommended. It looks more like a hotel than a dental hospital and has the latest equipment.

In the major tourist centres,

head to the recommended hospitals, all of which offer dental services; otherwise, get it fixed when you return to Bangkok, if you can.

Pharmacies

These are found everywhere in downtown Bangkok and in most island and beach destinations. In recent years, official control on prescription drugs has been more strongly enforced and requires the presence of a licensed pharmacist on the premises, especially in Bangkok. Nonetheless, most antibiotics and many other drugs that would require a prescription in the West are still available without one in Thailand.

Check the expiry date on all drugs you buy, and wherever possible, purchase them from an air-conditioned pharmacy. There are several branches of **Boots** and **Watson's** pharmacies in the centre of Bangkok.

Internet

Wi-fi zones are a fast-growing phenomenon, and the government has announced commitments to increase them around Bangkok. They are currently available at Bangkok airports and in some hotels and coffeeshops, including branches of Starbucks.

All the major hotels in Thailand offer broadband internet services, often free of charge, including in the rooms. Those that charge will be considerably more expensive than the public internet cafés. These days, even the smallest bungalow outfits on Thailand's relatively remote beaches have internet terminals for guests to use. Connection speeds at such places, however, can be painfully slow.

In Bangkok, internet cafés usually charge B30 per hour for broadband services. Be warned, though, that they tend to be full of teenagers playing games online and can be quite noisy. The Khao San area has more internet cafés than any other area in Bangkok,

but the Silom, Sukhumvit and Ploenchit areas have some internet cafés as well. Wi-fi is available at some shopping malls. Your hotel concierge should know the nearest location.

Left Luggage

Suvarnabhumi International Airport's left-luggage counters are found on Level 2 (Arrival), behind Exit 4, and Level 4 (Departure), behind check-in line Q. Cost is B100 per item per day. The airports at Phuket and Ko Samui also have left-luggage facilities; enquire at the information desks at the respective airports.

All hotels and guesthouses offer a left-luggage service; usually it is free but some may levy a small daily fee.

Lost Property

If you lose any valuable property, report it as soon as possible to the Tourist Police (see page 200) to get an insurance statement.
Airport: For property lost at Suvarnabhumi airport; tel: 0-2132 1888, and for Don Mueang Airport; tel: 0-2535 1253.

Public Transit: BMTA city bus service, tel: 0-2246 0973; **BTS Skytrain**, tel: 0-2617 6000; **MRTA subway**, tel: 0-2624 6200, **Hualamphong Railway Station**, tel: 1690.

Taxis: Bangkok taxi hotline (tel: 1644); drivers frequently listen to a radio station that has set up a lost property hotline, and it is surprising how often forgetful passengers get their lost items back: **JS100 Radio 100FM** hotline: 1137.

Maps

Basic maps of Bangkok are available for free at the **Tourism Authority of Thailand** (TAT) offices (see page 294) and also at the bigger hotels. More detailed ones can be found at bookshops. The Insight Fleximap and Nelles

Map of Bangkok are probably the best. Other more useful and offbeat insights to Bangkok's attractions can be found in Nancy Chandler's Map of Bangkok and Groovy Map's publications on Bangkok, Pattaya, Phuket and Samui, with sections on bars, dining, culture and shopping. At the larger islands such as Phuket, Ko Samui and Ko Chang, free maps are available at both hotels and tour agencies.

Media
Newspapers

Thailand has two long-standing English-language dailies. Both are quite conservative by Western press standards, but have some informative writers and are often more opinionated about government policies than in the past. The Nation, in recent years, has rebranded as a politics and business paper, with a much more limited lifestyle content. Most big hotels furnish one or the other free in their rooms. The Bangkok Post and The Nation cost B30 each.

Regional, advertisement-driven newspapers include the weekly Phuket Gazette (www.phuketgazette.net); Pattaya Mail (www.pattayamail.com); Pattaya Today (www.pattayatoday.net); and the monthly Hua Hin Today (www.huahintoday.com).

Magazines

There are several what's on and listings publications in English that cover events, nightlife, art galleries, restaurants, etc, although most are sparsely filled, unreliable and often consist of advertising copy disguised as editorial. The best free sheet is the weekly BK (www.bkmagazine.com). The glossy small-format monthly Bangkok 101 (www.bangkok101.com) costs B100, and has a good rundown of art shows and venues, along with events and restaurant and nightlife reviews.

New regional magazines geared toward the tourist or expat market are constantly appearing on the scene. Currently running are the monthly *Approach Magazine Hua Hin* (www.approach-thailand.com) and *Pattaya Trader* (www.pattayatrader.com).

Radio

AM radio is devoted entirely to Thai-language programmes. FM frequencies include several English-language stations with the latest pop hits. Some frequencies have bilingual DJs and play a mixture of Thai and English songs in the same programme.

• **97 MHz:** Radio Thailand has 4 hours of English-language broadcasts each day.
• **105.5 MHz:** Tourism Authority of Thailand offers useful tips to tourists every hour.
• **Fat FM 104.5:** Has the latest on Thailand's thriving indie-music scene.
• **Eazy FM 105.5 FM:** As the name suggests, mostly easy-listening middle-of-the-road music.
• **FMX 95.5 FM:** Contemporary dance and pop hits.

Television

Thailand has six Thai-language television channels. ITV, or Independent Television, specialises in news and documentaries. The rest mainly air soaps and game shows with a sprinkling of mostly domestically orientated news. There is also TRUEVISION, a cable television network that provides subscribers with a wide and increasing choice of international channels, including BBC world news, HBO, ESPN and MTV Thailand.

Money

The baht is the principal Thai monetary unit. Though it is divided into 100 units called satang, this is becoming outdated; only 50 and 25 satang pieces are used.

Banknote denominations include 1,000 (light brown), 500 (purple), 100 (red), 50 (blue) and 20 (green). There is a 10-baht coin (brass centre with silver rim), a 5-baht coin (silver with copper edge), a 2-baht coin (copper or silver coloured), a 1-baht coin (sil-ver), and two small coins of 50 and 25 satang (both brass-coloured).

At the time of press, US$1 was trading at B30.

Changing Money

Banking hours are Mon–Fri 9.30am–3.30pm, but nearly every bank maintains money-changing kiosks in the tourist areas of Thailand. Better hotels almost always have exchange facilities at their reception desks, but generally give poor exchange rates when compared with banks. ATM machines are widely available, except on smaller islands. Card cloning at ATM machines is an increasing problem throughout Thailand. Make sure you cover the keypad when you enter your pin.

Credit Cards

American Express, Diners Club, MasterCard, JCB and Visa are widely accepted throughout Bangkok and major resort towns such as Phuket, Ko Samui, Hua Hin and Pattaya. Smaller establishments, however, may impose a 3 percent surcharge on card transactions. Credit cards can be used to draw emergency cash at most banks. If you lose your credit card, contact your card company as soon as possible so that your card can be cancelled.

American Express: tel: 0-2273 5222.

Diners Club: tel: 0-2238 3660.
Visa: tel: 001-800 441 3485.
Mastercard: tel: 001-800 11 887 0663.

Warning: Credit-card fraud is a major problem in Thailand. Don't leave your credit card in safe-deposit boxes. When making a purchase, make sure that you get the carbon slips and dispose of them. When your card is swiped through the machine, make sure it is done in your presence.

Traveller's Cheques

Traveller's cheques can be cashed at all exchange kiosks and banks, and generally receive better exchange rates compared with cash. There is a nominal charge of B25 for each traveller's cheque cashed.

O pening Hours

Government offices in Thailand operate from 8.30am–4.30pm Mon–Fri. Most businesses are open 8am–5.30pm Mon–Fri while some are open 8.30am–noon on Sat. Banks are open 9.30am–3.30pm Mon–Fri,

Department stores are open 10am–9pm daily, though larger stores are open as late as 10pm. Ordinary shops open at 8.30am or 9am and close between 6pm and 8pm, depending on location and type of business.

Small open-air coffee shops and restaurants open at 7am and close at 8.30pm, though some stay open past midnight. Large restaurants generally have last orders at 10pm. In Bangkok, most hotel coffee shops close at midnight; some stay open 24 hours, and the city has several outdoor restaurants open as late as 4am for post-bar-hopping suppers.

Clubs and bars are subject to loosely applied licensing laws and may close anytime between midnight and 5am, depending on their location and political and policing climate. Generally, opening times are more flexible outside Bangkok.

P hotography

With over 20 million visitors per year, Thailand gets its photo taken an awful lot. The country and its people are very photogenic, and everything the photographer may need is readily available. Camera shops and photo-development outlets are commonly found in the tourist areas, and most now offer digital transfers on to CD and hard-copy photos from digital memory-cards. Prices are cheaper than in many other countries, at B3–4 per print, with enlargements being a real bargain.

Postal Services

The Thai postal service (www.thailandpost.com) is reasonably reliable, though mail seems to go more astray outside Bangkok and at Christmas time. Domestic mail can be sent registered or by EMS for a fee of B27 for a business-sized letter. EMS is supposed to guarantee that a letter reaches a domestic destination in one day, and it generally does, particularly in Bangkok. If you wish to send valuable parcels or bulky documents overseas, it is better to use a courier service.

In Bangkok, the **General Post Office** at Th. Charoen Krung, (tel: 0-2233 1050), is open Mon–Fri 8am–8pm, and Sat, Sun and holidays 8am–1pm.

Post offices elsewhere in Bangkok and Thailand usually open at 8am and close at 4pm on weekdays. Postal services are found at all tourist centres, even on small islands like Ko Samet.

In Bangkok, you can find mini post offices in some office buildings and hotels. Look for a red sign in English. These outlets offer basic mail services and accept small packages, but have no telecommunications services.

Courier Services

The usual global courier services are available in Bangkok. You can call direct or book online.
DHL: www.dhl.co.th; **Bangkok**; tel: 0-2631 2621; **Pattaya**; tel: 0-3871 1274; **Phuket**; tel: 0-7625 8500.
Fedex: www.fedex.com/th; **Bangkok**; tel: 0-2229 8800, or hotline: 1782; **Outside Bangkok**; tel: 1800-236-236 (toll free).
UPS: www.ups.com/th; **Bangkok**; tel: 0-2762 3300; **Pattaya**; tel: 0-3841 3440; **Phuket**; tel: 0 7626 3987; **Hat Yai**; tel: 0-7436 5596.

Public Holidays

Public holidays related to religion or royalty are often accompanied by restrictions on the sale of alcohol. This will not affect hotels, but may affect bars and shops, depending on local policing.
1 Jan: New Year's Day
Jan/Feb: (full moon) Makha Puja. Note: Chinese New Year is not an official holiday but many businesses close for several days.
6 Apr: Chakri Day
13–15 Apr: Songkran
1 May: Labour Day
5 May: Coronation Day
Late May–June: (full moon) Visakha Puja
Late July–Aug: (full moon) Asanha Puja and Khao Pansa
12 Aug: Queen's Birthday
23 Oct: Chulalongkorn Day
5 Dec: King's Birthday
10 Dec: Constitution Day

R eligious Services

Though it is predominantly Buddhist, Thailand has historically been tolerant of other religions. According to government census, 94 percent are Theravada Buddhists, 3.9 percent are Muslims, and 0.6 percent Christians, most of whom are Roman Catholic.

Buddhists will find no lack of temples to worship at. The further south you venture, the more mosques you will find. There is a handful of Christian churches, one major Hindu temple and at least one synagogue in Bangkok.

Christian

Bangkok: International Church of Bangkok, 67 Soi 19, Th. Sukhumvit; tel: 0-2258 5821. Services at 8am; and **International Christian Assembly**: Fl 11 Manoonpol Bldg, Th. Petchburi; tel: 0-2718 0603. Services at 10.30am and 6pm.
Phuket: Phuket Christian Centre, 74/123 Th. Phunphon, Phuket Town; tel: 0-7624 6380.
Pattaya: Victory Family Church, Pattaya Marriott Hotel, Th. Hat Pattaya; tel: 08-6688 5367.

Roman Catholic

Bangkok: Holy Redeemer Church, 123/19 Soi Ruam Rudi, Th. Withayu; tel: 0-2256 7262. Sunday Mass at 8.30am, 9.45am, 11am and 5.30pm; and **St Louis Church:** 215/2 Th. Sathorn Tai; tel: 0-2211 0220. Sunday Mass at 6am, 8am, 10am and 5.30pm.
Ko Samui: St. Anna Catholic Church, Na Thon; tel: 0-7742 1149.
Pattaya: St Nikolaus Church, Th. Sukhumvit; tel: 0-3841 6426.
Phuket: Phuket Catholic Church, Le Méridien Hotel, Phuket; tel: 0 7634 0480.

T axes

Thailand has a value-added tax (VAT) of 7 percent. This is added to most goods and services (but not goods sold by street vendors and markets). You can get the VAT refunded at the airport when you leave if you purchase at least B5,000-worth of goods at one go.

All major hotels and many others add 7 percent tax and 10 percent service charge to all bills for rooms and services.

Telephones
Public Phones

Even though Thais are heavy users of mobile phones, there are still plenty of coin- and card-operated telephones in booths in Bangkok. Public telephones accept B1, B5 and B10 coins. Phone cards for local calls in denominations of B50, B100, B200 and B400 can be purchased at convenience shops throughout Bangkok.

Local Calls

Area codes are merged with phone numbers and in theory do not exist anymore. The prefix 0 must be dialled for all calls made within Thailand, even when calling local numbers within the same city. So, when in Bangkok, dial 0 first, followed by the local 8-digit number; if you need **local directory assistance**, dial **1133**.

International Calls

The **country code** for Thailand is **66**. When calling Thailand from overseas, dial your local international access code, followed by 66 and the local Thai number without the preceding 0.

To make an international call from Thailand, dial 001 before the country and area code followed by the telephone number. Dial **100** for **international call assistance**.

Peak-hour calls from 7am–9pm are the most expensive, so it pays to call during non-peak hours from 5–7am and 9pm–midnight. The lowest call rates are from midnight to 5am.

Prepaid international phone cards (called Thaicard) of B300, B500 and B1,000 value can be used to make international calls. These can be bought at post offices, certain shops that carry the Thaicard sign or the office of the **Communications Authority of Thailand** in Bangkok; tel: 0-2950 3712; www.cat.or.th.

Mobile Phones

Mobile-phone numbers in Thailand have 10 digits, and most start with the prefix **08**. Just like fixed-line phones, dial the prefix 0 for all calls made within Thailand but drop the zero when calling from overseas.

Most international mobile-phone roaming services work in Thailand. Check with your service provider if you're not sure, especially if coming from US, Korea or Japan. Your phone will automatically select a local service provider and this enables you to make calls within Thailand at local rates. However, if someone calls your number, international call rates will apply. Charges will be billed to your account in your home country.

A much cheaper option is to buy a local SIM card, for which you will receive a local telephone number. These are widely available in mobile-phone shops, and cost as little as B50 in a promotion. Cheap 007, 008 and 009 international calls can be made with these prepaid cards, and local calls will be charged at local rates.

Time Zones

Thailand is 7 hours ahead of GMT. Since it gets dark between 6 and 7pm uniformly throughout the year, Thailand does not observe daylight saving time.

Tipping

Tipping is not a custom in Thailand, although it is becoming more prevalent. A service charge of 10 percent is included at the more expensive restaurants and is usually, though not always, divided among the staff. Do leave a small tip when service charge has not been included. When paying for a cab, it is customary to round up to the nearest 5 or 10 baht. There is no need to tip *tuk-tuk* drivers as you would have agreed on a flat fare before boarding. Porters are becoming used to being tipped but will not hover with their hand extended.

Toilets

There are few public toilets in Thailand, though Bangkok is beginning to address this in tourist areas. Public toilets are usually dirty and sometimes of the squat variety. Your best bet is to use hotels or shopping malls. Sometimes a fee of a few baht applies.

Tourist Offices

The **Tourism Authority of Thailand** (TAT) spends billions of baht every year to promote tourism domestically and abroad. They have information outlets in several countries and service kiosks within Thailand that offer basic maps and other promotional materials as well as advice on things to do and places to see. The main website, www.tatnews.org, has a wealth of information.

Bangkok

TAT Call Centre: tel: 1672. Daily 8am–8pm.
Tourism Authority of Thailand Main Office: 1600 Th. New Phetchaburi, Makkasan, Bangkok 10400; tel: 0-2250 5500. Daily 8.30am–4.30pm.
TAT Tourist Information Counter: Suvarnabhumi International Airport, Main Terminal and Baggage Claim Area, Level 2; tel: 0-2504 2701. Daily 8am–midnight.
TAT Tourist Information Counter (Ratchadamnoen): 4 Th. Ratchadamnoen Nok; tel: 0-2282 9774. Daily 8.30am–4.30pm.
Regional Offices
TAT Central Region office: 500/51 Th. Phetchkasem, Cha-am, Phetchaburi; tel: 0-3247 1005/6.
TAT Eastern Region office: 609

VAT REFUNDS

It is possible to get the 7 percent VAT refunded from your shopping if you purchase goods from stores displaying the "VAT Refund for Tourists" sign. Refunds can only be claimed on single purchases of B2,000 or more, with a minimum overall expenditure of B5,000. At the time of purchase, present your passport and ask the sales assistant to complete the VAT refund form. Before departure at the airport, present your goods together with the VAT refund form and sales invoice to the Customs

officers for inspection. After approval, present your claim to the Revenue officers at the airport's VAT Refund Counter.

Refunds not exceeding B30,000 will be made in cash (in Thai baht) or by bank draft or credit to your credit-card account. Refunds over B30,000 cannot be made in cash. In addition, there is an administrative fee of B100 for cash refunds; bank drafts and credit-card refunds will incur extra charges. See www.rd.go.th for more details.

Th. Phra Tamnak, Pattaya. Chonburi; tel: 0-3842 3990.
TAT Eastern Region office: 153/4 Th. Sukhumvit, Rayong; tel: 0-3865 5420/1.
TAT Eastern Region office: 100 Moo 1 Th. Trat-Laem Ngop, Laem-Ngop, Trat; tel: 0-3959 7259/60.
TAT Southern office: 1/1 Soi 2 Th. Niphatuthit 3, Hat Yai, Songkhla; tel: 0-7424 3747.
TAT Southern office: 73–75 Th. Phuket, Phuket Town; tel: 0-7621 2213.
TAT Southern office: 5 Th. Thalad Mai, Surat Thani; tel: 0-7728 8818/9.

Overseas Offices

UK: 1st Floor, 17 19 Cockspur Street, Trafalgar Square, London SW1Y 5BL, email: info@tourismthailand.co.uk.
USA: 61 Broadway, Suite 2810, New York, NY 10006; tel: 1-212 432 0433, email: info@tatny.com; and 611 North Larchmont Blvd, 1st Floor, Los Angeles, CA 90004; tel: 1-323 461 9814, email: tatla@ix.netcom.com.
Australia & New Zealand: Level 2, 75 Pitt Street, Sydney 2000; tel: 61-2 9247 7549, email: info@thailand.net.au.

▼ isas and Passports

Travellers should check visa regulations at a Thai embassy or consulate before starting their trip as visa rules vary for different nationalities. For an updated list, check the Thai **Ministry of Foreign Affairs** at www.mfa.go.th.

All foreign nationals entering Thailand must have valid passports, with at least six-month validity. At the airport, nationals from most countries will be granted a visa on arrival valid from 15–90 days, depending on the country. Officially you need an air ticket out of Thailand, but this is very rarely checked.

Longer tourist visas, obtained from the Thai consulate of your home country prior to arrival, allow for a 60-day stay. People seeking a work permit can apply

for a non-immigrant visa, which is valid for a total of 90 days. A letter of guarantee is needed from the Thai company you intend to work for and this visa can be obtained from a Thai consulate at home.

Visas can be extended by 30 days for a fee of B1,000 in Bangkok or at the regional immigration offices, or you can leave the country (even for half an hour) and return to receive another visa on entry. In total, tourists can stay in Thailand for a cumulative period not exceeding 90 days within any 6-month period from the date of first entry. Overstaying can carry a daily fine of B500 to a maximum of B20,000 on leaving the country, but if the police catch you before you are leaving, you may face imprisonment.

In Bangkok, the Thai **Immigration Bureau** is at 120 Moo 3, Th. Chaengwattana; tel: 0-2141 9889; www.immigration.go.th (Mon–Fri 8.30am–4.30pm).
Pattaya: Soi 5, Moo 12, Jomtien Beach Rd; tel: 0-3825 2750.
Phuket: Phuket Rd; tel: 0-7622 1905.
Ko Samui: Route 4169 Nathon; tel: 0-7742 1069.
Satun: Th. Burivanich, Satun Town; tel: 0-7471 1080.
Songkhla: Th. Phetchkasem, Hat Yai; tel: 0-7424 3019 or 6333.

▼ ebsites
Thailand

www.bangkokpost.com
Daily news from the *Bangkok Post* daily newspaper.
www.boi.go.th
The Thailand Board of Investment.
www.customs.go.th
The Thai Customs Department.
www.langhub.com/en-th
Audio and video files to learn Thai.
www.nationmultimedia.com
Daily news clips from *The Nation* newspaper.
www.tourismthailand.org
The official website of the Tourism Authority of Thailand.
www.thaiticketmajor.com
Sells tickets for all the major upcoming events.

www.utopia-asia.com
Gay resource for Thailand and Asia.

Bangkok

www.bangkok.coconuts.co
News, features and reviews covering the capital.
www.bkmagazine.com
Features and reviews from *BK*, the city's best listings freebie.
www.restaurantsofbangkok.com
Reviews of restaurants and bars in Bangkok, with cheap deals and vouchers for those who register.
www.siam2nite.com
All the latest Bangkok nightlife events.

Regional

Hua Hin
www.huahintoday.com
www.huahinafterdark.com
Ko Chang
www.koh-chang.com
Ko Phangan
www.kohphangan.com
www.phanganinfo.com
Ko Samui
www.kosamui.com
www.samui.org
www.samui.sawadee.com
Ko Si Chang
www.ko-sichang.com
Ko Tao
www.kohtao.com
www.on-koh-tao.com
Krabi
www.krabi-hotels.com
www.phi-phi.com
www.kolanta.net
Pattaya
www.pattaya-at-night.com
www.pattayainformation.com
Phuket
www.phuket.com
www.phuketgazette.net
www.phuket.net
Trang
www.trangonline.com

Weights and Measures

Thailand uses the metric system, except for their traditional system of land measurement (1 rai = 1,600 sq m) and the weight of gold (1 baht = 15.2 grammes).

A – Z

LANGUAGE

L ANGUAGE

UNDERSTANDING THE LANGUAGE

Origins and Intonation

For centuries, the Thai language, rather than tripping from foreigners' tongues, has been tripping them up. Its roots go back to the place Thais originated from, in the hills of southern China, but these are overlaid by Indian influences. From the original settlers come the five tones that seem designed to frustrate visitors. One sound can have five different tones: high (h), low (l), mid (m), rising (r) and falling (f), and each of these means something different (see text box below).

Therefore, when you mispronounce a word, you don't simply say a word incorrectly, you say another word entirely. It is not

THE FIVE TONES

Mid tone (m): Voiced at the speaker's normal, even pitch.
High tone (h): Pitched slightly higher than the mid tone.
Low tone (l): Pitched slightly lower than the mid tone.
Rising tone (r): Sounds like a questioning pitch, starting low and rising.
Falling tone (f): Sounds like an English speaker suddenly understanding something – "Oh, I see!"

unusual to see a semi-fluent foreigner standing before a Thai and running through the scale of tones until suddenly a light of recognition dawns on his or her companion's face. There are misinformed visitors who will tell you that tones are not important. These people are not communicating *with* Thais – they talk *at* them in a one-sided exchange.

Phonology

The way Thai consonants are written in English often confuses foreigners. An "h" following a letter such as "p" and "t" gives the letter a soft sound; without the "h", the sound is more explosive. Thus, "ph" is not pronounced "f" but as a soft "p"; without the "h", the "p" has the sound of a very hard "b". The word *thanon* (street) is pronounced "tanon" in the same way "Thailand" is not meant to sound like "Thighland". Similarly, final letters are often not pronounced as they look. A "j" on the end of a word is pronounced "t"; "l" is pronounced as an "n". To complicate matters further, many words end with "se" or "r", which are not pronounced at all.

Vowels are pronounced as follows: **i** as in *sip*, **ii** as in *seep*, **e** as in *bet*, **a** as in *pan*, **aa** as in *car*, **u** as in *pool*, **o** as in *so*, **ai** as in *pie*,

ow as in *cow*, **aw** as in *paw*, **iw** as in *you*, **oy** as in *toy*.

In Thai, the pronouns "*I*" and "*me*" are the same word, but it is different for males and females. Men use the word *phom* when referring to themselves, while women say *chan* or *diichan*. Men use *khrap* at the end of a sentence when addressing either a male or a female to add politeness, or in a similar manner as please (the word for "please", *karuna*, is seldom used directly) ie *pai* (f) *nai*, *khrap* (h) (where are you going sir?). Women add the word *kha* to their statements, as in *pai* (f) *nai*, *kha* (h).

To ask a question, add a high tone *mai* to the end of the phrase ie *rao pai* (we go) or *rao pai mai* (h) (shall we go?). To negate a statement, insert a falling tone *mai* between the subject and the verb ie *rao pai* (we go), *rao mai pai* (we don't go). "Very" or "much" are indicated by adding *maak* to the end of a phrase ie *ron* (hot), *ron maak* (very hot), or *phaeng* (expensive), *phaeng maak* (very expensive), and the opposite *mai phaeng* (not expensive).

Thai Names

From the languages of India have come polysyllabic names and words. Thai names are among the longest in the world. Every Thai person's first and surname has a meaning. By learning the meaning of the name of everyone you meet, you would acquire a formal, but quite extensive vocabulary.

There is no universal transliteration system from Thai into English, which is why names and street names can be spelt in three different ways. For example, the surname Chumsai is written Chumsai, Jumsai and Xoomsai, depending on the family. This confuses even the Thais. If you ask a Thai how they spell something, they may well reply, "how do you want to spell it?". Bangkok's thoroughfare of Ratchadamnoen is also spelled Ratchadamnern. Ko Samui can be spelled Koh Samui. The spellings will differ from map to map, and from book to book.

To address a person one has never met, the title khun is used for both male and female. Having long and complicated surnames, Thais typically address one another by their first name only, preceded by the title khun for formality, ie Hataichanok Phrommayon becomes Khun Hataichanok. Thais usually adopt nicknames from birth, often accorded to their physical or behavioural attributes as a baby ie Lek (small), Yai (big), Daeng (red), Moo (pig), etc. If the person is familiar – a friend, relative or close colleague – then according to the age relationship between the two people, they are addressed as Pii (if older), or Nong (if younger). So an older friend would be addressed Pii Lek, a younger one Nong Lek.

Numbers

0 soon (m)
1 nung (m)
2 song (r)
3 sam (r)
4 sii (m)
5 haa (f)
6 hok (m)
7 jet (m)
8 bet (m)

9 kow (f)
10 sip (m)
11 sip et (m, m)
12 sip song (m, r)
13 sip sam (m, r), and so on
20 yii sip (m, m)
30 sam sip (f, m), and so on
100 nung roi (m, m)
1,000 nung phan (m, m)

Useful Words and Phrases

Days of the Week

Monday Wan Jan
Tuesday Wan Angkan
Wednesday Wan Phoot
Thursday Wan Pharuhat
Friday Wan Sook
Saturday Wan Sao
Sunday Wan Athit
Today Wan nii (h)
Yesterday Meua wan nii (h)
Tomorrow Prung nii (h)

Colours

White sii kao
Black sii dum
Red sii daeng
Yellow sii leung
Blue sii num ngern
Green sii keeow
Orange sii som
Pink sii chompoo

Short Phrases

Hello, goodbye Sawadee (a man then says khrap; a woman says kha: thus sawadee khrap or sawadee kha)
How are you? Khun sabai dii, mai (h)
Well, thank you Sabai dii, khopkhun
Thank you very much Khopkhun maak
May I take a photo? Thai roop (f) noi, dai (f) mai (h)
Never mind Mai (f) pen rai
I cannot speak Thai Phuut Thai mai (f) dai (f)
I can speak a little Thai Phuut Thai dai (f) nit (h) diew
Where do you live? Khun yoo thii (f) nai (r)
What is this called in Thai? An nii (h), kaw riak aray phasa Thai
How much? Thao (f) rai

Directions and Travel

Go Pai
Come Maa
Where Thii (f) nai (r)
Right Khwaa (r)
Left Sai (h)
Turn Leo
Straight ahead Trong pai
Please slow down Cha cha noi
Stop here Jawt thii (f) nii (f)
Fast Raew
Slow Cha
Hotel Rong raem
Street Thanon
Lane Soi
Bridge Saphan
Police Station Sathanii Dtam Ruat
Ferry Reua
Longtail boat Reua haang yao
Train Rot fai
Bus Rot may
Skytrain Rot fai faa
Metro/subway Rot fai tai din
Pier Tha Reua
Bus stop Pai rot may
Station Sathanii (rot may), (rot fai), (rot fai faa)

Other Handy Phrases

Yes Chai (f)
No Mai (f) chai (f)
Do you have ...? Mii ... mai (h)
Expensive Phaeng
Do you have something cheaper? Mii arai thii thook (l) kwa, mai (h)
Can you lower the price a bit? Kaw lot noi dai (f) mai (h)
Do you have another colour? Mii sii uhn mai (h)
Too big Yai kern pai
Too small Lek kern pai
Do you have any in a bigger size? Mii arai thii yai kwa mai (h)
Do you have any in a smaller size? Mii arai thii lek kwa mai (h)
Do you have a girlfriend/boyfriend? Mii faen mai (h)
I don't want it Mai ao
Hot (temperature) Rawn (h)
Hot (spicy) Phet
Cold Yen
Sweet Waan (r)
Sour Prio (f)
Delicious Aroy
I do not feel well Mai (f) sabai

FURTHER READING

Travel and Culture

Culture Shock: Thailand by Robert Cooper and Nanthapa. Very useful look at Thai customs and how to avoid major faux pas.
Muay Thai: The Art of Thai Boxing by Joe Cummings. Excellent, well-illustrated book on the history and practice of Thai boxing.
9 Days in the Kingdom by Nicholas Grossman and William Warren. Stunning photographic exploration of Thailand, taken by 50 photographers in nine days.
Very Thai: Everyday Popular Culture by Philip Cornwel-Smith. If you've ever wondered why every compound in Thailand has a spirit house or why insect treats are such a hit, this book is for you.

Fiction

Bangkok 8, **Bangkok Tattoo**, and **Bangkok Haunts** by John Burdett. A bestselling trilogy about a half-Thai, half-American policeman who avenges his partner's death.
The Beach by Alex Garland. This inspired the film with Leonardo DiCaprio about backpackers trying to find their own paradise.
The Big Mango by Jake Needham. Action story about a hunt for millions of dollars that went missing during the fall of Saigon in 1975.
Sightseeing by Rattawut Lapcharoensap. Colourful novel that paints the real face of modern cross-cultural Thailand.
Sleepless in Bangkok by Ian Quartermaine. Funny thriller about an ex-SAS security consultant on a covert assignment to Siam.

History and Society

Thaksin: The Business of Politics in Thailand by Dr Pasuk Phongpaichit and Chris Baker. Carefully researched study of PM Thaksin Shinawatra and his impact on society.
Jim Thompson: The Legendary American by William Warren. Intriguing story of the American Thai-silk magnate, Jim Thompson.
Chronicle of Thailand: Headline News Since 1946. An EDM publication highlighting the country's recent history through articles culled from newspaper archives.
The King Never Smiles: A Biog-

SEND US YOUR THOUGHTS

We do our best to ensure that the information in our books is as accurate and up-to-date as possible. The books are updated on a regular basis using local contacts, who painstakingly add, amend and correct as required. However, some details (such as telephone numbers and opening times) are liable to change, and we are ultimately reliant on our readers to put us in the picture.

We welcome your feedback, especially your experience of using the book "on the road". Maybe we recommended a hotel that you liked (or another that you didn't), or you came across a great bar or new attraction that we missed.

We will acknowledge all contributions, and we'll offer an Insight Guide to the best letters received.

Please write to us at:
**Insight Guides
PO Box 7910
London SE1 1WE**
Or email us at:
insight@apaguide.co.uk

raphy of Thailand's Bhumibol Adulyadej by Paul M. Handley. An unauthorised portrait. This book is banned throughout Southeast Asia.
Bangkok Then & Now by Steve Van Beek. Hardcover book with photos both old and new showing how the city has changed but also remained the same.
A History of Thailand second edition, by Dr Pasuk Phongpaichit and Chris Baker. An informed history, mainly from the Rattanakosin period onwards.

Art

Architecture of Thailand by Nithi Sthapitanonda and Brian Mertens. Explores Thailand's architectural lineage, from bamboo huts to teak mansions and religious edifices.
Flavours: Thai Contemporary Art by Steven Pettifor. Full of colourful illustrations offering insights into Thailand's burgeoning contemporary visual arts scene.
The Grand Palace by Nngnoi Saksi, Naengnoi Suksri, and Michael Freeman. Beautifully illustrated account of Bangkok's Grand Palace and its surroundings.

Religion

A History of Buddhism in Siam by Prince Dhani Nivat. Written by one of Thailand's most respected scholars.
What the Buddha Taught by Walpola Rahula. Comprehensive account of Buddhist doctrine.

Cookery

Thai Food by David Thompson. Almost 700 pages of traditional recipes and food background from the famed chef.

ART AND PHOTO CREDITS

Aleenta 3, 4T, 155
Alamy 28, 31, 38, 40, 46, 56, 118, 126L, 132, 168, 176, 218L
Amari Trang Beach Resort 273
Austin Bush/Apa Publications 48, 270, 271, 272M, 273M, 274M, 275, 275M, 276, 277L/R, 278, 278M
AWL Images 170
Banyan Tree Bangkok 110
Bigstock 45, 84, 123, 149, 156, 171, 204, 220M, 222, 253M
Corbis 25
Derrick Lim/Apa Publications 222M
Devarana Spa 139
Dreamstime 20L, 52, 53, 62/63, 88, 169, 177, 212, 242
Francis Dorai/Apa Publications 80M, 82, 83M, 86, 227, 274
Fotolia 6BL, 19R, 36, 74, 76, 138, 140, 141, 150, 162, 163, 165, 173, 188, 190, 209, 282, 283
Getty Images 6R, 22, 30, 34, 35, 154, 178, 179, 203
iStock 27, 43, 50, 74R, 93, 175, 248
Jason Lang/Apa Publications 19, 41R, 73, 77, 77M, 85L/R, 85M, 86M, 89, 90, 92L/R, 95R, 97, 97M, 111, 128, 129, 129M, 146, 147, 149M, 150M, 151, 153
John W. Ishii/Apa Publications 1, 2/3, 4C, 4B, 5, 6L, 7L, 7C, 7BR,

8R, 9T, 10-11, 12/13, 14, 18, 20R, 21, 32/33, 42, 44, 51R, 57, 59, 61, 64-65, 66, 119, 120M, 121L/R, 124M, 125, 126B, 127, 130, 130M, 131B, 132M, 133, 134, 144, 145, 151M, 152L/R, 153M, 154M, 155M, 157, 158, 164, 166M, 167M, 169M, 170MT, 170MB, 172, 172M, 174M, 177M, 180, 180M, 181, 182, 182M, 183, 184, 187, 192, 194, 195, 196, 196M, 197L/R, 198, 198M, 199, 200, 200M, 201, 202, 202M, 203M, 205, 211, 213, 215M, 219M, 224M, 226, 227M, 241, 243, 244, 244M, 245, 246, 247M, 248M, 249, 250, 250M, 251L/R, 251M, 252, 253, 254, 254M, 255, 256, 257M, 258, 259, 259M, 260, 261, 264, 267, 268, 269, 279, 285, 286
JW Marriott Resort & Spa 220
Leonardo 105, 106
Marcus Wilson Smith/Apa Publications 39, 41L, 47, 51L, 58, 78, 79M, 83L, 84M, 87L/R, 88M, 89M, 90M, 93M, 124, 128M, 171M, 216, 217M, 218R, 219, 228M, 277M
Mary Evans Picture Library 26
Nikt Wong/Apa Publications 7TR, 60, 215, 217, 221, 223, 224, 229, 230, 230M, 230T, 233, 238
Oriental Hotel 94, 94M

Peter Stuckings/Apa Publications 49, 72, 75M, 79, 80, 81, 83, 91L/R, 95, 96, 101, 108, 115, 116
Pimalai Resort & Spa 257
The Art Archive 24, 29L
The Racha 9BR, 228
US National Archives 23

PHOTO FEATURES

Pages 36/37: Top row: Getty Images. Bottom row from left to right: Alamy, Dreamstime, Getty Images, Alamy
Pages 54/55: Top right iStock, all others Fotolia
Pages 98/99: Top middle Peter Stuckings/Apa Publications Top Right: Marcus Wilson Smith/Apa Publications, Marcus Wilson Smith/APA. Bottom row from left to right: Marcus Wilson Smith/Apa Publications, Marcus Wilson Smith/Apa Publications, Francis Dorai/Apa Publications, Marcus Wilson Smith/Apa Publications, Derrick/Apa Publications

Map Production: Apa Cartography Department

© 2014 Apa Publications (UK) Ltd
Production: Tynan Dean and Rebeka Davies

Cover Credits
Front Cover: Koh Samui island, 4Corners Images
Back Cover:
(top) Ang Thong National Park, John Ishii/Apa Publications
(middle): traditional dancers Peter Stuckings/Apa Publications

Front Flap: (from top) outdoor terrace of Sirocco Restaurant, Peter Stuckings/Apa Publications; Coconut drink John Ishii/Apa Publications; Sunset at Ao Nang, John Ishii/Apa Publications; coastal road between Senggigi and Dangsal, Lombok ,

Corrie Wingate/Apa Publications
Spine:
long tail in Maya bay Phi Phi Lei, John Ishii/Apa Publications

Index

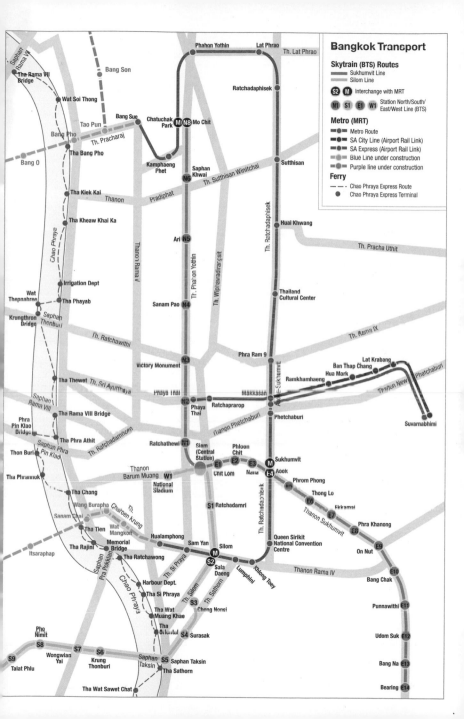

BANG PHLAD

Nonthaburi

Thanon Somdet

Phra Pin Klao

Soi Charan Sanit Wong 40

Amarin

Soi Suwannin

Wat Dao Wadung

PHRA PIN KLAO BRIDGE

THON BURI

National Museum of Royal Barges

Bangkok Noi

Bangkok Noi Thonburi Railway Station

Banphak Rotfai

Museum of Forensic Medicine

Ansorei Surinah

Thanon

Phrannok

Amulet Market

Th. Wang Lang

THA PHRANNOK

Soi Ban Chang Lo

Wat Rakhang

Amarin

THA CHANG

Wat Mahathat

Na Phra Lan

Wat Phra Kaew (Emerald Buddha)

Grand Palace

RATTANA KOSIN

Maharat

THA TIEN

Wat Pho (Reclining Buddha)

Thanon Itsaraphap

Th. Arun Amarin

S. Itsaraphap 40

Soi 49

Th. Wang Doem

Vichaiprasit (Old Fort)

Wat Arun (Temple of Dawn)

S. Itsaraphap 21

Bangkok Yai

THA WASUKRI

Wat Bowon Mongkhon

Th. Lukmanadthai

TH. THEWET

Wat Thewarat Kunchon

National Library

Saphan Rama VIII

Chao Phraya

TH. WISUTHI KASAT

Th. Si Ayutthaya

Th. Uthong Nok

Soi Samsen 9

Soi Samsen

SUANSAT

Vimanmek

National Assemb (Parliament)

Abhisek Dusit Throne

Dusit Zoo

DUSIT

AMPORN PARK

Ananta Samakhom (Royal Throne Hall)

Dusit Gate

Thanon Rama V

Th. Phitsanulok

Parusakkawan Palace

King Chulalongkorn

Wat Benjamabophit (Marble Temple)

Government House

Royal Turf Club

Thanon Sri Ayu

Th. Krung Kasem

Th. Luk Luang

Thanon Nakhon Pathom

Wat Mongkrut

Krasat Thiyaram

Ratchadamnoen Boxing Stadium

Wat Sommanat

Th. Luk Luang

Th. Lan Luang

Phaniang

Saphan Phra Pin Klao

National Theatre

National Museum

Thammasat University

SANAM LUANG

Th. Phra Chan

Th. Phra That

National Gallery

Khao San

Tanao

Wat Bowonniwet

Th. Ratchadamnoen

14 October Monument

Democracy Monument

Wat Mahan

Klang

Wat Ratchanatda

Loha Prasat

City Hall

Sao Ching Cha (Giant Swing)

Lak Muang (City Pillar)

Kanlaya Namit

Ratchapradit

Ratchabophit

Charoen

Wat Suthat

Dev Mandir Temple

Ban Baat

Phu Khao Thong (Golden Mount)

Wat Saket

Thanon Barum Muang

Thanon Lan Luang

Saen Saep

Damrong Rak

Th. Krung Kasem

Th. Phra Ya

Wat Chai Hatthka

Th. Rama

Wat Thepsirin

Wat Phlapphla Chai

Krung

Nakhon Kasem (Thieves' Market)

Sri Guru Singh Sabha

National Discovery Museum

Pahurat Market

Pak Khlong Talad (Flower Market)

THA RAJINI

Wat Ratchaburana

Wat Chakrawat

CHINATOWN

Th. Yaowarat

Leng Buai Ia Talad Kao

Talad Mai

Shanghai Mansion

Wat Mangkon Kamalawat

Wat Traimit (Golden Buddha)

Hualampho Railway Station

Hualamph

Rama IV

MEMORIAL BRIDGE

Saphan Pra Pokklao

THA RATCHAWONG

Th. Songwat

Wat Tian Fah

Wat Pathuma Kongkha

Thanon Charoen Krung (New Rd)

Th. Charoen

Th. Maha Phruthar

2nd State Expressway

Wat Prayunwongsawat

Thetsaban Sai 1

Th. Thetsaban

Thetsaban Sai 2

Thanon Itsaraphap

Thonburi Christian Hall

Soi 15

Thanon Prachathipok

Wat Yai Si Suphan

Thanon Phet Kasem

Th. Inthraraphitak

Thanon Thoet Thai

Suanphlu

THONBURI

Pho Ninjit

Th. Ratchaphruek

Soi 3

Soi 2

Wongwian Yai Railway Station

Soi 4

Soi 2

Wongwian Yai (King Taksin Mon.)

Thanon Somdet Phra Chao Taksin

Wongwian Yai

Thanon Krung Thonburi

Soi Saraphi 3

Thanon Krung Thonburi

Wat Thong Phleng

S. Saksin

Yenchit

Tr.

Wat Thong Thammachat

Chao Praya

Thanon Somdet Chao Praya

Soi 10

Soi Somdet Chao Praya 13

Th. Tha Din Daeng

Th. Itsaraphap

HARBOUR DEPT.

Patchamid Fort

THA SI PHRAYA

River City Shopping Complex

Royal Orchid

Wat Suwan Ubasikaram

Soi Charoen Nakhon 14

KHLONG SAN

Thanon Charoen Rat

Soi 13

Thanon Lad Ya

Th. Wiset San

Th. Charoen Nakhon

Soi 3

Soi 5

Soi 8

Soi 10

Soi 7

Soi 9

THA WAT UDANG KAA

Mandarin Oriental

THA ORIENTAL

Assumption Cathedral

Peninsula Hotel

Soi 13

Shangri-La

Saphan Taksin

THA SATHORN

Th. Sathorn

Krung Thonburi

Charoen Nakhon 18

Soi 15

Charoen 43

Surasak

Th. Silom

Soi Silom

BAN